The Practical Guide to HIPAA Privacy and Security Compliance

Second Edition

OTHER INFORMATION SECURITY BOOKS FROM AUERBACH

Anonymous Communication Networks: Protecting Privacy on the Web
Kun Peng
ISBN 978-1-4398-8157-6

Conducting Network Penetration and Espionage in a Global Environment
Bruce Middleton
ISBN 978-1-4822-0647-0

Cyberspace and Cybersecurity
George Kostopoulos
ISBN 978-1-4665-0133-1

Developing and Securing the Cloud
Bhavani Thuraisingham
ISBN 978-1-4398-6291-9

Ethical Hacking and Penetration Testing Guide
Rafay Baloch
ISBN 978-1-4822-3161-8

Guide to the De-Identification of Personal Health Information
Khaled El Emam
ISBN 978-1-4665-7906-4

Industrial Espionage: Developing a Counterespionage Program
Daniel J. Benny
ISBN 978-1-4665-6814-3

Information Security Fundamentals, Second Edition
Thomas R. Peltier
ISBN 978-1-4398-1062-0

Information Security Policy Development for Compliance: ISO/IEC 27001, NIST SP 800-53, HIPAA Standard, PCI DSS V2.0, and AUP V5.0
Barry L. Williams
ISBN 978-1-4665-8058-9

Investigating Computer-Related Crime, Second Edition
Peter Stephenson and Keith Gilbert
ISBN 978-0-8493-1973-0

Managing Risk and Security in Outsourcing IT Services: Onshore, Offshore and the Cloud
Frank Siepmann
ISBN 978-1-4398-7909-2

PRAGMATIC Security Metrics: Applying Metametrics to Information Security
W. Krag Brotby and Gary Hinson
ISBN 978-1-4398-8152-1

Responsive Security: Be Ready to Be Secure
Meng-Chow Kang
ISBN 978-1-4665-8430-3

Securing Cloud and Mobility: A Practitioner's Guide
Ian Lim, E. Coleen Coolidge, Paul Hourani
ISBN 978-1-4398-5055-8

Security and Privacy in Smart Grids
Edited by Yang Xiao
ISBN 978-1-4398-7783-8

Security for Service Oriented Architectures
Walter Williams
ISBN 978-1-4665-8402-0

Security without Obscurity: A Guide to Confidentiality, Authentication, and Integrity
J.J. Stapleton
ISBN 978-1-4665-9214-8

The Complete Book of Data Anonymization: From Planning to Implementation
Balaji Raghunathan
ISBN 978-1-4398-7730-2

The Frugal CISO: Using Innovation and Smart Approaches to Maximize Your Security Posture
Kerry Ann Anderson
ISBN 978-1-4822-2007-0

The Practical Guide to HIPAA Privacy and Security Compliance, Second Edition
Rebecca Herold and Kevin Beaver
ISBN 978-1-4398-5558-4

Secure Data Provenance and Inference Control with Semantic Web
Bhavani Thuraisingham, Tyrone Cadenhead, Murat Kantarcioglu, and Vaibhav Khadilkar
ISBN 978-1-4665-6943-0

Secure Development for Mobile Apps: How to Design and Code Secure Mobile Applications with PHP and JavaScript
J. D. Glaser
ISBN 978-1-4822-0903-7

AUERBACH PUBLICATIONS
www.auerbach-publications.com • To Order Call: 1-800-272-7737 • E-mail: orders@crcpress.com

The Practical Guide to HIPAA Privacy and Security Compliance

Second Edition

Rebecca Herold and Kevin Beaver

CRC Press
Taylor & Francis Group
Boca Raton London New York

CRC Press is an imprint of the
Taylor & Francis Group, an **informa** business

AN AUERBACH BOOK

CRC Press
Taylor & Francis Group
6000 Broken Sound Parkway NW, Suite 300
Boca Raton, FL 33487-2742

First issued in paperback 2021

ISBN 13: 978-1-03-209893-7 (pbk)
ISBN 13: 978-1-4398-5558-4 (hbk)

Library of Congress Cataloging-in-Publication Data

Herold, Rebecca, author.
    The practical guide to HIPAA privacy and security compliance / Rebecca Herold, Kevin Beaver. -- Second edition.
        pages cm
    Includes bibliographical references and index.
    ISBN 978-1-4398-5558-4 (hardback)
    1. Medical records--Law and legislation--United States. 2. Medical records--Access control--United States. 3. Medical care--Security measures--United States. 4. Health insurance continuation coverage--United States. I. Beaver, Kevin, author. II. Title. III. Title: HIPAA privacy and security compliance.

    KF3827.R4B43 2014
    344.7304'1--dc23   2014033165

Visit the Taylor & Francis Web site at
http://www.taylorandfrancis.com

and the CRC Press Web site at
http://www.crcpress.com

Limit of Liability and Disclaimer of Warranty

The authors have used their best efforts in the preparation of this book. The information and opinions provided in this book do not constitute or substitute for legal or other professional advice. The authors make no warranties or representations regarding the completeness or accuracy of this book and disclaim any implied warranties of merchantability or fitness for a particular purpose. No warranties exist that extend beyond the descriptions in this paragraph. The completeness and accuracy of the information and opinions provided in this book are not warranted or guaranteed to produce any particular results, including HIPAA compliance. Readers should consult their own legal or other professional advisors for individualized guidance regarding the application of the HIPAA laws to their particular situations and in connection with other compliance-related concerns. The authors shall not be liable for any loss, including fines or penalties, loss of profit, or any other commercial damages, including, but not limited to special, incidental, consequential, or other damages.

To my late father, who may be the only person who read every word of all my books and other publications.

To my late mother, who was the kindest, most wonderful person I have ever known.

And a huge "*thank you*" to both my parents for always expecting me to do my best and telling me I could accomplish anything, no matter what it was. They never put limitations on me because of my gender; I have only encountered that from others since starting my career. I am grateful my parents taught me that such gender-based limitations were ridiculous.

To my wonderful sons, Noah and Heath. You are both the joy in my life.

To my husband, Tom, even though he will never read a book like this.

To Stella, my Doberman, for being a warm, furry, faithful friend.

A huge thank you to my coauthor, Kevin Beaver! Yes, we did it! Looking forward to the next edition! :)

Thank you for your consistent patience, Laurie Schlags!

To Rich O'Hanley, for his unwavering patience while we finished this book, and for his support: Thank you!

To those who read these types of books and appreciate the work that goes into them.

Rebecca Herold

Hugs and kisses to Amy, Garrett, and Mary Lin. Thanks for your constant love, trust, and support!

Serious kudos and a major pat on the back to my coauthor, Becky Herold. You have been a true gem to work with on this new edition. We finally did it!

I would also like to thank Rich O'Hanley with Taylor & Francis for helping Becky and me get the original edition of this book off the ground over a decade ago. Thanks to Laurie Schlags, our project coordinator, and to Cynthia Klivecka, our project editor, at Taylor & Francis, and to Erika West, our editor with diacriTech. It's been a pleasure working with all of you. I really appreciate all of your help!

I want to also take this opportunity to say *Thanks!* to all of my clients who have trusted in me, the "*no-name-brand*" information security consultant, over the years. I really do appreciate your business!

Last but not least, to all of the people in business who are caught up in the relentless regulations the government keeps throwing your way. From the latest HIPAA mandates to the complexities of the "new and improved" U.S. health care system, the savvy, independent thinkers see what's going on. Keep up your spirits and put common sense into action—we shall prevail!

Kevin Beaver

Contents

PART III   HIPAA SECURITY RULE

Foreword

This is an important guide. It is important because there is widespread apprehension regarding the privacy and security regulations implementing HIPAA. This apprehension threatens to block the dissemination of individually identifiable health information in many situations in which the federal government never intended to do so.

There have been widespread media reports of fear in the offices of health care providers as to their ability to respond to requests for information from persons other than the patient. Each day those of us who practice in this area receive calls from confused and concerned providers, insurers, and persons seeking to perform services for those sectors. Those calls raise a remarkable array of tough issues.

How can research using health information gleaned across massive data sets continue to be conducted? How can the discovery process in litigation proceed? How can providers determine what disclosures of health information must be "accounted for"? How can insurers provide the information that their customers (that are employers) feel they need to answer employee questions and to design new benefits across HIPAA covered and noncovered employee welfare benefit plans? How must the electronic data be secured?

To answer these questions is not simple work. First, there are hundreds of pages of regulations to be parsed. The regulations are dense. In the context of privacy, they do not set forth a list of forbidden acts.

Instead, they attempt to define the thousands of ways individually identifiable health information could appropriately be used without obtaining the patient's or insured's special permission—the so-called "authorization." Although the public policy goal may be laudable, it is challenging in terms of ease of use.

However, the interpretative challenges do not stop there. The regulations are construed in thousands of pages of preamble. The regulations and the preamble are also constantly being interpreted through questions and answers published on websites by the Office of Civil Rights and the Centers for Medicare and Medicaid Services. Distilling this body of relevant information is a daunting task. Fortunately for the reader, Kevin Beaver and Rebecca Herold have both distilled much of that law and official statements and present it through this guide in a form that makes it understandable to the thousands of persons who must conform their clinical and business practices to its dictates.

Beaver and Herold first give the clinician or businessman an orientation to the purposes of the so-called Administrative Simplification provisions of the HIPAA statute and the scope of the privacy, security, and transactions and code set regulations that have emanated from it. The authors then instruct as to the elements of the privacy rule and provide practical guidance as to many issues faced by health care providers and plans. Affected parties are given useful checklists for privacy compliance programs and sample forms. The same approach is taken with respect to the security rule: orientation, analysis of areas of challenge, and implementation guidance. Later chapters continue to provide value through in-depth review of issues by industry segment and useful case studies.

The HIPAA regulations are transforming how providers and insurers think about the individually identifiable health information they create and receive every minute of every day. The notices and acknowledgments called for by the regulation are also awakening patients and insureds to the path information about them takes as they are cared for and seek payment for that care.

There is a potential for serious harm to service levels and even to patient health if misunderstandings as to the dictates of these regulations choke off the exchange of patient-health information. This guide is a good step toward erasing many of those misunderstandings. I commend the authors for their fine efforts at translating a difficult subject into practical terms. Additional material is available from the authors' own website: http://www.hipaaprivacyandsecurity.com.

Mark Lutes

Epstein Becker Green

Washington, DC

Preface

Introduction

The Practical Guide to HIPAA Privacy and Security Compliance is designed to help you understand what the Health Insurance Portability and Accountability Act (HIPAA) is about, what it requires, what you can do to work toward compliance, and how you can maintain compliance on an ongoing basis. We have designed this book to be the one-stop "how-to" practical reference for real-world HIPAA privacy and security advice that you can immediately apply to your organization's unique and specific situation, based upon the authors' actual experiences helping hundreds of covered entities (CEs) and business associates (BAs) to meet HIPAA compliance. This book describes the HIPAA Privacy and Security Rules and compliance tasks in easy to understand language. Although we provide actual definitions and passages from the regulatory text where appropriate, instead of focusing on technical and legal theory and jargon, we lay out what you actually need to do according to the final HIPAA Privacy and Security Rules, as well as the Health Information Technology for Economic and Clinical Health (HITECH) Act and the changes that came with the 2013 Omnibus Rule, to become compliant. All these HIPAA-related requirements are very complex. Privacy and security are also very complex. Given that, we don't claim to have coverage in this book on every possible topic or nuance related to these subjects. Our goal, though, is to provide you with guidance on the HIPAA requirements and more commonly discussed topics. We also provide you with a number of checklists and other reference materials to help you get started down the compliance path and point you in the right direction for references and resources when you need them in the future.

Who This Book Was Written For

This book is designed for anyone who needs to prepare their organization, or someone else's organization, for the HIPAA laws. This book is also designed to help you determine how HIPAA may impact you, even if your organization is not a HIPAA CE, BA, or subcontractor. Our target audience includes the following:

- Privacy officers
- Security officers
- Compliance officers
- Physicians
- Nurses
- Clinicians
- Office managers
- IT managers
- Network administrators
- Attorneys
- Consultants
- Auditors
- Compliance officers
- Chief information officers
- Chief information security officers
- All of the many types of BAs involved in the health care industry

Organizations ranging from rural health clinics to large insurance companies, in addition to cloud providers, health data vaults, medical device vendors and engineers, health care industry consultants, and any other type of business that handles patient information, can utilize the material contained in this book. From nontechnical office managers to noncomputer savvy doctors to highly technical

IT specialists, practically anyone who may be touched by HIPAA can benefit from this book.

How This Book Is Organized

Even if you do not read this book cover to cover, the pertinent information you need should be easy to find by simply referring to the particular section or chapter of interest. This book contains seven major sections as follows:

Part I: HIPAA Essentials
Part II: HIPAA Privacy Rule
Part III: HIPAA Security Rule
Part IV: Covered Entity Issues
Part V: HIPAA Technology Considerations
Part VI: Managing Ongoing HIPAA Compliance
Part VII: Appendices

Please refer to this book's website at **http://www.hipaaprivacyand security.com** for critical updates to the issues discussed within this book, along with updates and additions for various HIPAA resources and links. Our goal is to create a living HIPAA resource at our website and pass along helpful HIPAA compliance tips, information, and news.

Authors

Rebecca Herold has over 25 years of information privacy, security, and compliance expertise. She is CEO of Privacy Professor® and is a partner for Compliance Helper®. She has led the NIST SGIP Smart Grid Privacy Subgroup since June 2009. She has been an adjunct professor for the Norwich University Master of Science in Information Security and Assurance (MSISA) program since 2005. She has written 17 books and  hundreds of published articles. She has been invited to speak at a wide variety of events throughout the United States, and in other worldwide locations such as Melbourne, Australia; Bogotá, Colombia; and Naas, County Kildare, Ireland.

Rebecca is widely recognized and respected, and has been providing information privacy, security, and compliance services, tools, and products to organizations in an extensive range of industries for over two decades. Just a few of her awards and recognitions include the following:

- Rebecca was ranked #2 in the "Top 25 Female Infosec Leaders to Follow on Twitter" in 2014 by Information Security Buzz.
- Rebecca was named to the ISACA International Privacy Task Force in 2013.

- Rebecca was named on Tripwire's list of "InfoSec's Rising Stars and Hidden Gems: The Top 15 Educators" in July 2013.
- Rebecca was ranked #5 in the "Top 25 Female Infosec Leaders to Follow on Twiter" in 2013 by Information Security Buzz.
- Rebecca has been named one of the "Best Privacy Advisers in the World" multiple times in recent years by *Computerworld* magazine, most recently ranking third in the world in the last rankings provided.
- In 2012, Rebecca was named one of the most influential people and groups in online privacy by Techopedia.com.
- In 2012, Rebecca was named a Privacy by Design Ambassador by the Ontario, Canada Data Privacy Commissioner.

Rebecca is a partner for the Compliance Helper services for health care organizations and their business associates to meet their HIPAA, HITECH, and other legal requirements. She is a member of the IAPP Certification Advisory Board, and is an instructor for the IAPP's CIPM, CIPP/IT, CIPP/US, and CIPP foundations classes.

Rebecca currently serves on multiple advisory boards for security, privacy, and high-tech technology organizations. She is frequently interviewed and quoted in diverse broadcasts and publications such as *IAPP Privacy Advisor*, *BNA Privacy & Security Law Report*, *Wired*, *Popular Science*, *Computerworld*, *IEEE's Security and Privacy Journal*, *NPR*, and many others. She regularly appears on the Des Moines, Iowa-based *Great Day* morning television program on KCWI to discuss and provide advice for information security and privacy topics.

Rebecca was born and raised in Missouri and has degrees in math, computer science, and education. She has lived in Iowa on a farm with her family for the past couple of decades, where they raise corn, soy beans, and sunflowers, and make hay. They are currently renovating a house that is over 100 years old and had previously been occupied by raccoons and chipmunks for several years. See more about Rebecca, her work, services, and products at:

Rebecca Herold, CIPM, CIPP/IT, CIPP/US, CISSP, CISM, CISA, FLMI
Owner & CEO, The Privacy Professor (http://www .privacyguidance.com and http://www.privacyprofessor.org)

Co-Owner, CPO, and CISO, HIPAA Compliance Tools (http://www.hipaacompliance.org)
Partner, Compliance Helper (http://www.compliancehelper.com)
Adjunct Professor for the Norwich University Master of Science in Information Security and Assurance (MSISA) program (http://infoassurance.norwich.edu/)
Twitter ID: PrivacyProf (http://twitter.com/PrivacyProf)

Kevin Beaver is an independent information security consultant, writer, professional speaker, and expert witness with Atlanta, Georgia–based Principle Logic, LLC. He has worked in IT since 1989 and specializes in performing information security assessments for corporations, security product vendors, independent software developers, universities, government agencies, and nonprofit organizations. Before starting his information  security consulting practice in 2001, Kevin served in various information technology and security roles for several health care, e-commerce, financial, and educational institutions.

Kevin has appeared on CNN as an information security expert and has been quoted in *The Wall Street Journal*, *Entrepreneur*, *Fortune Small Business*, *Men's Health*, *Women's Health*, *Woman's Day*, and *Inc. Magazine*. His work has also been referenced by the PCI Security Standards Council in their *PCI DSS Wireless Guidelines*. He has given and participated in hundreds of highly rated presentations, panel discussions, seminars, and webcasts on information security and compliance.

Kevin has authored or coauthored 11 information security books, including *Hacking For Dummies* and *Hacking Wireless Networks For Dummies* (Wiley) as well as *Implementation Strategies for Fulfilling and Maintaining IT Compliance* (Realtimepublishers.com). He has written dozens of whitepapers and hundreds of articles and guest blog posts, and he is a regular contributor to SearchSecurity.com, SearchEnterpriseDesktop.com, SearchWindowsServer.com, and *Security Technology Executive* magazine.

Kevin is the creator and producer of the *Security On Wheels* audio-books, which provide security learning for IT professionals on the go (http://www.securityonwheels.com) and its associated blog (http://www.securityonwheels.com/blog). He also covers information security and related matters on Twitter (@kevinbeaver) and YouTube (PrincipleLogic). He earned his bachelor's degree in computer engineering technology from Southern College of Technology and his master's degree in management of technology from Georgia Tech. He obtained his CISSP certification in 2001 and also holds MCSE, Master CNE, and IT Project+ certifications.

Kevin can be reached through his website (http://www.principlelogic.com) and invites you to connect to him via LinkedIn (http://www.linkedin.com/in/kevinbeaver).

PART I
HIPAA
ESSENTIALS

1
INTRODUCTION TO HIPAA

All that may come to my knowledge in the exercise of my profession or outside of my profession or in daily commerce with men, which ought not to be spread abroad, I will keep secret and will never reveal. If I keep this oath faithfully, may I enjoy my life and practice my art, respected by all men and in all times; but if I swerve from it or violate it, may the reverse be my lot.

Hippocrates (460–370 BC), the Father of Terran Medicine—Excerpt from the Hippocratic Oath

1.1 How HIPAA Came to Be

HIPAA is a very well-known acronym in the health care industry these days. It consists of old-millennium ideas, yet it brings new-millennium realities. A few people love it, a fair amount of people understand the value it brings, and even more people dislike it. So, what is all the fuss about? HIPAA is the Health Insurance Portability and Accountability Act of 1996 and is also known as Public Law 104–191 and the Kennedy–Kassebaum Bill, named after its creators, Senators Edward Kennedy (D-MA) and Nancy Kassebaum (R-KS). This legislation was passed by the Congress, signed into law by Bill Clinton, and became effective on August 21, 1996.

The overall goal of HIPAA is to provide insurance portability, fraud enforcement, and administrative simplification for the health care industry. HIPAA was formed out of the growing concerns about keeping health care information private, the need to consolidate non-standard health care data and transaction formats, as well as the general consensus to streamline health care operations and reduce the cost of providing health care services. This legislation had been a long time coming for the health care industry—this was an industry known to be behind the times from a technology perspective when HIPAA was established.

There are still challenges to address as technology continues to evolve; as patient information is shared with more individuals and entities than ever before, and as privacy and security breaches continue to proliferate throughout the health care industry; and from the many times more numbers of business associates (BAs) doing work for covered entities (CEs). Appendix A demonstrates how these challenges are impacting the safeguarding of protected health information (PHI), and contains information about all the sanctions, penalties, breaches, and noncompliance statistics that have occurred through March 7, 2014.

There have been a wide range of breaches that have occurred, many of which were preventable. Here are just a few examples of the types of breaches that have occurred:

- November 2010: Seacoast Radiology, PA, discovered that an office server containing personal patient data and billing information had been hacked into. The server contained 231,400 patient names, Social Security numbers, addresses, phone numbers, as well as basic medical diagnosis codes and basic procedure codes for billing purposes.[1]
- November 2010: An unencrypted laptop containing the PHI of 4486 patients was stolen from an employee of Hanger Prosthetics & Orthotics, Inc. The PHI involved included names, addresses, and procedure codes.[2]
- April 2012: The South Carolina Department of Health and Human Services discovered that a Medicaid employee inappropriately transferred personal information for 228,435 Medicaid beneficiaries to his personal e-mail account, violating agency policy and HIPAA. The compromised data included names, addresses, birth dates, phone numbers, and Medicaid ID numbers.[3]
- January 2013: An emergency medical services supervisor and lieutenant in the New York Fire Department who admitted he posted a picture to Facebook of a computer screen containing confidential and privileged information about a 911 caller's complaint of a gynecological emergency was fired. The

picture also showed the caller's name, address, and telephone number.[4]

- May 2013: El Centro Regional Medical Center (ECRMC) was notified that x-rays ECRMC had provided to their BA, Digital Archive Management, were missing from a storage warehouse and may not have been properly destroyed. The missing documents included 189,489 patients' x-rays, paper jackets containing the films, and sometimes a written interpretation. The information involved may include patient names, dates of birth, addresses, medical record numbers, El Centro account numbers, physicians' names, diagnoses, radiology procedures, radiology interpretations, health insurance numbers, and in some instances Social Security numbers. ECRMC terminated the contract with Digital Archive Management following this incident.[5]
- July 2013: Six workers at Cedars-Sinai Medical Center where Kim Kardashian gave birth were fired for snooping into her patient medical records.[6]

The Third Annual Benchmark Study on Patient Privacy & Data Security conducted by the Ponemon Institute and published in December 2012 found that 94% of hospitals had experienced privacy breaches, and 45% experienced more than five breaches. At that point in time, it was determined that 21,210,439 individuals had been victims of health care organization breaches; 1.85 million had been victims in 2012 alone.[7] The public is understandably increasingly concerned about the privacy of their health information. On April 14, 2003, the Office for Civil Rights (OCR) began accepting complaints involving the privacy of personal health information in the health care system. As of October 31, 2013, the OCR had received 87,597 complaints.[8] Figure 1.1 provides a timeline showing how the number of complaints has generally increased over the years.

The Administrative Simplification section (Title II, Subtitle F) of HIPAA—the portion of HIPAA that we will explore in this book—was designed to help decrease the costs of health care administration with the goal of spending that money instead on increasing the quality of health care. This includes standardizing on electronic transactions, national identifiers, and ensuring the privacy and security of confidential health information.

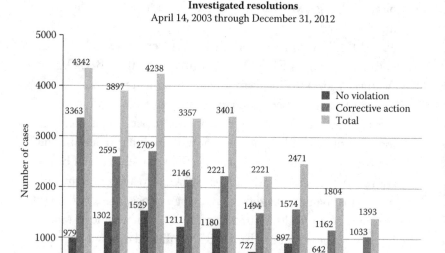

Figure 1.1   Investigated resolutions. (From U.S. Department of Health and Human Services, http://www.hhs.gov/ocr/privacy/hipaa/enforcement/highlights/indexnumbers.html, November 15, 2013.)

The Department of Health and Human Services (HHS) is the organization responsible for establishing the HIPAA standards. In February 2003, HHS Secretary Tommy G. Thompson concisely summarized HIPAA Administrative Simplification by stating the following on final release of the HIPAA Security Rule:

> Overall, these national standards required under HIPAA will make it easier and less costly for the healthcare industry to process health claims and handle other transactions while assuring patients that their information will remain secure and confidential. The security standards in particular will help safeguard confidential health information as the industry increasingly relies on computers for processing healthcare transactions.

As published in the final Privacy Rule, HHS states that HIPAA Administrative Simplification has three major purposes:

1. To protect and enhance the rights of consumers by providing them access to their health information and controlling the inappropriate use of that information
2. To improve the quality of health care in the United States by restoring trust in the health care system among consumers,

health care professionals, and the multitude of organizations and individuals committed to the delivery of care

3. To improve the efficiency and effectiveness of health care delivery by creating a national framework for health privacy protection that builds on efforts by states, health systems, and individual organizations and individuals

There are four administrative simplification subsections, or rules, which include mandates for the privacy and security of personal and confidential health care information, referred to as the Privacy Rule and the Security Rule; standardized electronic transactions and code sets, referred to as the Electronic Transactions and Code Sets Rule; and national identifiers, referred to as the Unique Identifier Rules. The Health Information Technology for Economic and Clinical Health (HITECH) Act was enacted as part of the American Recovery and Reinvestment Act of 2009, and signed into law on February 17, 2009, to promote the adoption and meaningful use of health information technology. Subtitle D of the HITECH Act addresses the privacy and security concerns associated with the electronic transmission of health information, in part, through several provisions that strengthen the civil and criminal enforcement and breach safeguards of the HIPAA rules.[9]

In this book, we provide a brief overview of the Electronic Transactions and Code Sets Rule, which you can find in Section 1.10, and in-depth coverage of the Privacy Rule, Security Rule, and the HITECH Act, with the associated modifications made to them as a result of the 2013 Omnibus Rule, throughout the rest of the book. Moving forward, unless noted otherwise, our references to HIPAA will focus solely on the 2013 Omnibus Rule versions of the Privacy and Security Rules and the HITECH Act.

1.2 What HIPAA Covers

In addition to the various transactions and code sets standards, HIPAA mandates protection of various forms of confidential health information referred to as PHI. PHI is considered any oral or recorded information relating to any past, present, or future physical or mental health of an individual, provision of health care to the individual, or the payment for the health care of that individual. With very few exceptions, oral or recorded PHI consists of individual health information that is spoken, written, or stored in hard copy or electronically in any way. Basically, PHI identifies or can be used to reasonably identify an individual. There are 18 identifiers originally defined by HIPAA that can be used to identify an individual, with a 19th item that was added in 2010 as a result of the Genetic Information Nondiscrimination Act (GINA).[10] Nineteen identifiers are collectively referred to as PHI when used in activities covered by HIPAA. See Section 1.8.2 for a list of specified PHI items.

Information that has been "de-identified" is not covered under HIPAA. We will go into additional detail about PHI in Chapter 6, where we cover the Privacy Rule in detail.

1.3 Current State of HIPAA Compliance

Between April 2003 and October 31, 2013, the HHS received over 87,597 HIPAA complaints.[8] Ninety-four percent of complaints received (over 82,698) were resolved as follows:

- Through investigation and enforcement (over 21,832)
- Through investigation and finding no violation (9,807)
- Through closure of cases that were not eligible for enforcement (51,059)

From the original HIPAA compliance dates to October 31, 2013, the compliance issues investigated most are the following, compiled cumulatively, in order of frequency:

- Impermissible uses and disclosures of PHI
- Lack of safeguards of PHI
- Lack of patient access to their PHI
- Uses or disclosures of more than the minimum necessary PHI
- Lack of administrative safeguards of electronic PHI

The most common types of CEs that have been required to take corrective action to achieve voluntary compliance are the following, in order of frequency:

- Private practices
- General hospitals
- Outpatient facilities

- Health plans (group health plans and health insurance issuers)
- Pharmacies

It is important to note that the previous numbers primarily represent investigations of CEs. Because the Omnibus Rule compliance requirements deadline for BAs and their subcontractors was September 23, 2013, as time goes on these numbers are expected to include significantly more data for those types of entities that, to date, have been largely uncollected.

1.4 Overview of the Omnibus Rule Updates

The final version of the Omnibus Rule was announced on January 17, 2013.[11] The HHS summarized the 526 pages of the Omnibus Rule as follows:[12]

> This omnibus final rule is comprised of the following four final rules:
> 1. Final modifications to the HIPAA Privacy, Security, and Enforcement Rules mandated by the Health Information Technology for Economic and Clinical Health (HITECH) Act, and certain other modifications to improve the Rules, which were issued as a proposed rule on July 14, 2010. These modifications do the following:
>   a. Make BAs of CEs directly liable for compliance with certain of the HIPAA Privacy and Security Rules' requirements.
>   b. Strengthen the limitations on the use and disclosure of PHI for marketing and fund-raising purposes, and prohibit the sale of PHI without individual authorization.
>   c. Expand individuals' rights to receive electronic copies of their health information and to restrict disclosures to a health plan concerning treatment for which the individual has paid out of pocket in full.
>   d. Require modifications to, and redistribution of, a CE's Notice of Privacy Practices.
>   e. Modify the individual authorization and other requirements to facilitate research and disclosure of child immunization proof to schools, and to enable access to decedent information by family members or others.
>   f. Adopt the additional HITECH Act enhancements to the Enforcement Rule not previously adopted in the October 30, 2009, interim final rule, such as the provisions addressing enforcement of noncompliance with the HIPAA Rules due to willful neglect.

2. Final rule adopting changes to the HIPAA Enforcement Rule to incorporate the increased and tiered civil money penalty structure provided by the HITECH Act, originally published as an interim final rule on October 30, 2009.
3. Final rule on Breach Notification for Unsecured Protected Health Information under the HITECH Act, which replaces the breach notification rule's "harm" threshold with a more objective standard and supplants an interim final rule published on August 24, 2009.
4. Final rule modifying the HIPAA Privacy Rule as required by the Genetic Information Nondiscrimination Act (GINA) to prohibit most health plans from using or disclosing genetic information for underwriting purposes, which was published as a proposed rule on October 7, 2009.

1.5 What the HITECH Act Covers

The HITECH Act[13] was authored by the OCR of the HHS and covers four main topics:

- Extension of the HIPAA Security Rule and the privacy and security provisions of the HITECH Act to BAs
- Modification of the Breach Notification Rule
- Changes to the HIPAA Privacy Rule requirements, some of which are mandated by the HITECH Act and some of which address problems with the original standards that have emerged over time
- Modifications to the HIPAA Enforcement Rule to implement the HITECH Act

The effective date of the rule was March 26, 2013, and the changes to the Enforcement Rule were implemented then. CEs and their BAs had to have been in compliance with all the other changes by September 23, 2013.

1.6 Pending Proposed Rules

1.6.1 Accounting of Disclosures Notice of Proposed Rulemaking

The HHS Centers for Medicare and Medicaid Services (CMS) issued a HIPAA Accounting of Disclosures Notice of Proposed Rulemaking

(NPRM) on May 31, 2011 with a goal to simplify the HIPAA Privacy Rule's requirements that CEs provide individuals with accountings of disclosures of their PHI.[14] However, the NPRM included a new requirement that CEs provide individuals, on request, with "access reports" concerning their PHI. The comments to the NPRM were due on August 1, 2011.

1.6.2 Patients' Access to Test Reports NPRM

The HHS/CMS issued a HIPAA Patients' Access to Test Reports NPRM on September 14, 2011 that would amend the Privacy Rule to provide individuals the right to receive their test reports directly from laboratories by removing the exceptions for Clinical Laboratory Improvement Amendments (CLIA)-certified laboratories and CLIA-exempt laboratories from the provision that provides individuals with the right of access to their PHI.[15] The comments to the NPRM were due on November 14, 2011.

1.6.3 Reporting Certain Information to the National Instant Criminal Background Check System NPRM

This NPRM, announced on January 7, 2014, would modify the HIPAA Privacy Rule to permit certain HIPAA CEs to disclose to the National Instant Criminal Background Check System (NICS) the identities of persons prohibited by federal law from possessing or receiving a firearm for reasons related to mental health.[16]

The proposal would give states and certain CEs added flexibility to ensure accurate but limited information is reported to the NICS, which would not include clinical, diagnostic, or other mental health information. Instead, certain CEs would be permitted to disclose the minimum necessary identifying information about individuals who have been involuntarily committed to a mental institution or otherwise have been determined by a lawful authority to be a danger to themselves or others or to lack the mental capacity to manage their own affairs. Importantly, the proposed permission focuses on those entities performing relevant commitments, adjudications, or data repository functions.

1.7 Organizations That Must Comply with HIPAA

1.7.1 Covered Entities

Virtually the entire health care industry, as well as a significant number of organizations in other industries, is affected by HIPAA in one way or another. Large insurance companies, hospitals, self-insured employers, small physician practices, and independent health insurance agents, to name a few, are required to comply with HIPAA. These organizations are called CEs. There are three main categories of CEs:

1. Health care providers: A health care provider can be an individual, a group, or an organization. An individual is a natural person licensed or authorized in some other way to perform or provide medical services, care, equipment, or supplies. A few examples include doctors, nurses, pharmacists, and physical therapists. A group is one that is typically made up of more than one person to provide patient care, including professional services such as billing and payment. For example, two physicians are practicing as a group by billing and receiving payments as a single entity. An organization is an entity composed of more than one person that is authorized to provide medical services, care, equipment, or supplies as part of their usual business. A few examples include hospitals, laboratories, pharmacies, nursing facilities, and health maintenance organizations (HMOs).

2. Health plans: Generally speaking, these are individual or group plans that provide or pay for medical care. Examples include private and governmental health insurance issuers such as HMOs, preferred provider organizations, Medicare and Medicaid programs, as well as employer-sponsored health plans with coverage for 50 or more employees. Health plans do not include workers' compensation programs, property and casualty programs, or disability insurance programs, even though they may pay health care costs.

3. Health care clearinghouses: These are public or private entities that process or facilitate the processing of nonstandard data elements of health information into a standard format, or convert from a standard format to one that is nonstandard, for electronic transactions. A few examples include billing services, repricing companies, value-added networks, and even some banks.

1.7.2 Business Associates

A BA is a person or organization, other than a member of a CE's workforce, that performs certain functions or activities on behalf of, or provides certain services to, a CE that involve the use or disclosure of PHI.[17] BA functions or activities on behalf of a CE include claims processing, data analysis, utilization review, and billing. BA services to a CE are limited to legal, actuarial, accounting, consulting, data aggregation, management, administrative, accreditation, or financial services. However, persons or organizations are not considered BAs if their functions or services do not involve the use or disclosure of PHI, and where any access to PHI by such persons would be incidental, meaning unintended, if at all. A CE can be the BA of another CE.

There is no size specification to be considered a BA. BAs vary in size from one-person businesses to businesses with hundreds of thousands of employees. BAs include start-ups and businesses that have been in existence for many decades. All must comply with all the HIPAA rules that are associated with the types of services and/or products they provide to CEs.

Entities specifically designated as being BAs under the HITECH Act include the following:

- Health information organizations
- E-prescribing gateways
- Data transmission vendors with routine access to PHI
- Personal health record (PHR) vendors that offer PHRs to individuals on behalf of a CE
- Subcontractors that create, receive, maintain, or transmit PHI for or on behalf of a BA

Figure 1.2 is a decision tree that can be used to identify BAs. Chapter 21 provides additional information about BAs.

1.7.3 Subcontractors

The 2013 Final Omnibus Rule defined a subcontractor as a BA to ensure any PHI the subcontractor creates or receives on behalf of the BA is appropriately safeguarded. As such, subcontractors are obligated to comply with all HIPAA regulatory requirements as appropriate for the services they are providing to the BAs. This includes the requirement for them to have a contract with each BA that meets the requirements of a BA Agreement. BA Agreements will be discussed in more detail in Chapter 5.

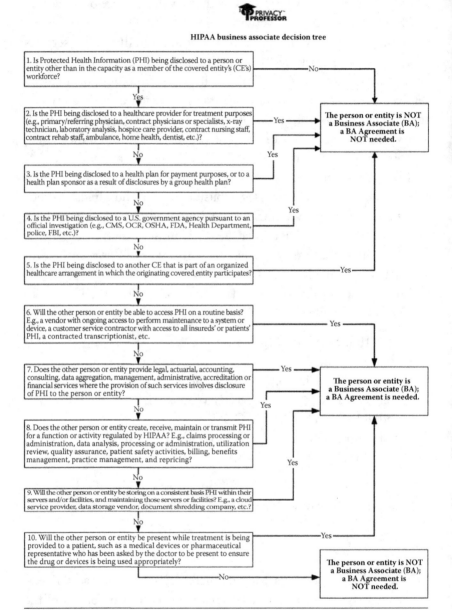

Figure 1.2 HIPAA business associate decision tree. (From The Privacy Professor®, http://www.privacyprofessor.org. With permission.)

A BA is liable, in accordance with the federal common law of agency, for a civil monetary penalty for a violation based on the act or omission of any subcontractor acting on behalf of the BA.

1.8 Organizations That Must Comply with the HITECH Act

CEs, BAs, and subcontractors, as previously described, must comply with the HITECH Act. The Federal Trade Commission's (FTC's) Health Breach Notification Rule (HBNR) was created under the HITECH breach regulations, and requires vendors of PHRs, who do not also fall under the HIPAA definition of a BA, to notify consumers and the FTC in the event that the security of personally identifiable health information in a PHR maintained by the PHR vendor is breached.[18]

HBNR applies to the following:

- Vendors of PHRs
- PHR-related entities
- Third-party service providers for PHR vendors and PHR-related entities

1.8.1 What Does Health Care Mean?

Health care is defined within 45 Code of Federal Regulations (CFR) § 160.103. Beyond care, the services and supplies related to an individual's health are all considered health care. A few examples, as discussed in the HIPAA regulations, include the following:

- A preventive, diagnostic, rehabilitative, maintenance, or palliative care, and counseling service, assessment, or procedure with respect to the physical or mental condition or functional status of an individual or that affects the structure or function of the body
- The sale or dispensing of a drug, device, equipment, or other item in accordance with a prescription

Note: For a complete set of definitions found throughout the HIPAA regulatory texts, see Appendix A.

1.8.2 What Is Protected Health Information?

1. HIPAA, under the Omnibus Rule, defines PHI to mean individually identifiable health information, with one exception (item 2), that is:
   a. Transmitted by electronic media
   b. Maintained in electronic media
   c. Transmitted or maintained in any other form or medium
2. PHI *excludes* individually identifiable health information in the following:
   a. Education records covered by the Family Educational Rights and Privacy Act, as amended, 20 U.S.C. 1232g
   b. Records described at 20 U.S.C. 1232g (a)(4)(B)(iv)
   c. Employment records held by a CE in its role as employer
   d. Regarding a person who has been deceased for more than 50 years

It is worth noting that item d was especially controversial. Many privacy groups have significant concerns about how the privacy of the deceased, and their descendants, may be significantly negatively impacted by having privacy protections expire after 50 years.

The term "individually identifiable health information" was essentially eliminated within the Omnibus Rule, and rolled into the definition of PHI.

The following 19 items are considered to be PHI items:

1. Names.
2. All geographic subdivisions smaller than a state, including street address, city, county, precinct, zip code, and their equivalent geocodes, except for the initial three digits of a zip code if, according to the current publicly available data from the Bureau of the Census:
   a. The geographic unit formed by combining all zip codes with the same three initial digits contains more than 20,000 people.
   b. The initial three digits of a zip code for all such geographic units containing 20,000 or fewer people are changed to 000.

3. All elements of dates (except year) for dates directly related to an individual, including birth date, admission date, discharge date, date of death; and all ages over 89 and all elements of dates (including year) indicative of such age, except that such ages and elements may be aggregated into a single category of age 90 or older.
4. Telephone numbers.
5. Fax numbers.
6. E-mail addresses.
7. Social Security numbers.
8. Medical record numbers.
9. Health plan beneficiary numbers.
10. Account numbers.
11. Certificate/license numbers.
12. Vehicle identifiers and serial numbers, including license plate numbers.
13. Device identifiers and serial numbers.
14. Web URLs.
15. IP address numbers.
16. Biometric identifiers, including finger and voice prints.
17. Full-face photographic images and any comparable images.
18. Any other unique identifying number, characteristic, or code, except as permitted by paragraph (c) of § 164.514.
19. Individually identifying genetic information.

Note: For a complete set of definitions found throughout the HIPAA regulatory texts, see Appendix A.

1.8.3 What Is Health Information Technology?

As defined by the HHS:[19]

> The term "health information technology" (health IT) is a broad concept that encompasses an array of technologies to store, share, and analyze health information.
>
> More and more, health care providers are using health IT to improve patient care. But health IT is not just for health care providers. You can use health IT to better communicate with your doctor, learn and share

information about your health, and take actions that will improve your quality of life. Health IT lets you be a key part of the team that keeps you healthy.

See more discussion of it at the HealthIT.gov site.[19]

Note: For a complete set of definitions found throughout the HIPAA regulatory texts, see Appendix A.

1.8.4 What Is a Health Information Exchange?

As defined by the HHS:[20]

> The term "health information exchange" (HIE) actually encompasses two related concepts:
>
>   Verb: The electronic sharing of health-related information among organizations
>
>   Noun: An organization that provides services to enable the electronic sharing of health-related information

Note: For a complete set of definitions found throughout the HIPAA regulatory texts, see Appendix A.

1.8.5 What Are Electronic Health Records and Electronic Medical Records?

As defined by the HHS:[21]

> Electronic medical records (EMRs) are a digital version of the paper charts in the clinician's office. An EMR contains the medical and treatment history of the patients in one practice. EMRs have advantages over paper records. For example, EMRs allow clinicians to
>
> - Track data over time
> - Easily identify which patients are due for preventive screenings or checkups
> - Check how their patients are doing on certain parameters—such as blood pressure readings or vaccinations
> - Monitor and improve overall quality of care within the practice

But the information in EMRs doesn't travel easily out of the practice. In fact, the patient's record might even have to be printed out and delivered by mail to specialists and other members of the care team. In that regard, EMRs are not much better than a paper record.

Electronic health records (EHRs) do all those things—and more. EHRs focus on the total health of the patient—going beyond standard clinical data collected in the provider's office and inclusive of a broader view on a patient's care. EHRs are designed to reach out beyond the health organization that originally collects and compiles the information. They are built to share information with other health care providers, such as laboratories and specialists, so they contain information from all the clinicians involved in the patient's care. The National Alliance for Health Information Technology stated that EHR data "can be created, managed, and consulted by authorized clinicians and staff across more than one healthcare organization."

See more discussion of EMRs and EHRs at the HealthIT.gov site (http://www.healthit.gov/buzz-blog/electronic-health-and-medical-records/emr-vs-ehr-difference/).[21]

Note: For a complete set of definitions found throughout the HIPAA regulatory texts, see Appendix A.

1.8.6 What Are Covered Transactions?

Covered transactions under HIPAA are those for which the secretary has adopted standards as described in 45 CFR Part 162. If a health care provider uses another CE (such as another provider, a health plan, or a clearinghouse) to conduct covered transactions in electronic form on its behalf, the health care provider is considered to be conducting the transaction in electronic form. A transaction is a covered transaction if it meets the regulatory definition for a covered transaction. You can find the complete regulatory definitions for each type of covered transaction as indicated in the following list:

- 45 CFR § 162.1101: Health care claims or equivalent encounter information transactions
- 45 CFR § 162.1201: The eligibility for a health plan transaction
- 45 CFR § 162.1301: The referral certification and authorization transaction
- 45 CFR § 162.1401: A health care claim status transaction
- 45 CFR § 162.1501: The enrollment and disenrollment in a health plan transaction
- 45 CFR § 162.1601: The health care payment and remittance advice transaction

- 45 CFR § 162.1701: The health plan premium payment transaction
- 45 CFR § 162.1801: The coordination of benefits transaction

Note: For a complete set of definitions found throughout the HIPAA regulatory texts, see Appendix A.

1.8.7 What Does Electronic Form Mean?

When HIPAA refers to information in "electronic form," it means using electronic media to store or transmit information. Such types of electronic media include CDs, disks, magnetic tapes, computer hard drives, dial-up lines, private networks, leased lines, the Internet, extranets that connect businesses with business partners, and so on. The term is defined in 45 CFR § 162.103.

Note: For a complete set of definitions found throughout the HIPAA regulatory texts, see Appendix A.

1.8.8 Are You a Covered Health Care Provider?

Do you furnish, bill, or receive payment for health care as part of your business?

- If NO, you are not a CE.
- If YES, do you execute covered transactions?
  - If NO, you are not a CE.
  - If YES, are the covered transactions transmitted in electronic form?
    - If NO, you are not a CE.
    - If YES, you *are* a CE health care provider. Be sure to read Chapter 16 for information specific to providers.

Note: For a complete set of definitions found throughout the HIPAA regulatory texts, see Appendix A.

1.8.9 Are You a Covered Health Care Clearinghouse?

Do you facilitate health information processing from a nonstandard format (or content) to a standard format? Or, do you convert standard format (or content) health information into a nonstandard format?

- If NO, you are not a CE clearinghouse.
- If YES, do you do these activities for another legal entity?
  - If NO, you are not a CE clearinghouse.
  - If YES, you *are* a CE clearinghouse. Be sure to read Chapter 18 for information specific to clearinghouses.

Note: For a complete set of definitions found throughout the HIPAA regulatory texts, see Appendix A.

1.8.10 Are You a Covered Entity Private Benefit Plan?

This is a somewhat detailed analysis best performed by using the decision chart shown in Exhibit 1.1, based on the one provided by CMS. Be sure to read Chapter 18 for information specific to health plans.

Exhibit 1.1   Covered Entity Decision Diagram

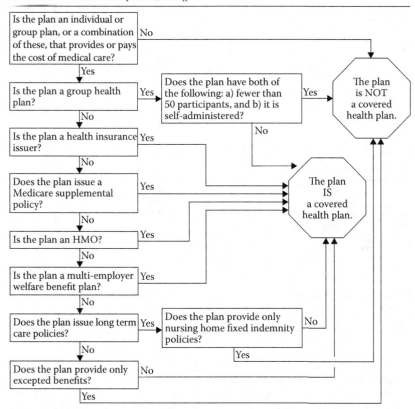

Note: For a complete set of definitions found throughout the HIPAA regulatory texts, see Appendix A.

1.8.11 Are You a Covered Government-Funded Health Plan Program?

This is also a detailed analysis and best presented in the decision chart shown in Exhibit 1.2, also based on a similar one provided by CMS.* Be sure to read Chapter 19 for information specific to covered health plans.

Exhibit 1.2   Health Plan Decision Diagram

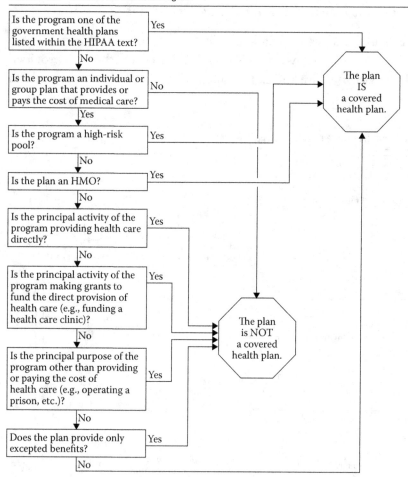

---

* CMS has a set of CE automated decision tools that can help health care organizations that are having an identity crisis decide whether or not HIPAA applies to them. These tools can be found at https://www.cms.gov/Regulations-and-Guidance/HIPAA-Administrative-Simplification/HIPAAGenInfo/AreYouaCoveredEntity.html.

Note: For a complete set of definitions found throughout the HIPAA regulatory texts, see Appendix A.

1.8.12 Hybrid Entities

Simply put, a hybrid entity is a CE whose covered functions are not its primary functions. An organization that is a single legal entity whose business activities include both covered and noncovered functions can designate itself as a hybrid entity. In that case, only the identified health care component is considered a CE.

It is very clear that some entities are CEs based on their business activities; for instance, networks of hospitals, or a nationwide health plan with millions of members. However, there are many large organizations that have health care components, but the organization itself is not primarily a health care entity. Consider state governments, for example. State governments support health care services, but they also support law enforcement, transportation, education, and other services. Large organizations that provide multiple services that include health care components are likely considered hybrid entities.

The Privacy Rule defines a hybrid entity as a single legal entity that also happens to be a CE, whose business services and activities include covered as well as noncovered functions, and that has portions of the organization designated as health care components. A hybrid CE must:

- Designate the components of the organization that perform health care-related activities.
- Ensure the health care component complies with requirements.
- Create adequate administrative, technical, and physical separations (also commonly called firewalls, not to be confused with technical Internet firewalls) between components.
- Ensure no disclosures between the health care component and other parts, except as allowed under HIPAA.
- Ensure workforce members with duties to both health care and non-health care components comply with the HIPAA requirements and not disclose PHI to the non-health care component.

The entire organization of which the hybrid entity is a part must still adhere to some of the CE requirements, such as the following:

- Implementing safeguards to protect PHI, and not disclose PHI to the non-health care components
- Establishing privacy and security policies and procedures
- Ensuring applicable language is included in BA agreements to protect PHI

There are advantages and disadvantages for an organization to declare itself a hybrid entity. The most apparent advantages are that as a hybrid entity the organization can do the following:

- Limit the scope, and thus expenses and efforts, for HIPAA compliance activities.
- Target the detailed compliance training and administrative procedures to only the identified health care component and not the entire organization.
- Designate otherwise noncovered areas of the organization that provide services to the health care component (such as legal, accounting) as part of the health care component to facilitate sharing of PHI with these areas, and also eliminate the need for BA agreements and individual authorizations with these components.

Some disadvantages for an organization to declare itself a hybrid entity include the following:

- Time, effort, and expense must be made to identify the health care components.
- Internal systems of administrative, technical, and physical firewalls and safeguards must be established and maintained between the health care and non-health care components.
- Information shared outside the health care component will likely need to be more limited, and disclosures to the non-health care component must be tracked.
- Workforce members' access to information must be completely evaluated and modified appropriately.

- Clients and business partners may potentially receive or believe they are receiving inconsistent treatment from the different components.
- There will likely be many more forms to administer and maintain.
- Staff confusion and compliance enforcement may be more difficult.
- Challenges may exist with overlapping and shared work areas, computer systems, and so on.

Each organization must weigh the advantages and disadvantages of declaring themselves a hybrid entity and make its decision based on its own unique situation.

Note: For a complete set of definitions found throughout the HIPAA regulatory texts, see Appendix A.

1.8.13 Business Associates

Individuals or organizations doing business with CEs, referred to as BAs, may be affected by HIPAA as well. To fall into the BA category, these individuals or organizations must perform an activity involving the use or disclosure of PHI on behalf of a CE. This does not include performing any activities as an employee of the CE.

CEs may also be BAs to other CEs. For any BA relationship that a CE has, a BA agreement that holds the BAs responsible for certain HIPAA requirements must be in place between the two parties. There are exceptions to this rule as well. These exceptions apply to CEs that disclose PHI to other CEs for purposes of treatment, payment, and operations in the course of normal business. We cover BA issues, including BA agreements, in more detail in Chapter 21.

Note: For a complete set of definitions found throughout the HIPAA regulatory texts, see Appendix A.

1.9 HIPAA Penalties and Enforcement

Like other laws affecting the health care industry, such as the Occupational Safety and Health Act, HIPAA must be taken seriously. There are civil penalties, as well as severe criminal penalties that include huge fines and possible prison time. If a complaint is lodged against an entity (CE, BA, or subcontractor) and an investigation or compliance review determines no violation exists, the secretary of HHS will inform both the entity and the person or organization filing the complaint in writing.

If a complaint is lodged against an entity and the resulting compliance review confirms noncompliance with the HIPAA rules, the entity will be informed in writing by the secretary, who will attempt to resolve the situation by informal means if possible. If the situation cannot be resolved in this manner, a formal noncompliance report will be issued to both the complainant and entity. The 2013 Omnibus Rule significantly increased the civil money penalties, as shown in Table 1.1, and introduced some new related terms defined within Sections 160.401, 160.402, and 160.404. The Omnibus Rule contains in-depth discussion of how these penalties will be applied, especially the upper limits, which it notes provide the secretary with flexibility to address the specific situation.

In 2009, HITECH gave state attorneys general the authority to bring civil actions on behalf of their state residents for violations of HIPAA. State attorneys general can sue in federal district court to obtain monetary damages on behalf of state residents and/or to enjoin further violations of HIPAA. Actions that have occurred since state attorneys general obtained this power include:

Table 1.1   Categories of Violations and Respective Penalty Amounts Available

VIOLATION CATEGORY— SECTION 1176 (A)(1)	EACH VIOLATION ($)	ALL SUCH VIOLATIONS OF AN IDENTICAL PROVISION IN A CALENDAR YEAR ($)
(A) Did not know	100–50,000	1,500,000
(B) Reasonable cause	1,000–50,000	1,500,000
(C)(i) Willful neglect—corrected	10,000–50,000	1,500,000
(C)(ii) Willful neglect—not corrected	50,000	1,500,000

- On May 26, 2012, the Massachusetts attorney general announced that it had settled a lawsuit filed against South Shore Hospital for $750,000. The lawsuit, which alleged violations of HIPAA and the Massachusetts Consumer Protection Act, arose out of South Shore's decision to send unencrypted backup tapes off-site to a data archiving vendor to be erased and resold as blank media. However, South Shore failed to notify the vendor that the tapes contained PHI and did not ensure that the vendor had the appropriate safeguards to protect the PHI.
- On July 30, 2012, the Minnesota attorney general announced a $2.5 million settlement with BA Accretive Health, Inc., a debt collection agency serving two Minnesota hospitals. The settlement arose out of a lawsuit filed in January 2012 alleging violations of HIPAA and other Minnesota state laws after Accretive lost a laptop containing the unencrypted PHI of over 23,000 Minnesota patients.
- On January 7, 2013, Massachusetts Attorney General Martha Coakley announced that several Massachusetts medical practices had agreed to a consent judgment and $140,000 payment to settle charges they improperly disposed of medical information. The defendants, who included several pathology practices and a firm that provided medical billing services to those practices, were accused of dumping hard-copy medical records at the Georgetown Transfer Station, a waste management facility open to the public. The records allegedly contained the names, Social Security numbers, and medical diagnoses of approximately 67,000 individuals.
- On July 12, 2013, Illinois Attorney General Lisa Madigan announced that she sent letters to operators of eight popular health-related websites requesting information about the websites' online data collection practices. The attorney general's press release underscored how individuals' health-related information shared online, which would be protected if disclosed in a traditional medical setting, "can be captured, shared and sold when online users enter their information into a website." The attorney general also stated that "website disclosure about the extent to which information is captured or shared is buried in privacy policies not found on the websites' main pages."

In addition, there may be more stringent state laws that could pre-empt HIPAA laws and result in different or additional penalties. We will discuss this in more detail in Chapter 9. Regarding the enforce-ment of HIPAA, the OCR of HHS is responsible for enforcing the Privacy Rule and Security Rule.

See Appendix B for a full set of detailed penalties and enforcement statistics that have occurred up through March 7, 2014.

1.10 Insight into the Electronic Transactions and Code Sets Rule

Although this book focuses on the HIPAA Privacy and Security Rules, it is important for privacy and information security professionals to understand the types and forms of information, as defined within the Electronic Transactions and Code Sets and Unique Identifiers Rules, for which they will need to implement privacy and security safeguards. They will need to include their information technology and services staff, in particular those responsible for implementing the Electronic Transactions and Code Sets Rules and the Unique Identifier Rules, when they are planning HIPAA privacy and security actions.

HHS issued the final electronic transaction standards in August 2000. The intent of these standards was to make the processing of health care claims more efficient, reduce the volume of paperwork, and provide better service for providers, insurers, and patients. They established a new standard by which data content, codes, and for-mats must comply within submitted electronic claims and adminis-trative health care transactions. HHS reports that if all health care entities follow these standards, the health care industry will realize a $29.9 billion net savings over a 10-year period by eliminating inefficient paper forms. While not required, all health care provid-ers will be encouraged to use this electronic standard for service billing. Also, all health plans are required to accept claims in this standard electronic form, in addition to accepting referral authori-zations and other defined health care transactions within this form. The rule is composed of standards for eight types of electronic transactions and for code sets to be used within these transactions. It also outlines the requirements for using the standards to which health plans, health care clearinghouses, and certain health care providers must adhere.

Because of the tremendous amount of software implementations and upgrades necessary to establish these electronic transaction standards, Congress adopted legislation in December 2001 that allowed most CEs to obtain a one-year extension to comply with the standards. If a qualified CE submitted its extension by the deadline, it had until October 16, 2003, to implement the electronic transaction standards. The compliance date for small health plans remained October 16, 2003. For those organizations that filed for an extension, transactions and code sets testing must have begun by April 16, 2003. The official government website for information about the HIPAA Electronics Transactions and Code Sets Standards is http://aspe.hhs.gov/admnsimp/bannertx.htm.

Section 1173 of the HIPAA Administrative Simplification requires "a standard unique health identifier for each individual, employer, health plan, and healthcare provider for use in the healthcare system." The wording makes it clear that multiple uses for identifiers would be necessary for multiple classifications of health care providers. The proposed unique identifier rules apply to health plans and clearinghouses, as well as any health care provider who electronically transmits HIPAA-covered transactions.

On August 24, 2012, the HHS announced a final rule for the standard for a national unique health plan identifier and a data element that will serve as an "other entity" identifier. This is an identifier for entities that are not health plans, health care providers, or individuals, but that need to be identified in standard transactions. The rule also specifies the circumstances under which an organization-covered health care provider, such as a hospital, must require certain noncovered individual health care providers who are prescribers to obtain and disclose a National Provider Identifier. You can find a copy of the final rule at http://www.gpo.gov/fdsys/pkg/FR-2012-09-05/pdf/2012-21238.pdf.

1.11 Conclusion

In this chapter, we have summarized what HIPAA is about. As you can see, it is quite comprehensive, and compliance will certainly take some time and resources to accomplish. In subsequent chapters on the Privacy and Security Rules, we will go into more detail that can provide you some guidance on how to move forward. At the end of each chapter, including this one, you will find practical checklists that will recap some of the major points in the chapter and can provide a quick reference of key items on which to focus.

Practical Checklist

- Does your organization supply, bill, or receive payment for health care services with payers or with CMS?
- Does your organization provide services that involve PHI on behalf of a CE or a BA?
- Have you identified all your organization's BAs and subcontractors, and received signed contracts from them?
- Do you know where to get information about the outstanding proposed rules, as soon as they are finalized?
- Are you aware of the penalties for noncompliance with the HIPAA rules?
- Have you performed a privacy and security assessment of your environment to determine your risks?
- Have you contacted your information systems and software vendors to ensure they have HIPAA-compliant software?
- Are your internal and in-house produced systems software HIPAA compliant?
- Are the cloud service providers that process and/or store PHI in compliance with all HIPAA requirements?
- If you use a claims clearinghouse, have you checked to ensure it is compliant with HIPAA?
- Have you updated your applicable documents to incorporate the required procedures and diagnosis code changes?
- Do you have procedures for obtaining the necessary demographic, charge, and diagnosis information?

2

RELATED REGULATIONS, LAWS, STANDARDS, AND GUIDANCE

2.1 Introduction

The Health Insurance Portability and Accountability Act (HIPAA) has had an impact on a wide range of existing laws and regulations, and also spawned many new data protection laws and regulations since it was signed into law in 1996. There have also been numerous guidance documents and advice provided by the Department of Health and Human Services (HHS) for various HIPAA compliance topics. This chapter provides an overview of some of the most significant.

2.2 ARRA and the HITECH Act

The American Recovery and Reinvestment Act of 2009 (ARRA, or Public Law 111–5), commonly referred to as the Stimulus or the Recovery Act, was an economic stimulus package enacted by the 111th U.S. Congress in February 2009 and signed into law on February 17, 2009, by President Barack Obama.

To respond to the Great Recession, the primary objective for ARRA was to save and create jobs almost immediately. Secondary objectives were to provide temporary relief programs for those most impacted by the recession and invest in infrastructure, education, health, and renewable energy.

The health objective included the creation of the Health Information Technology for Economic and Clinical Health (HITECH) Act. The purpose was to improve American health care delivery and patient care through an unprecedented investment in health information technology (HIT). The provisions of the HITECH Act are specifically designed to work together to provide the necessary assistance and technical support to providers, enable coordination and alignment within and among states, establish connectivity to the public health community in case of emergencies, and ensure the workforce is properly trained and equipped to be meaningful users of certified electronic health records (EHRs). These programs collaboratively build the foundation for every American to benefit from an EHR as part of a modernized, interconnected, and vastly improved system of care delivery.

Title IV, Division B of the HITECH Act establishes incentive payments under the Medicare and Medicaid programs for eligible professionals (EPs) and eligible hospitals (EHs) that meaningfully use certified EHR technology (CEHRT); these are commonly referenced as being "meaningful use" activities. The Centers for Medicare and Medicaid Services (CMS) are charged with managing the Medicare and Medicaid EHR Incentive Programs.

On April 17, 2009, HHS issued guidance specifying the technologies and methodologies that render protected health information (PHI) unusable, unreadable, or indecipherable to unauthorized individuals, as required by the HITECH Act passed as part of ARRA. This guidance was developed through a joint effort by the Office of Civil Rights (OCR), the Office of the National Coordinator for HIT, and CMS.

This guidance related to two breach notification regulations: one issued by HHS for covered entities (CEs) and their business associates (BAs) under HIPAA (Section 13402 of HITECH) and one issued by the Federal Trade Commission (FTC) for vendors of personal health records and other non-HIPAA CEs (Section 13407 of HITECH).

2.2.1 Meaningful Use

ARRA authorized the CMS to provide incentive payments to EPs and EHs, who adopt, implement, upgrade, or demonstrate meaningful use of CEHRT. CMS is making available up to $27 billion in EHR incentive payments, or as much as $44,000 (through Medicare) or $63,750 (through Medicaid) per eligible health care professional. EHs, including critical access hospitals, can qualify for incentive payments totaling approximately $2 million or more.

To receive the incentive payments, entities must demonstrate they have met the criteria for the EHR Incentive Program's privacy and security objective, among other requirements. This objective, "ensure adequate privacy and security protections for personal health information," is the fifth and final health policy priority of the EHR Incentive Program. The measure for Stage 1 aligns with HIPAA's administrative safeguard to conduct a security risk assessment and correct any identified deficiencies.

2.2.2 Breach Notice Requirements

The HIPAA Breach Notification Rule, 45 CFR § 164.400-414, requires HIPAA CEs and their BAs to provide notification following a breach of unsecured PHI.[1] Similar breach notification provisions implemented and enforced by the FTC apply to vendors of personal health records and their third-party service providers, pursuant to Section 13407 of the HITECH Act.

Subtitle D of Division A of the HITECH Act, entitled "Privacy," among other provisions, required the HHS to issue interim final regulations for breach notification by CEs subject to the Administrative Simplification provisions of HIPAA, and their BAs. These breach notification provisions are found in Section 13402 of the HITECH Act and apply to HIPAA CEs and their BAs that access, maintain, retain, modify, record, store, destroy, or otherwise hold, use, or disclose unsecured PHI.

The HITECH Act requires HIPAA CEs to provide notification to affected individuals and to the secretary of HHS following the discovery of a breach of unsecured PHI. In addition, in some cases, the HITECH Act requires CEs to provide notification to the media of breaches. In case of a breach of unsecured PHI at or by a BA of a CE, the Act requires the BA to notify the CE of the breach. Finally, it requires the secretary to post on an HHS website a list of CEs that experience breaches of unsecured PHI involving more than 500 individuals.

More about the HITECH Act and privacy breach requirements are found throughout the rest of this book. For a list of sanctions, including those resulting from breaches, that have been applied by HHS through March 7, 2014, see Appendix A.

2.2.3 Disposal Requirements

A significant number of HIPAA violations and breaches have occurred as a result of improper disposal practices. To address this significant compliance and breach problem, the HHS has, among other actions:

- Set up a "Disposal of Protected Health Information" page specifically to address and provide information disposal guidance to meet HIPAA compliance.[2]
- Recommended using the NIST SP 800-88 Rev. 1, *Draft Guidelines for Media Sanitization* for disposal of electronic data.[3]
- Implemented FCRA PART 682—Disposal of Consumer Report Information and Records, otherwise known as the Disposal Rule.[4]

2.2.4 Mental Health Guidance

The HIPAA Privacy Rule protects the privacy of patients' health information but is meant to provide ways to ensure that appropriate uses and disclosures of the information still may be made when necessary to treat a patient, to protect the nation's public health, and for other critical purposes, such as when a provider seeks to warn or report that persons may be at risk of harm because of a patient.

When a health care provider believes in good faith that such a warning is necessary to prevent or lessen a serious and imminent threat to the health or safety of the patient or others, the Privacy Rule allows the provider, consistent with applicable law and standards of ethical conduct, to alert those persons whom the provider believes are reasonably able to prevent or lessen the threat. The provider is presumed to have had a good faith belief when his or her belief is based on the provider's actual knowledge (i.e., based on the provider's own interaction with the patient) or in reliance on a credible representation by a person with apparent knowledge or authority (i.e., based on a credible report from a family member of the patient or other person). These provisions are in the Privacy Rule at 45 CFR § 164.512(j).

Under these provisions, a health care provider may disclose patient information, including information from mental health records, if necessary, to law enforcement, family members of the patient, or any other persons who may reasonably be able to prevent or lessen the risk of harm. For example, if a mental health professional has a patient who has made a credible threat to inflict serious and imminent bodily harm on one or more persons, HIPAA permits the mental health professional to alert the police, a parent or other family member, school administrators or campus police, and others who may be able to intervene to avert harm from the threat.

On March 7, 2014, the HHS released the "HIPAA Privacy Rule and Sharing Information Related to Mental Health" guidance.[5] This provides significantly more guidance advice related to mental health information, how it must be protected, and when it can be shared.

2.2.5 Payment Card Industry Data Security Standard

The Payment Card Industry Data Security Standard (PCI DSS) is a standard for credit card data security, established in 2004 by the major payment card brands (Visa, MasterCard, American Express, Discover, and JCB). PCI DSS contains more than 220 preventive and detective controls designed to protect credit card data. The security standard consists of 12 major sections of requirements covering security, management, policies, procedures, network architecture, software design, and other critical protection mechanisms.

There are many functions within the typical health care facility that accept credit cards and hence must be compliant with PCI DSS. For example, typical areas within a hospital that process credit card transactions include the following:

- Admitting/copayments
- Bill payment
- Doctors' offices
- Food services
- Fund-Raising/development
- Gift shop or florist
- Hospice facilities
- Hospital discharge areas

- Laboratories and radiology functions
- Outpatient clinics
- Parking
- Pharmacy

For more information about PCI DSS compliance see the PCI Security Standards Council site, https://www.pcisecuritystandards.org/.

2.2.6 State Health Information Laws

The National Conference of State Legislatures (NCSL) maintains a page that provides information on health information laws, and the impacts and actions taken by states for HIPAA. It is located at http://www.ncsl.org/research/health/hipaa-a-state-related-overview.aspx.

2.2.7 State Breach Notification Laws

The National Conference of State Legislatures maintains a page that provides information on the breach notification laws that exist within each U.S. state and territory. It is located at http://www.ncsl.org/research/telecommunications-and-information-technology/security-breach-notification-laws.aspx.

Practical Checklist

- Identify and document laws, standards, and regulations that you must follow.
- Review guidance documents from the HHS and other authoritative organizations.

3

PREPARING FOR HIPAA, HITECH, AND OTHER COMPLIANCE CHANGES

3.1 Background

The magnitude and impact of the Health Insurance Portability and Accountability Act (HIPAA) were much greater than most organizations ever anticipated. The magnitude of changes required by the Health Information Technology for Economic and Clinical Health (HITECH) Act was also unanticipated by most covered entities (CEs) and business associates (BAs). The resources and business process changes, along with the policies, procedures, and technology required to ensure the privacy and security of protected health information (PHI) have been overwhelming for many CEs and BAs that have been pursuing compliance, to say the least. Significant numbers of CEs, and most BAs and almost all their subcontractors, have not even started working on compliance, much less performed a proper information risk assessment. Most have expressed the opinion that they will get into compliance whenever they get an audit notice.*

There is a common myth that HIPAA compliance is about technology that can simply be bought and put in place, and magically make a CE, BA, or subcontractor HIPAA compliant. This is the furthest thing from the truth and any attempts at acquiring "compliance in a box" without applying any accompanying customization or thought

---

* This is based on the experiences of both authors. For instance, since 2003, Professor Herold has done over 250 BA HIPAA compliance audits and over 100 CE audits, and has accumulated these opinions and gathered compliance information for those organizations. In addition, she has obtained such compliance information from over 1000 attendees at her privacy and security classes and from directly working with over 200 of her Compliance Helper (http://www.compliancehelper.com) clients.

are not only futile, but likely will leave your organization with huge compliance gaps.

HIPAA compliance is not just about technology but rather people and their daily job activities. This includes everyone from your receptionist to the highest-ranking health care executive in your organization. Everyone must be involved in working toward HIPAA compliance. The success of any new and updated policies, procedures, and business processes that are put in place for HIPAA is completely dependent on the awareness and buy-in of everyone involved in daily health care operations. Initial HIPAA compliance cannot be achieved without the proper planning, project management, and change management practices in place. Ongoing HIPAA compliance cannot be effectively maintained without the proper culture and mind-set.

3.2 Managing Change

Change can be messy. Health care organizations are well known for their resistance to change. BAs and their subcontractors have not been required to make wide-sweeping changes to meet regulatory compliance requirements, for the most part. Quite often, things are complicated by multiple changes, differing priorities, conflicting interpretations of requirements, and lack of clarity about both short- and long-term goals. In addition, change is often overmanaged to the point where people are pushed too hard, too quickly. This can lead to loss of interest, lowered morale, or even severe burnout. When managing change, there are quite often many unfavorable decisions and transformations that must be made with which some people will not be happy. HIPAA has been known to strike a few chords in this area. The key to minimizing this is to properly set everyone's expectations in advance. This gets back to instilling the proper mind-set and culture.

Organizations must also consider the money issue. Change can be costly. A common occurrence is that upper management supports change yet does not want to finance those changes. This is often accompanied by the belief that change will not take much time, many human resources, or much financial output. The changes mandated by HIPAA and the HITECH Act can be, and must be, managed effectively in order to be rolled out and integrated properly with your business in a cost-effective manner.

Successful HIPAA change management will involve strong leadership, the decision to move forward with compliance efforts, and proactive planning and implementation. The outcome will be the creation of new HIPAA policies, procedures, supporting technologies, copious amounts of documentation, and organizational structures that foster new ways of thinking and doing business. Remember to monitor and readjust your policies and procedures if your business needs change or if problems arise.

It is human nature to fear change. The ways of providing health care mandated by HIPAA are new to a lot of organizations, and for those with little information security or privacy experience, it is a lot to take on. Even with a lot of experience, it can be, and has been, challenging for many HIPAA compliance experts. One key factor in helping to create a new way of "HIPAA thinking" is persuasion. The best way to persuade others is to motivate them and give them an incentive. Two motivating factors must be considered.

The first factor is an individual's desire to gain something and move ahead. You will need to articulate the value of HIPAA compliance requirements and put them in terms of the individual. Answer the question, "What's in it for me?" Then relay that answer to everyone, based on their daily job responsibilities and activities. Think of examples of how HIPAA can make everyone's job easier. For example, standardize one set of electronic health care transactions, have a formal documented procedure for more effectively and consistently communicating with patients and other health care professionals regarding PHI, and even reduce the number of passwords to remember by implementing a unified single-password user log-in system. When people see and hear these types of benefits, they can be motivated to consider and ultimately accept the changes.

The second motivating factor is a person's fear of losing something or falling behind because of new requirements. For example, if you can demonstrate to your staff just how easy it is to lose all of their hard work on their computer system when backups are not done properly or more frequently, and outline how serious and huge the HIPAA penalties are and have already been to many organizations, most employees can be motivated to help the organization, and thus their careers. Bottom line: you have to have an approach that puts it in their terms and their perspectives, and shows them what they stand to gain or lose.

3.3 Creating the Mind-Set

HIPAA requires a new way of thinking and performing daily tasks. Instilling the proper HIPAA-aware mind-set begins with creating the proper culture. This culture must be embraced by upper management and HIPAA officers, who must lead by example. As difficult as it may initially appear to be, HIPAA must be talked about within your organization in a positive light.

HIPAA should be embraced as a standard business practice moving forward, and top-down influence is very important. We are talking about the way people think here—perhaps the most difficult thing to change in the world. There must be buy-in, guidance, and strong leadership from upper managers if HIPAA compliance is going to work properly and effectively. Whether you are an office manager, an IT director, or in executive management, you must regularly educate yourself about HIPAA until you understand all the many requirements that apply to your organization. Reading this book is a great first step. You can also attend HIPAA seminars, webinars, and conferences, and immerse yourself in the excellent HIPAA resources found through information security, privacy, and health care compliance organizations, as well as a wide range of great resources on the Internet. See Appendix D for a listing of some of our favorites. You can then take your knowledge and start relating it to your job activities and your organization's overall mission. This type of activity is contagious. When you start working and behaving with HIPAA in mind, people will notice and, eventually, most will start doing the same.

One of the best ways to get buy-in on HIPAA in your organization is to demonstrate the business value that it brings. Embrace HIPAA with the future in mind and give examples of how HIPAA will pay off in the long term. No one wants to hear "we've got to become HIPAA compliant because the government is making us." You have got to look beyond that to understand and relay to others why the security and confidentiality of PHI is important. You must be able to relay the overall goal of HIPAA Administrative Simplification to everyone in your organization. Relay to them that HIPAA was designed to help lower costs while increasing the quality of health care. More specifically, you can tell them about how, with newer and more formal business policies and procedures, business operations can be streamlined, which can increase productivity and ultimately make their jobs easier.

You can also tell them about the specific risks involved when PHI is not kept secure, and when it is used or shared inappropriately. For example, the Ponemon Institute 2013 Third Annual Patient Privacy & Data Security Study found as follows:[1]

- The primary causes of breaches in this study were lost or stolen computing devices (46%), which were attributed in many cases to employee carelessness.
- The secondary causes of breaches for the study were employee mistakes or unintentional actions (42%).
- The next most common breach causes were those by third parties (42%).

The report also found that a major challenge for IT security is the continuing rise in criminal attacks, which has seen an increase from 20% in 2010 to 33% in 2012.

Another great resource for medical privacy and security breaches, and interesting reading for almost anyone, is "Medical Privacy Stories," published by the Health Privacy Project, which we mentioned in Chapter 1.[2] It is also a very effective tool to communicate the personal benefits of HIPAA requirements to your staff, and how it will ultimately help protect their own PHI that is processed by their corresponding physicians, insurance companies, and so forth. When people know they personally benefit from regulatory requirements, they are usually more open to making the necessary changes within their work environments.

Most information privacy and security surveys are not comprehensive, or not health care or HIPAA specific, but certainly provide good cross-section numbers and great insight into what is actually going on regarding threats and vulnerabilities to health care information. Information gleaned from surveys should certainly be considered as part of your organization's information protection program and HIPAA compliance efforts. The key here is to do your research and find specific real-world examples of how the side effects of HIPAA have helped other organizations and apply them to your environment. We outline several Internet resources in Appendix D where you can obtain this type of information.

3.4 It Is Up to You

For every health care system or business process that is knowingly affected by HIPAA, there may be many more that have not surfaced yet. Do not worry about getting everything right up front—just get started on your compliance efforts. Also, do not worry about having to make yourself a HIPAA expert overnight. Do not let your level of expertise, or lack thereof, in information privacy and security get in your way. Also, do not worry about having to change everyone's mind overnight. It simply will not happen. You can, however, be successful in the long term if you help influence others a little bit at a time.

Remember to start with yourself first. Do not expect others to change their ways of thinking and working. You have got to live and breathe HIPAA every day as well. Be sure to include everyone involved as significant contributors, not simply doers. Keep your eye on the horizon and your mind thinking long term so you can help effect these changes. What we have discussed in this chapter is only the tip of the iceberg regarding the importance of a HIPAA-aware culture. In Chapter 25, we go further into detail on creating ongoing training, education, and awareness programs that will help maintain a HIPAA mind-set and ways of providing and improving health care in the future.

Practical Checklist

- Establish a strong leadership role to drive the HIPAA changes.
- Has a shared vision of change to support effective security and privacy of information been created and communicated to everyone in the organization?
- Create a plan to monitor ongoing changes and readjust if necessary.
- Have you researched and studied HIPAA to the point where you feel that you really understand it?
- Is upper management leading by example?
- Are you leading by example?
- Can you honestly say that you understand your information risks?

- Be prepared to articulate the value that HIPAA brings.
- Have you explained how incorporating information security and privacy into everyday job activities will ultimately help the business?
- Have you explained breaches that have occurred and their impacts?
- Have you explained compliance fines that have been applied and the subsequent impact on the penalized organization?
- Focus on what motivates people: the desire to gain and the fear of loss.
- Consider tying employees' HIPAA change efforts and attitudes into performance evaluations.

4

HIPAA Cost
Considerations

4.1 Background

Actual costs for Health Insurance Portability and Accountability Act (HIPAA) compliance will vary among covered entities (CEs), business associates (BAs), and subcontractors, because of various factors such as size, type of business, organizational culture, geographic locations, and number, if any, of BAs or subcontractors they have. In addition, costs will depend on how "compliant" the CE, BA, or subcontractor can be and the amount of risk it can feasibly accept.

Obviously, costs will vary depending on whether the organization chooses to implement completely new systems and business processes, only the bare minimum requirements, or something in between. Unfortunately, there is no one good answer to how much HIPAA will cost. However, we believe it is safe to say that initial HIPAA compliance will most likely range from a few thousand dollars for small CEs, BAs, and subcontractors to a few hundred thousand dollars or more for larger CEs, BAs, and subcontractors.

According to research performed by the Department of Health and Human Services (HHS), the total costs of compliance with the requirements of the Final Omnibus Rule version of HIPAA and the Health Information Technology for Economic and Clinical Health (HITECH) Act for CEs, BAs, and subcontractors are:[1]

estimated to be between $114 million and $225.4 million in the first year of implementation and approximately $14.5 million annually thereafter. Costs associated with the rule include: (i) costs to HIPAA covered entities of revising and distributing new notices of privacy practices to inform individuals of their rights and how their information is protected; (ii) costs to covered entities related to compliance with breach notification requirements; (iii) costs to a portion of business associates to bring their subcontracts into compliance with business associate agreement requirements; and (iv) costs to a portion of business associates to achieve full compliance with the Security Rule.

Table 4.1 summarizes these costs.

It is important to note that these are the costs to meet the new Omnibus Rule requirements. The HHS expected that CEs and BAs should already be in compliance with the HIPAA and HITECH Act requirements that were in effect for many years (the Privacy Rule since 2003, the Security Rule since 2005, and the HITECH Act since 2010) prior to the release of the additional requirements created by the Omnibus Rule.

Before the Omnibus Rule, the HHS had estimated that original implementation of the Privacy Rule would have cost all the existing CEs a total of $17.6 billion over the first 10 years. At that time, the HHS performed a regulatory impact analysis on the Administrative Simplification standards and projected that HIPAA would have saved the industry $29.9 billion over 10 years. These estimates were made before the Privacy Rule Notice of Proposed Rulemaking changes that were released in August 2002, which, with eased requirements, will likely lower the cost estimates and possibly even raise the savings estimates.

In December 2000, Clinton administration officials did some number crunching of their own to determine what costs may be involved. Peter Swire, the chief privacy counsel for the administration at that time, projected the Privacy Rule cost would equate to $6.25 per year for every insured American. According to the administration's numbers, the electronic transactions and code sets requirements were projected

Table 4.1   Estimated Costs of the Final Rule

COST ELEMENT	APPROXIMATE NUMBER OF AFFECTED ENTITIES	TOTAL COST
Notices of Privacy Practices	700,000 covered entities (CEs)	$55.9 million
Breach notification requirements	19,000 CEs	$14.5 million
Business associate (BA) agreements	250,000–500,000 BAs of CEs	$21–$42 million
Security Rule compliance by BAs	200,000–400,000 BAs of CEs	$22.6–$113 million
Total		$114–$225.4 million

to save the industry $29.9 billion over 10 years, leaving a net savings of $12.3 billion after paying for privacy implementation costs. These numbers did not incorporate the Security Rule implementation costs.

Regardless of who turned out to be closest in their estimates of savings or costs related to implementing all the current HIPAA requirements, the fact remains that CEs, BAs, and subcontractors will need to spend at least a fair amount of time and money to implement all the current requirements. Time will tell if and when savings occur from HIPAA implementation activities.

4.2　Privacy Implementation Costs

Exhibit 4.1 contains the Privacy Rule implementation activities that will likely involve costs. Use the table to estimate and keep track of your organization's Privacy Rule implementation costs.

Exhibit 4.1　Estimated Privacy Rule Implementation Costs

PRIVACY RULE IMPLEMENTATION ACTIVITY	ESTIMATED COST
Performing a privacy gap analysis to establish your baseline compliance state	
Performing a privacy risk assessment to identify risks to protected health information (PHI)	
Creating and distributing a Notice of Privacy Practices (NPP)	
Creating required policies	
Creating required supporting procedures	
Creating supporting forms and other documentation tools	
Assigning personnel to be responsible for privacy	
Assigning personnel to be the point of contact for individuals with questions about their privacy rights, and to report complaints	
Providing initial personnel privacy training	
Implementing electronic technologies to provide safeguards	
Printing, paper, and other notice- and procedure-related costs	
Updating the provider facility directory	
Establishing PHI disclosure accounting mechanisms	
Establishing resources to archive and maintain necessary documentation for at least six years per document	
Establishing business continuity plans, including backup and recovery facilities and resources	
Establishing sanctions and the related resources	

(Continued)

Exhibit 4.1   Estimated Privacy Rule Implementation Costs (*Continued*)

PRIVACY RULE IMPLEMENTATION ACTIVITY	ESTIMATED COST
Establishing processes and tools to account for disclosures of PHI	
Implementing physical safeguards where necessary	
Reviewing and updating marketing and fund-raising plans	
Reviewing and updating research procedures and associated forms and documents	
Establishing identity verification mechanisms and practices	
Establishing mitigation mechanisms and practices	
Creating alternative communications methods to give individuals copies of their PHI	
Establishing mechanisms to update and correct PHI in response to individual requests	
Establishing mechanisms to review authorizations and ensure they are current	
Establishing mechanisms to obtain and document acknowledgment of receipt of notices	
Reviewing and updating BA agreements as necessary	
Establishing mechanisms to de-identify PHI	
Other expenses (provide descriptions)	
Total estimated costs	

The estimated costs will vary greatly among organizations, depending on (1) the type of CE, BA, or subcontractor and the associated services and/or products it provides; (2) the size (in employees, and locations) of the organization; (3) the amount of computer systems used; (4) the number of BAs and/or subcontractors the entity has; and (5) other aspects unique to each organization. There may be no cost involved with some of these activities if your organization already has the personnel or resources indicated.

4.3   Privacy Ongoing Maintenance Costs

Once you have implemented the Privacy Rule requirements, you will not be finished with your compliance obligations. There are ongoing responsibilities that are necessary to maintain compliance. Exhibit 4.2 will help estimate these costs.

Exhibit 4.2   Estimated Ongoing HIPAA Privacy Costs

PRIVACY RULE MAINTENANCE ACTIVITY	ESTIMATED COST
Performing regularly scheduled follow-up privacy gap analysis (recommended every 1–2 years, and when changes to regulations occur) to see where you may now be out of compliance	
Performing follow-up privacy risk assessments to identify new risks and to ensure previous risks have not reoccurred	
Creating and distributing an NPP	
Personnel resources to be responsible for privacy	
Personnel answering individuals' questions about their privacy rights, and to report complaints	
Providing ongoing personnel privacy training	
Maintenance of technologies to provide safeguards	
Printing, paper, and other notice-related costs	
Health plans establishing mechanisms to distribute notices on an ongoing basis (at least every three years and when significant changes occur within the notice)	
Performing PHI disclosure accounting activities	
Archiving and maintaining necessary documentation for at least six years	
Maintaining, testing, and updating business continuity plans, including backup and recovery facilities and resources	
Applying sanctions	
Maintaining and upgrading physical safeguards where necessary	
Maintaining identity verification mechanisms and practices	
Performing mitigation activities	
Utilizing alternative communication methods to give individuals copies of their PHI	
Updating and correcting PHI in response to individual requests	
Reviewing authorizations to ensure their currency	
Obtaining and documenting acknowledgment of receipt of notices	
Reviewing and updating BA agreements	
Maintaining mechanisms to de-identify PHI	
Keeping BA agreements updated and signatures renewed, as appropriate to the related contractual services	
Maintaining up-to-date lists and contact information for BAs and/or subcontractors	
Other expenses	
Total estimated costs	

4.4 Costs Related to Providing Access to PHI

One of the most hotly debated cost recoup issues is whether or not the Privacy Rule allows CEs to charge individuals who request copies of their records. The rule is clear about this: CEs are permitted to charge a cost that is based on the actual expenses involved with sending the copy of PHI to the requester. These costs include, but are not necessarily limited to, the following:

- Copy supplies (paper, toner cartridges, etc.)
- Postage
- Labor involved with the actual copying

If the individual wants a summary or explanation of PHI, the CE may also charge a fee for the actual clerical preparation of this summary or explanation. The CE must communicate this to the individual and obtain agreement to the cost before preparing this summary or explanation. However, this cost may not include the costs related to searching for and retrieving the information. Some states have established a cap on the fees that can be charged for the clerical time used. For example, California has set a limit of $6 per hour for the clerical charges incurred in the course of copying and providing access to the PHI. HIPAA does not allow a CE to charge for the time someone supervises an individual within facilities while the individual reviews the PHI. Even though some state laws may allow for such a charge, HIPAA preempts this allowance.

4.5 Privacy Officer Costs

One requirement of HIPAA is to appoint a person or position with the responsibility of ensuring compliance with the Privacy Rule. Even though the Privacy Rule has been in effect for over a decade, there are still many CEs that have not assigned this responsibility. Most BAs are not spending money to create new positions to meet this requirement, and they often simply have not accomplished this privacy compliance responsibility. Virtually all subcontractors have not formally assigned such responsibility.

It is likely that smaller organizations will need to assign the privacy responsibilities to existing staff because of their limited budgets.

However, in larger organizations it will probably be necessary to assign a person to dedicate his or her entire time to addressing the privacy requirements.

According to 2013 data from Simply Hired, the typical salary for a HIPAA privacy officer in the United States is $48,079–$77,561.[2] Contrast this with what their data showed as being the typical salary for a chief privacy and security officer in United States: $69,284–$131,093.[3] Considering the increased practical complexities of health care organizations, the lower average salary for a health care privacy officer compared to other industries often results in experienced privacy officers going to higher paying industries after they have established valuable, marketable experience.

Use Exhibit 4.2 to help you plan for and estimate all the various costs related to ongoing Privacy Rule compliance.

4.6   Security Implementation Costs

If you do not have thousands of dollars to completely harden your information systems, fear not. There are plenty of things you can do to secure your PHI that will not break the bank or your budget. A significant portion of safeguard activities are operational, physical, and administrative. And remember, there is no such thing as having 100 percent information security, and there will always be residual risks. You can, however, implement certain measures to reduce your exposure. The risks identified during your security risk analysis combined with security measures that are already in place will help you determine how much money will be spent on Security Rule compliance. Sure, HIPAA is a set of laws that must be adhered to, but the costs associated with protecting information (i.e., time, effort, and money) cannot exceed the value of the information or the consequences if the information is compromised. Your goal should be to align what is needed to reasonably protect PHI with your overall business objectives.

Do not worry about return on investment (ROI) on technology infrastructure and security spending. You have to spend money on HIPAA compliance anyway, right? Just make sure that you are spending it wisely. Besides, it is difficult changing the lens through which executives see IT and security investments. They need to see money spent on information security as a business expense or investment in meeting legal requirements, not just another IT expenditure. Why? Because it is a business expense—it is the cost of federal compliance, the cost of reasonably protecting confidential health information, the cost of demonstrating due diligence, and the cost of embracing IT to streamline operations and to provide higher-quality health care.

As discussed in the final Security Rule, HHS used Gartner Inc. to study the impact that changes in the health care industry might have on the expected impact of the final Security Rule. Gartner estimated that the cost of implementing the Security Rule standards in 2002 was less than 10% higher than it would have been in 1998. They go on to say that the preparation for the Security Rule that many CEs have begun offsets this cost difference, making it essentially the same now as it was in 1998. Gartner also determined that compliance with the Privacy Rule may even slightly reduce the overall cost impact of the Security Rule.

A really positive aspect of the Security Rule is its flexibility regarding costs. There are many security standards that are "addressable," meaning that CEs have some flexibility in determining how to implement these types of standards, depending on the associated risks and their specific situation. In addition, there are several information security best practices that can be put in place with relatively little or no cost at all, such as the following:

- Sending out periodic security reminders
- Providing short training sessions more frequently
- Applying critical patches
- Using stronger passwords
- Using encryption, especially for laptops and other mobile devices
- Turning on logging functions that are built into existing applications, databases, and operating systems (OSs)

There is specific verbiage in the Security Rule backing HHS's stance on the flexibility of this rule:

> While cost is one factor a covered entity may consider in determining whether to implement a particular implementation specification, there

is nonetheless a clear requirement that adequate security measures be implemented ...

Our decision to classify many implementation specifications as addressable, rather than mandatory, provides even more flexibility to covered entities to develop cost effective solutions ...

The implementation of these security requirements will reduce the potential overall cost of risk to a greater extent than additional security controls will increase costs.

With respect to security, covered entities will be able to blend security processes now in place with new processes. This should significantly reduce compliance costs.

You should keep these things in mind when the time comes to budget for and spend money on Security Rule compliance.

If you end up outsourcing some HIPAA initiatives to consultants, systems integrators, or large accounting firms, you can expect to be presented with a wide range of hourly rates. The rates will vary, depending on your location and the current state of the economy, but the following estimates should give you a good idea of the going rates:

- $50–$100 per hour for basic computer and network work
- $150–$250+ per hour for highly skilled information security experts
- $275–$350+ per hour for larger accounting/consulting and legal firms that can provide brand recognition

Exhibit 4.3 contains the Security Rule implementation activities that will likely involve costs. Use this to estimate and keep track of your organization's Security Rule implementation costs. Similar to the privacy costs outlined in Exhibit 4.1, these estimated costs will vary greatly or in some cases not even apply, depending on your needs.

4.7   Security Ongoing Maintenance Costs

Once you have implemented the Security Rule requirements, you will also have ongoing maintenance costs to consider. These ongoing costs of delivering secure information services that adhere to the Security

Exhibit 4.3   Estimated Security Rule Implementation Costs

SECURITY RULE IMPLEMENTATION ACTIVITY	ESTIMATED COST
Administrative security costs	
Performing a security gap analysis to establish your baseline state of Security Rule compliance	
Performing a security risk assessment to identify risks to PHI—this may include hiring outside experts to help with penetration testing and vulnerability assessments	
Hiring internal information security experts to build up your compliance team	
Establishing security incident plans, including specific technologies and external resources/expertise to assist in these efforts	
Establishing contingency plans, including backup and recovery systems and facilities and resources such as uninterruptible power supplies, generators, failover sites, backup devices, and backup media storage and retrieval services	
Creating, or purchasing, training for all employees, as well as for targeted groups (such as IT, marketing/sales, customer service, etc.) that need additional training for their specific types of job activities. General training is recommended for all employees at least once a year, and targeted training for subgroups should be provided as often as necessary to effectively mitigate the risks that exist within those groups based on their job activities	
Implementing security awareness reminders such as screen savers, posters, and mouse pads, along with the necessary training programs and materials	
Establishing employee sanctions along with the associated human and legal resources	
Reviewing and updating current BA agreements as necessary	
Creating required security policies and their supporting procedures	
Establishing resources to archive and maintain necessary documentation relating to Security Rule implementation for at least six years	
Physical security costs	
Implementing physical safeguards where necessary, including facility access controls such as card readers, biometrics, cameras, and alarm systems	
Implementing shredders or other physical media destruction mechanisms	
Implementing mobile device physical security controls, such as privacy screens, mobile computer alarms, computing device tracking labels, and laptop locks, for workers outside of the facilities and those that work while they travel	
Technical security costs	
Implementing network infrastructure technologies to facilitate confidential data transmission such as virtual private networks, firewalls, secure e-mail servers, and intrusion prevention systems	

Exhibit 4.3   Estimated Security Rule Implementation Costs (*Continued*)

SECURITY RULE IMPLEMENTATION ACTIVITY	ESTIMATED COST
Implementing computer and network strong authentication mechanisms, including tokens and biometrics	
Implementing encryption systems to ensure confidential data transmission	
Implementing secure fax servers and fax machines	
Identifying and contractually requiring cloud computing security requirements	
Establishing computer and network access control mechanisms such as new OS upgrades, policy servers, and possibly even routers and firewalls	
Establishing computer and network auditing mechanisms, including log monitoring and analysis software	
Other expenses (provide descriptions)	
Total estimated costs	

Rule and meet your customers' needs must be low enough so that it is not cost-prohibitive to continue with them. Rather than using theoretical models of total cost of ownership and ROI that do not always apply in the real world, look at the overall value that these security investments are bringing to your organization. Look at how they not only enable you to be compliant but also make your business better by enabling newer technologies that can streamline operations and ultimately lower overall IT costs.

4.8   Security Officer Costs

As with the mandated privacy officer position, HIPAA mandates that an individual be assigned as your HIPAA security officer for ensuring compliance with the Security Rule. Salaries for this position will vary greatly, depending on the size of the CE, BA, or subcontractor and specific needs. Most of the smaller CEs, BAs, and subcontractors cannot afford to hire a dedicated security officer. These CEs, BAs, and subcontractors will most likely make an existing position, typically the office manager, responsible for both privacy and security compliance. This is reasonable in a small environment, especially if most information security services are outsourced. Medium-sized CEs of 50 employees or more might consider hiring a dedicated HIPAA officer that is responsible for both privacy and security, and possibly other areas of IT or operations. Large CEs such as hospitals and health plans, as well as large BAs and subcontractors, will most likely want to have a dedicated security officer that focuses solely on security compliance efforts.

Based on various general surveys and job postings, the annual salary ranges for a security officer position can vary widely—anywhere from $30,000 to $300,000 and up. This position is new to many health care organizations, so there are no specific criteria to determine exactly how much the security officer should make. As the health care industry sees just how important this position is, more specific salaries and job descriptions will evolve. For comparative purposes, as mentioned earlier, 2013 study data from Simply Hired showed the typical salary for a chief privacy and security officer in United States was $69,284–$131,093.[3] Technology seems to pay significantly more. A study released in February 2013, conducted by the College of Healthcare Information Management Executives, reported health care chief information officers earned an average base salary of $208,417 in 2012.[4]

Exhibit 4.4 lists potential activities that will cost money for ongoing maintenance of Security Rule compliance. Moving ahead, you should always assess information security purchases in terms of what is the best fit for your organization—you might not be able to afford the best or need the solution with all the whistles and bells. The "best" for others might be the worst for your particular situation. Do not always assume that the highest priced, or even highest rated or most talked about by your peers, security products or services are the best ones for you. Shop around, try stuff out, and always make sure there is some sort of contingency in case the product or service ends up being a bad match. By all means, never, ever, make security purchasing decisions based on price alone.

Practical Checklist

- Decide how to staff your privacy officer and job positions that include privacy responsibilities.
- Decide how to staff your security officer and job positions that include security responsibilities.

Exhibit 4.4   Estimated Ongoing HIPAA Security Costs

SECURITY RULE MAINTENANCE ACTIVITY	ESTIMATED COST
Administrative security costs	
Performing ongoing security gap analyses (recommended every 1–2 years, and following regulatory changes) to ensure ongoing compliance with HIPAA	
Performing follow-up security risk assessments (recommended at least every year) to identify new risks and ensure previous risks have not reoccurred	
Performing risk mitigation activities	
Testing and maintaining your security incident plans to ensure they are still viable for new information systems and business changes	
Testing and maintaining your contingency plans to ensure they are still viable for new information systems and business changes	
Ongoing training costs for personnel, including class and conference registrations, publication subscriptions, and association dues	
Reviewing and updating BA agreements as necessary	
Maintaining security policies and their supporting procedures and documentation	
Establishing resources to archive and maintain necessary documentation relating to Security Rule implementation for at least six years	
Applying sanctions	
Ongoing maintenance of the risk management function	
Physical security costs	
Ongoing maintenance, and updates as work locations change, of physical safeguards and systems	
Management of facility maintenance records	
Technical security costs	
Administering and maintaining network infrastructure technologies	
Administering and maintaining computer and network authentication mechanisms	
Administering and maintaining encryption systems	
Administering and maintaining secure fax servers and fax machines	
Administering and maintaining computer and network access control mechanisms	
Administering and maintaining computer and network auditing mechanisms	
Other expenses (provide description)	
Total estimated costs	

- Do not position technology expenses required by HIPAA as IT expenses but rather as business and legal expenses.
- Budget for your Privacy Rule implementation activities.
- Budget for your Security Rule implementation activities.

- Budget for your Privacy Rule ongoing and maintenance activities.
- Budget for your Security Rule ongoing and maintenance activities.
- Obtain budget approval.
- Keep track of your Privacy Rule– and Security Rule–related spending.

5
RELATIONSHIP BETWEEN
SECURITY AND PRIVACY

5.1 Background

Although there has been some progress with unifying security and privacy roles in recent years, in many organizations the people responsible for privacy are still completely separated from and in entirely different departments than the people responsible for security. Often these departments do not communicate, or even acknowledge or understand the compelling relationship that essentially exists between the two. Too often privacy is considered a purely legal issue, the responsibility for which is often handed to organizational legal counsel. Or, it is ignored altogether as a separate issue, and management assumes it will be addressed by all the various business units during the course of doing business. Security is too often viewed as a purely technical issue, and the responsibility for security is more often than not placed within the information technology or networking support area—often buried beneath several layers of management. And the twain never meet. Security personnel must be actively involved in privacy issues and crafting privacy policies, and privacy personnel must be actively involved in security issues and crafting security policies.

Similarly, with regard to the Health Insurance Portability and Accountability Act (HIPAA), many organizations believe they can treat the HIPAA Privacy Rule and Security Rule as completely separate, independent regulations. Many organizations have created a HIPAA Privacy Rule compliance team and a HIPAA Security Rule compliance team, and, unfortunately, the two teams do not share any members, nor do they even communicate, except in some cases with compliance activities for the Health Information Technology for Economic and Clinical Health (HITECH) Act. It is mistakenly assumed that because the Security Rule only applies to electronic protected health information (PHI) there will be no overlap with the Privacy Rule, which applies to PHI in electronic and all other forms. Some business associates (BAs) and subcontractors are focusing solely on the Security Rule and the breach response requirements of the HITECH Act, and do not even plan to address the Privacy Rule.

So, to the crux of this topic: How is security different than privacy? It is really very simple: you must implement security safeguards to appropriately mitigate the risks to PHI to ensure privacy, as well as Privacy Rule compliance. You must use security to preserve and protect privacy. Security is a process; privacy is a consequence. Security is an action; privacy is a result of successful action. Security is a condition; privacy is the prognosis. Security is the strategy; privacy is the outcome. Privacy is a state of existence; security is the constitution supporting the existence. Security is a tactical strategy; privacy is a contextual strategic objective. Security is the sealed envelope; privacy is the successful delivery of the message inside the envelope. Rather than digress any further, we will stop the metaphors and assume you understand what we are trying to get across. The bottom line: company-wide privacy management strategies and security management practices and architecture must be effectively and actively integrated.

What is a common mistake an organization can make that can lead to potentially devastating public press, irreversible damage to personal lives, and huge fines and lawsuits? Often when the privacy responsibility lies in a different part of the organization from the security responsibility, or the two areas do not communicate, privacy policy notices are issued online, and to patients and insureds, and then no security policies, procedures, or mechanisms are implemented to ensure that the now-published privacy notices are enforced. These published privacy notices are legally binding contracts with your patients, customers, and consumers. The privacy notices are often the first and main point of contact between the public and your organization. If you are telling customers that your organization is performing certain activities to ensure their privacy, you had better well make sure your organizational personnel know what they have committed to, whether or not they were involved with the privacy choices.

Privacy, with respect to many of the current legislated regulations, such as HIPAA, means people are able to make informed choices when seeking care and reimbursement for health care based on how PHI may be used, or to make choices about how their personally identifiable financial information is used and shared by the organizations with which they do business. Privacy enables patients to find out how their information may be used and what disclosures of their information have been or may be made. Privacy enables consumers to find out how financial information is going to be protected and know that the people handling their information have been properly trained to protect their privacy. Privacy limits release of information to the minimum reasonably needed for the purpose of the disclosure. Privacy gives people the right to examine and obtain a copy of their own personal records and request corrections, as well as restrictions.

Security with respect to these same regulations constitutes those reasonable and prudent policies, processes, steps, and tools that are used to maintain confidentiality and privacy. It involves all methods, processes, and technology used to ensure the confidentiality and safety of the private information that has been entrusted to a third party by the customer or patient.

Closely reviewing the HIPAA Privacy Rule and Security Rule reveals many overlaps in requirements. To achieve compliance with all the Privacy Rule requirements you will need to understand and implement many of the Security Rule requirements. If you try to implement the safeguards required within the Privacy Rule without considering the Security Rule, you may end up making more work for yourself in the long run; if you implement a security procedure or mechanism to satisfy a Privacy Rule requirement, but that solution is in contradiction to a Security Rule requirement, you will need to redo the establishment and implementation of that security safeguard—spending precious money, time, and personnel resources—in essence, reinventing the wheel. You should plan to implement the security safeguards required in the Privacy Rule as they are required within the Security Rule.

5.2 Privacy Rule and Security Rule Overlaps

To most effectively achieve HIPAA compliance, you need to understand where the Privacy Rule and Security Rule overlap, and how they both relate to the HITECH Act. The Privacy Rule requires covered entities (CEs) to safeguard all PHI it has, regardless of the form the PHI is in, such as on paper, electronic, or spoken. The Security Rule applies to PHI in electronic form only, a subset of the PHI that the Privacy Rule covers. The Privacy Rule often directs CEs to restrict access to PHI; to implement these multiple directives you must implement security controls. The Privacy Rule also explicitly requires security safeguards. Exhibit 5.1 lists the significant Privacy Rule statements that specifically require security safeguards. Be sure to look at any omnibus changes in these sections.

Exhibit 5.1   Privacy Rule Statements Requiring Security Safeguards

(e) (2) *Implementation specifications:* Business associate contracts. A contract between the covered entity and a business associate must:

   i. Establish the permitted and required uses and disclosures of protected health information by the business associate. The contract may not authorize the business associate to use or further disclose the information in a manner that would violate the requirements of this subpart, if done by the covered entity, except that:

     A. The contract may permit the business associate to use and disclose protected health information for the proper management and administration of the business associate, as provided in paragraph (e)(4) of this section; and

     B. The contract may permit the business associate to provide data aggregation services relating to the health care operations of the covered entity.

   ii. Provide that the business associate will:

     A. Not use or further disclose the information other than as permitted or required by the contract or as required by law.

     B. Use appropriate safeguards and comply, where applicable, with subpart C of this part with respect to electronic protected health information, to prevent use or disclosure of the information other than as provided for by its contract.

     C. Report to the covered entity any use or disclosure of the information not provided for by its contract of which it becomes aware, including breaches of unsecured protected health information as required by § 164.410.

     D. In accordance with § 164.502(e)(1)(ii), ensure that any subcontractors that create, receive, maintain, or transmit protected health information on behalf of the business associate agree to the same restrictions and conditions that apply to the business associate with respect to such information.

     E. Make available protected health information in accordance with § 164.524.

     F. Make available protected health information for amendment and incorporate any amendments to protected health information in accordance with § 164.526.

G. Make available the information required to provide an accounting of disclosures in accordance with § 164.528.

H. To the extent the business associate is to carry out a covered entity's obligation under this subpart, comply with the requirements of this subpart that apply to the covered entity in the performance of such obligation.

I. Make its internal practices, books, and records relating to the use and disclosure of protected health information received from, or created or received by the business associate on behalf of, the covered entity available to the Secretary for purposes of determining the covered entity's compliance with this subpart.

J. At termination of the contract, if feasible, return or destroy all protected health information received from, or created or received by the business associate on behalf of, the covered entity that the business associate still maintains in any form and retain no copies of such information or, if such return or destruction is not feasible, extend the protections of the contract to the information and limit further uses and disclosures to those purposes that make the return or destruction of the information infeasible.

§ 164.514 Other requirements relating to uses and disclosures of PHI

c. 2. *Security.* The covered entity does not use or disclose the code or other means of record identification for any other purpose, and does not disclose the mechanism for re-identification.

§ 164.530 Administrative requirements

c. 1. *Standard: Safeguards.* A covered entity must have in place appropriate administrative, technical, and physical safeguards to protect the privacy of PHI.

2. *Implementation specification: Safeguards.*

i. A covered entity must reasonably safeguard PHI from any intentional or unintentional use or disclosure that is in violation of the standards, implementation specifications, or other requirements of this subpart.

ii. A covered entity must reasonably safeguard PHI to limit incidental uses or disclosures made pursuant to an otherwise permitted or required use or disclosure.

It should be clear that the Privacy Rule regulations require security to be implemented to achieve compliance; whenever you see the terms "protection" or "safeguards" within the text, think "security." From a topical view, how do security and privacy relate?

5.2.1 *Appropriate and Reasonable Safeguards*

Both the Privacy Rule and the Security Rule require CEs, BAs, and subcontractors to evaluate their organizational requirements and needs, and to identify security and privacy protections that are appropriate for their unique environment. In both rules CEs, BAs, and subcontractors are directed to perform a risk analysis to ensure the risk is balanced with the costs of the solutions.

5.2.2 Protecting Appropriate Information

The Privacy Rule requires all individually identifiable information, in any medium, collected and directly used in documenting health care or health status, to be adequately safeguarded. This covers a significant amount of information, many different types of PHI, and can be achieved only by incorporating appropriate security procedures and mechanisms in addition to the other tasks involved, such as using the correct forms, using correct wording, notifying appropriate people, and so forth.

5.2.3 Mapping PHI Data Flows

Both the Privacy and the Security Rules require CEs, BAs, and sub-contractors to identify their PHI, and to know and understand the flow of PHI through their organizations. Related to this is identifying where PHI comes into their organization, and where it leaves their organization. This encompasses the identification of BAs and/or subcontractors, as appropriate to the type of entity, who have access to, store, or process their PHI. To identify and implement appropriate security safeguards and procedures, you must know the flow of PHI.

5.2.4 Access Control and Information Integrity

The Privacy Rule contains many access control requirements, and access controls are fundamentally security mechanisms. For instance, the Privacy Rule requires the following:

- Role-based access controls to ensure that only appropriate people have access to the minimum necessary PHI to perform their job responsibilities. Thus, policies and procedures must be created to specify the groups and positions that need access to PHI to perform their job responsibilities, as well as the types of PHI to which they need access. Technological, procedural, and physical security controls will be required to implement and enforce these policies and procedures.
- Safeguards (security) to ensure that the PHI does not get altered or destroyed in an unauthorized manner.

- A formal process for ending a person's employment or a user's access so that inappropriate access to PHI does not occur. This will involve implementing security access controls and mechanisms.
- Consistent, secured control of media (such as papers, disks, tapes, laptops, personal digital assistants, CDs, etc.) containing PHI to ensure that unauthorized use or disclosure does not occur.
- Allowing only properly authorized persons to have physical access into your facilities where PHI is stored and resides.
- Definition of the appropriate functions for and locations of workstations to ensure PHI is not inappropriately stored or viewed on a workstation.
- A well-defined change control process to ensure information system changes do not result in the inappropriate use or disclosure of PHI.
- Regular audits of information system activity to ensure that PHI is being used or disclosed only by properly authenticated and authorized persons.
- Control of PHI sent across open systems, such as the Internet, such that it is protected from unauthorized access.

5.2.5 Assigned Security and Privacy Accountability

The Privacy and the Security Rules both require a specific position or group to be assigned responsibility to appropriately safeguard PHI. Referenced as "Designating a Privacy Official" in the Privacy Rule and as "Assigned Security Responsibility" in the Security Rule, assigning responsibility creates accountability and helps to ensure that a specific position or group is accountable for PHI use and disclosure.

5.2.6 Policies and Procedures

Both rules require CEs, BAs, and subcontractors to implement reasonable and appropriate policies and procedures to comply with the standards, specifications, and other requirements. In addition, both the privacy and security policies and procedures must be documented, maintained, and updated as appropriate, and retained for at least six years. The policies and procedures for security and privacy include the following similar issues:

- Identity verification
- Mitigation of security incident effects
- Risk analysis
- Background and security checks

5.2.7 Business Associate Agreements

Both rules require CEs, BAs, and subcontractors to establish agreements between themselves and all other entities with whom PHI is shared to protect the information they exchange. This is to ensure that PHI is safeguarded at all times, even when it is no longer under the CE's direct control. CEs, BAs, and subcontractors are also expected to periodically verify that the other entities are complying with the agreements. This principle is defined as a BA contract (often called the BA agreement throughout the health care industry) in both the Privacy Rule and the Security Rule.

5.2.8 Training and Awareness

The Privacy Rule and the Security Rule both require regular training and ongoing awareness and communications for protecting PHI to ensure all personnel understand why they must protect PHI, as well as how they must protect PHI. This is one of the most important aspects of safeguarding PHI.

5.2.9 Contingency Plans

The Privacy Rule and the Security Rule require contingency plans to ensure that you can effectively respond to incidents and disasters as soon as possible, and ensure the appropriate access and availability of PHI. Develop and implement security incident response procedures so that you can effectively detect, report, and respond to inappropriate use or disclosure of PHI. This includes procedures for handling security incidents at organizations with which your organization has exchanged PHI.

5.2.10 Compliance Monitoring and Audit

The Privacy Rule and Security Rule require you to monitor PHI access, audit activities, and audit logs to verify the appropriate use and disclosure of PHI. Related to this, both rules also require you to maintain an accounting of PHI disclosures and other applicable HIPAA-related documentation for at least six years. PHI will continue to be stored increasingly in electronic form. To keep comprehensive track of accounting, you need to develop and implement security policies, procedures, and mechanisms that will track, log, and maintain the use and disclosure of PHI.

5.2.11 Sanctions

Sanctions, meaning disciplinary actions, are required by both rules. You must document the sanctions in formal policies as well as document evidence that you support and follow the sanctions.

5.2.12 Individual Rights

5.2.12.1 Access and Amendment   Individuals have rights to access, view, request amendments to, and request restrictions over how their PHI is used. Both rules require that you document these disclosures and any subsequent changes, and maintain the documentation for such access to PHI. Both require, indirectly or specifically, secure methods for accessing PHI.

5.2.12.2 Uses and Disclosures   The Privacy Rule requires minimum necessary access to PHI. The Security Rule requires administrative, physical, and technical safeguards, all involving access based on minimum requirements as they relate to job responsibilities. Key concepts overlapping between the Privacy Rule and the Security Rule related to this issue include the following:

- Accounting for disclosures
- Minimum necessary requirements
- Restricting access
- Emergencies

5.3 Conclusion

The Privacy Rule and the Security Rule do not contradict each other, nor are they mutually exclusive of each other. The Security Rule requirements should be used to implement the safeguard requirements of the Privacy Rule. You should not delay implementing the Security Rule requirements simply because you think you've already addressed the Privacy Rule requirements; many of the Security Rule requirements need to be implemented as soon as possible to contribute to Privacy Rule compliance. In addition, by starting your Security Rule implementation now, you will have a head start on Security Rule compliance, which will help you avoid the potential civil suits that could be brought based on the Security Rule and associated noncompliance.

Practical Checklist

- You must have security to have privacy.
- The Privacy Rule and the Security Rule are not mutually exclusive. Each rule must be implemented by taking into account the requirements of the other rule.
- Privacy Rule safeguard requirements are basically security requirements.
- Many of the Security Rule requirements must be implemented to support the Privacy Rule safeguard requirements.
- Do not implement the Privacy Rule without reviewing and understanding the Security Rule.

PART II
HIPAA
Privacy Rule

6

HIPAA PRIVACY RULE REQUIREMENTS OVERVIEW

6.1 Background

In today's high-tech, network-connected, and increasingly device-connected (in the "Internet of Things") world, depending on locking file cabinets and passwords alone to protect the privacy of health information is not feasible. In addition to technology challenges, the laws in force to protect patient information have historically been, and continue to be, very patchwork and greatly diverse under the large collection of state and federal laws and regulations. In the distant past, patient and health information could be distributed without notice for almost any reason, including those not even related to health care or medical treatments. For example, such health information could be passed from an insurer to a lender, who subsequently could deny the person's application for a mortgage or a loan. The health information could even be sent to the person's employer, who could then consider it for making personnel decisions.

By signing the Health Insurance Portability and Accountability Act (HIPAA) into law in 1996, the president and Congress mandated that organizations must take specific actions to protect personally identifiable health information. HIPAA contains an important section called "Administrative Simplification." Provisions of this section are intended to reduce the costs and administrative burdens of health care by standardizing many administrative and financial forms and transactions. Administrative Simplification includes subsections on the privacy and security of patient information that mandate standards for safeguarding for physical storage and maintenance, transmission, and access of health information. The privacy requirements are collectively referred to as the Privacy Rule.

The Privacy Rule was passed on April 14, 2001, and updated on August 14, 2002, with compliance required by most health plans and health care providers by April 14, 2003. The Omnibus Rule, when it was enacted on March 23, 2013 and established a compliance date of September 23, 2013, expanded the compliance requirements to business associates (BAs) of covered entities (CEs), along with the associated subcontractors they used, as applicable to the services that were being performed. Those entities that do not comply with these regulations are subject to severe sanctions from the Department of Health and Human Services (HHS) and every state's attorney general office, in addition to potential civil and criminal penalties.

The Privacy Rule intends to safeguard protected health information (PHI) by:

- Giving patients more control over their health information
- Setting limitations on the use and release of health records
- Establishing safeguards CEs, BAs, and their subcontractors must implement to protect the privacy of health information
- Holding those in noncompliance responsible through sanctions and civil and criminal penalties for privacy violations
- Attempting to create a balance between public responsibility for disclosure of some forms of information and the personal information of individual patients
- Giving patients the opportunity to make informed choices when seeking care and reimbursement for care by considering how personal health information can be used
- Enabling patients to learn how their information can be used along with the disclosures of their information
- Limiting release to only the minimal amount of information needed for required disclosures
- Giving patients the right to examine and correct any mistakes in their personal health records

6.2 Uses and Disclosures

6.2.1 General Rules for PHI Uses and Disclosures

"Use" means the sharing, employment, application, utilization, examination, or analysis of PHI within a CE, BA, or subcontractor.

"Disclosure" means the release, transfer, provision of access to, or divulging of information in any manner outside the entity holding the information.

CEs may use or disclose PHI for living and deceased individuals only under certain conditions, including the following:

- To the individual about whom the PHI applies
- With individual authorization or other legal agreement
- Generally without individual authorization for treatment, payment, and operations (TPO), with a few exceptions

The Privacy Rule allows disclosure of medical information to parents if state law allows such disclosures. So, even if a minor has a legal right to certain types of medical care without parental consent, the Privacy Rule does not grant the child the right to withhold this information from parents or guardians.

When using, disclosing, or requesting PHI from another CE, reasonable precautions must be implemented to limit PHI access to only those people who need the access to accomplish their valid job responsibilities related to TPO. CEs and BAs may create and use aggregate information without authorization if the PHI cannot be connected to a specific individual, in other words ensuring "de-identification" of the individual PHI. De-identification is discussed in Section 6.5.

With exceptions related to health maintenance organizations (HMOs) and government programs, a CE generally may disclose PHI to a BA and allow a BA to create or receive PHI on its behalf if the CE can ensure the BA will provide adequate security over the PHI. The CE must have written documentation showing the evidence of adequate security within agreements or other types of contracts. When communicating PHI in any form, the CE must take measures to ensure the confidentiality of the PHI is maintained. PHI may not be used or disclosed in any way that conflicts with the entity's notice.

6.2.2 Uses and Disclosures: Organizational Requirements

There will be situations where a CE performs one or more other functions that are not related to or covered by the Privacy Rule. Such an organization is referred to within the regulation as a "hybrid entity." (Chapter 1 discusses hybrid entities at more length.) Legally, separate

CEs can be considered as a single affiliated CE if all of the CEs designated are under common ownership or control. A hybrid entity must ensure that the health care component of the organization complies with the Privacy Rule. For example, such a CE must ensure that the health care component does not disclose PHI to the other component of the entity in the same manner, as if the other component was distinctly and legally separate.

If a person within a hybrid organization has job responsibilities for both the health care component and another aspect of the organization, the person must not disclose PHI within the nonrelated role. To help ensure protection of PHI in this and similar types of situations, CEs must implement policies and procedures to ensure compliance and awareness of the Privacy Rule by all persons working with PHI.

Affiliates and BAs, along with any subcontractors of BAs, of a CE must also ensure that their use and disclosure of the entity's PHI comply with the Privacy Rule. The Privacy Rule includes model BA contract provisions. If a CE knows one of its affiliates or BAs is in violation of the Privacy Rule, then the CE will be considered in noncompliance if it does not take reasonable steps to end the violation. The same applies to BAs and their knowledge of the violations of their subcontractors. To help ensure such compliance, CEs must ensure that BA contracts clearly establish the permitted and required uses and disclosures of the entity's PHI by the BA. The regulations list specific activities that can and cannot be included within BA contracts. See Chapter 21 for more information.

The following are organizational tasks you need to address for your privacy provisions:

- Amend employee sanctions and disciplinary policies.
- Communicate employee HIPAA obligations.
- Apply disciplinary actions for improper use and disclosure of PHI.
- Confirm employee awareness and understanding of HIPAA policy.
- Appoint a privacy official, or at a minimum a position that has responsibility for privacy compliance, along with its other responsibilities.

- Develop complaint processes and sanctions.
- Implement personnel training and awareness programs.
- Establish a plan to comply with the minimum necessary requirement.
- Implement physical, administrative, and technical safeguards for PHI.
- Establish a minimum 6-year records retention policy.
- Implement procedures to ensure beneficiary rights.
- Ensure the covered plan participants receive the Notice of Privacy Practices (NPP).
- Obtain authorizations as applicable to HIPAA requirements.

If you are going to declare your organization as a hybrid entity, designate in writing the operations that perform covered functions as one or more health care components; if you do not do this, your entire organization is subject to the Privacy Rule. If your organization is affiliated by common ownership or control to another CE, you may designate in writing (including the health care components) as a single CE for Privacy Rule compliance; you must operate the different covered functions in compliance with the Privacy Rule provisions applicable to those covered functions.

If you are in an organized health care arrangement (OHCA), you can share PHI with others within the OHCA for joint health care operations. If you are a CE with multiple covered functions, you must operate the different covered functions in compliance with the Privacy Rule provisions applicable to those covered functions.

6.2.3 Uses and Disclosures: Consent for TPO

As stated within the original Privacy Rule, a consent agreement was intended to give health care providers who have a direct relationship with a patient permission to use and disclose all PHI for performing TPO. The consent purpose was to give permission to that specific provider and not to any other person.

The Privacy Rule as updated on August 14, 2002 no longer required health care providers to obtain a patient's written consent before using or disclosing the patient's PHI to carry out TPO. Prior to passage of the Privacy Rule, many health care providers routinely obtained a patient's consent for disclosure of information to insurance companies or for other purposes. The Privacy Rule originally mandated such practices by establishing a consistent standard for covered health care providers to obtain patient consent for uses and disclosures of PHI to carry out TPO. However, the requirement to obtain a signed consent for uses and disclosures of PHI to carry out TPO was removed. Patient authorizations are still required to use and disclose information for non-TPO purposes. It is important to note, however, that CEs may still choose to use consents if they believe the use of consents is beneficial to their business organization and environment, if required by their applicable state laws, or if they want to continue their existing consent agreement practices.

If a CE chooses to use consents for use or disclosure of PHI, the consents can be combined with other types of legal documents from the patient if the PHI consent is clearly separated from the other legal permissions, and if it is signed and dated by the individual.

Additional disclosures were allowed for certain types of payments and health care operations by a second CE. The original restrictions were removed and allowed the general sharing of TPO information between health care providers concerning a common patient.

The 2013 Omnibus Rule allowed a CE that participates in an OHCA to disclose PHI about an individual to other participants in the OHCA for any health care operations activities of the OHCA.

6.2.4 Uses and Disclosures: Authorization

As stated earlier, the Privacy Rule allows but does not require a CE to voluntarily obtain patient consent for uses and disclosures of PHI for TPO and to create associated processes that best serve their situation. In contrast, an authorization is more customized, detailed, and specific than a consent agreement. An authorization gives CEs permission to use specified PHI for specified purposes, generally other than TPO, or to disclose PHI to a specified third party. An authorization is required by the Privacy Rule for uses and disclosures of PHI not otherwise allowed by the Privacy Rule. It is critical for CEs to understand that voluntary consent is not sufficient to permit a use or disclosure of PHI unless it also satisfies the Privacy Rules requirements for an authorization.

An authorization is detailed and gives CEs permission to use PHI for the specific purposes listed within the document. These purposes are typically other than for TPO or for disclosing PHI to a third party. An authorization must include a description of the PHI to be used and disclosed, the name of the person authorized to make the use or disclosure, the name of the person to whom the CE may disclose the PHI, an expiration date, and, depending on the situation, the purpose(s) for which the PHI may be used or disclosed. CEs may generally not make authorization a condition for treatment or coverage for an individual, with a few specific exceptions.

Generally, an authorization is required for all purposes that are not part of TPO and are not described as acceptable uses and disclosures that do not require authorization. All CEs must obtain an authorization to use or disclose PHI for these purposes. A provider may have to obtain multiple authorizations from the same patient for different uses or disclosures. For example, an obstetrician may obtain an authorization from a patient for marketing, and need another authorization from the patient to have her participate in a research project.

A few examples of disclosures that require authorization include disclosures to the following:

- A life insurer for coverage purposes
- An employer for the results of a preemployment physical or laboratory test
- A pharmaceutical firm for their own marketing purposes

HIPAA allows the use of a single type of authorization form to get a patient's permission for a specific use or disclosure that otherwise would not have been permitted under the original Privacy Rule. Patients still need to grant permission in advance for each type of use or disclosure, but CEs do not need to use different types of forms to obtain advance permission.

The Privacy Rule requires providers to obtain authorization to use or disclose PHI maintained in psychotherapy notes for treatment by persons other than the originator of the notes, for payment, or for health care operations purposes.

Generally, authorization for use or disclosure of PHI may not be combined with any other document to create a compound authorization, except as follows:

- An authorization for the use or disclosure of PHI for a research study may be combined with any other type of written permission for the same or another research study. This exception includes combining an authorization for the use or disclosure of PHI for a research study with another authorization for the same research study, with an authorization for the creation or maintenance of a research database or repository, or with a consent to participate in research. Where a covered health care provider has conditioned the provision of research-related treatment on the provision of one of the authorizations, any compound authorization created must clearly differentiate between the conditioned and unconditioned components and provide the individual with an opportunity to opt in to the research activities described in the unconditioned authorization.

- An authorization for a use or disclosure of psychotherapy notes may only be combined with another authorization for a use or disclosure of psychotherapy notes.

- An authorization, other than an authorization for a use or disclosure of psychotherapy notes, may be combined with any other such authorization, except when a CE has conditioned the provision of treatment, payment, enrollment in the health plan, or eligibility for benefits on the provision of one of the authorizations. Individuals can revoke, in writing, authorizations at any time, except to the extent that the CE has taken action as a result of the authorization, or if the authorization was a condition of getting insurance coverage.

Here are some points to remember about authorizations:

- A CE must obtain an individual's written authorization for any use or disclosure of PHI that is not for TPO or otherwise permitted or required by the Privacy Rule.
- A CE may not condition TPO or benefits eligibility on receiving an individual's authorization, except in limited circumstances.
- An authorization must be written in specific terms. It may allow use and disclosure of PHI by the CE seeking the authorization or by a third party.

- Authorizations must be written in plain language, and must contain specific information regarding the information to be disclosed or used, the person(s) disclosing and receiving the information, expiration, right to revoke in writing, as well as other information, depending on the situation.
- The Privacy Rule contains transition provisions applicable to authorizations and other express legal permissions obtained prior to April 14, 2003.
- A CE must obtain an individual's authorization to use or disclose psychotherapy notes, with a few exceptions (see Section 6.2.10).
- A CE must obtain an authorization to use or disclose PHI for marketing, except for face-to-face marketing communications between a CE and an individual, and for a CE's provision of promotional gifts of nominal value. (No authorization is needed to make a communication that falls within one of the exceptions to the marketing definition, as discussed in Section 6.7.)
- An authorization for marketing must state that the CE is receiving direct or indirect remunerations from a third party, if applicable.

CEs may use and disclose PHI without individual authorization for certain activities. This is a long and detailed list; be sure you discuss these situations and how they apply to your organization with your legal counsel. A general listing of such purposes is shown in Exhibit 6.1.

Exhibit 6.1   General Listing of Purposes

Some examples of how PHI may be used and disclosed by CEs without an authorization include within the following situations:

- For its own TPO activities
- For the treatment activities of any health care provider
- For the payment activities of another CE and of any health care provider
- For the health care operations of another CE involving either quality or competency assurance activities or fraud and abuse detection and compliance activities, if both CEs have or had a relationship with the individual and the PHI pertains to the relationship
- For another CE that has, or had, a relationship with the individual
- For another CE that participates in an organized health care arrangement
- Use and disclosure for health oversight activities
- Disclosure to coroners and medical examiners

(Continued)

Exhibit 6.1   General Listing of Purposes (*Continued*)

- Use and disclosure for governmental health data systems
- Disclosure for facility directory information
- Disclosure for banking and payment processes
- Use and disclosure for research as described in Section 6.2.11 of this chapter
- In emergency circumstances
- For next-of-kin information
- As required by other laws
- For treatment by a CE that originated psychotherapy notes to use them for treatment
- A CE may use or disclose psychotherapy notes for its own training, and to defend itself in legal proceedings brought by the individual, for HHS to investigate or determine the CE's compliance with the Privacy Rules, to avert a serious and imminent threat to public health or safety, to a health oversight agency for lawful oversight of the originator of the psychotherapy notes, for the lawful activities of a coroner or medical examiner, or as required by law
- Communications to describe health-related products or services, or payment for them provided by or included in a benefit plan of the CE making the communication
- Communications about participating providers in a provider or health plan network, replacement of or enhancements to a health plan, and health-related products or services available only to a health plan's enrollees that add value to, but are not part of, the benefits plan
- Communications for treatment of the individual
- Communications for case management or care coordination for the individual, or to direct or recommend alternative treatments, therapies, health care providers, or care settings to the individual
- To the individual (unless required for access or accounting of disclosures)
- When the opportunity to agree or object provisions (discussed in Section 6.2.5) apply
- Incidental to an otherwise permitted use and disclosure
- When disclosure or use of the PHI is for public interest and benefit activities
- When creating and using a limited data set (discussed in Section 6.2.7) for the purposes of research, public health, or health care operations
- To funeral directors as needed, and to coroners or medical examiners to identify a deceased person, determine the cause of death, and perform other functions authorized by law
- To facilitate the donation and transplantation of cadaver organs, eyes, and tissue
- CEs may disclose PHI that they believe is necessary to prevent or lessen a serious and imminent threat to a person or the public, when such disclosure is made to someone they believe can prevent or lessen the threat (including the target of the threat)
- To law enforcement if the information is needed to identify or apprehend an escapee or violent criminal
- For certain essential government functions, including assuring proper execution of a military mission, conducting intelligence and national security activities that are authorized by law, providing protective services to the president, making medical suitability determinations for State Department employees, protecting the health and safety of inmates or employees in a correctional institution, and determining eligibility for or conducting enrollment in certain government benefit programs
- As authorized by, and to comply with, workers' compensation laws and other similar programs providing benefits for work-related injuries or illnesses
- For quality assurance reviews by authorized authorities
- For emergencies or concerns affecting public health or safety

Exhibit 6.1   General Listing of Purposes (*Continued*)

- For suspected abuse of the individual
- For research with documented authorization waiver approval from the institutional review board (IRB) or privacy board
- For reviews preparatory to research
- For research on decedent information
- For government health data and specialized functions
- For financial institution payment processing for health care
- For utilization review
- For credentialing
- When mandated by other laws
- For other activities that are part of ensuring appropriate TPO
- To public health authorities authorized by law to collect or receive such information for preventing or controlling disease, injury, or disability and to public health or other government authorities authorized to receive reports of child abuse and neglect
- To entities subject to Food and Drug Administration (FDA) regulation regarding FDA-regulated products or activities for purposes such as adverse event reporting, tracking of products, product recalls, and postmarketing surveillance
- To individuals who may have contracted or been exposed to a communicable disease when notification is authorized by law
- To employers, regarding employees, when requested by employers, for information concerning a work-related illness or injury or workplace-related medical surveillance, because such information is needed by the employer to comply with the Occupational Safety and Health Administration, the Mine Safety and Health Administration, or similar state law
- In certain circumstances, to appropriate government authorities regarding victims of abuse, neglect, or domestic violence
- To health oversight agencies (as defined in the Privacy Rule) for purposes of legally authorized health oversight activities, such as audits and investigations necessary for oversight of the health care system and government benefit programs
- In a judicial or administrative proceeding if the request for the information is through an order from a court or administrative tribunal. Such information may also be disclosed in response to a subpoena or other lawful process if certain assurances regarding notice to the individual or a protective order are provided
- To law enforcement officials for law enforcement purposes under the following six circumstances, and subject to specified conditions:
    - As required by law (including court orders, court-ordered warrants, subpoenas) and administrative requests
    - To identify or locate a suspect, fugitive, material witness, or missing person
    - In response to a law enforcement official's request for information about a victim or suspected victim of a crime.
    - To alert law enforcement of a person's death, if the CE suspects that criminal activity caused the death
    - When a CE believes that PHI is evidence of a crime that occurred on its premises
    - By a covered health care provider in a medical emergency not occurring on its premises, when necessary to inform law enforcement about the commission and nature of a crime, the location of the crime or crime victims, and the perpetrator of the crime

6.2.5 Uses and Disclosures Requiring Opportunity for the Individual to Agree or Object

HIPAA allows a CE to use or disclose PHI without the written authorization of the individual in certain situations if the individual is informed in advance of the use or disclosure. Informal permission may be obtained by asking the individual outright, or by circumstances that clearly give the individual the opportunity to agree or object. Where the individual is incapacitated, in an emergency situation, or not available, CEs generally may make such uses and disclosures, if in the exercise of their professional judgment, the use or disclosure is determined to be in the best interests of the individual.

In general, individuals must be given the opportunity in advance to agree or object to uses and disclosures of PHI in the situations listed in Exhibit 6.2. The CE may orally inform the individual and obtain oral agreement or objection to use or disclosure.

Individuals may ask a CE to restrict further use and disclosure of PHI (with the exception of uses or disclosures required by law).

Exhibit 6.2   Uses and Disclosures Requiring Opportunity to Agree or Object

- Disclosure of name, location, general condition, and religion within the entity's facility directory or to clergy or persons asking for the individual by name; the provider may then disclose the individual's condition and location in the facility to anyone asking for the individual by name, and also may disclose religious affiliation to any clergy inquiring about patients with certain religious affiliations
- Disclosure of medical condition and location to a family member, other relative, or a close personal friend of the individual, or any other person identified by the individual
- To an individual's family, relatives, friends, or other persons identified by the individual, for notification and other purposes directly relevant to that person's involvement in the individual's care or payment for care; for example, this allows a pharmacist to dispense filled prescriptions to a person acting on behalf of the patient
- Notifying (including identifying or locating) family members, personal representatives, or others responsible for the individual's care of the individual's location, general condition, or death
- For notification purposes to public or private entities authorized by law or charter to assist in disaster relief efforts
  - If the individual is not present, or the opportunity to agree or object to the use or disclosure cannot practicably be provided because of the individual's incapacity or an emergency circumstance, the CE may, in the exercise of professional judgment, determine whether the disclosure is in the best interests of the individual and, if so, disclose only the PHI that is directly relevant to the person's involvement with the individual's care or payment related to the individual's health care or needed for notification purposes.

(Continued)

Exhibit 6.2   Uses and Disclosures Requiring Opportunity to Agree or Object

- A CE may use or disclose PHI to a public or private entity authorized by law or by its charter to assist in disaster relief efforts, for the purpose of coordinating with such entities the uses or disclosures permitted under HIPAA, to the extent that the CE, in the exercise of professional judgment, determines that the requirements do not interfere with the ability to respond to the emergency circumstances.
- If the individual is deceased, a CE may disclose to a family member, or other persons allowed under HIPAA who were involved in the individual's care or payment for health care prior to the individual's death, PHI of the individual that is relevant to such person's involvement, unless doing so is inconsistent with any prior expressed preference of the individual that is known to the CE.

The CE does not have to agree to such a request. But, if the CE and the individual agree to such a restriction, the CE is then bound by the agreement, even when the agreement is given orally.

It is also important to note that although HIPAA allows CEs to use or disclose PHI in these specific situations, it does not mean the CE must do so. Each entity must decide what is best and what is in compliance with the applicable state laws for each situation and act accordingly.

6.2.6 Other Requirements Relating to Uses and Disclosures of PHI

The Privacy Rule contains many other requirements for a vast array of situations relating to virtually every conceivable type of PHI use and disclosure. Again, it is important for CEs and their legal counsel to thoroughly review and understand the Privacy Rule and these many requirements. These issues are explored in detail throughout this chapter. Following is an overview of the other requirements:

- PHI must be handled in specific ways for de-identification requirements.
- CEs must ensure minimum necessary requirements are implemented related to PHI use and disclosure.
- PHI may not be used for marketing purposes without the specified authorizations described within the Privacy Rule.
- A CE may use or disclose demographic information relating to an individual and dates of health care provided to an individual for its own fund-raising purposes without authorization to a BA or to a related foundation.

- PHI used by a health plan for underwriting, premium rating, or other activities relating to the creation, renewal, or replacement of a contract of health insurance or health benefits, may not be used or disclosed for any other purpose, except as may be required by law, if such PHI is not placed with the health plan.
- Before CEs disclose PHI, they must verify the identity and authority of the person requesting the PHI.

6.2.7 *Limited Data Set*

A limited data set is PHI that excludes the specific direct identifiers of the individual and the relatives, employers, or household members of the individual as outlined within the Privacy Rule. A CE may use or disclose a limited data set if the recipient of the data set signs a data-use agreement promising specified safeguards for the PHI within the limited data set, and ensures that any agents to whom it provides the limited data set agree to the same restrictions and conditions on the limited data set that have been established. A limited data set may only be used for the purposes of research, public health, or health care operations. CEs and BAs must ensure that anyone using the limited data set agrees to all the same restrictions and conditions specified within the data-use agreement, and the entity must not identify the information or contact the individuals.

If, prior to January 25, 2013, a CE has entered into and is operating under a data-use agreement with a recipient of a limited data set from which it receives remuneration, the CE may continue to disclose a limited data set in exchange for such remuneration from or on behalf of the recipient of the PHI until the earlier of the following:

- The date such agreement is renewed or modified on or after September 23, 2013
- September 22, 2014

If a CE discloses only a limited data set to a BA to carry out a health care operations function, the CE satisfies the Privacy Rule requirement to obtain satisfactory assurances from the BA with the data-use agreement. A separate BA agreement is not also necessary.

A good example provided by the HHS Office of Civil Rights (OCR) is if a state hospital association receives only limited data sets of PHI from member hospitals for the purposes of conducting and sharing comparative quality analyses with these hospitals, then the member hospitals need only have data-use agreements in place with the state hospital association.

A CE may contract with a BA to create a limited data set the same way it can use a BA to create de-identified data. The OCR provides another great example: If a researcher needs county data, but the CE's information contains only the postal address of the individual, a BA may be used to convert the CE's geographical information into the form needed by the researcher. In addition, the CE may hire the intended recipient of the limited data set as the BA for this purpose in accordance with the BA requirements.

A CE can combine the data-use agreement and BA contract to hire the intended recipient of a limited data set to also create the limited data set as a BA. Because the CE is providing the recipient with PHI that includes direct identifiers, a BA agreement is required in addition to the data-use agreement to protect the information. The agreement must require the recipient to return or destroy the information that includes the direct identifiers once it has completed the conversion for the CE.

6.2.8 Fund-Raising

Fund-raising for the CE's own benefit is defined as part of the CE's health care operations. CEs and BAs may use or disclose the demographic information and date of health care for an individual to a BA or an institutionally related foundation for the purpose of its own fund-raising efforts for mailings and similar communications. An authorization is not necessary in these types of situations. However, the individual must be given the opportunity to opt out of receiving any further types of communications.

The HHS does not define demographic information within the Privacy Rule but indicates that for the purpose of fund-raising, it generally includes name, address and other contact information, age, gender, and insurance status. HHS further clarifies the meaning of demographic information and the use of nondemographic information in fund-raising as follows:

- HHS limits the information that can be used or disclosed for fund-raising, and excludes information about diagnosis, nature of services, or treatment.
  - *Permissible information.* (Note: There is no regulatory source for this advice, other than the Preamble to the 2000 Final Rule.) PHI that can be utilized for fund-raising purposes without obtaining a patient's authorization includes the following:
    - Date of service (45 CFR § 164.514[f][1]).
    - Demographic information (45 CFR § 164.514[f][1]) (all of the previously mentioned are discussed as "demographic information" in the Preamble to the 2000 Final Rule).
    - Name.
    - Address.
    - Other contact information (phone numbers, e-mail addresses, etc.).
    - Age.
    - Gender.
    - Insurance status.
  - *Impermissible use and disclosure.* PHI that cannot be used without a patient first signing an authorization includes the following:
    - Diagnosis.
    - Nature of services.
    - Treatment.
    - Place within health care provider where patient receives treatment that identifies the treatment, such as the following:
      - Department of psychiatry.
      - Department of obstetrics.
      - Department of radiation oncology.
  - *Questionable use and disclosure.* Although not discussed in the regulations or any of the preambles to the proposed or adopted regulations, a CE may be able to use information about the department in which the patient was

treated to filter patient names for fund-raising purposes if the department name does not identify the type or nature of treatment. For example, when a patient is treated by the medical/surgery or another type of general department, using or disclosing this information for fund-raising filtration purposes would not appear to reveal the diagnosis or nature of the services or treatment received by the affected individuals, and would appear to fit within the minimum necessary information to accomplish the goal: fund-raising.

- Implement policies to ensure that fund-raisers receive only limited PHI, while allowing them to request some other department of the health care provider to review patient PHI to ensure that data received fits within the limitation. Using procedures to ensure that individuals with access to PHI limit the information given to fund-raisers to only that which is appropriate should be consistent with the responsibility of the health care provider to use reasonable efforts to limit use of PHI to the minimum necessary to accomplish the task.
- Always keep in mind that the Privacy Rule does not preempt state laws that are more restrictive than HIPAA, or other federal laws. While HIPAA permits limited disclosure of health care provider directory information, other federal laws may prohibit a health care provider from even responding to an inquiry about a patient receiving treatment for substance abuse, and applicable state laws on the privacy of medical records must be considered by the fund-raising entity. However, in most cases, the most common information used for fund-raising (name, age, gender, date of treatment, and address) can be used safely for fund-raising efforts. See Chapter 9 for full discussion of state preemption issues.

The 2013 Omnibus Rule changed the fund-raising communications requirements.

- A CE must still provide the individual with an opportunity to opt out, but now can decide what method of opt-out to use, provided the method is not excessively burdensome or costly.
- A CE must include a statement in the NPP that indicates the individual has the right to opt out.

- A CE may choose whether it wants the individual to opt out of all fund-raising communications or only those directed at a specific fund-raising campaign.
- A CE is prohibited from sending fund-raising communications once the individual has opted out of receiving such communications.

The 2013 Omnibus Rule also created new categories of PHI that can be used by CEs for targeted fund-raising communications. These categories include the following:

- Department of service (general department of treatment)
- Treating physician information
- Outcome information (including information on death and suboptimum outcome)

These categories are added to the already existing demographic statistics and health insurance status on the list of items the Privacy Rule allows to be used for fund-raising. The anticipated result of these new categories was to allow CEs to use PHI to develop more focused fund-raising programs.

6.2.9 Underwriting Purposes

When group health plans, health insurance issuers (including HMOs), and issuers of Medicare supplemental policies receive PHI for the purpose of underwriting, premium rating, or other activities relating to the creation, renewal, or replacement of a health insurance contract or health benefits, and if such health insurance or health benefits are not placed with the group health plan, health insurance issuer, or issuer of Medicare supplemental policies, it may not use or disclose the PHI for any other purpose, except as may be required by law. Under the 2013 Omnibus Rule, group health plans, health insurance issuers (including HMOs), and issuers of Medicare supplemental policies are prohibited from using or disclosing genetic information for underwriting purposes.

Prior to any disclosure of PHI, a CE must verify the identity of the person requesting PHI and validate their authority to access the PHI. The CE must also obtain any documentation, statements, or representations, whether oral or written, from the person requesting the PHI when it is a condition of the disclosure.

6.2.10 Public Health

The Privacy Rule allows but does not require CEs to share PHI with public health authorities that are authorized by law to collect the information when necessary to protect the health of the public. CEs and BAs may disclose PHI for public health activities and purposes such as the following:

- A public health authority authorized by law to collect or receive PHI for the purpose of preventing or controlling disease, injury, or disability. Such activities include, but are not limited to, reporting disease, injury, vital events such as birth or death, and the conduct of public health surveillance, public health investigations, and public health interventions. The activities may also be directed by a public health authority to a foreign government agency official acting in collaboration with a public health authority.
- A public health authority authorized by law to receive reports of child abuse or neglect.
- A person who may have been exposed to a communicable disease or may otherwise be at risk of contracting or spreading a disease or condition, if the CE or public health authority is authorized by law to notify such a person as necessary in the conduct of a public health intervention or investigation.
- A person subject to the jurisdiction of the FDA with respect to an FDA-regulated product or activity for which that person has responsibility, for the purpose of activities related to the quality, safety, or effectiveness of such FDA-regulated product or activity.
- A person who may have been exposed to a communicable disease or may otherwise be at risk of contracting or spreading a disease or condition, if the CE or public health authority is authorized by law to notify such person as necessary in the conduct of a public health intervention or investigation.

- An employer, about an individual who is a member of the workforce of the employer, if:
  - The CE is a covered health care provider who provides health care to the individual at the request of the employer:
    - To conduct an evaluation relating to medical surveillance of the workplace.
    - To evaluate whether the individual has a work-related illness or injury.
- A school, about an individual who is a student or prospective student of the school, if:
  - The PHI that is disclosed is limited to proof of immunization.
  - The school is required by state or other law to have such proof of immunization prior to admitting the individual.

  - The CE obtains and documents the agreement to the disclosure from:
    - A parent, guardian, or other person acting in loco parentis of the individual, if the individual is an unemancipated minor.
    - The individual, if the individual is an adult or emancipated minor.

6.2.11 Research

Research is not considered as TPO under the Privacy Rule. Therefore, unless an exception applies, as listed earlier, authorizations are generally required for use or disclosure of PHI for research purposes. These authorizations may be combined with any other type of written permission for the same research study, including other authorizations for the use or disclosure of PHI or consents to participate in such research.

A CE may combine conditioned and unconditioned authorizations for research, provided that the authorization clearly differentiates between the conditioned and unconditioned research components and clearly allows the individual the option to opt in to the unconditioned research activities. This provision allows for the use of compound authorizations for any type of research activities, and not solely for clinical trials and bio-specimen banking, except to the extent the research involves the use or disclosure of psychotherapy notes. For research that involves the use or disclosure of psychotherapy notes, an authorization for a use or disclosure of psychotherapy notes may only be combined with another authorization for a use or disclosure of psychotherapy notes.

Health care providers may also condition the provision of research-related treatment on receipt of a prior authorization for the use or disclosure of PHI. Any compound authorization created must clearly differentiate between the conditioned and unconditioned components and provide the individual with an opportunity to opt in to the research activities described in the unconditioned authorization.

There are many ways PHI may be obtained for research purposes. For instance, CEs may use or disclose PHI for research, regardless of funding, when they obtain documentation that a waiver of the individual authorization required for use or an IRB or a privacy board has approved disclosure of PHI. CEs may also use or disclose PHI if a researcher demonstrates that the PHI is necessary to prepare a research protocol, or if the researcher demonstrates the PHI is needed exclusively for research on decedents.

Limited data sets are applicable to PHI for research. Limited data sets are similar to de-identified data sets except they have 15 identifiers removed instead of 18. Limited data sets may include the following identifiers: date of birth; dates of hospital admissions and discharges; and an individual's residence by city, county, state, and five-digit zip code. Researchers using PHI via limited data sets must enter into data-use agreements with CEs. These researchers may serve as BAs to CEs, however, and create limited data sets from fully identifiable health information.

Accounting is not required when PHI is disclosed to researchers pursuant to an authorization or as part of a limited data set. Research performed under IRB or privacy board waivers, reviews in preparation for research, or research on decedents are subject to accounting requirements for disclosures. Research disclosures prior to the regulatory compliance date of April 14, 2003 are not subject to the accounting requirement.

CEs and BAs need to accomplish one of the following to use PHI for research purposes:

- Obtain documentation that an alteration or waiver of the authorization for the use or disclosure of PHI about an individual for research purposes has been approved by an IRB or privacy board.
- Obtain documented representations from the researcher that the use or disclosure of the PHI is solely to prepare a research protocol or for similar purpose preparatory to research, that the researcher will not remove any PHI from the CE, and that PHI for which access is sought is necessary for the research.
- Obtain documented representations from the researcher that the use or disclosure sought is solely for research on the PHI of decedents, that the PHI sought is necessary for the research, and, at the request of the CE, documentation of the death of the individuals about whom information is sought.
- CEs and BAs may use or disclose a limited data set of PHI or de-identified information for research purposes without authorization. See Section 6.2.7 for more information.

What should you consider if you perform research with PHI?

- Obtain an authorization whenever possible to use or disclose PHI for research protocols.
- Authorizations should be combined with informed consent documents, if you use them.
- Consider using de-identified PHI and limited data sets. They do not need IRB/privacy board approval and have no accounting requirement. Limited data sets require data-use agreements between researchers and CEs.

6.2.12 Workers' Compensation

Unless they are also CEs, the Privacy Rule does not apply to workers' compensation insurers, workers' compensation administrative agencies, or employers. Regardless, these entities need access to individuals' health information to process workers' compensation claims and to coordinate care under workers' compensation systems. This information is typically obtained from the health care providers treating the individuals. The Privacy Rule likely covers these providers. The Privacy Rule recognizes the need of insurers and other entities involved in the workers' compensation systems to have access to individuals' health information as authorized by state or other applicable laws. Because of the vast differences between these other laws, the Privacy Rules allow disclosures of health information for workers' compensation purposes in a number of different ways that tend to vary depending on the type of organization. These issues are explored in more detail in Part IV, Covered Entity Issues.

6.3 Incidental Uses and Disclosures

The nature of many customary health care communications and practices and the various environments in which individuals receive health care create the potential for health information to be disclosed incidentally. However, these types of communications are often necessary to ensure prompt health care treatment. For example, someone visiting in a hospital may overhear the physician's confidential discussion with a patient in the same room. The Privacy Rule was written so it would not prevent these customary communications. The Privacy Rule does not require that 100 percent of all risks of incidental use or disclosure be eliminated; this would be impractical. The Privacy Rule allows certain incidental uses and disclosures of PHI if there are reasonable safeguards and minimum necessary policies and procedures in place to protect an individual's privacy to the greatest possible practical extent.

The Privacy Rule permits certain incidental uses and disclosures that occur as a result of other acceptable uses or disclosures if reasonable safeguards have been implemented according to the minimum necessary standard. Safeguards cannot guarantee the privacy of PHI from all potential risks. Reasonable safeguards depend on many factors, such as size, location, and nature of the business. What are considered reasonable safeguards will vary from organization to organization. An incidental use or disclosure is a secondary use or disclosure that cannot reasonably be prevented as a result of an acceptable use or disclosure, and is limited in nature. An incidental use or disclosure is not permitted if it results from a violation of the Privacy Rule.

Here are some examples of reasonable safeguards CEs should consider implementing:

- Speak quietly when discussing a patient's condition with family members in a public area such as a waiting room.
- Avoid using patients' full names in public locations, such as elevators and public hallways.
- Post signs reminding employees to protect patient privacy.
- Physically isolate or lock file cabinets or records rooms.
- Secure workstations and computers containing personal information by requiring passwords and other security mechanisms as detailed in this book.

It is important to understand that if the disclosure was intentional, it will not be considered incidental. Among the other pointers from the Privacy Rule on this topic, the directive for incidental disclosures is a long-standing, original HIPAA Security Rule requirement:

§ 164.530 Administrative requirements.

(2)(ii) A covered entity must reasonably safeguard protected health information to **limit incidental uses or disclosures** made pursuant to an otherwise permitted or required use or disclosure.

As the HHS has explained in numerous publications and venues, HIPAA is not intended to impede customary and essential communications and practices associated with health care, and so does not require that all risk of incidental use or disclosure be eliminated to satisfy its standards. Instead, HIPAA allows certain unintended, accidental, incidental uses and disclosures of PHI to occur when the CE, BA, and subcontractor have in place reasonable safeguards and minimum necessary policies and procedures to appropriately protect privacy.

Here is an example of an incidental disclosure from the HHS website:

For example, a hospital visitor may overhear a provider's confidential conversation with another provider or a patient, or may glimpse a patient's information on a sign-in sheet or nursing station whiteboard.

The following is an example of what is *not* considered to be an incidental disclosure, meaning it is intentional:

When sales reps are asked to be present during patient care, and provide advice and/or guidance about the use of medical devices to the providers/doctors during such provision of care.

For an expanded discussion of this topic, see Rebecca's blog post at: http://privacyguidance.com/blog/if-it-was-intentional-it-is-not-incidental/.

6.4 Minimum Necessary Requirement

The minimum necessary requirement applies when using or disclosing PHI or when requesting PHI from another CE or BA; a CE or BA must make reasonable efforts to limit PHI to the minimum necessary to accomplish the intended purpose of the use, disclosure, or request.

The minimum necessary requirement is based on the premise that PHI should not be used or disclosed when it is not necessary to perform job responsibilities or health care-related activities. CEs and BAs need to examine and evaluate their health information handling practices to meet the minimum necessary requirements to ensure safeguards exist to limit unnecessary or inappropriate access to PHI.

CEs and BAs must take reasonable actions to limit the use and disclosure of PHI to the minimum necessary to accomplish a necessary task. The minimum necessary requirement does not apply to the following situations:

- Disclosures to or requests by a health care provider for treatment purposes
- Disclosures to the individual who is the subject of the information
- Uses or disclosures made with an individual's authorization
- Uses or disclosures required for compliance with HIPAA
- Disclosures to HHS for Privacy Rule enforcement purposes
- Uses or disclosures required by other laws

The Privacy Rule requirements necessitate the development and implementation of policies and procedures appropriate for each CE's and BA's own unique organization, business practices, and personnel. Use the following guidance to help develop the policies and procedures necessary for your organization. Chapter 8 describes two important policies you must create. For full sets of policies, and policy examples, see http://www.hipaacompliance.org.

- Develop and implement policies and procedures that identify the persons, positions, groups, or departments who need access to PHI to perform job responsibilities, and the conditions appropriate for the access. For example, hospitals may implement policies that permit doctors, nurses, or others involved in treatment to have access to the entire medical record, as needed. Where the entire medical record is necessary, the CE's policies and procedures must state so explicitly and include a justification.

- Develop criteria for determining and limiting the disclosure of PHI necessary for nonroutine disclosures and requests to only the minimum amount to accomplish the purpose. Nonroutine disclosures and requests must be reviewed on an individual basis in accordance with these criteria and limited accordingly.

- Standard protocols for routine or recurring requests and disclosures must limit the PHI disclosed or requested to the minimum necessary for that particular type of disclosure or request. Individual review of each disclosure or request is not required.

- The Privacy Rule permits a CE and BA to rely on the judgment of the requester asking for the minimum amount of information necessary in the following circumstances:
  - A public official or agency who states that the information requested is the minimum necessary for a purpose permitted, such as for public health purposes.
  - Another CE.
  - A workforce member or BA of the CE holding the information and who indicates the information requested is the minimum necessary for the stated purpose.
  - A researcher with appropriate documentation from an IRB or privacy board (Note: The Privacy Rule does not require disclosure or use under these circumstances. It is still at the discretion of the CE to decide upon the minimum necessary determination for disclosures it makes and to which the standard applies.)

- Implement policies and procedures that limit how much PHI is used, disclosed, and requested for certain purposes. These must limit who within the entity has access to PHI, and under what conditions, based on job responsibilities and the nature of the business.
- Uses and disclosures that are authorized by the individual are exempt from the minimum necessary requirements.
- The Privacy Rule does not prohibit the use, disclosure, or request of an entire medical record, and a CE or BA may use, disclose, or request an entire medical record without a case-by-case justification, if the CE or BA has documented in its policies and procedures that the entire medical record is the amount reasonably necessary for certain identified purposes. For uses, the policies and procedures would identify those persons or classes of person in the workforce that need to see the entire medical record and any conditions that are appropriate for such access. Policies and procedures for routine disclosures and requests and the criteria used for nonroutine disclosures and requests would identify the circumstances under which disclosing or requesting the entire medical record is reasonably necessary for particular purposes.

The minimum necessary standard does not apply to the following situations:

- Disclosures to or requests by a health care provider for treatment purposes
- Disclosures to the subject of the information
- Uses or disclosures made pursuant to an individual's authorization
- Uses or disclosures required for compliance with the HIPAA Privacy and Security Rules
- Disclosures to HHS when disclosure of information is required under the Privacy Rule for enforcement purposes
- Uses or disclosures that are required by other laws

For a discussion of how this topic related to a significant breach and associated $865,000 fine, see Rebecca's blog post at http://privacyguidance.com/blog/ucla-health-system-pays-865k-to-settle-celebrity-privacy-hipaa-violations/.

6.4.1 Reasonable Reliance

There are certain circumstances where the Privacy Rule permits a CE and BA to rely on the judgment of the requester as to the minimum amount of information that is needed. These circumstances are called reasonable reliance, and must be reasonable under the particular circumstances of the request. Reasonable reliance is allowed for requests made by the following:

- A public official or agency that indicates that the information requested is the minimum necessary for a purpose permitted under the Privacy Rule, such as for public health purposes
- Another CE
- A professional who is a workforce member BA of the CE holding the information and who states that the information requested is the minimum necessary for the stated purpose of providing services to or for the CE
- A researcher with appropriate documentation from an IRB or privacy board

The Privacy Rule does not require reasonable reliance allowances. CEs and BAs may make its own minimum necessary determination for disclosures to which the standard applies.

6.5 De-Identification

CEs can generally use de-identified information for any of their health care purposes without seeking authorization or other agreements. De-identified information is health information that does not identify a specific individual, so there is no reasonable basis to believe that the information can be used to identify an individual. De-identified information is not necessarily anonymous information. The purpose of de-identification is to ensure there is a reasonable and feasible balance between the risks of identifying individuals using the information and the usefulness of the information.

CEs and BAs must remove the following pieces of information from a designated record set to appropriately de-identify the PHI:

- Name
- Geographic subdivisions smaller than a state

- Dates (excluding year) of:
  - Birth
  - Admission
  - Discharge
  - Death
- Telephone number
- Fax number
- E-mail address
- Social Security number
- Medical records numbers
- Health plan beneficiary numbers
- Account numbers
- License and certificate numbers
- Vehicle identifiers (such as license plate number)
- Device identifiers (such as serial numbers)
- Internet URLs
- IP addresses
- Biometric identifiers (such as finger and voice prints)
- Genetic data that is individually identifying
- Full-face photographic images (and any comparable images)
- Other unique identifiers that can be attributed to a specific individual

CEs and BAs may need to modify the data set even more if the CE believes the information could still be used to identify the individual after the 19 items are removed.

Removing the 19 items and any further information as previously indicated is commonly referenced as the "Safe Harbor" method of de-identification. Age is allowed in de-identified information; however, all dates that might be directly related to the individual must be removed or aggregated to the level of year to prevent the determination of birth date because this could be used to help identify an individual. The Safe Harbor method does not allow a month or day of any date, so does not allow for judgment calls about what to include in a data set based on what may or may not be deduced from the data. For an expanded discussion of this topic, see Rebecca's blog post at http://privacyguidance.com/blog/implementing-a-data-de-identification-framework/.

6.6 Business Associates

A BA is a person or business that performs a function or activity for a CE, or for an organized health care arrangement in which the CE participates, involving the use or disclosure of PHI, where PHI is created, received, maintained, or transmitted. This includes claims processing and administration; data analysis, processing, or administration; utilization reviews; quality assurance; patient safety activities; billing; benefits management; practice management; repricing; or any other activity HIPAA covers. A BA is also a person, not a member of the CE's workforce, who provides legal, actuarial, accounting, consulting, data aggregation, management, administrative, accreditation, or financial services for a CE or for an OHCA in which the CE participates, and where the service involves the disclosure of PHI. CEs and BAs may be a BA of another CE.

A BA includes the following:

- A health information organization, e-prescribing gateway, or other person that provides data transmission services with respect to PHI to a CE and that requires access on a routine basis to such PHI
- A person that offers a personal health record to one or more individuals on behalf of a CE
- A subcontractor that creates, receives, maintains, or transmits PHI on behalf of the BA

A BA does not include the following:

- A health care provider, with respect to disclosures by a CE to the health care provider concerning the treatment of the individual
- A plan sponsor, with respect to disclosures by a group health plan (or by a health insurance issuer or HMO with respect to a group health plan) to the plan sponsor
- A government agency, with respect to determining eligibility for, or enrollment in, a government health plan that provides public benefits and is administered by another government agency, or collecting PHI for such purposes, to the extent such activities are authorized by law

- A CE participating in an OHCA that performs a function or activity as described by HIPAA on behalf of such OHCA, or that provides a service for such OHCA

It is important to understand that a subcontractor means a person or entity to whom a BA delegates a function, activity, or service, other than in the capacity of a member of the workforce of such BA. A subcontractor is also considered to be a BA under HIPAA, and must follow all BA requirements. Chapter 21 discusses BA issues at length.

6.7 Marketing

HIPAA originally required an authorization to send marketing communications, with a few exceptions for certain health-related communications. The 2013 Omnibus Rule changed the marketing requirements. If the CE is receiving payment from a third party to send a marketing communication, called a "subsidized communication," then the CE must obtain authorizations. CEs no longer have to include information about these communications in their NPPs because the authorizations are required. CEs do not have to include information in their NPPs about the following:

- Appointment reminders
- Treatment alternatives
- Other services that are for treatment and operations

The marketing authorization is valid if it does the following:

- Meets the general requirements for all HIPAA authorizations
- Notifies the individual he or she may revoke the permission at any time
- Notifies the individual that a third party is paying the CE to make the communication

The notice may be either general, situation-specific, or product- specific, and provide a general explanation of the intended purpose of the use or disclosure.

The HIPAA Omnibus Rule created an exception for refill reminders, adherence reminders, and delivery system instructions.

If remuneration received by the CE is reasonably related to the cost of making the communication and the CE does not make a profit, then these types of reminders are not considered marketing communications.

6.8 Notice of Privacy Practices for PHI

Health plans and health care providers must provide individuals a notice document specifying their information use and disclosure practices. The notice must include information describing how the information is protected, stored, and used, and the conditions under which it is shared. More specifically, the notice must:

- Contain the following statement, prominently displayed:

  THIS NOTICE DESCRIBES HOW MEDICAL INFOR-MATION ABOUT YOU MAY BE USED AND DISCLOSED AND HOW YOU CAN GET ACCESS TO THIS INFOR-MATION. PLEASE REVIEW IT CAREFULLY.

- Contain a description, including at least one example, of the types of uses and disclosures that the CE is permitted to make for TPO.
- Contain separate statements if the entity will use and/or disclose PHI: (1) for appointment reminders; (2) in information about treatment alternatives; (3) to raise funds for the entity; (4) in information sent to the HMO or health insurance insurers; (5) to raise funds for the CE, and that the individual has a right to opt out of receiving such communications; (6) to the sponsor of the plan; and (7) for underwriting purposes, a statement that the CE is prohibited from using or disclosing PHI that is genetic information of an individual.
- Contain a statement that other uses and disclosures not described in the notice will be made only with the individual's written authorization, and a statement that the individual may revoke authorization.
- Contain a statement that the individual may request to revoke or restrict authorization for the CE to use PHI, along with a statement that the CE is not required to agree to a requested restriction, except in the case of specific disclosures.

- Contain a statement that the CE is required by law to maintain the privacy of PHI, to provide individuals with notice of its legal duties and privacy practices with respect to PHI, and to notify affected individuals following a breach of unsecured PHI.
- Describe the patient's right to inspect and copy PHI.
- Describe the patient's right to amend PHI.
- Describe the patient's right to receive an accounting of PHI disclosures and make formal complaints.
- Contain a statement that the CE is required by law to maintain the privacy of PHI.
- Contain the name, or title, and telephone number of a person or office to contact for further information regarding the handling of PHI.
- Be made available at enrollment, within 60 days of a material revision to the notice, and not less than every three years.
- If there is a material change to the notice:
  - A health plan that posts its notice on its website must prominently post the change or its revised notice on its website by the effective date of the material change to the notice, and provide the revised notice, or information about the material change and how to obtain the revised notice, in its next annual mailing to individuals then covered by the plan.
  - A health plan that does not post its notice on a website must provide the revised notice, or information about the material change and how to obtain the revised notice, to individuals then covered by the plan within 60 days of the material revision to the notice.

A CE must revise and distribute its notice without delay whenever there is a material change to the uses or disclosures, the individual's rights, the CE's legal duties, or other privacy practices stated in the notice. Except when required by law, a material change to any part of the notice cannot be implemented prior to the effective date of the notice in which such material change is reflected.

If a CE provides information about its customer services or benefits on a website, it must prominently post the notice on the website in addition to allowing requests for the notice from the website. The requested notice can be sent by e-mail if the requestor agrees to this type of response. If the CE knows that an e-mail transmission failed, a paper copy of the notice must be sent to the individual. CEs must document compliance with the notice requirements by retaining all copies of the issued notices.

Keep the following points in mind with regard to your NPP:

- Each health plan and health care provider that is a CE must have an NPP.
- The NPP must contain the elements previously listed.
- A covered health care provider with a direct treatment relationship with individuals must deliver the NPP to patients.
- All CEs must give an NPP to anyone on request.
- CEs and BAs must post the NPP on any website it maintains for customer service or benefits information.
- CEs in an OHCA may use a joint NPP, as long as each agrees to abide by the NPP content with respect to the PHI created or received in connection with participation in the OHCA.
- Distribution of a joint NPP by any CE participating in an OHCA arrangement at the first point that an OHCA member has an obligation to provide notice satisfies the distribution obligation of the other participants in the OHCA.
- A health plan must distribute its NPP to each enrollee by the Privacy Rule compliance date. Following this, the health plan must give the NPP to each new enrollee at enrollment, and send a reminder to every enrollee at least once every 3 years that the NPP is available on request. A health plan satisfies the distribution obligation by giving the NPP to the "named insured," or subscriber, for coverage that also applies to spouses and dependents. See Chapter 18 for further discussion.
- A covered health care provider with a direct treatment relationship with individuals must make a good-faith effort to obtain written acknowledgment from patients of receipt of the NPP. The Privacy Rule does not describe particular content for the acknowledgment. However, the provider must document the reason for any failure to obtain the patient's written acknowledgment in such situations. Providers do not need to request acknowledgment in emergency treatment situations.

See Chapter 8, Writing Effective Privacy Policies, for further discussion of the NPP.

6.9 Individual Rights to Request Privacy Protection for PHI

CEs must permit an individual to request restrictions for uses or disclosures of PHI about the individual to carry out TPO and other disclosures. CEs and BAs are not required to agree to a restriction request. However, if the entity agrees to a restriction, then the entity is bound to comply with the restriction for that individual except for emergency situations and as required by other laws. CEs and BAs may terminate agreement to a restriction if:

- The individual agrees to or requests the termination in writing.
- The individual orally agrees to the termination and the oral agreement is documented.
- The CE informs the individual that it is terminating its agreement to a restriction. The termination is only effective with respect to PHI created or received after it has informed the individual.

Covered health care providers must permit individuals to request and must accommodate reasonable requests by individuals to receive communications of PHI from the covered health care provider by alternative means or at alternative locations if the individual indicates that disclosure of all or part of the PHI could endanger the individual. For example, an individual may request that a CE communicate using a method other than through the use of the telephone or a specific telephone number, perhaps through a specific mailing address or alternate phone number. An individual may also request CEs to send printed communications in sealed envelopes instead of on postcards. Health plans must also accommodate reasonable requests from individuals indicating that disclosure of all or part of the PHI could put them in danger. A health plan may not question the individual's statement of endangerment. All CEs may condition compliance with a confidential communication request on the individual specifying an alternative address or method of contact and explaining how any payment will be handled.

The 2013 Omnibus Rule expanded an individual's right to restrict the disclosure of PHI to a health plan in the following circumstances:

- Disclosure is for health care operations or payment and disclosure is not otherwise required by law.
- PHI relates solely to a product or service for which the individual or a third party paid in full, out of pocket.

On such a request, CEs must comply, make this restriction, and not disclose the restricted information to the individual's health plan(s). BAs of the health plan are also prohibited from receiving the restricted PHI.

6.10 Individual Access to PHI

An individual generally has a right to access, inspect, and obtain a copy of his or her own PHI in a CE's designated record set for as long as the PHI is maintained. The designated record set is the group of records maintained by or for a CE that is used, in whole or part, to make decisions about individuals, or that is a provider's medical and billing records about individuals or a health plan's enrollment, payment, claims adjudication, and case or medical management record systems. There are a few exceptions, including the following:

- Psychotherapy notes
- Information that is, or could be used for, a civil, criminal, or administrative action or legal proceeding
- PHI that is subject to access prohibitions described in the Clinical Laboratory Improvements Amendments of 1988
- PHI held by certain research laboratories

For further discussion of designated record sets, see Rebecca's blog post at http://privacyguidance.com/blog/designated-record-sets -know-what-they-are-ad-nprm-discussion-1/.

CEs and BAs can deny an individual access to PHI without providing an opportunity for review under certain circumstances. For instance, providers for correctional institutions can deny an inmate's request to access PHI if it could jeopardize the health, safety, security, custody, or rehabilitation of the individual or of other inmates, or the safety of any officer, employee, or other person at the correctional institution or responsible for the transporting of the inmate. Access can also be denied if the health care professional believes the access could cause harm to the individual or some other person. The individual can also be denied access if the PHI was used for research that does not allow such access, if the access is subject to the denial of access requirements within the Privacy Act, or if the PHI was obtained from another provider with the condition the PHI cannot be given to anyone else.

Individuals have the right to have such denials reviewed by a licensed health care professional designated by the CE to act as a reviewing official. The reviewer must be someone who did not participate in the original decision to deny. Such circumstances include the following:

- Access is likely to endanger the life or physical safety of the individual or another person.
- PHI references another person and the access would likely cause substantial harm to the other person.
- Request for access is made by the individual's personal representative, and access to the individual's PHI is likely to cause substantial harm to the individual or another person.

CEs and BAs must provide or deny an access request in writing generally no later than 30 days after receipt of the request for PHI it maintains on-site, and generally no later than 60 days for PHI maintained off-site. In a denial, it must explain, in plain language, the basis for the denial, and if applicable, the individual's review and complaint rights. The CE must provide the individual with access to the PHI in the form requested by the individual if it already exists in that form, or, if it does not, in another form agreed to by the CE and the individual. When providing an individual a copy of PHI, the CE may impose a reasonable, cost-based fee, but the fee must be based on the actual costs to provide the information.

For paper records, the fee can only include the costs of supplies and labor, postage, and preparation of a summary of the contents. For electronic records, the fee can include labor costs, and, where requested by the individual, the costs for the electronic media on which the records are transferred (such as a CD or a USB drive), postage (when the electronic media is mailed), and a summary of the contents. The CE cannot add on computer costs or data storage costs to the fee.

If a CE does not maintain the PHI requested but knows where it is maintained, it must inform the individual where to direct the request for access. CEs and BAs must document the PHI files that are subject to access by individuals, in addition to the titles of the persons or offices responsible for receiving and processing individual requests for access.

The 2013 Omnibus Rule created the following additional requirements:

- CEs must provide individuals with a copy of the PHI that is maintained in a designated record set in the form and format requested by the individual, and if that is not possible, to reach an agreement with the individual for the provision of that information electronically. The requested information must be provided within 30 days. CEs are allowed one 30-day extension if circumstances are justified for a delay.
- Individuals may designate third parties to receive their information, and the CE is required to send the information to that person on a signed written request. CEs are not required to investigate each request to ensure the third party seeking the records is doing so scrupulously. However, the CE is required to have policies and procedures in place to verify the third party's identity when they request access to the PHI, as well as to protect the PHI as it is shared.

6.11 Amendment of PHI

The CE must permit an individual to request amendment to PHI maintained in a designated record set. The CE may require the requests to be in writing and require a reason to support a requested amendment. A CE must accept requests to amend PHI for individuals as long as it maintains PHI records. A CE can deny an individual's amendment request if the PHI was not created by the CE (unless the originator of PHI is no longer available), if the PHI is not part of the designated record set, or if the PHI is determined to be accurate and complete.

A CE must make the requested amendment, or deny the amendment, no later than 60 days after receipt of the amendment request. If the CE denies in part or in whole the requested amendment, the entity must give the individual a written denial. If the CE is unable to act on the amendment within 60 days, the CE can extend the time to take action by no more than 30 days, provided the entity gives the individual a written statement of the reasons for the delay and the date by which action will be completed on the request. The CE can have only one extension of time for action on a request for an amendment.

If the CE accepts the requested amendment, in whole or in part, the entity must make the appropriate amendment to the PHI by, at a minimum, identifying the records that are affected by the amendment, and appending or otherwise providing a link to the location of the amendment. Then the CE must inform the individual that the amendment is accepted and obtain the individual's identification of and agreement to have the entity notify the relevant persons with which the amendment needs to be shared. Notice of the amendment must be made to persons identified by the individual as having received PHI about the individual and needing the amendment, and all persons that the CE knows have the PHI that is the subject of the amendment.

If the CE denies the requested amendment, it must provide the individual with a written denial. The denial must describe the basis for the denial in plain language and describe the individual's right to submit a written statement disagreeing with the denial. The denial must also state that if the individual does not submit a statement of disagreement, the individual may request the CE provide the individual's request for amendment and the denial with any future disclosures of the PHI, and contain a description of how the individual can submit formal complaints. The description must include the name, or title, and telephone number of the designated contact person or office.

A CE must permit the individual to submit a written statement disagreeing with a denial of a requested amendment describing the basis of the disagreement, and the entity can prepare a written rebuttal to the individual, but this is not a required action. Whenever a rebuttal is prepared, the CE must provide a copy to the individual who submitted the statement of disagreement. The CE must also identify the PHI that is the subject of the disputed amendment and amend it with information regarding the individual's request for amendment, related denial, and any resulting statement of disagreement and rebuttal. These amendments must then be included with any subsequent PHI disclosures related to the disagreement.

A CE that is informed by another CE of an amendment to an individual's PHI must amend the PHI in designated record sets. A CE must document and retain the titles of the persons or offices responsible for receiving and processing requests for amendments.

6.12 Accounting Disclosures of PHI

An individual generally has a right to receive an accounting of disclosures of PHI made by a CE and the CE's BAs in the six years prior to the date on which the accounting is requested. The exceptions to this include accounting of disclosures:

- To carry out TPO
- To individuals of PHI about them
- To the personal representatives of individuals
- For notification of or to persons involved in an individual's health care or payment for health care
- For disaster relief
- For the facility's directory or to persons involved in the individual's care or other notification purposes
- For national security or intelligence purposes
- To correctional institutions or law enforcement officials for certain purposes regarding inmates or individuals in lawful custody
- That occurred prior to the compliance date for the CE
- For incidental disclosures
- For disclosures made pursuant to an authorization
- For limited data sets

The CE must temporarily suspend an individual's right to receive an accounting of disclosures to a health oversight agency or law enforcement official if the agency or official indicates in writing that such an accounting to the individual would impede the agency's activities.

If, during the period covered by the accounting, the CE has made multiple disclosures of PHI to the same person or entity for a single purpose, the accounting may include the number of the disclosures made during the accounting period and the date of the last disclosure during the accounting period.

A CE must act on the individual's request for an accounting no later than 60 days after receipt of the request. The action must provide the individual with the accounting requested or a written statement explaining the reason for delay. If there is a delay, the time can be extended no more than 30 days, and the CE must provide the individual a written statement explaining the reasons for the delay and the date by which the CE will provide the accounting.

The CE must provide the first accounting to an individual in any 12-month period without charge. However, the CE may impose a reasonable, cost-based fee for each subsequent request for an accounting by the same individual within the 12-month period, provided that the CE informs the individual in advance of the fee and provides the individual with an opportunity to withdraw or modify the request for a subsequent accounting to avoid or reduce the fee. In addition, a CE must document the information that will be included in an accounting, including the specific pieces of information and the titles of the persons or offices responsible for receiving and processing requests for an accounting by individuals. A patient who has signed an authorization to disclose the results of a preemployment physical to a prospective employer will not see this event in a disclosure-accounting report.

6.13 PHI Restrictions Requests

The Privacy Rule gives individuals the right to request CEs to restrict use or disclosure of PHI for TPO, disclosure to persons involved in the individual's health care or payment for health care, or disclosure to notify family members or others about the individual's general condition, location, or death. The 2013 Omnibus Rule established rights of individuals to keep certain health information and associated activities confidential. It required that a CE must agree to the request of an individual to restrict disclosure of PHI about the individual to a health plan if:

- The disclosure is for the purpose of carrying out payment or health care operations and is not otherwise required by law.
- The PHI pertains solely to a health care item or service for which the individual, or person other than the health plan on behalf of the individual, has paid the CE in full.

Other than these situations, a CE is not obligated to agree to restriction requests. If a CE agrees to a restriction request, however, it must comply with the specified and agreed-upon restrictions, except for purposes of medical emergency treatment for the individual.

6.14 Administrative Requirements

CEs and BAs (as applicable to their BA contract with each of their CEs for whom they provide services) are required to implement basic administrative procedures to protect PHI. Some high-level descriptions of administrative requirements include obligations to

- Designate a privacy official responsible for the development and implementation of the entity's policies and procedures.
- Designate a contact person or office responsible for receiving complaints and answering questions related to the notice.
- Document the associated personnel designations (e.g., privacy official, or positions that were assigned these responsibilities, contact person, etc.).
- Train all personnel and workforce members on the privacy policies and procedures with respect to PHI as necessary and appropriate to carry out their job responsibilities. Workforce members include employees, volunteers, trainees, and may also include other persons whose conduct falls under the CE's and BA's direct control, whether or not they are paid by the entity.
- Document training that has occurred.
- Implement appropriate administrative, technical, and physical safeguards to protect the privacy of PHI.
- Safeguard PHI from any intentional or unintentional unauthorized use or disclosure.
- Maintain reasonable and appropriate administrative, technical, and physical safeguards to prevent intentional or unintentional use or disclosure of PHI in violation of the Privacy Rule and to limit incidental use and disclosure resulting from otherwise permitted or required use or disclosure. A safeguard example is shredding documents containing PHI before having a trash service haul it away, locking access to physical

printout of medical records, allowing access to electronic PHI only with passwords and user IDs, and so on. These safeguards are typically detailed within the information security policies and procedures.

- Provide a process for individuals to make complaints concerning the policies and procedures; CEs and BAs, as appropriate, must explain these procedures in the NPP.
- Document all complaints received and their resolution.
- Consistently apply and document sanctions against personnel who fail to comply with the privacy policies and procedures, and document applied sanctions.
- Mitigate as much as possible any harmful effect that is known to the CE of a use or disclosure of PHI in violation of its policies and procedures by the CE or a BA.
- Maintain, until at least six years after the later of the date of the creation or last effective date, the CE's and BA's, as applicable, privacy policies and procedures, NPP(s), documentation of complaints, and other actions, activities, and designations that the Privacy Rule requires to be documented.

CEs may not intimidate or take any type of retaliatory action against any individual for exercising the right to submit a complaint, request a review, request an amendment for their PHI, or any other type of action described previously as being a right of the individual under the Privacy Rule. In addition, CEs may not require individuals to waive their rights as a condition of medical treatment, payment, enrollment in a health plan, or eligibility for benefits.

CEs must implement documented PHI privacy policies and procedures designed to comply with the Privacy Rule. The policies and procedures must be designed to take into account the size of and the type of activities that relate to the CE's and BA's PHI. When developing policies and procedures to meet Privacy Rule compliance, a CE needs to

- Review and change its existing policies and procedures as necessary and appropriate.
- Promptly document and implement a revised policy and procedure whenever there is a change in the law that necessitates a change. If the change affects the content of the notice, the

CE and BA must promptly make the appropriate revisions to the notice.
- Maintain the policies, procedures, and related communications in written or electronic form for at least six years from the date of creation or the date when it last was in effect, whichever is later.

A group health plan is not subject to most of these aforementioned requirements if it provides health benefits solely through an insurance contract with a health insurance issuer or an HMO, and does not create or receive PHI other than summary health information or information indicating whether the individual is participating in the group health plan, or is enrolled in or has disenrolled from a health insurance issuer or HMO offered by the plan.

The only administrative obligations with which a fully insured group health plan that has no more than enrollment data and summary health information is required to comply are:

- Bans on retaliatory acts and waiver of individual rights
- Documentation requirements with respect to plan documents if such documents are amended to provide for the disclosure of PHI to the plan sponsor by a health insurance issuer or HMO that services the group health plan

6.14.1 Privacy Officer

CEs and BAs must designate a privacy officer, or an existing position to have the responsibilities of a privacy officer in addition to the other responsibilities of that position, to be responsible for developing and implementing the CE's and BA's privacy policies and procedures. A contact person or office must also be designated to be responsible for receiving complaints and answering questions about the entity's privacy practices, notices, and HIPAA compliance. See Appendix B for a job description of a privacy officer.

6.14.2 Training

All CE and BA personnel must receive initial and ongoing training that covers the privacy policies and procedures to ensure they perform their job responsibilities in compliance with the requirements. Although not specifically required within the HIPAA text, you should consider the following action items as part of your training project plan:

- Establish a timeline for mandatory initial HIPAA privacy training.
- Establish procedures to train new personnel as soon as feasible following their employment.
- Provide training that helps personnel relate the policy to their working environment.
- Provide training on how to report a privacy problem.
- Consider competency tests or quizzes to evaluate and ascertain the training effectiveness.
- Require regular follow-up training and training following significant changes in policies and procedures. Train the personnel who are most impacted as soon as possible, either immediately before or immediately following these changes.
- Document the training in written or electronic form and retain the records for at least six years.

See Chapter 25 for a detailed discussion of awareness and training.

6.14.3 Safeguards

CEs and BAs must establish appropriate and reasonable administrative, technical, and physical safeguards to protect PHI. These safeguards must protect PHI from any intentional or unintentional use or disclosure that is in violation of the standards, implementation specifications, or other requirements of the Privacy Rule. Perform a risk analysis and, based on the results, create and implement a risk management plan for both electronic and nonelectronic information assets. Request the privacy officer to work closely with the security officer, and other personnel as appropriate, to determine the most feasible safeguards for your organization.

6.14.4 Complaints

CEs and BAs must establish policies and processes for adequately taking and responding to complaints from individuals concerning the

CE's privacy policies and procedures, or concerns with its compliance with the policies and procedures. All complaints received must be documented, along with the associated actions that were taken to address the complaints. Documentation must be retained for at least six years.

6.14.5 Sanctions

Sanction policies and procedures must be established and applied when appropriate. The procedures must ensure disciplinary actions are taken against personnel who do not comply with the CE's or BA's privacy policies and procedures or the requirements of the Privacy Rule. Assign an individual or group to review policy and procedural violations and specify corrective and disciplinary action. Apply disciplinary action as necessary and appropriate. Each sanction that is applied must be documented.

Some suggestions to consider for sanctions are the following:

- Make sanctions progressive and appropriate for the severity, frequency, and intent of violations.
- Apply sanctions equitably without regard to the person's role or position within the CE.
- Include termination of employment or contract relationship and criminal prosecution as possible sanctions.
- Include provisions for sanctions within contract and labor agreements.
- Coordinate sanctions with your human resources department.
- Consider establishing progressive sanctions, such as verbal warning, written warning, and termination, and determine when progressive sanctions are appropriate.
- Make sure workforce members are aware of the sanction procedures.

6.14.6 Mitigation

CEs and BAs must mitigate as much as possible any harm that occurs as a result of a use or disclosure of PHI that occurred in violation of its policies and procedures or the requirements of the Privacy Rule by the CE or any BA.

Here are just a few of the methods you can consider using for mitigating (and containing) the damage from inappropriate disclosure of PHI. Keep in mind that mitigation procedures also include those that help to mitigate (prevent) a PHI disclosure from occurring.

- Use a fax cover sheet for all PHI transmittals and include a notice asking people who have received the fax in error to contact you immediately and to destroy the information.
- Inform the area responsible for the policy or procedural breach to determine if it needs to be updated to prevent future actions that would have harmful effects.
- Meet with your legal counsel to determine if inappropriate use or disclosure may in itself constitute a harmful effect with regard to HIPAA and other applicable legal requirements.
- Discuss with your legal counsel how and when your organization should notify individuals if misuse or inappropriate disclosure of PHI will likely lead to a harmful effect.
- Consult with your legal counsel to determine appropriate contract language to use to transfer the potential financial burden of harm to BAs.
- Notify the individual immediately when an improper disclosure has occurred. Determine if there is anything you can do to prevent further unauthorized spread of the PHI.
- Prohibit employees from posting PHI to online social media sites.
- Perform security and privacy compliance audits for any cloud service or other outsourced entity prior to engaging their services.
- Require mobile computers and mobile digital storage devices to encrypt all data stored within them.
- Maintain an inventory of all computing and digital storage devices containing PHI.

6.14.7 Refraining from Intimidating or Retaliatory Acts

Establish policies and procedures to make sure members of your workforce do not intimidate, threaten, coerce, discriminate against, or take other retaliatory action against any individual who exercises any of the rights established by the Privacy Rule, such as filing a complaint with regard to privacy practice compliance.

6.14.8 Waiver of Rights

Individuals cannot be required to waive their rights provided by the Privacy Rule as a condition for providing treatment, payment, enrollment in a health plan, or to be eligible for benefits.

6.14.9 Policies and Procedures

CEs and BAs must create and implement privacy policies and procedures designed to ensure the entity's compliance with the standards, implementation specifications, or other Privacy Rule requirements.

6.14.10 Documentation

Documented privacy policies and procedures must be maintained in written and electronic form, and kept available for at least six years from the date of its creation or the date when it was last in effect, whichever is later.

6.15 Personal Representatives

A CE must treat a personal representative of an individual the same as the individual with respect to uses and disclosures of the individual's PHI, as well as the individual's rights under the Privacy Rule. A personal representative is a person legally authorized to make health care decisions on an individual's behalf or to act for a deceased individual or the individual's estate. The Privacy Rule permits an exception when a CE believes the personal representative may be abusing or neglecting the individual, or that treating the person as the personal representative could otherwise endanger the individual.

6.16 Minors

In most cases, parents are personal representatives for their minor children. And, in most cases, parents can exercise individual rights, such as access to the medical record, on behalf of their minor children. However, in certain exceptional cases, the parent is not considered the personal representative. In these situations, state and other applicable laws determine the rights of parents to access and control the PHI of their minor children. If state and other laws do not address parental access to a minor's PHI, a licensed health care professional on behalf of the CE has discretion to provide or deny a parent access to the minor's PHI.

6.16.1 Some Points from HHS regarding Personal Representatives and Minors

An individual given a health care power of attorney has the right to access PHI of the individual related to this representation to the extent permitted by the Privacy Rule. However, when a CE believes that an individual, including an unemancipated minor, has been or may be subjected to domestic violence, abuse, or neglect by the personal representative, or that treating a person as an individual's personal representative could endanger the individual, the CE may choose not to treat that person as the individual's personal representative.

With the exception of decedents, a CE must treat a personal representative as the individual only when that person has authority under other law to act on the individual's behalf on matters related to health care. A power of attorney that does not include decisions related to health care in its scope would not, therefore, authorize the holder to exercise the individual's rights under the Privacy Rule. In addition, a CE does not have to treat a personal representative as the individual if it believes doing so would not be in the best interest of the individual because of a reasonable belief that the individual has been or may be subject to domestic violence, abuse, or neglect by the personal representative, or that doing so would otherwise endanger the individual.

With respect to personal representatives of deceased individuals, the Privacy Rule requires a CE to treat the personal representative as the individual as long as the person has the authority under law to act for the decedent or the estate for 50 years following death. The power of attorney needs to be valid after the individual's death to qualify the holder as the personal representative of the decedent.

An individual who is the subject of PHI can exercise all rights granted by the Privacy Rule with respect to all corresponding PHI, including information obtained while the individual was an unemancipated minor, consistent with state or other applicable law. Generally, the parent would no longer be the personal representative of his or her child once the child reaches the age of majority or becomes emancipated, and therefore, would no longer control the PHI about the child. Any individual can have a personal representative, including a parent, who can exercise rights on his or her behalf.

A deceased individual's PHI may be relevant to a family member's health care. The Privacy Rule provides two ways for a surviving family member to obtain the PHI of a deceased relative:

- Disclosures of PHI for treatment purposes, including the treatment of another individual, do not require an authorization. A CE may disclose a decedent's PHI without authorization to the health care provider who is treating the surviving relative.
- A CE must treat a deceased individual's legally authorized executor or administrator, or a person who is otherwise legally authorized to act on the behalf of the deceased individual or his estate, as a personal representative with respect to PHI relevant to the representation for 50 years following death. If it is within the scope of the personal representative's authority under other law, the Privacy Rule permits the personal representative to obtain the information or provide the appropriate authorization for its disclosure.

6.17 Transition Provisions

A CE may continue to use or disclose PHI under consent, an authorization, or other type of legal permission that was obtained from an individual before the April 14, 2003, compliance date, as long as the entity complies with all limitations placed by the permission. For example, a provider that obtained consent for use or disclosure for billing purposes would be able to continue to use PHI obtained prior to the compliance date and covered by the consent form for all TPO activities to the extent not expressly excluded by the terms of the consent.

If a permission obtained prior to April 14, 2003 is a general consent to participate in a research project, and a CE is conducting or participating in the research, the entity may continue to make use or disclosure of PHI for purposes of that project. If a CE agrees to a restriction requested by an individual, subsequent use or disclosure of PHI is subject to that restriction.

6.18 Compliance Dates and Penalties

The following were the compliance dates for initial implementation of the HIPAA Privacy Rule standards:

- Health care providers: No later than April 14, 2003
- Health plans: No later than the following date, as applicable:
  - Health plans other than small health plans: April 14, 2003
  - Small health plans: April 14, 2004
- Health care clearinghouses: No later than April 14, 2003

If a complaint is lodged against an entity and an investigation or compliance review determines no violation exists, the secretary of HHS will inform both the entity and complainant in writing. If a complaint is lodged against an entity and the resulting compliance review confirms noncompliance with the Privacy Rule, the CE or BA will be informed by the secretary in writing, who will attempt to resolve the situation by informal means if possible. If the situation cannot be resolved in this manner, a formal noncompliance report will be issued to both the person filing the complaint and the CE or BA.

There are four tiers of penalties:

1. Not knowing: The CE or BA did not know and reasonably should not have known of the violation.
2. Reasonable cause: The CE or BA knew, or should have known that the act was a violation, but the CE did not act with willful neglect.

3. Willful neglect, corrected: The violation resulted from an intentional failure or reckless indifference to HIPAA obligations, but the violation was corrected within 30 days of discovery.

4. Willful neglect, not corrected: The violation resulted from an intentional failure or reckless indifference to HIPAA obligations, and the violation was not corrected within 30 days of discovery.

Penalties for each of the tiers are as follows:

1. Not knowing: $100–$50,000 for each violation
2. Reasonable cause: $1,000–$50,000 for each violation
3. Willful neglect, corrected: $10,000–$50,000 for each violation
4. Willful neglect, not corrected: at least $50,000 for each violation

In each circumstance, the total civil monetary penalty for violations of the same type in a calendar year is capped at $1.5 million.

The HHS will take several factors into account in determining the amount of the penalty. Such factors include the nature and extent of the violation, including the number of individuals impacted; the nature and extent of the harm from the violation, including whether the breach impacted the ability to obtain health care; the history of prior violations, if any; and the financial condition of the CE or BA.

Civil monetary penalties are not the only remedy for violations of HIPAA. Criminal penalties may apply in some circumstances. HHS may resolve issues through informal methods, and may provide technical assistance to violators.

With the Omnibus Rule, CEs are reminded that HIPAA compliance is a required part of the sponsorship of a group health plan. The large civil monetary penalties encourage compliance with all aspects of HIPAA privacy and security requirements.

The Health Information Technology for Clinical and Economic Health (HITECH) Act, part of the American Recovery and Reinvestment Act of 2009, gave state attorneys general the authority to bring civil actions on behalf of state residents for violations of the HIPAA Privacy and Security Rules. The HITECH Act permits state attorneys general to obtain damages on behalf of state residents or to enjoin further violations of the HIPAA Privacy and Security Rules.

Practical Checklist

- Assign, document, and communicate with your privacy official.
- CEs include health care providers, health plans, and health care clearinghouses.
- BAs must follow the Privacy Rule requirements that are applicable to the services and products they provide.
- Subcontractors of BAs are also considered to be BAs, and as such must comply with HIPAA.
- Creating an NPP is the action that will be the most obvious to the public.
- You may want to create more than one NPP based on your locations and jurisdictions.
- HIPAA gives individuals many explicit rights to their corresponding PHI; create procedures to support these rights.
- Know the circumstances under which you must obtain signed authorizations, as well as those requiring you to give an individual the opportunity to agree or object to a use or disclosure.
- Penalties are significantly higher than under the first version of HIPAA.
- Each state attorney general can bring action for HIPAA penalties, greatly increasing the potential sanctions that can occur against CEs and BAs.
- Document! Document!! Document!!!

7

PERFORMING A PRIVACY
RULE GAP ANALYSIS
AND RISK ANALYSIS

7.1 Introduction

Considering the potential costs and effort associated with Health
Insurance Portability and Accountability Act (HIPAA) compliance, it is a mistake to install a HIPAA solution without first understanding your current organizational HIPAA compliance situation.
Your organization may already have in place policies, procedures,
systems, and technology that adequately address at least some of the
HIPAA requirements.

To determine where HIPAA compliance requirements must
be addressed, or your HIPAA gaps, you must perform a HIPAA
Privacy Rule gap analysis and risk analysis. Using the results of
these analyses, along with any existing business and financial plans,
your organization will be ready to develop a HIPAA compliance
plan, including a listing of compliance priorities. Use the following
checklist to help you perform your own Privacy Rule gap analysis and
identify privacy risks.

7.2 Gap Analysis and Risk Analysis

1. *Is someone within your organization responsible for addressing
   privacy issues and compliance?* This should be someone who
   has been assigned privacy official responsibilities, often designated as the privacy officer. This may also be an existing
   role that has been given the privacy officer responsibilities,
   but continues to maintain his or her current title. The privacy officer, or equivalent, should be someone who knows

not only your business well but also is very familiar with the health care industry, is experienced with security and privacy activities, and is knowledgeable in the HIPAA regulations. Typically, this person has filled one or more of the following positions:

- Information security officer
- Chief privacy officer
- Director of information technology
- Director of medical records
- Director of patient accounting
- Director of patient registration/admitting
- Compliance officer

2. *Do you have an inventory of all your organizational policies, procedures, training, and technical controls?* Besides collecting all these documents from within your organization, also collect HIPAA plans from your business associates (BAs), including vendors, clearinghouses, payers, cloud providers, and so on. Obtain copies of all forms related to release of protected health information (PHI) or authorizations to release or disclose PHI to third parties. Document and inventory everything you collect.

3. *Have you reviewed all your documents and identified the directives and practices that apply to PHI?* Determine and document the following:

- What rules, if any, exist for protecting health information?
- Identify all current non-IT-specific policies and procedures related to information access, disclosure, and integrity.
- What are the procedures for allowing access to PHI and medical records?
- What are the procedures for responding to complaints?
- How is your Notice of Privacy Practices (NPP), if it applies to your organization, worded?
- What PHI-related security and privacy training do you provide and require?
- What types of ongoing security and privacy awareness communications do you provide?

- If written policies and procedures for the privacy of PHI meeting the HIPAA Privacy Rule exist, have they been completely implemented?
- Are any existing privacy policies and procedures monitored, incidents documented, and corrective action taken?
- Identify the policies, procedures, and forms that need to be revised to comply with HIPAA requirements.
- Identify which policies, procedures, or forms do not currently exist and need to be created to comply with HIPAA.
- Identify all reports containing PHI that are distributed on paper, electronically, faxed, e-mailed, or using some other method (technical or nontechnical).
- Identify all organized health care arrangements.
- Interview key staff to confirm or expand upon findings.
- What reports need to be changed to comply with HIPAA requirements?

Do not forget to review your websites to see if you have any forms or databases with health information. It is typical in many organizations for the web administrators to place forms or databases onto Internet websites at the request of almost any manager within the organization. Marketing areas in particular have a tendency to collect as much information from website visitors as possible, very possibly including PHI. Review carefully the information collected from and stored on your Internet web servers to determine if any is PHI. Be sure to check *all* web pages—some sites have thousands of web pages. Include review of the web pages of your BAs, if they are also collecting information for you.

4. *Have you determined the security and privacy practices of your BAs?* Carefully review your BA contracts. If you are a BA, this includes your subcontractors; as a result of the 2013 Omnibus Rule, they are also your BAs. How does your organization ensure privacy protection by BAs? Do you have a standard BA agreement that has been executed by all BAs? Have you obtained the appropriate assurances that your BAs are in compliance with their applicable HIPAA requirements? Have the noncompliant BAs been replaced?

Determine HIPAA compliance and the adequacy of BA privacy practices; ask each of your BAs to provide the following information:

- Copies of their information security and privacy policies.
- Validation that they have performed a recent (within the past year) risk assessment.
- Validation that they provide their employees appropriate training and ongoing awareness communications.
- Executive summaries of any compliance audits they have had performed.
- Identify all electronic data interchange (EDI) transactions and their associated purposes and types.
- Identify all EDI standards used by your BAs.
- Identify and document BA systems that process your organization's PHI.
- Obtain and review copies of BA and third-party agreements involving the transmission of PHI in any form.
- Identify code sets used.
- Document how identifiers are used.
- Identify third parties and BAs receiving or sending PHI. This includes information received or sent via export, file transfer, e-mail, paper, disk, tape, web, or transactional interface.
- Meet with third parties and BAs receiving or sending PHI. Are they aware of HIPAA requirements? What are their plans for meeting HIPAA compliance?
- Identify contracts that need to be revised to comply with HIPAA. Include BA agreements as appropriate to meet HIPAA requirements for third-party data processing vendors.
- Meet with vendors to determine their HIPAA compliance plans. Will they offer system upgrades? At a cost? Will new products be offered? In what time frame?
- If applicable, meet with your health care clearinghouse to determine their plans. Review your contract with the clearinghouse to ensure appropriate language exists for exchange of data.

- Identify legal counsel with HIPAA expertise within your organization. You will need their help to make business and third-party contract revisions.
- Determine and document HIPAA compliance for your BAs and third-party partners based on all your previous research.

Implement a methodology to identify all your organization's BA and third-party contracts. Include the following in your methodology:

- Develop standard contract terminology to ensure consistency for BA provisions to help ensure HIPAA compliance.
- While you are reviewing your BA contracts, identify terminology and HIPAA requirements that must be included.
- Update your contract renewal process to incorporate HIPAA BA terminology and requirements into existing contracts.

Note: A solution for this activity is provided at http://www.privacyprofessor.org.

5. *Have you conducted a security review to determine what security technology and practices exist to help ensure health information privacy?* Have you reviewed the security of PHI during transmission and in storage of all forms to ensure privacy and security? For example, if you send PHI over the Internet, carefully consider implementing encryption to prevent unauthorized interception. Most of the privacy requirements for a security review will be met when you perform your security risk analysis. At a high level, you must determine the following:

- What administrative security exists for PHI?
- What physical security exists for PHI?
- What technical security exists for PHI?

However, there are a few additional security review actions you should perform that fall under these categories:

- Identify all information systems (including web servers, cloud locations, and mobile devices) containing PHI.

- Identify all PHI code sets and determine those that are not in compliance with HIPAA requirements.
- Determine the systems and related software applications that must be upgraded or changed to comply with HIPAA EDI requirements.
- Assess the functionality, changes, and upgrades that must be made. For example, have you added security breach and incident tracking and reporting capabilities? Do you have a way to track and report new code releases? Do you have capabilities for tracking data access and changes?
- Identify all current policies and procedures related to system security, privacy, and information sharing.
- Identify contingency and disaster planning practices.
- Determine how your organization's websites need to be modified based on code set and reporting changes.
- Document your overall architecture, including internal and external networks, and identify potential security risks and issues.
- Verify the use of malware detection software, firewalls, and other security and intrusion detection mechanisms.
- Identify, document, and evaluate the effectiveness of the applications and operating system security features.
- Identify how information communications are secured. For instance, how does your organization secure e-mail, texts, social media communications, fax transmissions, Internet connections, and so on? Are encryption, digital signatures, and other such privacy-enhancing technologies used?
- Identify and document access points to your networks and systems, both internal and external.
- Map the PHI data flows through your systems and applications, documenting all points from the time of collection or creation through to where data is shared outside of your organization, and then where the data is destroyed/removed from further use.
- Identify and review backup systems and procedures.
- Identify and determine the purposes for your Internet and intranet websites.
- Identify user security policies and practices such as log on/log off, passwords, and so on.

- Determine where workstations, cloud providers, and mobile users that can access PHI are located, and the policies and practices that govern their use.
- Identify the physical security mechanisms that help to protect access to PHI; for example, locks, badges, pass codes, guards at entrances, and so on.
- Identify your organization's incident-reporting and follow-up procedures.

6. *Have you documented your organization's uses and disclosures of PHI?* When you do your gap analysis and risk analysis correctly you will discover all the ways that PHI is used and disclosed. To determine risks that exist during use and disclosure, and then determine how to address those risks, you must know what use and disclosure means. Use means the sharing, employment, application, utilization, examination, or analysis of individually identifiable information *within* an entity. Disclosure means the release, transfer, provision of access to, or divulging of information *outside* the entity holding the information.

   Use and disclosure typically occur during face-to-face communications, mail, faxes, e-mails, text messages, online social communications sites, phone calls, or access to your computer systems. To effectively mitigate unauthorized use and disclosure, you must implement good policies and procedures and train your workforce well.

- Understand current uses and disclosures.
- List all privacy measures in place.
- Forms of notice in use.
  - Authorization forms in use.
  - Disclosure request forms in use.
  - Copies of all agreements in use.
  - Copies of all consent forms in use.
- Obtain operational procedure documentation.
- Examine security and privacy policies in place.

7. *Have you identified uses and disclosures that require authorizations? Does your organization follow the promises made within the authorizations?* Authorizations give covered entities (CEs) permission

to use or disclose indicated PHI for indicated purposes that are typically other than treatment, payment, and operations. Except as otherwise permitted or required by the HIPAA Privacy Rule (see Chapter 6), your organization may not use or disclose PHI without a valid authorization as indicated by the HIPAA regulations. When you obtain or receive a valid authorization for the use or disclosure of PHI, the use or disclosure must be consistent with, and not go beyond, the authorization.

8. *Have you identified your organization's uses and disclosures of health information that do not require authorizations, but allow for opportunity to object?* Your organization may use or disclose PHI without the written authorization of the individual, or the opportunity for the individual to agree or object, in several situations as detailed within the HIPAA Privacy Rule. When your organization is required by the HIPAA Privacy Rule to inform the individual of a use or disclosure permitted by the HIPAA Privacy Rule, or when the individual may agree to such, the individual's agreement may be given orally. A couple of the situations for which authorizations are not required, but opportunity to agree or object must be presented to the individual, for use or disclosure of PHI, include the following:

   • Name, location, condition, and religion within the entity's facility directory or to clergy or persons asking for the individual by name
   • Medical condition to a family member, other relative, or a close personal friend of the individual, or any other person identified by the individual

   See Chapter 6 for detailed information on uses and disclosures of health information that do not require authorizations, but allow for the opportunity to object.

9. *Have you determined which PHI needs to be de-identified?* Identify PHI that must be de-identified per HIPAA Privacy Rule requirements (see Chapter 6) so that it does not identify an individual and with respect to which there is no reasonable basis to believe that the information can be used to identify an individual. Eighteen specific types of information must be removed from a data set for it to be de-identified.

10. *Have you established procedures for using PHI for marketing purposes to meet HIPAA requirements?* Your organization may not use or disclose PHI for marketing without an authorization that meets the applicable HIPAA Privacy Rule requirements, and you must provide information about this within your NPP, if applicable to your organization (see Chapter 6). Generally, a CE may use or disclose PHI for marketing communication in the following three situations:

1. The communication occurs in a face-to-face encounter with the individual.
2. The products or services have a "nominal" value, for example, when giving calendars, pens, and so on.
3. To direct or recommend alternative treatments, therapies, health care providers, care settings, or similar topics within a case management or care coordination situation, but only when the provider discloses that remuneration was provided in return.

You must also prohibit the sale of PHI for fund-raising without individual authorization.

11. *Have you identified all the uses and disclosures of PHI for fund-raising purposes?* Your organization must provide an opt-out method for individuals to deny your use of their PHI for fund-raising purposes, and you must provide information about this within your NPP, if applicable to your organization. You must take reasonable steps to ensure that opt-outs are honored throughout all areas of your organization. You must prohibit the sale of PHI for fund-raising without individual authorization. In addition, you must maintain a record of disclosures made for fund-raising purposes. Review your organization's privacy practices notice to determine whether it permits the use of other PHI for fund-raising.

12. *If you are a health plan organization, do you have policies and procedures governing the use of health information received for policy processing purposes?* This is covered in detail in Chapter 6. Generally, health plans that receive PHI for the purposes of underwriting, premium rating, or other activities relating to

the creation, renewal, or replacement of a contract of health insurance or health benefits may not use or disclose the PHI for any other purpose, except as may be required by law, if health insurance or health benefits are not placed with the health plan.

13. *Have you identified all of your organization's uses of PHI for which authorization and opportunity to object are not needed?* This is covered in detail in Chapter 6. Generally, these special situations include the following:

   - Uses and disclosures required by law
   - Uses and disclosures for public health activities
   - Disclosures about victims of abuse, neglect, or domestic violence
   - Uses and disclosures for health oversight activities
   - Disclosures for judicial and administrative proceedings
   - Disclosures for law enforcement purposes
   - Uses and disclosures about decedents
   - Uses and disclosures for cadaveric organ, eye, or tissue donation purposes
   - Uses and disclosures to avert a serious threat to health or safety
   - Uses and disclosures for specialized government functions
   - Disclosures for workers' compensation

14. *Has your organization established and implemented identity verification policies and procedures to use when it receives requests for PHI?* Your organization must develop policies and procedures to verify the identity and authority of people requesting PHI. We recommend you consider using the following activities as appropriate for your situation and organization:

   - Require requesters to provide documentation detailing the purpose for requesting the PHI.
   - Verify the identity of persons requesting PHI before giving them access.
   - Confirm that persons acting on behalf of a public official have appropriate statements on official letterhead or credentials before giving them the PHI.

- Establish a policy that legal authority is presumed when a request is made in relation to a legal proceeding, warrant, subpoena, or order.
- Develop a formal procedure to authorize disclosure of PHI using other verification items in the absence of a written verification.
- Establish procedures requiring your personnel to make every effort to identify and document the people requesting disclosure and the circumstances of disclosure as detailed within the HIPAA Privacy Rule.
- Develop policies that clearly define the sources of identification and documents of authority that are acceptable to verify permission for disclosure.
- Provide your personnel with training for these procedures, along with comprehensive guidelines and backup resources to help them obtain answers to their verification questions.
- When PHI is released to a legal authority, send a cover letter with the information to remind the recipients that the information is PHI and must be handled in a confidential manner. Retain a copy of the letter for your records.
- Inform frequent requestors of PHI of the procedural changes required by the HIPAA Privacy Rule.

15. *Does your organization provide individuals with an NPP that meets HIPAA requirements?* Except as provided by the HIPAA Privacy Rule, individuals have a right to adequate notice of the uses and disclosures of their PHI that may be made by your organization, in addition to a right to know their rights and your organization's legal duties with respect to PHI. Your organization must document compliance with the notice requirements by retaining copies of the notices issued.

- Include a brief, easy-to-read explanation of the primary points within the notice along with the detailed version. This will help to reinforce individuals' understanding of their privacy rights.
- Incorporate the privacy practice notice into your organization "patient rights" literature and procedures to minimize

the expense and inconvenience and maximize the informational impact.

- Develop a procedure to account for the delivery of the privacy practices notice as your organization delivers it.

16. *Have you identified your organization's confidential communications requirements and established procedures to fulfill requests for alternative communications methods?* Review your organization's facilities to verify that all areas of your organization enable privacy when communicating patient information. A covered health care provider must permit individuals to request and must accommodate reasonable requests by individuals to receive communications of PHI from the covered health care provider by alternative means or at alternative locations. A health plan must permit individuals to request and must accommodate reasonable requests by individuals to receive communications of PHI from the health plan by alternative means or at alternative locations, if the individual clearly states that the disclosure of all or part of that information could endanger the individual. Consider the following, as appropriate for your organization:

- Establish procedures for patients or plan members to request alternative means of communication for PHI, and accommodate the requests when feasible.
- Establish procedures and training for all personnel who receive and fulfill requests from patients for PHI so they are aware of the need for and use of alternate means of communication, as appropriate.
- Document the most common causes for requests for special restrictions, and determine a set of restriction methods to accommodate these situations—for example, for celebrities, government officials, social stigma, physical danger, and so on.
- Establish a way to communicate the restrictions quickly and effectively to workforce members. Remember, some workforce members may not yet have received training on this issue when they receive the restriction request.

- Keep the communications restrictions as simple as possible.
- When an individual asks for restrictions you cannot make, refer them to a facility that can honor their request, if appropriate.
- Identify how to provide aliases for patients when using them to comply with this provision.

17. *Does your organization have procedures in place to archive your PHI and allow authorized individuals access to their corresponding information?* With the few exceptions detailed within the HIPAA Privacy Rule, individuals have a right to inspect and obtain a copy of their corresponding PHI for as long as the PHI is maintained in the designated record set. Your organization must develop and document policies and procedures to receive and act upon an individual's request to access, inspect, and receive a copy of PHI, including the denial of such requests. Be sure you

- Respond to access requests within the time frame specified within the HIPAA Privacy Rule as is appropriate to the situation, typically 30 days, with an allowance for an additional 30 days under specific circumstances.
- Develop procedures to release required PHI to verified requestors.
- Develop documented and legally defensible grounds for denials of information requests.
- Develop procedures to review denial of information access requests.
- Develop procedures to allow for the appeal of access denial decisions.
- Identify a person within your organization with the authority to release PHI, and a person authorized to process denials and appeals.

We recommend you include a temporary suspension of the patient's right of access to research records within your research authorization and consent forms, if applicable.

18. *Do you have procedures in place to allow individuals to amend their PHI?* An individual has the right to ask your organization to amend PHI or a record about the individual in a designated record set for as long as the PHI is maintained in the designated record set.

A designated record set is a group of records you maintain that consists of medical records and billing records about individuals maintained by or for a covered health care provider; enrollment, payment, claims adjudication, and case or medical management record systems maintained by or for a health plan; or is being used, in whole or in part, by or for your organization to make decisions about individuals.

- Develop and document policies and procedures to receive and act upon these requests, as well as policies and procedures providing guidance and directives on when to deny such requests.
- Respond to amendment requests within the time frame specified for the specific situation within the HIPAA Privacy Rule.
- Consider providing resources from your organization to assist patients with their record reviews.
- Establish procedures for retrieving PHI about individuals following a request to amend information.
- Establish procedures for evaluating and accepting or rejecting requests for correction and implementing corrections.
- Establish procedures to amend paper and electronic records (including accepted requests for removal of a record).

We recommend you date-stamp PHI amendment requests.

19. *Do you have procedures and mechanisms implemented to record the disclosures of PHI and maintain them for at least six years as required by HIPAA?* Individuals have a right to receive an accounting of disclosures of their PHI made by your organization in the six years prior to the date on which they request the accounting. You need to establish policies and procedures to ensure these disclosure records are retained.

- Maintain a record of all individuals requesting reports of disclosure as required by the HIPAA Privacy Rule, as well as the nature of those requests.
- Identify a person or group to determine on a case-by-case basis whether disclosures must, may optionally, or must not be reported in accordance with the HIPAA Privacy Rule.
- Establish a procedure to ensure all covered disclosures are reported as quickly as possible in accordance with HIPAA Privacy Rule requirements.
- Ensure your BAs are also keeping track of such disclosures, and will provide them to you upon request.
- If an extension of the time limit for providing an accounting is needed, notify the requestor of the delay as required by the HIPAA Privacy Rule, and ensure the extension does not exceed permissible limits.

20. *Does your organization have someone to handle HIPAA- and privacy-related complaints and questions?* Your organization must designate a contact person or department to be responsible for receiving and addressing HIPAA-related complaints, in addition to being able to provide further information in response to HIPAA- and privacy-related issues and questions.

- Designate an individual or department to receive complaints and provide information about issues covered in your NPP (if applicable), as well as questions or complaints regarding your organization's compliance with HIPAA policies and procedures.
- Document the contact information within your NPP.
- Document and maintain this personnel designation.
- Establish a reporting structure and procedures to involve persons with appropriate authority to investigate and track complaints.
- Ensure the procedures for responding to complaints are consistent with good public relations practices as well as good privacy policy.
- Maintain a record of complaints and brief explanations of how they were resolved.

- Establish procedures governing how the person or department that receives complaints will handle them, and under what circumstances they will triage them to be handled by others.
- Establish time frames and procedures for handling and reporting complaints.
- Use complaints to evaluate your HIPAA compliance procedures to improve upon them where warranted.
- Identify the person or position responsible for reviewing and accessing complaint information and for what purposes.
- Establish a method to track complaints.
- Create reports to periodically communicate to appropriate management complaint resolutions.
- Ensure your complaint procedures are synchronized with your NPP and your organization's Patient Rights policy, if applicable.

21. *Do you require all personnel to participate in ongoing privacy training?* A CE must train all members of its workforce on the policies and procedures with respect to PHI required by the HIPAA Privacy Rule as necessary to allow personnel to perform their job responsibilities. See Chapter 25 for additional training and awareness guidance.

- Establish a timeline for mandatory initial HIPAA privacy training.
- Establish procedures to train new personnel as soon as feasible following their employment.
- Require regular follow-up training and training following significant changes in policies and procedures. Train the personnel who are most impacted as soon as possible either immediately before or immediately following these changes.
- Document the training in written or electronic form and retain the records for at least six years.
- Give copies of the NPP to each workforce member.
- Require each member to sign an acknowledgment that they have received, read, and understand their responsibilities with regard to the privacy practices.

- Provide training that relates the privacy practices to how personnel are expected to perform their job responsibilities.
- Train personnel on how to report a privacy problem.
- Provide ongoing refresher training and periodic reminders for workforce members about privacy practices.
- Consider competency tests or quizzes to evaluate training effectiveness.
- Additional tools are available at http://www.privacyprofessor .org.

22. *Have you implemented administrative, technical, and physical safeguards to help ensure the privacy of PHI?* Your organization must establish administrative, technical, and physical safeguards to protect the privacy of PHI from unauthorized use or disclosure. These safeguards must be appropriate and reasonable.

- Perform a risk analysis and, based on the results, create and implement a risk management plan for both electronic and nonelectronic PHI.
- Request that the privacy officer works closely with the security officer and other personnel as appropriate to determine the safeguards appropriate and feasible for your organization.
- Establish the privacy and security positions at a high enough level within your organization to ensure they have the authority to implement effective safeguards.
- Document reasonably anticipated threats and hazards to the privacy of PHI and unauthorized uses or disclosures.
- Meet with the appropriate areas of your organization to gather details about how they address specific aspects of the safeguard requirements (e.g., training, sanctions, complaints).
- Be sure to dispose of PHI appropriately (e.g., shred papers or reformat hard drives of PCs you are no longer going to use).

23. *Does your organization have enforced sanctions for policy noncompliance?* Develop sanctions to consistently apply for workforce members who do not comply with your organization's privacy policy and privacy practices.

- Identify an individual or group to review policy and procedural violations and to determine the appropriate disciplinary action.
- Document corrective and disciplinary action taken.
- Make the sanctions appropriate to the violation.
- Discuss the sanctions with your legal counsel and obtain their approval for the wording.
- Apply sanctions equitably without regard to an offender's role or position within the organization.
- Include termination of employment or contract relationship, criminal prosecution, or both as possible sanctions.
- Include provision for sanctions in contract and labor agreements.
- Coordinate sanctions with your human resources department.
- Communicate the sanctions policy and possible disciplinary actions to your personnel.

24. *Does your organization have mitigation procedures to address unauthorized use or disclosure of PHI?* Consider using the following methods for containing or minimizing the damage, or potential for damage, and stopping further compromise:

- Have you established documented privacy breach response and notification policies and procedures?
- Have you created a breach response team, and provided them with training?
- Inform the area responsible for the policy or procedural breach to determine if the policy needs to be updated to prevent future actions that would have harmful effects.
- Meet with your legal counsel to determine if inappropriate use or disclosure may in itself constitute a harmful effect with regard to HIPAA and other applicable legal requirements.
- Discuss with your legal counsel how and when your organization should notify individuals if misuse or inappropriate disclosure of PHI will likely lead to a harmful effect.

- Consult with your legal counsel to determine appropriate contract language to use to transfer the potential financial burden of harm to BAs as appropriate to situations where the unauthorized use or disclosure occurred at a BA.

25. *Has your organization implemented procedures to prohibit intimidation following patient requests allowed by HIPAA?* Establish policies and procedures that prohibit intimidation, threats, coercion, discrimination, or retaliatory action against individuals who exercise their rights under this provision.

26. *Has your organization established policies prohibiting your personnel from requiring individuals to waive their rights if they file complaints?* Your organization cannot require individuals to waive their rights to file a complaint or their other rights under the privacy standards as a condition of treatment, payment, and enrollment in a health plan or eligibility for benefits. Do not put waivers of rights on consent forms if you use them. CEs cannot ask patients to waive their privacy rights.

27. *Has your organization developed and implemented policies and procedures to address all the HIPAA Privacy Rule requirements?* A CE must implement policies and procedures with respect to PHI that are designed to comply with the standards, implementation specifications, or other requirements of this subpart. The policies and procedures must be reasonably designed, and take into account the size and the type of activities that relate to PHI within your organization. You cannot create policies and procedures that would violate any of the HIPAA requirements, or any other applicable privacy regulations.

28. *Has your organization established and implemented procedures to update your policies whenever changes in the law occur, or when your organization makes changes in your practices or your NPP?* A CE must change its policies and procedures as necessary and appropriate to comply with changes in the law, including the standards, requirements, and implementation specifications

of the privacy regulations. When you change your NPP, you must update your policies and procedures appropriately, and make the changes effective for PHI that was created or received before the effective date of the notice revision if you included in the notice a statement reserving the right to make such a change in the privacy practices. You can make changes to your other policies and procedures at any time if you document them and meet the HIPAA requirements.

- Consider reserving the right to change your privacy policy within your NPP.
- When creating your privacy policies, procedures, and notices, take into consideration how you will need to communicate any necessary updates.
- Consider your organization's size and complexity when creating and updating your policies and procedures.

29. *Does your organization maintain your policies and procedures in written or electronic form, and keep copies for at least six years from the effective date?* You must maintain your privacy policies, notices, and related procedures for at least six years. You must also retain related communications for this period.

- Document required communications, designations, actions, and activities.
- Record the creation date and last effective date of documents.
- Maintain the documentation for at least six years from date of creation or the date when the policy or procedure was last in effect, whichever is later.
- Assign responsibility for policies and procedures documentation.
- Indicate the expiration and review dates for documentation.
- Centralize retention of policy and procedure documentation so that it is easily accessible.
- Communicate to appropriate personnel the importance of documentation, and that lack of documentation is considered a HIPAA noncompliance action.

- Organize documentation in such a way that it can be identified when necessary.

30. *Have you identified existing consents, authorizations, and other legal permissions that are not in compliance with the HIPAA Privacy Rule requirements?* You may continue to use or disclose PHI under a consent, authorization, or other type of legal permission obtained from an individual permitting the use or disclosure of PHI that does not comply with HIPAA, depending on when it was created.

  - Decide whether or not to treat PHI created or received before the HIPAA compliance date with a different set of privacy consents and authorizations from PHI created or received after the HIPAA compliance date.
  - If PHI will be handled in different ways depending on the date it was created or received, clearly identify the PHI that existed before the HIPAA compliance date.
  - Handle PHI in accordance with the consent, authorization, or other documented wishes of the individual that were effective at the time the PHI was created or received.

31. *Have you identified all PHI, and developed and implemented procedures to limit access to the PHI to only that which is minimally necessary to perform job responsibilities?* Is PHI accessed, used, and disclosed based on the minimum amount of information necessary to accomplish the required purpose? Are patient information access, use, and disclosure by personnel based only on a need-to-know basis, to accomplish the required business purpose?

  - Document all PHI access allowed and the relationship to job functions.
  - Identify PHI that can be de-identified without interfering with needed functions.
  - Calculate personnel and technology costs for limiting information disclosure and de-identifying PHI.
  - Identify appropriate persons to determine what PHI should be used, disclosed, and requested consistent with the minimum necessary standard.

- Create methods to determine minimum access allowances on an individual basis.
- Define and implement policies and procedures that are reasonable and appropriate for your organization.

Have you ensured your BAs, and their subcontractors, are also limiting access to the minimum necessary for their employees as well?

32. *Analyze your responses to the previous questions to identify the gaps between your organization's current state and the HIPAA Privacy Rule requirements. Do you have gaps?* Use your inventory to assess and document compliance levels, gaps, and vulnerabilities.

- Rank the gaps according to their immediacy. It is usually most efficient and effective to use a "high, medium, or low" ranking system.
- Include your applicable state regulatory requirements within the gap analysis.
- Identify situations requiring de-identification of PHI.

33. *Have you created a summary risk analysis report and created an action plan to close gaps and address the risks?* This will establish your current baseline compliance status. Prepare the final report, with details on specific areas of observed and potential risk.

- Include dates.
- Label this as your first, or baseline, risk assessment.
- Set a target date to perform the next gap analysis.
- Clearly identify the noncompliance items.
- Document the observed and potential risks.
- Identify disparities between procedure, practice, and culture, and HIPAA requirements.
- Determine the availability of archived PHI.
- Determine the impact of potential HIPAA-related changes on secondary uses of PHI; for instance, in clinical systems, medical devices, support applications, and so on.

- Indicate opportunities for operational streamlining and cost savings.
- Use any existing analysis of security risk management strategies.
- Consider applicability of HIPAA provisions for hybrid and affiliated CEs.
- Indicate alternative HIPAA solutions, including beneficial EDI advances and their costs.
- Note available resources for performing remediation activities.
- Identify opportunities for HIPAA-related changes that will facilitate your business goals.
- Carry out recommended HIPAA-related remediation and strategic actions.

Practical Checklist

- Perform a Privacy Rule gap analysis and risk analysis now to determine your current and baseline compliance status.
- Perform another gap analysis after you have completed all your compliance activities.
- Continue performing gap and risk analyses following Privacy Rule changes, major organizational changes, and major technology changes.
- Always communicate results to organization leaders, appropriate compliance officers, and legal counsel.

8

WRITING EFFECTIVE
PRIVACY POLICIES

8.1 Introduction

The Health Insurance Portability and Accountability Act (HIPAA) requires two kinds of privacy policies. People sometimes consider the required Notice of Privacy Practices (NPP) the only necessary privacy policy. HIPAA also requires covered entities (CEs), business associates (BAs), and their subcontractors to document their organizational privacy policies and procedures that will support the multiple requirements of the HIPAA Privacy Rule and applicable privacy requirements from the Health Information Technology for Economic and Clinical Health (HITECH) Act. First we will address the NPP and then address writing organizational privacy policies.

8.2 Notice of Privacy Practices

The NPP is covered within 45 CFR § 164.520 parts (a), (b), (c), and (d). The notice requires CEs to inform covered individuals (e.g., patients, insureds) of their rights for accessing and modifying their protected health information (PHI), in addition to describing the security that the CE has established to protect individuals' privacy. CEs must make the NPP available to generally any individual who asks, and CEs must take the initiative to make their NPP available and known to individuals for whom they process or handle PHI. Generally, most BAs and subcontractors are not required to provide NPPs, unless their services include those described within 45 CFR § 164.520 "Notice of privacy practices for protected health information." We will look at the specific distribution and communication issues related to the notices in the chapters specific to each type of CE in Part IV of this book.

On January 17, 2013, the Department of Health and Human Services (HHS) released the Omnibus Final Rule pursuant to the HITECH Act of 2009 and the Genetic Information Nondiscrimination Act of 2008. The Omnibus Final Rule expanded the NPP requirements to include provisions designed to provide individuals with a better understanding of the following:

- The patient's right to restrict disclosures
- The types of uses and disclosures that require individual authorization
- The patient's right to opt out of certain disclosures
- Rights to notice in the event of a breach
- Rights with respect to the use of their genetic information for health plan underwriting purposes

Here we will examine specifically how to write an NPP compliant with the Omnibus Final Rule requirements.

8.3 Example NPP

8.3.1 Header

The HIPAA Privacy Rule requirements are very specific and straightforward when it comes to specifying the wording for the heading of the privacy notice (45 CFR § 164.520(b)(1)(i)). The header, or a prominently displayed message, must be written exactly as follows:

THIS NOTICE DESCRIBES HOW MEDICAL INFORMATION ABOUT YOU MAY BE USED AND DISCLOSED AND HOW YOU CAN GET ACCESS TO THIS INFORMATION. PLEASE REVIEW IT CAREFULLY.

8.3.2 Content of the Notice

There are three requirements related to the content of an NPP.

1. Your NPP must be written clearly, in plain language, describing the following:
   a. How your organization may use and disclose PHI. You must include at least one example of each use and disclosure.

b. All the individual's rights with regard to the corresponding PHI, and how an individual may execute his rights; this includes the right to submit formal complaints to your organization. This section may be quite lengthy, depending on other state laws that have more stringent requirements related to health information privacy.

c. Your organization's legal duties for handling PHI, including a statement clearly stating your organization is required by law to maintain the privacy of PHI.

d. The name of the person to contact when an individual wants more information about your organization's privacy policies.

2. Your organization's notice must include an effective date.

3. Your organization must revise and distribute its notice promptly following material changes to its privacy practices.

8.3.3 Layered Notices

CEs are allowed to use "layered" notices to implement the HIPAA Privacy Rule notice requirements. When a layered notice is used, all of the elements listed in Section 8.3.2 must still be present within the notice. For example, your organization can choose to create a short notice that briefly summarizes individuals' rights regarding their PHI, but then also provide the longer, more detailed, full version of the notice as an attachment or addendum to the brief summary. The brief summary is in effect similar to an executive summary, and the full details provide elaboration and expand on the summary points. By using a layered approach you may get more individuals to read the summary page, realize the importance of their rights regarding their PHI, and then continue to read on to discover the details of their full rights.

It is important to understand that you will *not* satisfy the HIPAA Privacy Rule requirements by providing individuals with only the summary of the notice, and by not including the full details of the NPP. CEs are not required to provide layered notices; it is an allowable option that they can choose to help facilitate individuals' understanding of their privacy rights. However, if you want individuals to actually read your notice, and you want to help ensure their under-standing, we encourage you to use a layered notice.

When writing your notice, be very careful to sufficiently detail your organization's uses and disclosures of PHI. The uses and disclosures will vary, often dramatically, from CE to CE, so do not depend on getting a copy of another CE's notice and using it verbatim. Not only could you be making some promises that your actual procedures do not support, but also you could be opening up your organization to some potentially nasty legal actions.

HHS provides models of layered NPPs, as well as models of other kinds of NPPs, on their site, http://www.hhs.gov/ocr/privacy/hipaa/modelnotices.html.

8.3.4 *Before You Post or Distribute Your Notice*

If you are the person responsible for HIPAA compliance within your organization, you probably know more about your organization's pri-vacy policies and practices than other coworkers. So, you are also most likely the best person to write the NPP and detail the uses and dis-closures of PHI. However, upon finishing the document, do not post or publish the notice until you have been in touch with your legal counsel! This notice is a legal contract, and as such you want a lawyer to review it to ensure you have not inadvertently worded something in a way that could be misinterpreted or lead to litigation against your organization. After your lawyer has reviewed and expressed any con-cerns, make the necessary changes, get approval from the lawyer and any other necessary executives and personnel within your organiza-tion, and then post and publish.

8.3.5 *Example Notice*

We cannot stress enough that your organization's NPP must be based on your actual practices, as documented within your policies, proce-dures, standards, and so forth, prior to publishing your notice. You should not write a notice indicating you are performing procedures and practices that do not exist or that are not formally documented.

Also, what we are providing is strictly an example within which virtually all possible uses and disclosures are listed and explained.

Please do not use this notice verbatim; chances are your organization would not be in compliance. The intent is to give you an idea of what your NPP will look like, and make your job a little easier by giving you a model to build on. Some points to keep in mind when using this example are as follows:

- This is *not* an example of a layered notice, but an example of a fully detailed notice.
- In the example shown in Exhibit 8.1, you will need to change the descriptions of the uses and disclosures if your state law, or any other legal requirements, further limits or prohibits any of the described uses and disclosures.

Exhibit 8.1   Notice of Privacy Practices

THIS NOTICE DESCRIBES HOW MEDICAL INFORMATION ABOUT YOU MAY BE USED AND DISCLOSED AND HOW YOU CAN GET ACCESS TO THIS INFORMATION. PLEASE REVIEW IT CAREFULLY.

Company XYZ is required by law to protect the privacy of your health information, to provide you with notice of its legal duties and privacy practices with respect to your health information, and to follow the terms of our notice that is currently in effect. If you have questions about any part of this notice, or if you want more information about the privacy practices at Company XYZ, please contact:

Joe Doe, HIPAA Compliance Director
Street XXX
City, State 99999
Phone: (000) 000-0000

Effective date of this notice: April 14, 2014 (Note: Use the date applicable to your organization; it may initially be different than the compliance date, and it will be different after you change your notice.)

I. How Company XYZ may use or disclose your health information

Company XYZ collects health information from you and stores it on printed paper and on electronic computer systems. The collection of your health information is considered your medical record. The medical record is the property of Company XYZ, but the information within the medical record containing information about you belongs to you. Company XYZ cares about and protects the privacy of your health information. Law allows Company XYZ to use or disclose your health information for the following purposes:

1. *Treatment.* Put a description here of the provision, coordination, or management of health care and related services. Also include, as appropriate, a description of consultation between health care providers that relates to patients, and referrals of patients from one health care provider to another. Include at least one example of a treatment, for example, if a treatment is provided by a specialist who asks a primary care doctor to share the patient's PHI.

(Continued)

Exhibit 8.1   Notice of Privacy Practices (*Continued*)

2. *Payment.* Describe the activities to obtain premiums and to determine or fulfill responsibility for coverage and provision of benefits, or to obtain or provide reimbursement for providing health care, whichever is appropriate. The activities may include such things as determinations of eligibility of coverage, risk adjusting amounts, billing, claims management, review of health care services with respect to medical necessity, utilization review activities, disclosure of PHI to consumer reporting agencies, and so forth. Include at least one example applicable to your organization. For example, complete a claim form to obtain insurer payment.

3. *Health care operations.* Describe the health care operations your organization provides, if applicable. For example, you may conduct quality assessment and improvement activities, review the competence or qualifications of health care professionals, underwriting, premium rating, conducting or arranging for medical reviews, legal services, auditing functions, fraud and abuse detection, business planning and development, business management and general administrative activities, and so forth. Include at least one example. For example, another type of health care operations activity is to engage in quality review activities, such as performing audits or implementing compliance programs. We may also use and disclose information to make sure the care you receive is of the highest quality.

4. *Information provided to you.* Describe the type of information you provide to the individual, if applicable. Include at least one example.

5. *Appointment reminders, treatment alternatives, and health-related benefits and services.* We may use and disclose health information to contact you to remind you that you have an appointment with us. We also may use and disclose health information to tell you about treatment alternatives or health-related benefits and services that may be of interest to you.

6. *Individuals involved in your care or payment for your care.* When appropriate, we may share health information with a person who is involved in your medical care or payment for your care, such as your family or a close friend. We also may notify your family about your location or general condition or disclose such information to an entity assisting in a disaster relief effort.

7. *Research.* Under certain circumstances, we may use and disclose health information for research. For example, a research project may involve comparing the health of patients who received one treatment to those who received another, for the same condition. Before we use or disclose health information for research, the project will go through a special approval process. Even without special approval, we may permit researchers to look at records to help them identify patients who may be included in their research project or for other similar purposes, as long as they do not remove or take a copy of any health information.

SPECIAL SITUATIONS

1. *As required by law.* We will disclose health information when required to do so by international, federal, state, or local law.

2. *To avert a serious threat to health or safety.* We may use and disclose health information when necessary to prevent a serious threat to your health and safety or the health and safety of the public or another person. Disclosures, however, will be made only to someone who may be able to help prevent the threat.

Exhibit 8.1   Notice of Privacy Practices (*Continued*)

3. *Business associates.* We may disclose health information to our BAs that perform functions on our behalf or provide us with services if the information is necessary for such functions or services. For example, we may use another company to perform billing services on our behalf. All of our BAs are obligated to protect the privacy of your information and are not allowed to use or disclose any information other than as specified in our contract.

4. *Organ and tissue donation.* If you are an organ donor, we may use or release health information to organizations that handle organ procurement or other entities engaged in procurement, banking, or transportation of organs, eyes, or tissues to facilitate donation and transplantation.

5. *Military and veterans.* If you are a member of the armed forces, we may release health information as required by military command authorities. We also may release health information to the appropriate foreign military authority if you are a member of a foreign military.

6. *Workers' compensation.* We may release health information for workers' compensation or similar programs. These programs provide benefits for work-related injuries or illness.

7. *Public health risks.* We may disclose health information for public health activities. These activities generally include disclosures to prevent or control disease, injury, or disability; to report births and deaths; to report child abuse or neglect; to report reactions to medications or problems with products; to notify people of recalls of products they may be using; to prevent a person who may have been exposed to a disease or may be at risk for contracting or spreading a disease or condition from spreading it to the public; and to report to the appropriate government authority if we believe a patient has been the victim of abuse, neglect, or domestic violence. We will only make this disclosure if you agree or when required or authorized by law.

8. *Health oversight activities.* We may disclose health information to a health oversight agency for activities authorized by law. These oversight activities include, for example, audits, investigations, inspections, and licensure. These activities are necessary for the government to monitor the health care system, government programs, and compliance with civil rights laws.

9. *Data breach notification purposes.* We may use or disclose your PHI to provide legally required notices of unauthorized access to or disclosure of your health information.

10. *Lawsuits and disputes.* If you are involved in a lawsuit or a dispute, we may disclose health information in response to a court or administrative order. We also may disclose health information in response to a subpoena, discovery request, or other lawful process by someone else involved in the dispute, but only if efforts have been made to tell you about the request or to obtain an order protecting the information requested.

11. *Law enforcement.* We may release health information if asked by a law enforcement official if the information is (1) in response to a court order, subpoena, warrant, summons, or similar process; (2) limited information to identify or locate a suspect, fugitive, material witness, or missing person; (3) about the victim of a crime even if, under certain very limited circumstances, we are unable to obtain the person's agreement; (4) about a death we believe may be the result of criminal conduct; (5) about criminal conduct on our premises; and (6) in an emergency to report a crime, the location of the crime or victims, or the identity, description, or location of the person who committed the crime.

12. *Coroners, medical examiners, and funeral directors.* We may release health information to a coroner or medical examiner. This may be necessary, for example, to identify a deceased person or determine the cause of death. We also may release health information to funeral directors as necessary for their duties.

(*Continued*)

Exhibit 8.1   Notice of Privacy Practices (*Continued*)

13. *National security and intelligence activities.* We may release health information to authorized federal officials for intelligence, counterintelligence, and other national security activities authorized by law.

14. *Protective services for the president and others.* We may disclose health information to authorized federal officials so they may provide protection to the president, other authorized persons, or foreign heads of state, or conduct special investigations.

15. *Inmates or individuals in custody.* If you are an inmate of a correctional institution or under the custody of a law enforcement official, we may release health information to the correctional institution or law enforcement official. This release would be, if necessary, (1) for the institution to provide you with health care, (2) to protect your health and safety or the health and safety of others, or (3) to protect the safety and security of the correctional institution.

16. *Change of ownership.* In the event that Company XYZ is sold or merged with another organization, your health information will become the property of the new owner. (Note: Be sure your lawyer reviews and approves of this statement; its applicability is based on a wide range of differing state laws.)

USES AND DISCLOSURES THAT REQUIRE US TO GIVE YOU AN OPPORTUNITY TO OBJECT AND OPT OUT

1. *Individuals involved in your care or payment for your care.* Unless you object, we may disclose to a member of your family, a relative, a close friend, or any other person you identify, your PHI that directly relates to that person's involvement in your health care. If you are unable to agree or object to such a disclosure, we may disclose such information as necessary if we determine that it is in your best interest based on our professional judgment.

2. *Disaster relief.* We may disclose your PHI to disaster relief organizations that seek your PHI to coordinate your care, or notify family and friends of your location or condition in a disaster. We will provide you with an opportunity to agree or object to such a disclosure whenever we practically can do so.

YOUR WRITTEN AUTHORIZATION IS REQUIRED FOR OTHER USES AND DISCLOSURES.

The following uses and disclosures of your PHI will be made only with your written authorization:

1. Uses and disclosures of PHI for marketing purposes
2. Disclosures that constitute a sale of your PHI

II. When Company XYZ may not use or disclose your health information

Company XYZ will not use or disclose your health information without your written authorization, except as described in this NPP. If you authorize Company XYZ to use or disclose your health information for another purpose, you may revoke your authorization in writing at any time by submitting a written revocation to our privacy officer and we will no longer disclose PHI under the authorization. But disclosure that we made in reliance on your authorization before you revoked it will not be affected by the revocation.

III. Your health information rights

(Note: Be sure you make the explanation of these rights appropriate for your organization. An individual reading your notice needs to understand that these rights are subject to certain unavoidable limitations and conditions, as are most legal rights, so that each "right" is not an absolute. Also, be sure you have procedures in place to support these activities.)

Exhibit 8.1   Notice of Privacy Practices (*Continued*)

You have the following rights regarding health information we have about you:

1. *Right to inspect and copy.* You have a right to inspect and copy health information that may be used to make decisions about your care or payment for your care. This includes medical and billing records, other than psychotherapy notes. To inspect and copy this health information, you must make your request, in writing, to _____. We have up to 30 days to make your PHI available to you and we may charge you a reasonable fee for the costs of copying, mailing, or other supplies associated with your request. We may not charge you a fee if you need the information for a claim for benefits under the Social Security Act or any other state of federal needs-based benefit program. We may deny your request in certain limited circumstances. If we do deny your request, you have the right to have the denial reviewed by a licensed health care professional who was not directly involved in the denial of your request, and we will comply with the outcome of the review.

2. *Right to an electronic copy of electronic medical records.* If your PHI is maintained in an electronic format (known as an electronic medical record or an electronic health record), you have the right to request that an electronic copy of your record be given to you or transmitted to another individual or entity. We will make every effort to provide access to your PHI in the form or format you request, if it is readily producible in such form or format. If the PHI is not readily producible in the form or format you request, your record will be provided in either our standard electronic format or if you do not want this form or format, a readable hard copy form. We may charge you a reasonable, cost-based fee for the labor associated with transmitting the electronic medical record.

3. *Right to get notice of a breach.* You have the right to be notified of a breach of any of your unsecured PHI.

4. *Right to amend.* If you feel that health information we have is incorrect or incomplete, you may ask us to amend the information. You have the right to request an amendment for as long as the information is kept by or for our office. To request an amendment, you must make your request, in writing, to _____.

5. *Right to an accounting of disclosures.* You have the right to request a list of certain disclosures we made of health information for purposes other than treatment, payment, and health care operations or for which you provided written authorization. To request an accounting of disclosures, you must make your request, in writing, to _____.

6. *Right to request restrictions.* You have the right to request a restriction or limitation on the health information we use or disclose for treatment, payment, or health care operations. You also have the right to request a limit on the health information we disclose to someone involved in your care or the payment for your care, such as a family member or friend. For example, you could ask that we do not share information about a particular diagnosis or treatment with your spouse. To request a restriction, you must make your request, in writing, to _____. We are not required to agree to your request unless you are asking us to restrict the use and disclosure of your PHI to a health plan for payment or health care operation purposes and such information you wish to restrict pertains solely to a health care item or service for which you have paid us "out of pocket" in full. If we agree, we will comply with your request unless the information is needed to provide you with emergency treatment.

7. *Out-of-pocket payments.* If you paid out of pocket (or in other words, you have requested that we do not bill your health plan) in full for a specific item or service, you have the right to ask that your PHI with respect to that item or service not be disclosed to a health plan for purposes of payment or health care operations, and we will honor that request.

(*Continued*)

Exhibit 8.1   Notice of Privacy Practices (*Continued*)

8. *Right to request confidential communications*. You have the right to request that we communicate with you about medical matters in a certain way or at a certain location. For example, you can ask that we only contact you by mail or at work. To request confidential communications, you must make your request, in writing, to _____. Your request must specify how or where you wish to be contacted. We will accommodate reasonable requests.

9. *Right to a paper copy of this notice*. You have the right to a paper copy of this notice. You may ask us to give you a copy of this notice at any time. Even if you have agreed to receive this notice electronically, you are still entitled to a paper copy of this notice. You may obtain a copy of this notice at our website, www._____. To obtain a paper copy of this notice, you must make your request, in writing, to _____. If you would like to have a more detailed explanation of these rights or if you would like to exercise one or more of these rights, contact:

> Joe Doe, HIPAA Compliance Director
> Street XXX
> City, State 99999
> Phone: (000) 000-0000

IV. Changes to this NPP

Company XYZ reserves the right to amend this NPP at any time in the future, and to make the new provisions effective for all information that it maintains, including information that was created or received prior to the date of such amendment. Until such amendment is made, Company XYZ is required by law to comply with this notice.

Company XYZ will send updates of this notice by (add a description of the update distribution methods here).

V. Complaints

Complaints about this NPP or how Company XYZ handles your health information should be directed to:

> Joe Doe, HIPAA Compliance Director
> Street
> City, State 99999
> Phone: (000) 000-0000

All complaints must be made in writing. You will not be penalized for filing a complaint.

If you are not satisfied with the manner in which this office handles a complaint, you may submit a formal complaint to:

> Department of Health and Human Services
> Office of Civil Rights
> Hubert H. Humphrey Building
> 200 Independence Avenue, SW
> Room 509F HHH Building
> Washington, DC 20201

You may also address your complaint to one of the regional Offices for Civil Rights. A list of these offices can be found online at http://www.hhs.gov/ocr/office/about/rgn-hqaddresses.html.

8.4 Organizational Privacy Policies

You must formally document, communicate, and maintain the policies and procedures you implement internally for your personnel to follow to comply with the HIPAA Privacy Rule requirements. At a minimum, you must create a privacy policy for your organization that directs personnel on how to handle and process PHI and that describes the practices that are allowed and disallowed. Your policy will set the boundaries around which your personnel activities occur with respect to PHI. It is likely you will need multiple policies, and probably even more supporting procedures, to adequately address and communicate your organization's requirements with regard to protecting health information. How many policies you have will depend on what type of services and/or products you provide, the size of your organization, and how widely dispersed your offices are geographically.

First create your privacy policies draft. An example is provided in this chapter to give you a basis from which to work. Each organization is unique, so you must create policies based on your unique situation, business, and legal requirements. Please review the example carefully and make changes everywhere that is appropriate, so it will apply to your specific organization. It is likely your policies will look significantly different from the example!

When you have created your privacy policy you will then need to work with the appropriate members of your organization to create procedures that support the policies. The details of *how* to achieve compliance will be found within the procedures. The details of *what* needs to be the result must be described within the policy. Policy statements should not contain many, if any, "how to" statements; those belong in procedure documents.

Be sure to include "sanctions," or disciplinary consequences, within your policy. Besides being a Privacy Rule requirement, personnel must understand what actions they can expect if they do not comply with the policies, and your organization must follow through with these documented sanctions for personnel to take the policies seriously. Some organizations like to have a separate sanctions policy; however, including sanction descriptions with each privacy policy is also an acceptable alternative.

After you have finished your privacy policies, you need to have your executive management, legal department, human resources department, and any other appropriate management review them and give their approval. The personnel must know that your organizational leaders support the policies. Your leaders should communicate to the organization personnel that they support the policies and they will ensure sanctions are enforced for those who break the policies. Exhibit 8.2 is a sample set of privacy policies.

Exhibit 8.2 Organizational Privacy Policies

Purpose: Company XYZ personnel must comply with the following privacy policies to ensure the privacy of the information Company XYZ processes and handles, and also to ensure that Company XYZ complies fully with all applicable federal and state privacy protection laws and regulations. Protecting customer and patient information is of utmost importance to Company XYZ. Personnel violating this policy are subject to disciplinary action up to and including possible termination of employment and possible criminal prosecution.

Effective Date: This policy is in effect as of April 14, 2014. (Note: Put whatever date is applicable to your organization.)

Expiration Date: This policy has no expiration date. This policy will remain in effect until personnel are notified otherwise.

Policy Owner: (Name) owns and maintains this policy. Please direct questions regarding this policy to (name and contact information).

Assigning Privacy and Security Responsibilities

Specific positions within Company XYZ are assigned the responsibility of implementing and maintaining the HIPAA Privacy Rule requirements. These positions will be provided sufficient resources and authority to fulfill their responsibilities. There will be one individual or job position designated as the privacy officer. There will also be one individual or job position designated as the HIPAA compliance manager.

Uses and Disclosures of Protected Health Information (PHI)

Company XYZ customer and patient information may only be used or disclosed in the following situations:

1. The individual who is the subject of the information has authorized the use or disclosure.
2. The individual who is the subject of the information has received the Company XYZ Notice of Privacy Practices (NPP) and has acknowledged receipt of the notice. This allows use or disclosure for treatment, payment, or health care operations.
3. The individual who is the subject of the information agrees or does not object to the disclosure to persons involved in the health care of the individual.
4. The disclosure is to the individual who is the subject of the information or to HHS for compliance-related purposes.
5. The use or disclosure is for a HIPAA "public purposes" exception.

Deceased Individuals

Company XYZ privacy protections and procedures apply to information concerning deceased individuals.

Exhibit 8.2   Organizational Privacy Policies (*Continued*)

Notice of Privacy Practices

Company XYZ will publish an NPP and provide it to all individuals at the earliest practicable time. All uses and disclosures of PHI will be done according to the Company XYZ NPP. Company XYZ will attempt to gain written acknowledgment of the receipt of the Notice from all individuals to whom it provides the NPP. Company XYZ will document our attempts to gain this acknowledgment if we cannot successfully obtain written receipt of the Notice.

Restriction Requests

Company XYZ will give serious consideration to all requests for restrictions on uses and disclosures of PHI as published in the NPP and follow its procedures for addressing such requests. When Company XYZ agrees to a restriction, personnel with Company XYZ must observe and comply with the restriction.

Minimum Necessary Disclosure of PHI

Except for disclosures made for treatment purposes, all disclosures of PHI must be limited to the minimum amount of information necessary to accomplish the purpose of the disclosure. All requests for PHI (except requests made for treatment purposes) will be limited to the minimum amount of information needed to accomplish the purpose of the request.

Access to PHI

Company XYZ will grant access to PHI to each employee or contractor based on the assigned job functions. The access privileges will not exceed those necessary to accomplish the assigned job function.

Access to PHI by the Individual

Company XYZ will provide access to PHI to the person who is the subject of such information when the individual requests access within the time frames required by the HIPAA Privacy Rule. Company XYZ will inform the person requesting access of the location of their PHI if Company XYZ does not physically possess the PHI but knows where it is located.

Amendment of Incomplete or Incorrect PHI

Company XYZ will respond to all requests for amendment of PHI in a timely manner following its procedures for updating PHI. If requests reveal the PHI is incorrect, Company XYZ will amend the PHI appropriately within the time frame dictated by the HIPAA Privacy Rule and will document the amendment. A notice of corrections will be given to any organization with which the PHI has been shared.

Access by Personal Representatives

Company XYZ will grant access to PHI to personal representatives of individuals in the same manner as if they were the individuals themselves, except in cases of abuse where granting the access could endanger the individual or someone else. We will observe the relevant state, local, and other applicable laws when disclosing information about minors to parents.

Confidential Communication Channels

Company XYZ will use confidential communication channels whenever possible, and when requested by individuals.

Disclosure Accounting

Company XYZ will provide an accounting of all disclosures of PHI subject to HIPAA Privacy Rule requirements to an individual on the individual's request in accordance with the company accounting of disclosures procedure.

(*Continued*)

Exhibit 8.2 Organizational Privacy Policies (*Continued*)

Marketing Activities

Company XYZ will use or disclose PHI for marketing activities only after obtaining a valid written authorization. The written authorization must contain the specific PHI information items that will be used for the marketing purposes. The authorization must state that financial remuneration is involved, if applicable.

Company XYZ considers marketing as any communication to purchase or use a product or service where an arrangement exists in exchange for direct or indirect payment, or where Company XYZ encourages purchase or use of a product or service. Company XYZ does not consider the communication of alternate forms of treatment, or the use of products and services in treatment to be marketing. Company XYZ will not obtain an authorization when a face-to-face communication is made by us to the patient, or when giving an individual a promotional gift of nominal value.

Judicial and Administrative Proceedings

Company XYZ will disclose PHI for judicial or administrative proceedings only when

- Accompanied by a court or administrative order or grand jury subpoena
- Accompanied by a subpoena or discovery request that includes either the authorization of the individual to whom the information applies, documented assurances that good faith effort has been made to adequately notify the individual of the request for their information and there are no outstanding objections by the individual, or a qualified protective order issued by the court

If a subpoena or discovery request is submitted to Company XYZ without one of these requirements, it will seek to notify the individual, obtain his or her authorization, or obtain a qualified protective order before disclosing any information. It will not disclose information other than that required by the court order, subpoena, or discovery request.

De-Identified Data and Limited Data Sets

Company XYZ will disclose de-identified data only after it has been properly de-identified. Limited data sets will be used only after the relevant identifying data has been removed, and released only to organizations that have signed adequate data-use agreements. Limited data sets will be used only for research, public health, or health care operations purposes.

Authorizations

Company XYZ will obtain a valid authorization for all disclosures, other than those for treatment, payment, health care operations, to the individual or their personal representative, to persons involved with the individual's care, to BAs and their subcontractors in their legitimate duties, to facility directories, or for public purposes. The authorization will include all the HIPAA-required statements. Authorizations from outside this organization will be checked to confirm validity.

Complaints

Company XYZ will investigate and resolve all complaints relating to the protection of health information within the time limits required by the HIPAA Privacy Rule. The privacy officer will investigate all complaints made to Company XYZ related to privacy practices and implement resolutions as appropriate.

Prohibited Activities

No Company XYZ employee or contractor may engage in any intimidating or retaliatory acts against persons who file complaints or otherwise exercise their rights under HIPAA regulations. No Company XYZ employee or contractor may condition treatment, payment, enrollment, or eligibility for benefits on the provision of an authorization to disclose PHI.

Exhibit 8.2   Organizational Privacy Policies (*Continued*)

Responsibility

The privacy officer is responsible for designing and implementing procedures to comply with the Company XYZ privacy policies.

Verification of Identity

Company XYZ will verify the identity of all persons who request access to PHI before such access is granted.

Mitigation

Company XYZ will follow mitigation procedures to minimize the effects of any unauthorized use or disclosure of PHI that may occur.

Safeguards

Company XYZ will implement security procedures to appropriately safeguard physical and electronic PHI from intentional or unintentional use or disclosure that is in violation of the HIPAA Privacy Rule. The security procedures will include directives for physically protecting Company XYZ facilities and PHI, establishing technical security for electronic PHI, and establishing administrative security and access control protection. These procedures will include safeguarding the oral communication of PHI to the greatest extent possible.

Business Associates

Company XYZ BAs will be contractually required to protect health information to the same degree as Company XYZ personnel. Company XYZ will deal with BAs who violate their agreement by first attempting to correct the situation; if the situation cannot be resolved, the BA agreement will be terminated, and the services provided by the BA will be discontinued.

Training and Awareness

Company XYZ provides information security and privacy training related to HIPAA Privacy Rule requirements to all personnel. New personnel will receive training during the first week of their start date. Existing personnel will receive ongoing awareness messages covering the privacy and security requirements for customer and patient information, and must attend formal training soon after the Company XYZ privacy policies are changed, and at least once a year. Company XYZ will document the training in which each personnel member participates, including the date and topic of the training.

Sanctions

Company XYZ will apply disciplinary sanctions to any personnel member who violates these policies, or any procedures implemented to support these policies. Sanctions include disciplinary actions up to and possibly including termination of employment and possible criminal prosecution.

Retention of Records

Company XYZ will retain, secure, and maintain all records identified within the HIPAA Privacy Rule for at least six years using procedures that allow for access when necessary within a reasonable amount of time as determined by the privacy officer. Company XYZ will extend the records retention time requirement as necessary to comply with other governmental regulations, laws, or requirements made by the Company XYZ professional liability carrier.

(*Continued*)

Exhibit 8.2   Organizational Privacy Policies (*Continued*)

Cooperation with Privacy Oversight Authorities

Company XYZ will fully support and cooperate with oversight agencies such as the Office for Civil Rights of HHS and the offices of state attorneys general during investigations and other efforts to ensure the protection of health information. All Company XYZ personnel will cooperate fully with all privacy compliance reviews and investigations.

Practical Checklist

- Does the NPP you give to your customers or patients contain all the sections required by the HIPAA Privacy Rule?
- Have you decided whether to use a layered NPP?
- Has your lawyer reviewed and approved your NPP?
- Have you communicated your NPP to your personnel?
- Do you have procedures established to support the promises made within the NPP?
- Does your marketing authorization form include a field to list the specific PHI information items that will be used for marketing purposes?
- Have you created internal privacy policies for your personnel and BAs that cover the HIPAA Privacy Rule requirements?
- Has your lawyer reviewed your organizational privacy policies and signed off on them?
- Do you have the visible support of your executive management and other organization leaders for the policies?

9

STATE PREEMPTION

9.1 Introduction

Covered entities (CEs), business associates (BAs), and subcontractors will not only need to be in compliance with the Health Insurance Portability and Accountability Act (HIPAA) Privacy Rule requirements, but also with the privacy and confidentiality state laws that are not preempted by the Privacy Rule. The Privacy Rule does not replace federal, state, or other laws that grant greater privacy protections than are stipulated within the Rule. Additionally, CEs, BAs, and subcontractors are free to retain or adopt more protective privacy policies and practices. The HIPAA Privacy Rule defines "state law" to include statutes, regulations, case laws, and other state actions having binding legal effect. Preemption of state law is addressed in Part 160, Subpart B of the Privacy Rule. It is interesting to note that this section of the regulation was constructed not only to address the privacy issues, but also the preemption issues in the already-issued Transactions Rule, which did not cover this issue.

During the comment period for the 2002 Privacy Rule Notice of Proposed Rulemaking, many health care plans and providers expressed concern that the preemption provision would be overly burdensome, ineffective, and that without a complete preemption of all the various and sundry state privacy laws, they would be hard to implement and enforce. Many commenters expressed concern that the proposed preemption provisions would result in litigation. It was feared that the exception determination process as outlined would be very costly and result in inconsistent handling from state to state. The Department of Health and Human Services (HHS) noted that many commenters asked to have the wording changed so that the rule would preempt all state privacy laws. On the other end of the spectrum, there were also many commenters that recommended there should be no exceptions granted to the federal standards, with the opinion that such exceptions defeat the goal of promoting uniform transactions.

Since the Privacy Rule went into effect, the preemption provision has caused confusion to many CEs, BAs, and subcontractors. This is often because it is not always apparent whether the state requirements are more or less stringent than the HIPAA requirements. When it is not readily apparent if a state legal requirement is more or less stringent than HIPAA, involve your legal counsel to do a preemption analysis. This is a sophisticated exercise, discussed in Section 9.4, which depends on full understanding of the laws involved. Complete preemption analysis must also take into account analogous court decisions as well as the details of the statutes.

9.2 What Is Contrary?

A state law is considered "contrary to" a HIPAA privacy standard, requirement, or implementation specification in one of the following two situations (45 CFR § 160.202):

- The CE, BA, or subcontractor cannot possibly comply with both the state and federal requirements. So, compliance with a state requirement would prevent compliance with the HIPAA requirement.
- A provision of state law stands as an "obstacle" to the accomplishment and execution of the full purposes of the HIPAA legislation related to administrative simplification. This language is far from clear-cut but anticipates situations in which state and federal law do not directly conflict, but state and federal requirements nevertheless compete with one another.

Other situations that imply there may be a contrary situation, but upon further analysis reveal there is not, include the following:

- When state law privacy requirements are not contrary to the Privacy Rule, a CE, BA, and subcontractor must abide by both laws.
- When the state imposes a requirement for which there is no analogous federal requirement, then the state law applies.

For example, when the HIPAA Privacy Rule allows, but does not require, a specific disclosure that is prohibited by state law, the state law is considered not contrary to HIPAA because the decision can be made to comply with both by not disclosing the information.

State laws are considered to be in agreement with, or not contrary to, HIPAA standards, requirements, and implementation specifications in the following situations:

- When both a state law and the Privacy Rule permit, or both require, the same use or disclosure
- When both a state law and the Privacy Rule prohibit, expressly or implicitly, the same use or disclosure
- When both a state law and the Privacy Rule permit, both require, or both prohibit the same use or disclosure, but the state law is more restrictive or detailed in its requirements, or vice versa
- When a use or disclosure is required by state law and permitted by the Privacy Rule, or vice versa

State laws are considered to be in opposition to, or contrary to, HIPAA standards, requirements, and implementation specifications in the following situations:

- When a state law expressly or implicitly prohibits a use or disclosure that is permitted by a HIPAA standard, requirement, or implementation specification, or vice versa
- When a state law requires a use or disclosure, but it is prohibited by the Privacy Rule, or vice versa

Preemption criteria that must be considered include the following:

- What criteria must be used to determine the state's laws that need to be reviewed?
- Is it the state in which the group health plan is registered?
- Is it the state in which medical treatment was obtained?
- Is it the state in which the patient resides?
- Is it to the state in which the patient resides, and whose laws provide privacy protection to the patient?

The answer is a definite "it depends!" In some states, the jurisdiction of the Department of Insurance is based on the membership covered under the master contracts used in that state, and also covered under master contracts used in out-of-state trusts. There is a need to have federal law, such as HIPAA, control competing state and local laws with respect to the specifications for the use of certain health transactions and associated information. The HIPAA rules for information transactions and the security of health information override any contrary provision of state law unless expressly excluded by the secretary of HHS.

The Privacy Rule is treated slightly differently than the Security Rule and Transactions and Code Sets Standards. The Privacy Rule does not fully preempt state privacy laws. The Privacy Rule does not supersede a contrary provision of state law, if the state law imposes requirements, standards, or implementation specifications that are more stringent than the requirements, standards, or implementation specifications imposed under the Privacy Rule. The Privacy Rule sets the minimum privacy requirements that must be met by CEs, BAs, and subcontractors in all states. Any Privacy Rule standard, requirement, or implementation guideline that is contrary to state law will preempt that state law unless one of the exceptions to preemption applies. (See 45 CFR § 160.203.)

9.3 Exceptions to Preemption

Some state laws that may be contrary to HIPAA and the Privacy Rule may not be preempted if the law falls under an exception established within the HIPAA legislation or Privacy Rule. The following are the state law HIPAA and Privacy Rule preemption exception categories:

- *Public health and vital statistics.* This allows providers to report diseases or injuries, child abuse, births, or deaths, or those that authorize public health surveillance, or public health investigation or intervention.
- *Health plan regulation and monitoring.* This allows for the application of state laws that require a health plan to report or provide access to information for regulatory management audits, financial audits, program monitoring and evaluation, facility licensure or certification, or individual licensure and certification.

- *Determination by the secretary of HHS.* The secretary has the discretion to determine that HIPAA will not preempt contrary state laws that are necessary to prevent fraud and abuse related to health care payment; to ensure appropriate state regulation of insurance and health plans; to permit state reporting on health care delivery or cost; or to serve a compelling need related to public health, safety, or welfare.
- *More stringent health privacy protections.* HIPAA does not preempt provisions of state laws that cover the privacy of individually identifiable health information and impose requirements that are more stringent than the requirements, standards, or specifications imposed under the HIPAA Privacy Rule.

Requests for an exception may be submitted to the secretary with information indicating, among other things, the specific state law and corresponding HIPAA privacy standard, requirement, or implementation specification for which the exception is requested. A request by a state must be submitted through its chief elected official or that person's designated representative. Until the secretary makes a determination, the HIPAA rule will continue to preempt state law (see 45 CFR § 160.204).

9.4 Preemption Analysis

Thousands of questions were posed during the public comment period regarding the interpretation, implications, and consequences of the preemption directives. Organizations will need to obtain significant advice and technical assistance about all of the regulatory requirements on an ongoing basis as they strive to maintain continued compliance.

HHS does not have the statutory authority under HIPAA to preempt state laws that impose more stringent privacy requirements on CEs, BAs, and subcontractors. HIPAA provides that the rule promulgated by the secretary may not preempt state laws that are in conflict with the regulatory requirements and that provide greater privacy protections.

Thus, it becomes imperative for CEs, BAs, and subcontractors to conduct a preemption analysis for the laws of the states in which they have or process protected health information (PHI). Such an analysis will identify the state law requirements for which continued compliance is necessary, along with the HIPAA requirements. As with any law or regulation that impacts your organization, be sure to discuss this issue thoroughly with your legal counsel. It will be important for you to identify and discuss with your legal counsel the technical, operational, and procedural issues related to the handling of PHI so the most applicable interpretation of state law can be made.

How do you approach this state preemption analysis? There are a few ways to accomplish this, but it will probably be easiest for you to decide first which states you can eliminate as having privacy laws that are in direct opposition with, or that have less restrictive privacy laws than, the HIPAA laws. In these cases, the HIPAA requirements will take precedence. In general, there are four broad situations within which state privacy laws may fall. These include when the state laws

1. Have been identified by the secretary of HHS as specifically not being preempted by the HIPAA Privacy Rule
2. Are more stringent with regard to privacy and confidentiality requirements than the corresponding HIPAA requirement, standard, or implementation specification
3. Allow disease, injury, child abuse, birth, death, or public health surveillance, investigation, or intervention to be reported
4. Govern the access to, or how to report, the information health plans possess

Generally you can disregard from analysis the state laws that fall into situations 1, 3, and 4; these generally are exceptions to preemption. Now you are ready to perform your preemption analysis. For each HIPAA requirement, use the decision tree shown in Exhibit 9.1.

9.4.1 Framework for Analyzing HIPAA Preemption Issues

- Prepare an inventory of applicable state law requirements and the Privacy Rule.
- Review policies, procedures, and operations in relation to both state law and the Privacy Rule.
- Use the decision tree shown in Exhibit 9.1.

Exhibit 9.1   HIPAA State Preemption Decision Tree

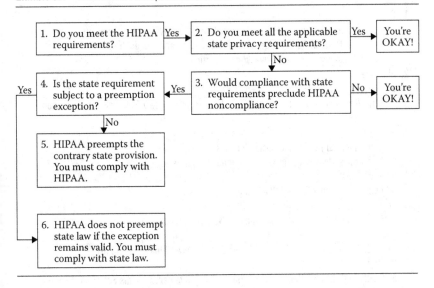

9.5 Conclusion

State preemption issues are extremely complex. The laws in each state are worded vastly differently, and each part must be analyzed and compared to the Privacy Rule. It is often difficult to determine which law, state or federal Privacy Rule, is more stringent with regard to privacy protections. For example, some state laws allow patients copies of their records with no exceptions. The Privacy Rule has several exceptions. The decision of what actions to take in such a situation, perhaps hinging on the life or death of the patient versus the general welfare of the public, can be extremely hard to determine. It is up to CEs, BAs, and subcontractors to know ahead of time how they will approach preemption issues in general, and then to address each situation with their legal counsel, based on the unique factors involved.

Use the sites in Exhibit 9.2 as beginning points for your state law preemption research. Not all will have specific preemption information, but at the time this book was written, all had links to other sites with such information.

Exhibit 9.2   State-by-State HIPAA Preemption-Related Information Websites

1. General information
   a. Government Information Value Exchange for States (GIVES); http://www.hipaagives.org/
   b. Center on Medical Record Rights and Privacy summaries for each state; http://hpi.georgetown.edu/privacy/records.html
2. Alabama
   a. Alabama Medicaid; http://medicaid.alabama.gov/CONTENT/7.0_Fraud_Abuse/7.3_Consumer_Protection _Privacy.aspx
3. Alaska
   a. Department of Health and Social Services; http://dhss.alaska.gov/dhcs/Pages/hipaa/default.aspx
4. American Samoa
   a. No resources specific to HIPAA found
5. Arizona
   a. Arizona Health Care Cost Containment System; http://www.azahcccs.gov/privacy/
6. Arkansas
   a. Arkansas Department of Human Services; http://www.hipaa.state.ar.us/
7. California
   a. Southern California Health Information and Management Systems Society (HIMSS); http://www.himss-socal.org/index.html
   b. Department of Health Services; http://www.dhs.ca.gov/hipaa/
   c. Medi-CAL; https://files.medi-cal.ca.gov/pubsdoco/hipaa/
   d. Office of Health and Information Integrity; http://www.ohii.ca.gov/calohi/PrivacySecurity/HIPAA/Preemption.aspx
   e. Office of HIPAA Implementation; http://www.ohii.ca.gov/calohi/
   f. Department of Developmental Services; http://www.dds.ca.gov/HIPAA/Home.cfm
   g. Department of Mental Health; http://www.dhcs.ca.gov/formsandpubs/laws/hipaa/Pages/default.aspx
8. Colorado
   a. Department of Health Care Policy and Financing; http://www.colorado.gov/cs/Satellite/HCPF/HCPF/1197364086675
   b. Division of Insurance; http://cdn.colorado.gov/cs/Satellite?c=Page&childpagename= DORA-HealthIns%2FDORALayout&cid=1251623077023&pagename=CBONWrapper
   c. Colorado Department of Human Resources, Alcohol and Drug Abuse Division; http://www.colorado.gov/cs/Satellite/CDHS-Ops/CBON/1251591540090
9. Connecticut
   a. Department of Information Technology; http://www.doit.state.ct.us/HIPAA/HIPAA.htm
   b. Department of Social Services; http://www.ct.gov/dss/site/default.asp?agingservicesNavPage=%7C
10. Delaware
    a. HIPAA Information; http://dhss.delaware.gov/dph/hipaa.html
11. District of Columbia
    a. No resources specific to HIPAA found
12. Florida
    a. Agency for Health Care Administration; http://ahca.myflorida.com/hipaa/

Exhibit 9.2 State-by-State HIPAA Preemption-Related Information Websites (*Continued*)

13. Georgia
    a. Georgia Department of Community Health; http://dch.georgia.gov/hipaa-privacy-notices
14. Guam
    a. No resources specific to HIPAA found
15. Hawaii
    a. Hawaii Health Information Corporation; http://hhic.org/training-materials.asp
16. Idaho
    a. Idaho Optometric Physicians; http://idaho.aoa.org/x4837.xml
    b. Department of Health and Welfare; http://www2.state.id.us/dhw/hipaa
17. Illinois
    a. Department of Healthcare and Family Services; http://www.hfs.illinois.gov/hipaa/
18. Indiana
    a. Indiana State Department of Health; http://www.in.gov/isdh/23501.htm
19. Iowa
    a. Iowa Department of Human Services;
       http://www.dhs.state.ia.us/Consumers/Health/HIPAA/Home.html
    b. Iowa Medical Society; http://www.iowamedical.org/legal/hipaa.cfm
    c. Iowa Department of Public Health; http://www.idph.state.ia.us/hipaa_statement.asp
20. Kansas
    a. HIPAA Awareness and Readiness for Kansas; http://www.hark.info/
    b. Workers Compensation and HIPAA; http://www.dol.ks.gov/WorkComp/Hipaa.aspx
21. Kentucky
    a. Cabinet for Health and Family Services; http://dbhdid.ky.gov/kdbhdid/hipaa.aspx
22. Louisiana
    a. Department of Health and Hospitals; http://new.dhh.louisiana.gov/index.cfm/faq/category/36
23. Maine
    a. Department of Human Services; http://www.maine.gov/dhhs/privacy/
24. Maryland
    a. Maryland Health Care Commission;
       http://mhcc.dhmh.maryland.gov/SitePages/Home.aspx
    b. Department of Health and Mental Hygiene;
       http://dhmh.maryland.gov/HIPAA/SitePages/Home.aspx
25. Massachusetts
    a. Massachusetts Health Data Consortium; http://www.mahealthdata.org/
    b. Health and Human Services;
       http://www.mass.gov/eohhs/gov/laws-regs/privacy-security/masshealth/
26. Michigan
    a. Department of Community Health;
       http://www.michigan.gov/mdch/0,4612,7-132-2945_24020—,00.html
27. Minnesota
    a. Information Policy Analysis Division; http://www.ipad.state.mn.us/docs/hipaa.html
    b. Department of Human Services; http://mn.gov/dhs/
28. Mississippi
    a. Division of Medicaid; https://www.medicaid.ms.gov/hipaaNoticeOfPrivacy.aspx

(*Continued*)

Exhibit 9.2   State-by-State HIPAA Preemption-Related Information Websites (*Continued*)

29. Missouri
    a. Department of Health and Senior Services; http://health.mo.gov/information/hipaa/
30. Montana
    a. Department of Public Health and Human Services; http://www.dphhs.mt.gov/hipaa.shtml
31. Nebraska
    a. Department of Health and Human Services; http://dhhs.ne.gov/
32. Nevada
    a. Department of Insurance; http://doi.state.nv.us/
33. New Hampshire
    a. New Hampshire Insurance Department; http://www.nh.gov/insurance/consumers/health.htm
34. New Jersey
    a. No resources specific to HIPAA found
35. New Mexico
    a. No resources specific to HIPAA found
36. New York
    a. Department of Health; http://www.health.ny.gov/regulations/hipaa/
37. North Carolina
    a. Office of Privacy and Security; http://www.ncdhhs.gov/pso/
    b. North Carolina Healthcare Information Communications Alliance (NCHICA);
       http://www.nchica.org/
38. North Dakota
    a. Department of Health; http://www.nd.gov/dhs/
39. Northern Marianas Islands
    a. No resources specific to HIPAA found
40. Ohio
    a. HIPAA Statewide Project;
       http://privacy.ohio.gov/Portals/0/pdf/GuidetotheHIPAAPrivacyRule.pdf
41. Oklahoma
    a. State Department of Health;
       http://www.ok.gov/health/Organization/HIPAA_Privacy_Rules/
42. Oregon
    a. Public Health;
       http://public.health.oregon.gov/DISEASESCONDITIONS/COMMUNICABLEDISEASE
       /LOCALHEALTHDEPARTMENTS/Pages/hipaa.aspx
43. Pennsylvania
    a. Department of Health;
       http://www.portal.state.pa.us/portal/server.pt/community/department_of_health
       _information/10674/health_insurance_portability_and_accountability_act
       _(hipaa)/559367
44. Puerto Rico
    a. No resources specific to HIPAA found

Exhibit 9.2   State-by-State HIPAA Preemption-Related Information Websites

45. Rhode Island
    a. Department of Health and Human Services;
       http://www.eohhs.ri.gov/ProvidersPartners/ProviderManualsGuidelines/
       HealthInsurancePortabilityAccountabilityAct.aspx
46. South Carolina
    a. South Carolina Department of Health and Environmental Control;
       http://www.scdhec.gov/administration/phsis/scccr/Legislation.htm
47. South Dakota
    a. Department of Social Services; http://dss.sd.gov/hipaa/
48. Tennessee
    a. Department of Health; https://health.state.tn.us/hipaa/
49. Texas
    a. Texas Department of State Health Services; http://www.dshs.state.tx.us/hipaa/
50. Utah
    a. Utah Health Information Network; http://www.uhin.org/
51. Vermont
    a. Agency of Human Services;
       http://humanservices.vermont.gov/policy-legislation/hipaa/
52. Virginia
    a. Department of Behavioral Health and Developmental Services;
       http://www.dbhds.virginia.gov/adm-hipaa.htm
53. Virgin Islands
    a. The Governor's Office; http://www.governordejongh.com/
54. Washington
    a. Washington State Department of Labor & Industries;
       http://www.lni.wa.gov/ClaimsIns/Providers/Claims/HIPAA/
55. West Virginia
    a. State Privacy Office; http://www.privacy.wv.gov/HIPAA/Pages/default.aspx
56. Wisconsin
    a. HIPAA Collaborative of Wisconsin (COW); http://www.hipaacow.org/
    b. Department of Health and Family Services; http://www.dhfs.state.wi.us/HIPAA/
57. Wyoming
    a. Department of Health; http://www.health.wyo.gov/default.aspx

Note: The URLs (online addresses) of websites can change, and some change often. While the
    URLs in this section were valid at the time of publication, it is possible that they may no
    longer work at some point after this book is published.

Practical Checklist

- Identify state and local laws applicable to your organization that have requirements that are contrary to, but more stringent than portions of the HIPAA Privacy Rule requirements. These laws are generally not preempted.
- Identify state and local laws applicable to your organization that have requirements that are contrary to, but are less stringent than portions of the HIPAA Privacy Rule requirements. These laws will generally be preempted.
- Identify state and local laws applicable to your organization that have requirements that are not contrary to the HIPAA Privacy Rule requirements. These laws are generally not preempted.
- Incorporate noncontrary laws into your HIPAA Privacy Rule authorization, privacy notice practices, and the policies and procedures of your organization.
- *Very important:* Discuss state preemption issues with your legal counsel to determine how this issue affects your particular organization.

10

CRAFTING A PRIVACY IMPLEMENTATION PLAN

10.1 Introduction

Preparing for Health Insurance Portability and Accountability Act (HIPAA) (including the Health Information Technology for Economic and Clinical Health [HITECH] Act) compliance is complex and must be thoroughly planned. Planning should involve the entire organization; it is not just an information technology issue, nor just a business application issue. It certainly involves these issues, but also much more. HIPAA compliance is both a project to be implemented, as well as an ongoing practice and a set of tasks and processes to oversee. Most organizations will already meet some of the HIPAA requirements. Other requirements will still need to be addressed. Organizations must accurately review their state of HIPAA compliance, identify the outstanding requirements, and create a functional plan for implementation. A baseline compliance assessment (Chapter 7) needs to occur to determine where the organization is presently at with regard to HIPAA compliance. A successful assessment will have the beneficial side effect of creating an information flow document.

Many organizations struggle with the initial approach to creating an implementation plan. Exhibit 10.1 shows a plan to help you get started; modify it to best meet your organization's business environment.

Exhibit 10.1 Privacy Rule Implementation Plan

1. Determine your covered entity (CE) status.
   a. Are you a CE? What kind? A health care provider? A health plan? A health care clearinghouse? A hybrid entity?
   b. Are you a business associate (BA)?
   c. Are you a BA who has subcontractors that access protected health information (PHI) in some way? If yes, then they are considered to be your BAs, and must follow all the applicable Security Rule, Privacy Rule, and HITECH Act requirements.
   d. See Chapter 1, as well as Chapters 17–21, to help you make these determinations. Then, discuss with your legal counsel.

(Continued)

Exhibit 10.1 Privacy Rule Implementation Plan (*Continued*)

2. Establish a HIPAA privacy project. Start planning for your compliance activities.
   a. Determine who will sponsor the project.
   b. Establish a steering committee to oversee and guide the HIPAA compliance effort.
   c. Organize a team of people to track and manage the HIPAA activities. Develop a project management environment.
   d. Assign a HIPAA compliance team.
   e. Develop a strategic plan so that everyone in the organization understands the mission, goals, and objectives of the effort.
   f. Confirm your scope and establish your due diligence documentation method and repository.
   g. Develop initiative-level roles and responsibilities so that each major component of the organization knows who is doing what in the effort.
   h. Develop detailed work plans for at least the next phase of your effort and a master plan for the initiative.
   i. Establish a HIPAA compliance budget and timeline.
3. Understand the activities covered by HIPAA.
   a. Read and understand the HIPAA regulations (see Chapters 6 and 7).
   b. Analyze the requirements as they relate to your organization.
   c. Know the compliance timelines and penalties (see Chapter 4).
   d. Analyze the HIPAA regulations against potentially preemptive, superseding, or conflicting privacy regulations and other types of legal requirements with which you must comply (see Chapter 9):
      i. State
      ii. Other federal
      iii. International
   e. Identify which parts of your organization are impacted by the regulations and legal requirements.
   f. Is your organization a CE or a hybrid entity under HIPAA?
   g. If a hybrid entity, identify the covered functions that are within your organization.
   h. Obtain regulatory guidance materials (see Appendix D).
   i. Make top management aware of the issues and obtain their documented commitment to compliance.
4. Identify a privacy officer and privacy contact for HIPAA questions and complaints.
   a. Identify and appoint a qualified privacy officer to address HIPAA and other privacy-related issues if you are a CE, BA, or subcontractor to a BA.
   b. Identify privacy and security officers within each health care component of a hybrid-covered entity.
   c. Identify a contact person to receive complaints about policies, privacy, and HIPAA compliance, to provide information about the Notice of Privacy Practices (NPP), and to answer general related questions.
   d. Train the privacy officer(s) and privacy contact(s).
   e. Visit websites often to obtain new and updated HIPAA privacy information (see Appendix D).
   f. Assign members of the HIPAA compliance team specific responsibilities for addressing each of the HIPAA gap analysis action items.

Exhibit 10.1 Privacy Rule Implementation Plan (*Continued*)

5. Perform a HIPAA requirements gap analysis and determine the baseline compliance status for the organization.
   a. Develop an assessment method. You will likely need a different method for each regulation area (see Chapter 7).
   b. Collect and review printed documentation.
   c. Conduct interviews to collect unwritten methods and procedures.
   d. Review electronic information.
   e. Create an inventory of all current policies, procedures, and documentation related to HIPAA privacy requirements.
   f. Analyze the HIPAA regulations against your existing organizational policies, rules, procedures, directives, and so forth.
   g. Create an inventory of all information that is considered individually identifiable health information (see Chapter 6). Classify the information that is PHI under HIPAA definitions.
   h. Create an inventory of all your medical devices that collect, derive, process, or store PHI.
   i. Create an inventory of all your BAs (vendors, contractors, etc.) and electronic trading partners with whom your organization shares health information.
   j. Identify all BAs who have remote access capabilities to your facilities (for example, dial-in, virtual private network, etc.) for support purposes.
   k. Map data flows with BAs.
      i. Identify paper systems and forms.
      ii. Identify information systems.
      iii. Identify mobile devices that BAs use.
      iv. Identify all BA contracts.
      v. Identify all BAs' policies and procedures related to health information.
      vi. Determine existing responsibilities within BAs for the privacy function.
   l. Document the uses and disclosures for PHI within your organization and by your BAs.
   m. Test information systems to determine if access controls are implemented.
   n. Conduct assessment activities to establish baseline HIPAA compliance and a risk assessment summary.
   o. Analyze the HIPAA regulations against existing organization-specific rules, directives, enterprise policies, and so forth.
   p. Analyze gaps between the existing organizational (human) environment and HIPAA requirements.
   q. Analyze gaps between the existing technical and networking environment and HIPAA requirements.
   r. Analyze gaps between the existing information policies and procedures and HIPAA requirements.
   s. Document and date all identified gaps.
   t. Create a compliance plan for closing gaps and meeting compliance.
   u. Maintain the compliance plan and gap analysis for future reference.
   v. Document potential impacts the gaps present to your organization.
6. Plan remediation strategies.
   a. Document your business compliance strategy and implementation plan.
   b. Document your technical compliance strategy and implementation plan.
   c. Refine your budget estimates as necessary.
   d. Seek additional funding commitment if necessary.

(*Continued*)

Exhibit 10.1 Privacy Rule Implementation Plan (*Continued*)

---

    e. Organize or recruit the staff necessary to close the gaps.

    f. Determine if you can meet HIPAA Privacy Rule compliance on your own, or if you will need outside help. Consider hiring temporary workers or outside consultants experienced with HIPAA remediation if you do not have the staff, resources, or experience available in-house.

    g. Consider using other resources as well:

       i. Professional associations

      ii. Software

     iii. Forms

7. Remediate the organization.

    a. Update existing policies and procedures and develop new policies and procedures as necessary.

    b. Update organizational procedures, systems, and documentation to match policy and procedure requirements.

    c. Develop training for the workforce covering HIPAA privacy requirements.

    d. Conduct appropriate levels of training for implementation staff as well as designated privacy and security officers.

    e. Give all personnel awareness communications to support retention of what they learned during training, as well as to emphasize how to best safeguard PHI in areas of risk within your organization.

    f. Document privacy training and the personnel who attended.

    g. Establish and update BA contracts as necessary to provide detailed directives for protecting PHI.

    h. Modify business processes, business application systems, and technical infrastructure as necessary to comply.

    i. Test information systems; modify as necessary and pilot modifications.

    j. Conduct training relating to modifications or specific compliance issues.

    k. Implement and install changes.

    l. Transition the maintenance of new processes and products to the responsible parties.

    m. Determine the appropriate administrative, physical, and technical security measures to apply to medical devices.

    n. Create operating procedures for secure medical equipment use.

    o. Develop privacy notices and any necessary accompanying forms and documents.

    p. Develop consent forms and documents (if applicable for your organization). Consent forms are not required by HIPAA; however, some state or international regulations may require them, and your organization may choose to use them based on your legal counsel advice.

    q. Develop authorization forms and documents.

    r. Develop accounting for disclosure forms and documents.

    s. Develop formal documentation procedures and standards to ensure information is adequately maintained for the appropriate time limits.

    t. Implement and maintain the use of notice, consent (if applicable), and authorization forms.

    u. Get the new and updated BA agreements signed.

    v. Perform due diligence on your business relationships.

    w. If applicable to your organization, create or update your NPP appropriately.

    x. Communicate your NPP to your patients and health plan members.

    y. Establish compliance systems and a plan for ongoing compliance.

    z. Create and maintain HIPAA compliance activities documentation.

Exhibit 10.1 Privacy Rule Implementation Plan (*Continued*)

---

8. Monitor progress and changes in HIPAA rules and update your organizational policies, procedures, and technologies appropriately.
   a. Keep current with changes in the HIPAA regulations.
   b. Keep current with new and updated state, federal, and international regulations related to privacy.
   c. Update policies and procedures as necessary to meet new requirements and to reflect organizational changes.
   d. Monitor organizational procedures and follow-up of activities falling out of compliance.
   e. Manage BAs and other relationships related to processing and handling health information.
   f. Perform periodic gap analysis (at least annually and following major organizational and systems changes).
   g. Perform regular privacy risk assessments to discover and address new risks.
   h. Review audit and activity logs for health information.
   i. Perform regular internal audits for each aspect of Privacy Rule compliance.
   j. Maintain ongoing training and awareness.
   k. Document all your activities related to HIPAA compliance and maintain the documentation in a central location.

10.2 Some Points to Keep in Mind

Here are some Privacy Rule compliance facts related to common questions and concerns you need to keep in mind when creating and applying your Privacy Rule implementation plan:

- Physicians and nurses can discuss PHI. They need to take care not to discuss PHI in locations outside their facilities where others can hear. However, discussing within their facilities (such as in a hospital room shared by patients) is considered acceptable even if the possibility exists that someone may overhear their discussion, since this would be considered an incidental (or unintentional) disclosure.
- CEs are now encouraged by the Department of Health and Human Services (HHS) to oversee, as is feasible and practical for the relationship and the associated risks to PHI, how BAs apply safeguards to the PHI they are processing. The same goes for BAs and their subcontractors, who are now considered to also be BAs under the 2013 Final Omnibus Rule. CEs and BAs must include safeguard requirements in their BA contracts, and must discontinue the associations (if possible) if they notice a BA is in violation of the safeguards and does not correct the violation.

- The Privacy Rule does not prevent the use of sign-in sheets or calling names of patients in the waiting room.
- The Privacy Rule does not require the use of specific technologies or operating systems.
- The Privacy Rule does not prohibit faxing PHI. However, CEs must use appropriate administrative, technical, and physical safeguards to protect the PHI in the faxes. Also keep in mind that many organizations now use electronic faxing, which delivers the faxes to servers and e-mail accounts, so appropriate safeguards must be in place for those locations as well.
- The Privacy Rule permits disclosure of PHI that is required by other applicable laws.
- The Privacy Rule permits disclosures to researchers and law enforcement; however, it does not require the disclosures. In some cases (such as for research), authorization may be required. Even when an authorization is not required and the Privacy Rule permits a disclosure, there may be other limitations or laws preventing such disclosures, as well as the discretion of the CE.
- Unless a patient objects, a physician can discuss a patient's condition with family or friends involved with the patient's care.
- The Privacy Rule allows hospitals and disaster relief agencies to notify family members that a family member has been admitted to a hospital or has been involved in a disaster.
- An organization cannot and is not expected to be perfect. Organizations are expected to identify mistakes and correct them as best as possible to meet HIPAA compliance. Noncompliance issues arise when an organization recognizes it has problem or noncompliance areas and does not take corrective action.

10.3 Conclusion

The HIPAA compliance plan will require ongoing maintenance. HIPAA compliance does not have a termination point. HIPAA requirements will impose strict penalties for noncompliance from the compliance date forward. You cannot expect to meet all the HIPAA compliance requirements by one date and be done; this must be a long-term commitment your organization makes.

Practical Checklist

- Determine your CE or BA status.
- Establish a HIPAA compliance project.
- Understand your HIPAA obligations.
- Assign privacy responsibilities.
- Perform a gap analysis and identify risks.
- Create a remediation plan.
- Implement the plan.
- Monitor ongoing compliance.

11

PRIVACY RULE
COMPLIANCE CHECKLIST

11.1   Introduction

When striving for Health Insurance Portability and Accountability Act (HIPAA) Privacy Rule compliance, keep all the information in the previous chapters in mind. To make your efforts a little easier to keep track of, use the following checklist (Exhibit 11.1) to identify the HIPAA activities you have fulfilled and those that you still need to address. To help you determine specific regulatory requirements, the corresponding location within the regulatory text is noted, and the wording from within the text has been preserved as much as possible, with some modification for clarification.

Exhibit 11.1   Privacy Rule Compliance Checklist

A. Prohibited disclosures

_____   1. Privacy protection

§ 164.502(a): A covered entity and business associate may not use or disclose protected health information (PHI) except as provided in the HIPAA privacy rule. Those provisions include uses and disclosures to the individual himself or herself; for treatment, payment, and operations; as authorized by the individual; for research, public health or health care operations in the form of limited data sets; for listings in facility directories or disclosures to those involved in the individual's care provided that the individual does not object; incidental to an otherwise permitted use; to business associates; as required by law for health oversight activities, compliance investigations, or other public purposes.

_____   2. Deceased individuals

§ 164.502(f): A covered entity and business associate must protect the protected health information of a deceased individual for a period of 50 years following the death of the individual.

(Continued)

Exhibit 11.1   Privacy Rule Compliance Checklist (*Continued*)

_____   3. Consistency with notice

§ **164.502(i):** A covered entity, and a business associate if applicable to the services it provides, may not use or disclose protected health information in a manner that is inconsistent with its notice of information practices. A specific statement must be included in its notice if it intends to engage in an activity listed in § 164.520(b)(1)(iii)(A)-(C). It may not use or disclose protected health information for such activities unless the required statement is included in the notice.

_____   4. Physician–patient privilege

§ **164.512(j)(2):** A covered entity may not disclose protected health information if the information is obtained as part of treatment to reduce the possibility for the criminal activity to occur.

_____   5. Underwriting disclosures

§ **164.514(g):** A health plan that receives protected health information for the purposes of underwriting, premium rating, etc., may not use or disclose this information for any other purpose, and may not use genetic information for underwriting purposes.

_____   6. Access locked by agency or official

§ **164.528(a)(2)(i):** A covered entity and business associate must temporarily suspend an individual's right to receive an accounting of disclosures for the duration specified by the agency or official if a health oversight agency or law enforcement official provides a written statement that an accounting of the disclosures a covered entity or business associate made to such agency or official about an individual (patient or health plan member) would interfere with official business.

B. Disclosures requiring opportunity to agree or object

_____   7. Listings in facility directories

§ **164.510(a)(2):** A covered entity must inform an individual that protected health information relating to them may be listed in a facility directory and provide the individual with the ability to object, except in emergencies or if the individual is incapacitated.

§ **164.510(a)(1)(i):** A facility directory may contain name, location, general condition, and religious affiliation.

§ **164.510(a)(1)(ii)(A):** A covered entity may disclose religious affiliation only to members of the clergy.

§ **164.510(a)(1)(ii)(B):** A covered entity may disclose facility directory information only to persons who ask for the individual by name, with certain exceptions (for example, clergy members).

_____   8. Disclosures to persons involved with the individual

§ **164.510(b):** A covered entity must provide an individual with an opportunity to object prior to revealing protected health information to family, friends, or others involved with the care of the individual.

§ **164.510(b)(3):** If a covered entity (CE) uses professional judgment to disclose information to a person involved in the individual's care when the individual is not present, then the CE may disclose only the protected health information directly relevant to the person's involvement with the individual's care.

Exhibit 11.1   Privacy Rule Compliance Checklist (*Continued*)

C. Disclosures for treatment, payment, and operations (TPO)

_____ 9. Health care operations disclosures

§ **164.506(c)(4):** A covered entity (CE) may disclose protected health information to another CE only under certain allowed conditions; for example, when each has a relationship with the individual, the information disclosed must pertain to that relationship.

_____ 10. Restrictions on use and disclosure for treatment, payment, and operations

§ **164.522(a)(1)(i):** A covered entity (CE) must permit an individual to request restriction of uses and disclosures of protected health information for treatment, payment, and operations or to family, friends, or others involved in the health care of the individual. The CE is not required to agree to the requested restriction.

§ **164.502(c):** If a covered entity (CE) agrees to a restriction on the use of protected health information, the CE is bound by that restriction, except in emergency situations.

§ **164.522(a)(2):** A covered entity may terminate its agreement to a restriction request only under certain circumstances. For example, the individual agrees, termination applies only to information collected after the termination, etc.

D. Disclosures requiring authorization

_____ 11. Disclosures must be consistent with authorizations

§ **164.508(a)(1):** When a covered entity uses or discloses protected health information for a purpose that requires authorization, the information must be used or disclosed in a way that is consistent with the terms of the authorization.

_____ 12. Authorization is required for disclosure of psychotherapy notes

§ **164.508(a)(2):** Authorization is required for any use or disclosure of psychotherapy notes, with certain exceptions (for example, by the originator of the psychotherapy notes for treatment, for the covered entity's mental health student training under supervision, or for the covered entity to defend itself in a legal action brought by the corresponding individual).

_____ 13. Mandatory contents of authorization

§ **164.508(c):** An authorization must have certain elements in it, for example, it must be in plain language, it must describe the information to be used or disclosed, contain an expiration date or expiration event, etc. Be sure to work with your legal counsel to ensure you address all legal requirements.

§ **164.508(a)(3)(ii):** A covered entity must obtain authorization to use and disclose Protected Health Information for marketing purposes unless it is face-to-face communication between the covered entity and the individual, or a promotional gift of nominal value provided by the covered entity. The authorization must state that remuneration is involved if the covered entity receives any form of payment from a third party resulting from marketing activity allowed by the authorization.

_____ 14. Individual retains a copy of the authorization

§ **164.508(c)(4):** If the covered entity seeks an authorization from an individual, the individual must be given a copy of the authorization.

(Continued)

Exhibit 11.1   Privacy Rule Compliance Checklist (*Continued*)

_____   15. Authorizations may be defective

> **§ 164.508(b)(2):** A covered entity may not use or disclose protected health information (PHI) using a defective authorization. Authorization is defective if it has expired, it is incomplete, it has been revoked, it is known to be false, it is part of a compound authorization or treatment, or if payment, enrollment, or eligibility has been conditioned on obtaining the individual's signature.

_____   16. Compound authorizations not allowed

> **§ 164.508(b)(3):** An authorization may not be combined with another document to create a compound authorization; such as where one authorization conditions the provision of treatment, payment, enrollment in a health plan, or eligibility for benefits. There are certain exceptions; here are two examples: for the use or disclosure of protected health information for a research study combined with any other type of written permission for the same research study; or the use or disclosure of psychotherapy notes combined with another authorization for a use or disclosure of psychotherapy notes.

_____   17. Revocation

> **§ 164.508(b)(5):** An individual may revoke an authorization at any time with certain exceptions. For example, if the covered entity has already taken action based on the authorization, or if the authorization was obtained as a condition of obtaining insurance coverage.

E. Minimum necessary disclosure

_____   18. Disclosure limitations

> **§ 164.502(b):** A covered entity and business associate must make reasonable efforts to limit the amount of protected health information used or disclosed to the minimum necessary to accomplish the purpose of the use or disclosure with certain exceptions. For example, disclosures to or requests by a health care provider for treatment, or uses or disclosures made pursuant to an authorization.

> **§ 164.512(j)(3):** A covered entity that discloses information to law enforcement about an individual who admits participation in a violent crime may reveal only the admission and certain specified information.

> **§ 164.514(d)(3)(i):** A covered entity and business associate must implement policies and procedures for routine disclosures to limit the information disclosed to that needed to accomplish the purpose of the disclosure.

> **§ 164.514(d)(3)(ii):** A covered entity and business associate (CE) must develop criteria for non-routine disclosures to limit the information disclosed to the minimum necessary to accomplish the purpose of the disclosure. The CE must review non-routine requests for disclosure on an individual basis.

> **§ 164.514(d)(5):** A covered entity and business associate may not use, disclose, or request an entire medical record unless the entire medical record is specifically justified as the amount of information needed to accomplish the purpose of the use, disclosure, or request.

_____   19. Minimum necessary requests for disclosure

> **§ 164.514(d)(4)(i):** A covered entity and business associate must limit its own requests for protected health information to the minimum necessary to accomplish the purpose for which the request is made.

Exhibit 11.1   Privacy Rule Compliance Checklist (*Continued*)

---

§ 164.514(d)(4)(ii): A covered entity and business associate must implement policies and procedures for its own routine requests for protected health information to ensure that it requests the minimum information needed to accomplish the intended purpose.

§ 164.514(d)(4)(iii): A covered entity and business associate must develop criteria to limit each of its non-routine requests for information to the minimum information necessary to accomplish the purpose of the request. The entity must review each of its own non-routine requests for protected health information with respect to those criteria.

____ 20. Minimum necessary access privileges

§ 164.514(d)(2): A covered entity (CE) and business associate must identify classes of persons who need access to protected health information to carry out their duties and must establish the levels of access needed by each. A CE must make reasonable efforts to limit access to the minimum information required to perform an assigned job function.

F. Notice

____ 21. Individual's right to notice

§ 164.520(a)(1): A covered entity, with certain exceptions, must provide a notice of information practices. An example of an exception is providing notice to an inmate.

§ 164.520(a)(2)(ii): A group health plan that provides benefits through an insurance issuer or health management organization (HMO) and that creates or receives protected health information, must maintain a notice of information practices and provide it to any person who requests it.

____ 22. Timeliness

§ 164.520(c)(1)(i): A health plan must provide notice no later than the compliance date for the health plan to individuals covered by the plan, to new enrollees at the time of enrollment, and to individuals who are new enrollees. A health plan that posts its notice on its website must prominently post the revised notice or change by the effective date of the change, along with information about how to obtain the revised notice in its next mailing to insureds. A health plan that doesn't post the notice on their website must provide notice to all individuals covered by the plan within 60 days of a material revision to the notice.

§ 164.520(c)(1)(ii): A health plan must notify all individuals covered by the plan at least once every 3 years that the notice of information practices is available. The health plan must also advise them of how to obtain a copy of the notice of information practices.

§ 164.520(c)(2)(i): A health care provider that has a direct treatment relationship with an individual must provide notice of information practices no later than the date of the first service delivery following the compliance date for the provider or as soon as possible after an emergency treatment situation.

____ 23. Location of notice

§ 164.520(c)(2)(iii): A health care provider that maintains a physical service delivery site must have copies of the notice of information practices available that individuals may take with them. The provider must also post the notice where individuals seeking service may read it.

(*Continued*)

Exhibit 11.1   Privacy Rule Compliance Checklist (*Continued*)

_____   24. Notice of revised practices

§ **164.520(c)(2)(iv):** A health care provider must make a revised Notice of Privacy Practices available on request on or after the effective date of the revision. If the covered entity maintains a physical service delivery site, it must prominently post the notice where patients may see it and make copies of the notice available.

_____   25. Electronic notice

§ **164.520(c)(3)(i):** A covered entity that maintains a website providing information about the entity's services must post its Notice of Privacy Practices on the website.

§ **164.520(c)(3)(ii):** If a covered entity (CE) attempts to provide a Notice of Privacy Practices electronically and knows that the transmission has failed, then the CE must provide a paper copy.

§ **164.520(c)(3)(iii):** If the first service to an individual is delivered electronically, a copy of the Notice of Privacy Practices must be delivered, and an attempt must be made to gain a written acknowledgment that it has been received, at the same time in response to the request for service.

§ **164.520(c)(3)(iv):** A covered entity must honor a request for a paper copy of the notice of information practices when the notice has previously been delivered electronically.

_____   26. Mandatory content of notice

§ **164.520(b):** The Notice of Privacy Practices that a covered entity provides must contain certain mandatory elements.

_____   27. Acknowledgment

§ **164.520(c)(2)(ii):** A covered entity must make a good faith effort to obtain a written acknowledgment of receipt of the notice except in an emergency situation and must document the efforts to obtain the acknowledgment if it cannot get the acknowledgment itself.

G. Access

_____   28. Individual's right to access and copy protected health information (PHI)

§ **164.524(a)(1):** A covered entity (CE) must grant access to protected health information to the corresponding individual with certain exceptions. One example of an exception is a CE that is a correctional institution or a covered health care provider acting under the direction of the correctional institution.

§ **164.524(c)(1):** A covered entity must provide access to protected health information to the individual in designated record sets.

§ **164.524(c)(2)(i):** A covered entity must provide access to protected health information to the individual in the form requested by the individual, if it is readily producible in such form and format; or, if not, in a readable hard copy or other form as agreed to by the covered entity.

_____   29. Denial of an individual's request for access

§ **164.524(d)(1):** If a covered entity (CE) denies an individual's request to access certain protected health information, the CE must allow access to all information for which the reason for the rejection does not apply.

Exhibit 11.1 Privacy Rule Compliance Checklist (*Continued*)

§ 164.524(d)(2): If a covered entity denies an individual's request to access certain protected health information, the denial must be in writing and must contain: the basis for the denial; a statement of the individual's rights; and a description of how the individual may appeal the decision.

§ 164.524(a)(4): If a covered entity (CE) has denied access to protected health information to the individual, the CE must allow review of the denial by a licensed health care professional and must abide by the reviewer's decision.

_____ 30. Miscellaneous rules governing access by the individual

§ 164.524(d)(3): If a covered entity (CE) does not possess the protected health information requested by an individual, but knows where it is, the CE must inform the individual of where to direct the request.

§ 164.524(b)(2)(i): A covered entity (CE) must act on a request for access to protected health information (PHI) by the individual within 30 days, with certain exceptions. For example, if the request for access is for PHI that is not maintained or accessible to the CE on-site, the CE must take an action by no later than 30 days from the receipt of such a request with specific provisions.

§ 164.524(c)(4): A covered entity may not charge fees for granting access to protected health information to the individual in excess of the cost of the supplies for copying, postage, and preparation of summaries or explanations, or for creating in electronic form and the associated portable media.

H. Amendment

_____ 31. Individual's right to request amendment

§ 164.526(a)(1): A covered entity (CE) must honor an individual's request to amend incorrect or incomplete protected health information (PHI), with certain exceptions. For example, if the CE determines that the PHI or record that is the subject of the request is accurate and complete.

_____ 32. Timeliness

§ 164.526(b)(2)(i): A covered entity (CE) must act on an individual's request for amendment of protected health information within 60 days of the submission of the request. The CE is entitled to one 30-day extension if it provides the individual with the reasons for the delay.

_____ 33. Denial of individual's request for amendment

§ 164.526(b)(2)(i)(B): A covered entity that denies a request for amendment of protected health information must notify the requestor in writing.

§ 164.526(d): If a covered entity denies a request for amendment, the denial must have certain mandatory elements.

_____ 34. Acceptance of request

§ 164.526(c)(1): If a covered entity accepts a request for amendment of protected health information, it must make the appropriate amendment or provide a link to the amendment in the designated record set.

§ 164.526(c)(2): If a covered entity accepts a request for amendment of protected health information, it must inform the individual and obtain a list of persons with whom the amendment needs to be shared.

(*Continued*)

Exhibit 11.1   Privacy Rule Compliance Checklist (*Continued*)

§ 164.526(c)(3): If a covered entity (CE) accepts a request for amendment of protected health information, it must make reasonable efforts to provide the amendment to all persons identified by the individual. The CE must also inform business associates known to have a copy of the inaccurate or incomplete information.

____ 35. Transitivity

§ 164.526(e): A covered entity (CE) that is informed by another CE of an amendment to an individual's health information must make the same amendment to its own copies of the information.

I. Personal representatives

____ 36. Personal representative rights to access or amend PHI

§ 164.502(g)(1): A covered entity must treat a personal representative of an individual as the individual for the purposes of protecting health information concerning that individual, with certain exceptions.

§ 164.502(g)(2): A covered entity must treat a person as a personal representative of an individual (such as an adult or emancipated minor) if that person has the authority to act on behalf of the individual in making health care decisions.

____ 37. Parents and guardians are personal representatives

§ 164.502(g)(3): A covered entity (CE) must treat a parent, guardian, or person acting with parental rights of an unemancipated minor as a personal representative of that minor, unless the minor may lawfully obtain the health care without parental consent. If the minor may lawfully obtain the health care without parental consent, then the CE must follow state law with respect to disclosures to parents, guardians, and persons acting with parental rights. If state law is unclear on this matter a licensed health care professional may exercise his or her professional judgment.

____ 38. Executors are personal representatives

§ 164.502(g)(4): A covered entity must treat a representative of a deceased person as a personal representative for the purposes of health information protection.

J. Confidential communications channels

____ 39. Individual's right to request alternate communication channels

§ 164.522(b)(1)(i): A health care provider must permit individuals to request and must accommodate reasonable requests by individuals to receive communications of protected health information by alternate means or at alternate locations.

§ 164.522(b)(1)(ii): A health plan must permit individuals to request and must accommodate reasonable requests by individuals to receive communications of protected health information by alternate means or at alternate locations if the individual clearly states that disclosure could endanger the individual.

K. Accounting of disclosures

____ 40. Individual's right to an accounting of disclosures

§ 164.528(a)(1): A covered entity must provide an individual with an accounting of disclosures of protected health information on request, with certain exceptions; for example, pursuant to an authorization. Business associates must maintain an accounting of disclosures for associated access to PHI services they provide to CEs.

Exhibit 11.1   Privacy Rule Compliance Checklist (*Continued*)

---

§ 164.528(b): When a covered entity provides an accounting of disclosures, it must include certain mandatory elements. Business associates must maintain these mandatory elements within an accounting of disclosures for associated access to PHI services they provide to CEs.

L. Complaint process

____   41. Individual's right to file a complaint

§ 164.530(d)(1): A covered entity (CE) must provide a process for individuals to make complaints concerning the CE's policies and procedures.

M. Prohibited activities

____   42. Intimidation

§ 164.530(g): A covered entity may not engage in any intimidating or retaliatory acts against persons who file complaints or otherwise exercise their rights under HIPAA regulations.

____   43. Conditioning

§ 164.530(h): A covered entity may not require an individual to waive the right to file a complaint as a condition of the provision of treatment, payment, enrollment, or eligibility for benefits.

§ 164.508(b)(4): A covered entity may not condition treatment, payment, enrollment, or eligibility for benefits on the provision of an authorization to disclose protected health information (PHI) by the individual, with certain exceptions. For example, a covered health care provider may condition the provision of research-related treatment on provision of an authorization for the use or disclosure of PHI for such research.

§ 164.522(b)(2)(iii): A covered health care provider may not require an individual to explain their reasons for requesting communications be done in a confidential manner.

____   44. Employment-related disclosures

§ 164.504(f)(3)(iv): A group health plan may not disclose protected health information to a plan sponsor for the purpose of employment-related actions.

N. Safeguards

____   45. Specific actions must be taken to implement HIPAA regulations

§ 164.530(c)(1): A covered entity and business associate must have in place appropriate administrative, technical, and physical safeguards to protect the privacy of protected health information.

§ 164.530(i)(1): A covered entity and business associate must implement policies and procedures with respect to protected health information to comply with all HIPAA standards.

§ 164.530(i)(2): A covered entity and business associate must promptly change its policies and procedures to comply with changes in the law and document such changes.

____   46. Responsibility assignment

§ 164.530(a)(1)(i): A covered entity and business associate must designate a privacy official who is responsible for development and implementation of privacy policies and procedures.

(*Continued*)

Exhibit 11.1 Privacy Rule Compliance Checklist (*Continued*)

---

§ **164.530(a)(1)(ii):** A covered entity and business associate must designate a contact person responsible for receiving and addressing complaints.

O. Training

____ 47. Workforce training

§ **164.530(b)(1):** A covered entity and business associate must train all members of its workforce on its policies and procedures with respect to protected health information.

P. Authentication

____ 48. Requestor identity and authority verification

§ **164.514(h)(1)(i):** A covered entity must verify the identity of a person who requests protected health information and the authority of the person to have access to the information they request. A business associate that provides such access services on behalf of covered entities must also establish such identity verification procedures.

§ **164.514(h)(1)(ii):** A covered entity and business associate must obtain from the requestor any documents, statements, or representations required before disclosing protected health information. A business associate that provides such access services on behalf of covered entities must also establish such identity verification procedures.

Q. Mitigation

____ 49. Policy or procedure violation

§ **164.530(f):** A covered entity and business associate must mitigate to the extent possible the harmful effects of a violation of its privacy policies and procedures.

____ 50. Emergency disclosures

§ **164.522(a)(1)(iv):** If a covered entity (CE) discloses protected health information for emergency treatment, the CE must request that the health care provider not further use or disclose the information.

§ **164.512(c)(2):** A covered entity (CE) that discloses protected health information to a government authority concerning a victim of abuse must promptly notify the individual, with certain exceptions. For example, if the CE believes informing the individual would place the individual at risk of serious harm, or if the CE would be informing a personal representative, and the CE believes the personal representative is responsible for the abuse, neglect, or other injury, and that informing such person would not be in the best interests of the individual.

R. Mandatory documentation

____ 51. General

§ **164.530(j)(1)(ii):** A covered entity and business associate is required to keep copies of all communications that are required to be in writing.

§ **164.530(j)(1)(iii):** A covered entity and business associate is required to keep records of all actions, activities, and designations that are required to be documented.

____ 52. Personnel

§ **164.524(e)(2):** A covered entity and business associate must maintain documentation on the titles and offices of personnel responsible for receiving requests to access protected health information.

Exhibit 11.1   Privacy Rule Compliance Checklist (*Continued*)

§ **164.526(f):** A covered entity and business associate must maintain documentation on the titles of persons or offices responsible for processing requests for amendment of protected health information.

§ **164.528(d)(3):** A covered entity and business associate must retain records of the titles of persons or offices responsible for receiving and processing requests for an accounting of disclosures.

§ **164.530(b)(2)(ii):** A covered entity and business associate must maintain records of training that has been provided.

§ **164.530(e)(2):** A covered entity and business associate must maintain records of sanctions that are applied to members of its workforce who have failed to comply with its privacy and security policies and procedures.

_____   53. Access

§ **164.524(e)(1):** A covered entity and business associate must maintain documentation of the designated record sets (information used to make decisions about the individual) for which an individual may submit a request for access.

_____   54. Disclosures

§ **164.528(d)(1):** A covered entity and business associate must retain documentation on each disclosure of protected health information that could be the subject for a request for an accounting of disclosures. The information maintained must include all items that are required to be part of a disclosure accounting.

§ **164.528(d)(2):** A covered entity and business associate must maintain a record of written accountings of disclosures provided to individuals.

§ **164.508(b)(6):** A covered entity and business associate must document and retain all signed authorizations.

§ **164.522(a)(3):** A covered entity and business associate that agrees to restrictions on the use or disclosure of protected health information for treatment, payment, and operations must maintain written records of such agreements.

_____   55. Notice history

§ **164.520(e):** A covered entity must maintain copies of all published Notice of Privacy Practices and acknowledgments, and attempts to gain acknowledgment, of the receipt of such notices as part of the required documentation.

_____   56. Complaints

§ **164.530(d)(2):** A covered entity and business associate must maintain records of all complaints received and the disposition of each complaint.

§ **164.530(j)(1)(i):** A covered entity and business associate must document all policies and procedures adopted to protect the privacy of protected health information.

_____   57. Retention

§ **164.530(j)(2):** A covered entity and business associate must maintain all required documentation for a period of at least 6 years following its creation date or last date in effect.

(Continued)

Exhibit 11.1   Privacy Rule Compliance Checklist (*Continued*)

____   58. Business associate (BA) agreements

     § 164.502(e)(2): A covered entity and business associate must document the satisfactory assurances given by a business associates in the form of a contract, agreement, or other arrangement.

     § 164.504(e)(2): A business associate's agreement with a covered entity and business associate describing their satisfactory assurances must contain certain mandatory elements, including permitted uses and disclosures, appropriate safeguards, etc.

____   59. Hybrid and affiliated entities

     § 164.504(c)(3)(iii): A hybrid entity is responsible for designating the health care components of the organization.

     § 164.504(d)(2): If two or more covered entities are designated as affiliated (i.e., acting as a single covered entity), documentation of this designation must be maintained.

S. Demonstrating compliance

____   60. Mandatory disclosure

     § 164.502(a)(2)(ii): A covered entity and business associate must disclose protected health information to an individual when requested, and in accordance with § 164.524 or § 164.528, and if required to do so as part of a compliance review or investigation.

____   61. Record keeping

     § 160.310(a): A covered entity and business associate must keep appropriate records and submit appropriate reports to demonstrate HIPAA compliance, as directed by the Department of Health and Human Services.

____   62. Cooperation

     § 160.310(b): A covered entity and business associate must cooperate with compliance reviews and investigations.

     § 160.310(c)(1): A covered entity and business associate (CE) must permit HHS to inspect its facilities, books and records, and other information, including protected health information, that are pertinent to determining whether or not the CE is in compliance with HIPAA regulations.

T. Business Associate Agreements

____   63. Covered entity (CE) agreement compliance

     § 164.504 (e)(1)(ii): A covered entity is not in compliance with agreement requirements if it knew of a pattern of activity or practice of the business associate that violated the agreement, unless the covered entity took reasonable steps to cure the breach or end the violation, or to terminated the contract or arrangement, if feasible, if the violations and breaches were not cured.

____   64. BA agreement compliance

     § 164.504 (e)(1)(iii): A business associate is not in compliance an agreement if the business associate knew of a pattern of activity or practice of a subcontractor breached or violated the subcontractor's contract or other arrangement, unless the business associate took reasonable steps to cure the breach or end the violation, or to terminated the contract or arrangement, if feasible, if the violations and breaches were not cured.

Exhibit 11.1   Privacy Rule Compliance Checklist (*Continued*)

____   65. CE's BA contracts

§ 164.504 (e)(2)(i): A contract between the covered entity and a business associate must establish the permitted and required uses and disclosures of protected health information by the business associate. The contract may not authorize the business associate to use or further disclose the information in violation of the contract. The contract may permit the business associate to disclose protected health information to subcontractors to support the management, administration, and/or data aggregation services relating to the health care operations of the covered entity.

____   66. BA's contracts with subcontractors

§ 164.504 (e)(2)(ii): Business associates (BAs) must not further disclose the information to a subcontractor other than allowed by the BA contract or as required by law. BAs must have contracts with subcontractors to whom access or possession of PHI is provided that generally has the same requirements within it that the CE's contract with the BA has. The subcontractor is essentially a BA of the BA.

a. Termination of contract

§ 164.504 (e)(iii): A BA contract must be terminated if the CE or BA determines the terms of the contract have been violation. Authorize termination of the contract by the covered entity, if the covered entity determines that the business associate has violated a material term of the contract.

b. Governmental entities contracts

§ 164.504 (e)(3)(i): If a covered entity (CE) and its business associate (BA) are both governmental entities the CE may comply with the contract requirement by using a memorandum of understanding with the business associate that contains all the terms required of a BA contract. The CE may also comply if other law requirements accomplish same the objectives.

c. Governmental PHI disclosures to BAs

§ 164.504 (e)(3)(ii): If a business associate (BA) is required by law to perform a function or activity on behalf of a covered entity (CE), the CE may disclose protected health information to the BA as necessary to comply with the law without having a BA contract in place, provided the CE attempts to obtain satisfactory safeguards assurances. If the CE cannot obtain such assurance, it must document the attempt and reasons why the assurances could not be obtained.

d. Governmental termination contract clauses

§ 164.504 (e)(3)(iii): A covered entity may omit the termination authorization from the contract if it is if inconsistent with the legal obligations of the covered entity or its business associate.

e. Governmental use of limited data sets

§ 164.504 (e)(3)(iv): A covered entity may disclose only a limited data set to a business associate to carry out a health care operations function if the covered entity has a data use agreement with the business associate.

(Continued)

Exhibit 11.1   Privacy Rule Compliance Checklist (*Continued*)

_____   67. PHI to BAs for management and legal requirements

§ **164.504 (e)(4)(i):** The contract/arrangement between the covered entity and the business associate may permit the business associate to protected health information if necessary for BA management and administration responsibilities, or to comply with legal requirements.

   a. Permitted BA disclosures

§ **164.504 (e)(4)(ii):** The BA contract may permit the business associate (BA) to disclose the protected health information as required by law; or if the BA obtains reasonable assurances the PHI disclosed will be safeguarded and disclosed only as required by law; and if the recipient agrees to notify the BA in the event of a PHI breach.

   b. Business associate contracts with subcontractors

§ **164.504 (e)(5):** Implementation specifications: The requirements within a contract between a business associate (BA) and a BA that is a subcontractor are the same as the requirements between a covered entity and business associate.

U. Disclosures for research, marketing, and fund-raising

_____   68. Fund-raising communications—no authorization necessary

§ **164.514 (f)(1):** A covered entity may use, or disclose to a business associate or to an institutionally related foundation, certain specified protected health information for the purpose of raising funds for its own benefit, without an authorization.

   a. Fund-raising requirements

§ **164.514 (f)(2):** A covered entity may not use or disclose protected health information unless a statement that such use may occur is included in the covered entity's notice of privacy practices. The covered entity must provide the individual with an opportunity to opt-out of receiving further fundraising communications, and the covered entity must comply with that request unless the individual opts-back in. A covered entity may not condition treatment or payment upon the receipt of fundraising communications.

   b. Uses and disclosures for research purposes

§ **164.512 (i):** A covered entity may use or disclose protected health information without the written authorization of the individual only under certain specific situations. The covered entity is otherwise required to inform the individual of research activities and allow the individual to agree to allowing their protected health information to be used.

_____   69. Authorization required for marketing

§ **164.508(a)(3):** A covered entity and business associate must obtain an authorization to use protected health information for marketing activities, with certain exceptions. For example, except if the communication is in the form of a face-to-face communication made by a covered entity and business associate to an individual; or a promotional gift of nominal value provided by the covered entity and business associate.

Exhibit 11.1   Privacy Rule Compliance Checklist (*Continued*)

V. Hybrid entities

_____   70. Wall between regulated and unregulated business components

§ **164.504(c)(2):** A hybrid entity must ensure that health care components do not disclose protected health information to non-health care components of the organization.

W. Group health plans

_____   71. Disclosures to plan sponsors

§ **164.504(f)(1)(i):** A group health plan, a health insurer, or an HMO, with respect to the group health plan, must ensure that the plan documents restrict uses and disclosures of protected health information by plan sponsors before such information may be disclosed to the plan sponsor, with certain exceptions. For example, the group health plan may disclose summary health information to the plan sponsor, if the plan sponsor requests the summary health information for the purpose of obtaining premium bids from health plans for providing health insurance coverage under the group health plan; or modifying, amending, or terminating the group health plan.

§ **164.504(f)(2):** Plan documents of group health plans must contain certain mandatory elements.

§ **164.504(f)(3)(iii):** A group health plan may not disclose protected health information to a plan sponsor unless its notice of information practices contains a separate statement to that effect.

X. Health care clearinghouses

_____   72. Compliance requirements

§ **164.500(b)(1):** A health care clearinghouse that is a business associate (BA) of a covered entity may use or disclose protected health information only as permitted in the BA's agreement. Additionally, it must comply with sections of the privacy rule specific to clearinghouses.

§ **164.500(b)(2):** A health care clearinghouse that creates or receives protected health information other than as a business associate of another covered entity must comply with all HIPAA standards and requirements.

Y. Public interest disclosures

_____   73. Disclosures for law enforcement purposes

§ **164.512(f):** A covered entity may disclose only certain kinds of protected health information for law enforcement purposes to law enforcement officials.

_____   74. Disclosures about victims of abuse

§ **164.512(c)(1):** A covered entity may disclose protected health information concerning suspected victims of abuse, neglect, or domestic violence to appropriate government authority only if the individual agrees to the disclosure, the disclosure is required by law, or the disclosure is authorized by state statute and is necessary to prevent harm.

_____   75. Judicial and administrative proceedings

§ **164.512(e)(1):** A covered entity and business associate may disclose protected health information in the course of a judicial or administrative proceeding only in certain circumstances.

(*Continued*)

Exhibit 11.1   Privacy Rule Compliance Checklist (*Continued*)

§ **164.512(e)(1)(i):** A covered entity and business associate that discloses protected health information in response to a court order may disclose only that information expressly authorized by the order.

§ **164.512(e)(1)(ii):** A covered entity and business associate may disclose protected health information in response to a subpoena or discovery request only when accompanied by a written statement and accompanying documentation demonstrating certain satisfactory assurances that contain certain mandatory elements.

_____ 76. Disclosures about decedents

§ **164.512(g):** A covered entity may disclose protected health care information to coroners, medical examiners, and funeral directors only as necessary to carry out their duties.

_____ 77. Averting a serious threat to health or safety

§ **164.512(j):** A covered entity and business associate may disclose information to avert a serious threat to health or safety only if the disclosure is necessary and is made to a person able to prevent or reduce the threat.

Z. De-identified data disclosures

_____ 78. De-identified data

§ **164.514(b):** A covered entity may disclose de-identified information only if the de-identification procedure meets certain basic requirements.

_____ 79. Use and disclosure of de-identified PHI

§ **164.502(d):** A covered entity and business associate may do the following with de-identified PHI:

(1) Uses and disclosures to create de-identified information. A covered entity may use protected health information to create information that is not individually identifiable health information or disclose protected health information only to a business associate for such purpose, whether or not the de-identified information is to be used by the covered entity.

(2) Uses and disclosures of de-identified information. Health information that meets the standard and implementation specifications for de-identification under § 164.514(a) and (b) is considered not to be individually identifiable health information, i.e., de-identified. The requirements of this subpart do not apply to information that has been de-identified in accordance with the applicable requirements of § 164.514, provided that:

(i) Disclosure of a code or other means of record identification designed to enable coded or otherwise de-identified information to be re-identified constitutes disclosure of protected health information; and

(ii) If de-identified information is re-identified, a covered entity may use or disclose such re-identified information only as permitted or required by this subpart.

_____ 80. Limited data sets

§ **164.514(e)(2):** A covered entity and business associate may disclose information contained in a limited data set only if certain data identifiers are removed.

§ **164.514(e)(3):** A covered entity and business associate may disclose information contained in a limited data set only for specific purposes.

Exhibit 11.1   Privacy Rule Compliance Checklist (*Continued*)

§ **164.514(e)(4):** A covered entity and business associate may disclose information contained in a limited data set only if it at first obtains a data use agreement with certain mandatory provisions.

AA. Organized health care arrangements

____   81. Joint notice

§ **164.520(d)(1):** Covered entities that participate in an organized health care arrangement must publish a joint Notice of Privacy Practices.

§ **164.520(d)(2):** The notice provided by an organized health care arrangement (OHCA) must include a description of the entities or classes of entities to which the notice applies. It must also contain a description of the service delivery sites and state that the covered entities in the OHCA will share protected health information with each other.

PART III
HIPAA
SECURITY RULE

12

SECURITY RULE
REQUIREMENTS OVERVIEW

12.1 Introduction to the Security Rule

The Health Insurance Portability and Accountability Act (HIPAA) Security Rule was originally published in a proposed form on August 12, 1998. The long anticipated final Security Rule made its way to the Federal Register on February 20, 2003. Subsequently, the Breach Notification Rule (part of the Health Information Technology for Economic and Clinical Health [HITECH] Act of 2009[1]) and the HIPAA Omnibus Rule,[2] published in the Federal Register on January 25, 2013, contain further updates to the Security Rule.

The Security Rule covers all protected health information (PHI) that a covered entity (CE), business associate (BA), or any BA subcontractor creates, receives, maintains, or transmits in an electronic format. In the text of the original Security Rule, the Department of Health and Human Services (HHS) summarized it as follows:

This final rule adopts standards for the security of electronic PHI to be implemented by health plans, health care clearinghouses, and certain health care providers. The use of the security standards will improve the Medicare and Medicaid programs, and other federal health programs and private health programs, and the effectiveness and efficiency of the health care industry in general by establishing a level of protection for certain electronic health information.[3] Overall, even with the latest updates from the 2013 Omnibus Rule, the Security Rule can be characterized as follows:

- A set of information security "best practices" that make good business sense
- A minimum security baseline that is intended to help prevent unauthorized use and disclosure of PHI
- An outline of what to do

- Something that encourages health care organizations to embrace e-business and leverage the benefits that an improved technology infrastructure can provide
- Standards to reduce the threats, vulnerabilities, and overall risks to PHI along with their associated costs and negative impact on the organization

On the other hand, the Security Rule is not:

- A prescriptive set of how-to instructions covering exactly how to secure PHI
- A set of rules that must be implemented the same way for every organization

The overall goals of the Security Rule revolve around the confidentiality, integrity, and availability of electronic PHI. These terms are defined as follows:

- *Confidentiality*: The requirement that data stored or transmitted is revealed only to those authorized to see it.
- *Integrity*: The requirement that data remains free from unauthorized creation, modification, or deletion.
- *Availability*: The requirement that data is available when it is needed.

When the proper policies, procedures, and technologies are in place, PHI can be reasonably protected against known threats and vulnerabilities. This will allow all organizations (CEs, BAs, and their subcontractors) to protect against unauthorized uses and disclosures of PHI—a main consideration of the HIPAA Privacy Rule. We go into detail on some of the specific policies, procedures, and technologies that businesses should consider implementing in Chapters 14 and 22.

The Security Rule was designed to be:

- *Technology neutral*: Focuses on what needs to be done rather than how to do it or what technologies to use
- *Scalable*: Does not require all organizations to implement the same exact policies, procedures, and technologies—an organization's information systems' complexity will essentially define its Security Rule implementation complexity

- *Flexible*: Allows organizations to take their size, capabilities, risks, and costs into consideration when trying to determine whether or not to implement certain security systems
- *Comprehensive*: Covers the technical, business, and behavioral issues related to securing PHI

HHS references several key terms in the Security Rule that deserve mentioning. As defined in the Security Rule, these terms are as follows:

- *Facility*: The physical premises and interior and exterior of a building.
- *Security incident*: The attempted or successful unauthorized access, use, disclosure, modification, or destruction of information or interference with system operations in an information system.
- *System*: An interconnected set of information resources under the same direct management control that shares common functionality. A system normally includes hardware, software, information, data, applications, communications, and people.
- *Workstation*: An electronic computing device, for example, a laptop or desktop computer or any other device that performs similar functions, and electronic media stored in its immediate environment.

Note: For a full glossary of all terms that are defined within all the HIPAA rules, see Appendix B.

As we noted in Chapter 1, the HITECH Act covers four main areas—three of which impact security directly:

1. The extension of the HIPAA Security Rule and the privacy and security provisions of the HITECH Act to BAs
2. Modification of the Breach Notification Rule
3. Changes to the HIPAA Privacy Rule requirements, some of which are mandated by the HITECH Act and some of which address problems with the original standards that have emerged over time
4. Modifications to the HIPAA Enforcement Rule to implement the HITECH Act

The 2013 Omnibus Rule also made changes to the definition of breach (see the definition provided later in this section) as well as any needed risk assessment requirements after a breach. If any impermissible use or disclosure of PHI occurs, then it must be presumed to be a breach unless the CE or BA can demonstrate (and document) the low probability that PHI was exposed. Therein lies the dilemma.

When a security breach occurs, unless and until you have all the necessary security controls in place, such as event logging and monitoring, and can somehow "prove" that PHI was encrypted on the system or systems in which it was accessed, it is going to be difficult to make your case.[4] This is why it is so important to ensure you have the proper technical controls and business processes in place *before* something happens.

Related Omnibus Rule requirements for PHI breaches revolve around risk assessment of what actually occurred. At least three of the following must be considered:

1. The nature and extent of the PHI presumed to be breached
2. The unauthorized party who gained access
3. Whether the PHI was actually viewed or acquired
4. The extent to which the risk has been mitigated

A key requirement that began with the HITECH Act, and was further clarified with the 2013 Omnibus Rule, is the Safe Harbor provided when PHI is encrypted. With Safe Harbor, if a breach occurs but it can be shown that PHI was encrypted using one of the specified methods, then a risk assessment does not have to be performed and breach notifications to the affected parties are not required. So, you have a sort of free pass if, and only if, you implement encryption controls for systems that house PHI such as databases, workstations, and mobile devices.

A good example of what can happen when PHI is not encrypted occurred in the fall of 2013 when two laptops containing PHI of over 800,000 patients were stolen from Horizon Blue Cross Blue Shield of New Jersey.[5] Apparently the laptops had physical locks on them but no disk encryption. Ironically, the cost to encrypt the laptop drives could very well have been less than the cost of the laptop locks (which tend to be priced at around $30 each).

Make no mistake: encryption (full disk encryption, database encryption, etc.) is not the ultimate solution for protecting PHI. It can have its own weaknesses if not implemented and managed properly. However, encryption can buy you some good peace of mind if it is done the right way. We provide further guidance on what it takes to build a HIPAA-compliant technology infrastructure in Chapter 22.

Some additional terms relating to security and compliance introduced in the HITECH Act and the 2013 Omnibus Rule include the following:

- *Reasonable cause*: an act or omission in which a covered entity or business associate knew, or by exercising reasonable diligence would have known, that the act or omission violated an administrative simplification provision, but in which the covered entity or business associate did not act with willful neglect.
- *Reasonable diligence*: the business care and prudence expected from a person seeking to satisfy a legal requirement under similar circumstances.
- *Willful neglect*: conscious, intentional failure or reckless indifference to the obligation to comply with the administrative simplification provision violated.
- *Breach*: the acquisition, access, use, or disclosure of protected health information in a manner not permitted ... which compromises the security or privacy of the protected health information.

These terms are important for management and other decision makers to fully understand given the ramifications of noncompliance with HIPAA.

The Security Rule, similar to all other HIPAA Administrative Simplification rules, has a set of effective dates and compliance deadlines. The effective date for the original Security Rule was April 21, 2003. Most CEs had two years to implement and comply with the rule, which made the effective deadline April 21, 2005. The exception to this was small health plans with annual receipts of $5 million or less. They were required to be in compliance by April 21, 2006. Technically, the majority of the Security Rule requirements were to be in place by April 14, 2003, to meet the Privacy Rule requirements of having certain administrative, physical, and technical safeguards in place to protect PHI. Given these age-old deadlines, we still see both CEs and BAs that have yet to perform *proper* security assessments of their environments.

The latest deadline for Security Rule compliance as specified in the HIPAA Omnibus Rule was September 23, 2013. CEs and BAs alike must comply with this deadline. Again, based on what we have seen in our work, many organizations have a long way to go—especially BAs that have largely been disconnected from compliance to this point.

12.2 General Rules for Security Rule Compliance

In § 164.306 of the Security Rule, there are various general rules to which every CE must adhere:

- Ensure the confidentiality, integrity, and availability of all electronic PHI that the CE creates, receives, maintains, or transmits.
- Protect against any reasonably anticipated threats or hazards to the security or integrity of PHI.
- Protect against any reasonably anticipated uses or disclosures of PHI.
- Ensure that its workforce complies with the Security Rule.
- Comply with the Security Rule standards with respect to all electronic PHI.
- Review and modify security measures as needed to ensure reasonable and appropriate protection of electronic PHI.

In addition, as outlined in § 164.316 of the Security Rule, CEs must consider the following security policy, procedure, and documentation requirements:

- CEs must implement reasonable and appropriate policies and procedures to comply with the standards, implementation specifications, or other requirements of the Security Rule.
- CEs may change their policies and procedures at any time provided that they document the changes and implement them in accordance with the Security Rule.

- CEs must maintain their Security Rule policies and procedures in written or electronic form.
- CEs must maintain a written or electronic record of any actions, activities, or assessments related to the Security Rule.
- CEs must retain all of this documentation for at least six years from the date it was created or 6 years from the date when it was last in effect, whichever is longer.
- CEs must make this documentation available to anyone responsible for implementing itsassociated procedures.
- CEs must review this documentation periodically, and update as needed based on any environmental or operational changes that may affect the security of electronic PHI.

In addition, regarding the flexible characteristic of the Security Rule, CEs may use any security measures that allow them to reasonably and appropriately implement the standards and implementation specifications of the Security Rule. When deciding which security measures to use, CEs must consider the following factors:

- Their size, complexity, and capabilities
- Their geographic locations
- Their technical infrastructure, hardware, and software security capabilities
- The cost of security measures
- The probability and criticality of potential risks to electronic PHI

12.2.1 Required versus Addressable

Another general rule that deserves closer attention is that of required versus addressable implementation specifications. The 18 Security Rule standards contain a total of 42 implementation specifications that are either required or addressable. There are a total of 20 required implementation specifications that must be implemented by all CEs regardless of the outcome of their risk analysis, and a total of 22 addressable implementation specifications that must be considered based solely on the outcome of their risk analysis. These factors include the CE's size, existing security controls in place, and the cost to mitigate the risks that are discovered. CEs have the options listed in Exhibit 12.1 when handling these addressable implementation specifications.

The steps in Exhibit 12.1 have been a considerable source of confusion and discussion within the industry. The addressable option does not imply that CEs can simply make their own rules or ignore the implementation specifications altogether if an implementation specification simply does not seem like a good fit or may be an inconvenience. It means that CEs have the flexibility to make their own choices based on their risks, but there must be genuine and documented business reasons behind these decisions.

Exhibit 12.1   Scenarios

Scenario 1
IF:
- The implementation specification is reasonable and appropriate for the CE

THEN:
- It must be implemented

Scenario 2
IF:
- The specification is unreasonable and inappropriate for the CE, but the overall standard cannot be met otherwise

THEN:
- The CE must:
  1. Implement an alternate security measure to accomplish the same goal
  2. Document the decision not to implement the specification
  3. Document why it is unreasonable and inappropriate
  4. Document how the overall standard is being met otherwise

Scenario 3
IF:
- The specification is unreasonable and inappropriate for the CE, but the overall standard can be met without alternate measures

THEN:
- The CE must:
  1. Document the decision to not implement the specification
  2. Document why it is unreasonable and inappropriate
  3. Document how the overall standard is being met otherwise

Our take on handling addressable implementation specifications is that CEs should consider treating every implementation specification as if it is required yet scalable and flexible. The time spent trying to determine whether or not something should be implemented based on the results of a risk analysis may very well be more difficult than implementing the specification itself. The key here is to document everything to support your decisions.

12.3 Insight into the Security Rule

The Security Rule is broken down into three major sections, as shown in Exhibit 12.2. As you will see in Exhibit 12.2, HHS outlines what needs to be done, but does not give specifics on how to do it. In the information in Exhibit 12.2, we outline the actual Security Rule verbiage for each standard and implementation specification, whether each implementation specification is required or addressable, and some tips on what you can use to meet each standard or specification. Keep in mind these are not the only possible solutions to meet each particular standard or implementation specification—just some information security best practices that have worked for us and others in the past. Also, just because we list it does not necessarily mean you should use it. We will not go into technical detail in these tips, so be sure to refer to Chapter 21 for more specific technical information and practical advice on certain technologies you can implement in your HIPAA compliance efforts. In addition, Appendix C contains a listing of some vendors and products that you may be able to use and benefit from as well.

12.4 Other Organizational Requirements

The Security Rule outlines specific organizational requirements in addition to the overall administrative, physical, and technical safeguards we outlined earlier. These requirements are for hybrid entities, affiliated CEs, and governmental entities, and are covered in Security Rule sections § 164.105 and § 164.314. If your organization

Exhibit 12.2 Interpretation of the Security Rule

---

1. Administrative safeguard requirements
   a. Security management process
       i. Defined in the rule as
           "Implement policies and procedures to prevent, detect, contain, and correct security violations."
       ii. Implementation specifications
           A. Risk analysis (required)
               What the rule says
               "Conduct an accurate and thorough assessment of the potential risks and vulnerabilities to the confidentiality, integrity, and availability of electronic protected health information held by the covered entity."
               What can be used to assist in meeting this specification
               Chapter 13 of this book
               NIST Special Publication 800-30 Guide for Conducting Risk Assessments or similar methodology
               Risk analysis software
               Network and application vulnerability assessment software and expertise for performing the necessary manual validation and analysis
           B. Risk management (required)
               What the rule says
               "Implement security measures sufficient to reduce risks and vulnerabilities to a reasonable and appropriate level to comply with § 164.306(a)."
               What can be used to assist in meeting this specification
               Chapter 12 of this book
               NIST Special Publication 800-30 Guide for Conducting Risk Assessments or similar methodology
               Risk analysis software
               Security policy management software
           C. Sanction policy (required)
               What the rule says
               "Apply appropriate sanctions against workforce members who fail to comply with the security policies and procedures of the covered entity."
               What can be used to assist in meeting this specification
               Chapter 14 of this book
               Security policy management software to store and help train everyone on the policy
               Various books and Internet resources on security policy development
           D. Information system activity review (required)
               What the rule says
               "Implement procedures to regularly review records of information system activity, such as audit logs, access reports, and security incident tracking reports."
               What can be used to assist in meeting this specification
               Intrusion prevention system (IPS)
               Logging capabilities built into your operating systems (OSs) and/or applications
               Third-party managed security services provider that can handle these functions for you

Exhibit 12.2   Interpretation of the Security Rule (*Continued*)

b. Assigned security responsibility
   i. Defined in the rule as:
       "Identify the security official who is responsible for the development and
       implementation of the policies and procedures required by this subpart for the entity."
   ii. Implementation specifications
       A. None
           What can be used to assist in meeting this specification
       B. The security officer job description found in Appendix B of this book
c. Workforce security
   i. Defined in the rule as:
       "Implement policies and procedures to ensure that all members of its workforce
       have appropriate access to electronic protected health information, as provided
       under paragraph (a)(4) of this section, and to prevent those workforce members
       who do not have access under paragraph (a)(4) of this section from obtaining
       access to electronic protected health information."
   ii. Implementation specifications
       A. Authorization and/or supervision (addressable)
           What the rule says
           "Implement procedures for the authorization and/or supervision of workforce
           members who work with electronic protected health information or in loca-
           tions where it might be accessed."
           What can be used to assist in meeting this specification
           OS, application, and database access controls
           User IDs and passwords
           Biometrics, tokens, or other authentication devices
           Event auditing and logging software
           HR, supervisor, and manager education on what to look for
       B. Workforce clearance procedure (addressable)
           What the rule says
           "Implement procedures to determine that the access of a workforce member
           to electronic protected health information is appropriate."
           What can be used to assist in meeting this specification
           Workforce member job descriptions
           HR, supervisor, and manager education on what to look for
       C. Termination procedures (addressable)
           What the rule says
           "Implement procedures for terminating access to electronic protected health
           information when the employment of, or other arrangement with, a workforce
           member ends or as required by determinations made as specified in para-
           graph (a)(3)(ii)(B) of this section."
           What can be used to assist in meeting this specification
           HR, supervisor, and manager education on what to look for
           Strong line of communication between HR and IT
d. Information access management
   i. Defined in the rule as:

(Continued)

Exhibit 12.2   Interpretation of the Security Rule (*Continued*)

"Implement policies and procedures for authorizing access to electronic protected health information that are consistent with the applicable requirements of subpart E of this part."

ii. Implementation specifications

   A. Isolating health care clearinghouse functions (required)

   What the rule says

   "If a healthcare clearinghouse is part of a larger organization, the clearinghouse must implement policies and procedures that protect the electronic protected health information of the clearinghouse from unauthorized access by the larger organization."

   What can be used to assist in meeting this specification

   Network perimeter devices such as firewalls, routers, and switches that can be configured to segment the network

   OS, application, and database access controls.

   B. Access authorization (addressable)

   What the rule says

   "Implement policies and procedures for granting access to electronic protected health information, for example, through access to a workstation, transaction, program, process, or other mechanism."

   What can be used to assist in meeting this specification

   HR, supervisor, and manager education on what to look for

   Strong line of communication between HR and IT

   Security policy management software to store the policies and procedures and maintain a record of user awareness and sign-off

   C. Access establishment and modification (addressable)

   What the rule says

   "Implement policies and procedures that, based upon the entity's access authorization policies, establish, document, review, and modify a user's right of access to a workstation, transaction, program, or process."

   What can be used to assist in meeting this specification

   HR, supervisor, and manager education on what to look for

   Strong line of communication between HR and IT

   Security policy management software to store the policies and procedures and maintain a record of user awareness and sign-off

e. Security awareness and training

   i. Defined in the rule as

   "Implement a security awareness and training program for all members of its workforce (including management)."

   ii. Implementation specifications

   A. Security reminders (addressable)

   What the rule says

   "Periodic security updates."

   What can be used to assist in meeting this specification

   Screen savers

   Periodic security awareness e-mails

   Log-in banners

Exhibit 12.2   Interpretation of the Security Rule (*Continued*)

Periodic classroom training

Lunch and learns

Newsletter or magazine articles

Pamphlets and brochures

Posters around the office

Promotional trinkets such as coffee mugs, mouse pads, sticky notes, and so forth

Intranet website

B. Protection from malicious software

What the rule says

"Procedures for guarding against, detecting, and reporting malicious software."

What can be used to assist in meeting this specification

Anti-malware software on all systems

Personal firewall software

C. Log-in monitoring (addressable)

What the rule says

"Procedures for monitoring log-in attempts and reporting discrepancies."

What can be used to assist in meeting this specification

Logging capabilities into your OSs, applications, and databases

HR, supervisor, and manager education on what to look for

Strong line of communication between HR and IT

D. Password management (addressable)

What the rule says

"Procedures for creating, changing, and safeguarding passwords."

What can be used to assist in meeting this specification

Password features built into OSs and/or applications

Directory services software

Single sign-on management software

User education on this matter

f. Security incident procedures

  i. Defined in the rule as:

  "Implement policies and procedures to address security incidents."

  ii. Implementation specifications

    A. Response and reporting (required)

What the rule says

"Identify and respond to suspected or known security incidents; mitigate, to the extent practicable, harmful effects of security incidents that are known to the covered entity; and document security incidents and their outcomes."

What can be used to assist in meeting this specification

Chapter 23 of this book

IPS

Miscellaneous forensics analysis tools

(*Continued*)

Exhibit 12.2   Interpretation of the Security Rule (*Continued*)

g. Contingency plan
   i. Defined in the rule as:
      "Establish (and implement as needed) policies and procedures for responding to an emergency or other occurrence (for example, fire, vandalism, system failure, and natural disaster) that damages systems that contain electronic protected health information."
   ii. Implementation specifications
      A. Data backup plan (required)
          What the rule says
          "Establish and implement procedures to create and maintain retrievable exact copies of electronic protected health information."
          What can be used to assist in meeting this specification
          Chapter 23 of this book
          Tape or disk-to-disk backup
          CD, DVD, or other optical backup
          Cloud-based backup
          Redundant computer systems
      B. Disaster recovery plan (required)
          What the rule says
          "Establish (and implement as needed) procedures to restore any loss of data."
          What can be used to assist in meeting this specification
          Chapter 23 of this book
          Offsite failover facilities
          Uninterruptible power supplies
          Backup generators
      C. Emergency mode operation plan (required)
          What the rule says
          "Establish (and implement as needed) procedures to restore any loss of data."
          What can be used to assist in meeting this specification
          Chapter 23 of this book
          Offsite failover facilities
          Uninterruptible power supplies
          Backup generators
      D. Testing and revision procedure (addressable)
          What the rule says
          "Establish (and implement as needed) procedures to enable continuation of critical business processes for protection of the security of electronic protected health information while operating in emergency mode."
          What can be used to assist in meeting this specification
          Chapter 23 of this book
      E. Applications and data criticality analysis (addressable)
          What the rule says
          "Assess the relative criticality of specific applications and data in support of other contingency plan components."
          What can be used to assist in meeting this specification
          Chapters 13 and 23 of this book

Exhibit 12.2   Interpretation of the Security Rule (*Continued*)

The results of your risk analysis
NIST Special Publication 800-30 Guide for Conducting Risk Assessments or similar methodology
Risk analysis software

h. Evaluation
  i. Defined in the rule as:
  "Perform a periodic technical and nontechnical evaluation, based initially on the standards implemented under this rule, and subsequently, in response to environmental or operational changes affecting the security of electronic protected health information, which establishes the extent to which an entity's security policies and procedures meet the requirements of this sub-part."
  ii. Implementation specifications
    A. None
    What can be used to assist in meeting this specification
    Chapter 12 of this book
    The results of your initial risk analysis
    NIST Special Publication 800-30 Guide for Conducting Risk Assessments or similar methodology
    Risk analysis automation and management software
    Network and application vulnerability assessment software
    Security policy management software to store the policies and procedures and maintain a record of user awareness and sign-off

i. Business associate contracts and other arrangement
  i. Defined in the rule as:
  "A covered entity, in accordance with § 164.306, may permit a business associate to create, receive, maintain, or transmit electronic protected health information on the covered entity's behalf only if the covered entity obtains satisfactory assurances, in accordance with § 164.314(a), that the business associate will appropriately safeguard the information. This standard does not apply with respect to:
    (i) The transmission by a covered entity of electronic protected health information to a health care provider concerning the treatment of an individual;
    (ii) The transmission of electronic protected health information by a group health plan or an HMO or health insurance issuer on behalf of a group health plan to a plan sponsor, to the extent that the requirements of § 164.314(b) and § 164.504(f) apply and are met; or
    (iii) The transmission of electronic protected health information from or to other agencies providing the services at § 164.502(e)(1)(ii)(C), when the covered entity is a health plan that is a government program providing public benefits, if the requirements of § 164.502(e)(1)(ii)(C) are met.
    A covered entity that violates the satisfactory assurances it provided as a business associate of another covered entity will be in noncompliance with the standards, implementation specifications, and requirements of this paragraph and § 164.314(a)."
  ii. Implementation specifications
    A. Written contract or other arrangement (required)
    What the rule says

(Continued)

Exhibit 12.2   Interpretation of the Security Rule (*Continued*)

"Document the satisfactory assurances required by paragraph (b)(1) of this section through a written contract or other arrangement with the business associate that meets the applicable requirements of § 164.314(a)."

What can be used to assist in meeting this specification

Chapter 21 of this book

Outside consulting or legal counsel

2. Physical safeguard requirements

   a.   Facility access controls

      i. Defined in the rule as:

"Implement policies and procedures to limit physical access to its electronic information systems and the facility or facilities in which they are housed, while ensuring that properly authorized access is allowed."

     ii. Implementation specifications

         A.   Written contract or other arrangement (required)

            What the rule says

"Establish (and implement as needed) procedures that allow facility access in support of restoration of lost data under the disaster recovery plan and emergency mode operations plan in the event of an emergency."

What can be used to assist in meeting this specification

Chapters 14 and 23 of this book

Offsite failover facilities

Uninterruptible power supplies

Backup generators

         B.   Facility security plan (addressable)

            What the rule says

"Implement policies and procedures to safeguard the facility and the equipment therein from unauthorized physical access, tampering, and theft."

What can be used to assist in meeting this specification

Chapters 14 and 22 of this book

Various books and Internet resources on security policy development

ID badges, biometrics, locks, and other physical security devices

Security policy management software to store the policies and procedures and maintain a record of user awareness and sign-off

         C.   Access control and validation (addressable)

            What the rule says

"Implement procedures to control and validate a person's access to facilities based on their role or function, including visitor control, and control of access to software programs for testing and revision."

What can be used to assist in meeting this specification

Chapters 14 and 22 of this book

ID badges, biometrics, locks, and other physical security devices

         D.   Maintenance records (addressable)

            What the rule says

"Implement policies and procedures to document repairs and modifications to the physical components of a facility which are related to security (for example, hardware, walls, doors, and locks)."

Exhibit 12.2   Interpretation of the Security Rule (*Continued*)

What can be used to assist in meeting this specification

Chapter 13 of this book

Various books and Internet resources on security policy development

Security policy management software to store the policies and procedures

b.   Workstation use

   i.   Defined in the rule as:

"Implement policies and procedures that specify the proper functions to be performed, the manner in which those functions are to be performed, and the physical attributes of the surroundings of a specific workstation or class of workstation that can access electronic protected health information."

   ii.   Implementation specifications

      A.   None

What can be used to assist in meeting this specification

Chapters 14 and 22 of this book

The results of your risk analysis

Various books and Internet resources on security policy development

Security policy management software to store the policies and procedures

c.   Workstation security

   i.   Defined in the rule as:

"Implement physical safeguards for all workstations that access electronic protected health information, to restrict access to authorized users."

   ii.   Implementation specifications

      A.   None

What can be used to assist in meeting this specification

Chapter 22 of this book

The results of your risk analysis

Moving computers or monitors

Secured rooms

Curtains

Partitions

Standard user ID and passwords

Biometrics, tokens, or other authentication devices

OS, application, and database access controls

d.   Device and media controls

   i.   Defined in the rule as:

"Implement policies and procedures that govern the receipt and removal of hardware and electronic media that contain electronic protected health information into and out of a facility, and the movement of these items within the facility."

   ii.   Implementation specifications

      A.   Disposal (required)

What the rule says

"Implement policies and procedures to address the final disposition of electronic protected health information, and/or the hardware or electronic media on which it is stored."

What can be used to assist in meeting this specification

Chapters 14 and 22 of this book

Media cross shredder

Full disk encryption

(Continued)

Exhibit 12.2   Interpretation of the Security Rule (*Continued*)

Bulk eraser or degausser

Physical destruction

Various books and Internet resources on security policy development

Security policy management software to store the policies and procedures

B.   Media reuse (required)

What the rule says

"Implement procedures for removal of electronic protected health information from electronic media before the media are made available for reuse."

What can be used to assist in meeting this specification

Full disk encryption

Bulk eraser or degausser

Disk wiping tools

C.   Accountability (addressable)

What the rule says

"Maintain a record of the movements of hardware and electronic media and any person responsible therefore."

What can be used to assist in meeting this specification

Chapter 14 of this book

Various books and Internet resources on security policy development

Security policy management software to store the policies and procedures

D.   Data backup and storage (addressable)

What the rule says

"Create a retrievable, exact copy of electronic protected health information, when needed, before movement of equipment."

What can be used to assist in meeting this specification

Chapter 23 of this book

Tape or disk-to-disk backup

CD, DVD, or other optical backup

Cloud-based backup

Redundant computer systems

3. Technical safeguard requirements

    a.   Access control

       i.   Defined in the rule as:

"Implement technical policies and procedures for electronic information systems that maintain electronic protected health information to allow access only to those persons or software programs that have been granted access rights as specified in § 164.308(a)(4)."

      ii.   Implementation specifications

         A.   Unique user identification (required)

What the rule says

"Assign a unique name and/or number for identifying and tracking user identity."

What can be used to assist in meeting this specification

User ID management built into OSs, applications, and databases

Directory services

Single sign-on software

Exhibit 12.2   Interpretation of the Security Rule (*Continued*)

      B. Emergency access procedure (required)

          What the rule says

          "Establish (and implement as needed) procedures for obtaining necessary electronic protected health information during an emergency."

          What can be used to assist in meeting this specification

          Chapter 23 of this book

          Uninterruptible power supplies

          Backup generators

      C. Automatic log-off (addressable)

          What the rule says

          "Implement electronic procedures that terminate an electronic session after a predetermined time of inactivity."

          What can be used to assist in meeting this specification

          Screen savers built into OSs, applications, and databases

          Timeout configuration settings built into OSs or applications

          Proximity sensors

      D. Encryption and decryption (addressable)

          What the rule says

          "Implement a mechanism to encrypt and decrypt electronic protected health information."

          What can be used to assist in meeting this specification

          Chapter 22 of this book

          Encryption hardware and software for protected data in transit (i.e., SSL/TLS) and data at rest (i.e., full disk encryption)

          Public key infrastructure (PKI) systems

          S/MIME, SMTPS, and POP3S support built into e-mail applications

          E-mail firewalls with encryption support

          Cloud-based e-mail security providers

          SFTP and FTPS for file transfers

  b. Audit controls

    i. Defined in the rule as:

       "Implement hardware, software, and/or procedural mechanisms that record and examine activity in information systems that contain or use electronic protected health information."

    ii. Implementation specifications

      A. None

          What can be used to assist in meeting this specification

          Chapter 22 of this book

          Logging capabilities into your OSs, applications, and databases

  c. Integrity

    i. Defined in the rule as:

       "Implement policies and procedures to protect electronic protected health information from improper alteration or destruction."

    ii. Implementation specifications

      A. Mechanism to authenticate electronic PHI (addressable)

          What the rule says

(*Continued*)

Exhibit 12.2   Interpretation of the Security Rule (*Continued*)

"Implement electronic mechanisms to corroborate that electronic protected health information has not been altered or destroyed in an unauthorized manner."

What can be used to assist in meeting this specification

Chapter 22 of this book

Encryption hardware and software for protected data in transit (i.e., SSL/TLS) and data at rest (i.e., full disk encryption)

PKI systems

S/MIME, SMTPS, and POP3S support built into e-mail applications

E-mail firewalls with encryption support

Cloud-based e-mail security providers

SFTP and FTPS for file transfers

d. Person or entity authentication

   i. Defined in the rule as:

   "Implement procedures to verify that a person or entity seeking access to electronic protected health information is the one claimed."

   ii. Implementation specifications

   A. None

   What can be used to assist in meeting this specification

   Chapter 22 of this book

   User IDs and passwords

   Biometrics, tokens, or other authentication devices

e. Transmission security

   i. Defined in the rule as:

   "Implement technical security measures to guard against unauthorized access to electronic protected health information that is being transmitted over an electronic communications network."

   ii. Implementation specifications

   A. Integrity controls (addressable)

   What the rule says

   "Implement security measures to ensure that electronically transmitted electronic protected health information is not improperly modified without detection until disposed of."

   What can be used to assist in meeting this specification

   Chapter 22 of this book

   Encryption hardware and software for protected data in transit (i.e., SSL/TLS) and data at rest (i.e., full disk encryption)

   PKI systems

   S/MIME, SMTPS, and POP3S support built into e-mail applications

   E-mail firewalls with encryption support

   SFTP and FTPS for file transfers

   B. Encryption (addressable)

   What the rule says

   "Implement a mechanism to encrypt electronic protected health information whenever deemed appropriate."

   What can be used to assist in meeting this specification

   Chapter 22 of this book

Exhibit 12.2   Interpretation of the Security Rule (*Continued*)

Encryption hardware and software for protected data in transit (i.e., SSL/TLS) and data at rest (i.e., full disk encryption)

PKI systems

S/MIME, SMTPS, and POP3S support built into e-mail applications

E-mail firewalls with encryption support

SFTP and FTPS for file transfers

is considered as, or does business with, hybrid entities, affiliated CEs, and governmental entities, we recommend that you review these specific sections of the Security Rule with your legal counsel to see how it may affect your organization.

12.5   Reasons to Get Started on Security Rule Initiatives

If you have followed the Privacy Rule requirements, you are probably well on your way to achieving Security Rule compliance. As if you do not have enough other issues to worry about outside HIPAA, if you have not started working toward Security Rule compliance, it may be time to take that leap—especially if you are a BA and have not done anything about HIPAA compliance.

You may already have a lot of the policies, procedures, and technologies in place that are necessary to become compliant. Regardless of your situation, here are a few reasons to consider moving forward:

- Security Rule compliance now extends to all HIPAA BAs and their subcontractors who create, receive, maintain, or transmit electronic PHI. The CE is not required to enter into a BA agreement with the BA's subcontractors. This is instead a requirement of the BAs themselves.
- Electronic media includes storage material such as hard drives, tapes, and memory cards as well as transmission media such as the Internet, virtual private networks, and the physical transportation of storage media. For all intents and purposes, everywhere electronic PHI exists, even if it is for mere seconds, falls into the scope of compliance.
- You do not need perfection; perform a risk analysis, create a good plan, and show that you are working on it.

- Security Rule compliance is more about culture and business processes than anything else. The sooner you get started, the sooner your workforce will be working with a security-aware state of mind.
- The sooner you get started doing just a few small things at a time to become compliant, the easier and cheaper it will be.
- The Security Rule is all about well-known (and well-documented) best practices and common sense—nothing more and nothing less.
- Your PHI is at risk now. You should not wait to protect it until that dreaded security incident occurs.
- Security compliance does not have to be that expensive or complicated—keep things simple.
- You need a response plan and so do your BAs and their subcontractors. The inevitability of a PHI breach exists. What matters most is what you are doing now to minimize the impact once the breach occurs.

The bottom line is that if you get started now, you can integrate your Security Rule compliance efforts with your Privacy Rule compliance efforts and kill two huge birds with one stone.

Practical Checklist

- The Security Rule and the 2013 Omnibus Rule updates are nothing more than best practices that are intended to protect the confidentiality, integrity, and availability of PHI.
- The Security Rule requires both technical and nontechnical systems, policies, and procedures to be in place.
- You cannot secure what you do not acknowledge, so perform a risk analysis as your first step.
- The flexibility characteristic of the Security Rule does not absolve you of reasonable efforts to comply and protective measures for PHI, regardless of your organization's size.
- Seriously consider treating all implementation specifications as required so that you do not have to explain why you did not implement a particular specification when a security incident occurs.

- Remember to document all of your decisions. If you choose not to implement a certain security control, then document why the decision was made in the event you are ever audited or a breach occurs.
- Get started on Security Rule compliance as soon as possible to save time, effort, and future stress once the rule is enforced.

13

PERFORMING A SECURITY
RULE RISK ANALYSIS

13.1 Background

Security Rule compliance is only possible when an appropriate risk analysis (sometimes referred to as a risk assessment) is performed on your information systems—specifically the systems and physical locations where protected health information (PHI) is stored, processed, accessed from, or transmitted. Stated another way, you must know what you are trying to protect and what you are trying to protect against before you can actually protect anything. The Department of Health and Human Services (HHS) states in the Security Rule that:

> The most appropriate means of compliance for any covered entity can only be determined by that entity assessing its own risks and deciding upon the measures that would best mitigate those risks.

In fact, the first step listed and recommended by HHS in the Security Rule is a required risk analysis. We must say they are generally right on target with this. You absolutely cannot secure what you do not acknowledge. For most organizations, a risk analysis typically needs to be done before starting any of your Health Insurance Portability and Accountability Act (HIPAA) security compliance efforts. One exception is when you do not have any documented information security or privacy policies and procedures to begin with; these are also key requirements, and those policies that are explicitly required (e.g., for passwords and the assignment of information security responsibilities, just to name a couple) can be created prior to or while you are performing your risk analysis. Also, some of the tiniest business associates (BAs) and subcontractors (e.g., one to three people in the organization) can often use a standardized set of policies and procedures that are specific to that size and type of business, and the similar types of risks they face. That said, they all still need to perform a formal and documented risk analysis.

A risk analysis is the only realistic way to determine where your technical and operational (nontechnical) risks are. As we have seen, there are many covered entities (CEs) and BAs that have implemented all their security policies and procedures before doing a risk analysis. Although there are core policies and procedures that can be implemented based on demonstrated effective security practices, a large portion of the policies and procedures, such as for operating systems (OSs) and the physical characteristics of your work areas, need to be based on the results of the risk analysis.

It is no secret that you have to ensure the confidentiality, integrity, and availability of PHI, but you have to get more specific than that. A risk analysis will help you determine the following:

- What PHI your organization has.
- Where the PHI is stored and transmitted.
- Who has access to the PHI and the locations from where they access it.
- Where PHI enters your network and where it leaves your network.
- What specific threats and vulnerabilities are associated with the PHI?
- What could happen to the PHI if unauthorized uses or disclosures occur?
- When and how the PHI needs to be protected.
- Whether or not encryption is needed.
- What security policies need to be developed?
- What specific security controls need to be in place to enforce your policies?
- What areas of security need to be assessed or audited on an ongoing basis?
- How detailed security incident and contingency plans should be.
- What physical security controls are necessary to ensure the protection of PHI?

This information can be used to supplement an existing information security infrastructure or to create a new one from scratch. Taking the *information risk management* approach to addressing your security risks—instead of focusing solely on compliance—is the wisest way to go about it.

Part of this overall process is determining where you currently stand versus where you need to be—analyzing your gaps—with regard to HIPAA compliance. We encourage you to refer to Chapter 7, where we have detailed questions that must be answered as part of your overall risk analysis and gap analysis for Privacy Rule compliance; most of this applies to the Security Rule as well. Chapter 15 also outlines some specific areas to focus on to come up with a solid implementation plan for Security Rule compliance. In this chapter, we provide an overview of the risk analysis process and the steps involved with managing information risks.

13.2 Risk Analysis Requirements According to HIPAA

The Security Rule requires CEs, BAs, and subcontractors (also considered to be BAs under HIPAA) to perform an initial risk analysis to determine specific unauthorized uses, disclosures, and data integrity losses that could occur to PHI if the proper security systems and safeguards are not in place. This is part of the Security Management Standard that falls under the Administrative Safeguards. In fact, a risk analysis is a required implementation specification that all CEs and BAs must perform. Still, so many organizations have yet to do this.

As we covered in Chapter 12, the Security Rule is flexible and scalable based on what is derived from the risk analysis. What this means is that a risk analysis must be used to determine whether or not all of the other addressable implementation specifications must be implemented. Depending on the results, a CE or BA may come to the following conclusions:

- The PHI threats and vulnerabilities are not significant enough to worry about.
- The cost to mitigate those threats and vulnerabilities is too high.
- Their IT capabilities are not sufficient to warrant implementing all of the required security measures.

Not so fast though—we cannot imagine any scenario where an organization would come to the conclusion that its PHI is at no risk whatsoever. There are bound to be certain threats and vulnerabilities that exist that just may not be so obvious. In fact, we have found many vulnerabilities (both technical and nontechnical) in our security assessment work that *should* have already been uncovered. Hopefully, the threats and vulnerabilities to PHI we list in this chapter will make you aware of just how easily PHI can be at risk. On another note, the Security Rule does not apply to information in any risk analysis documentation unless it specifically contains PHI. Just make sure that you secure these records as you would any other critical business document.

13.3 Risk Analysis Essentials

Before we go any further, we need to define some key terms associated with information risk in the context of HIPAA, as follows:

- *Threat*: An indication or intent to cause disturbance or harm to PHI
- *Vulnerability*: An information system weakness that can be exploited to cause disturbance or harm to PHI

There is an indefinite number of threats and vulnerabilities associated with PHI. We have listed some of the more common ones in Exhibit 13.1 of which you should be aware.

Exhibit 13.1   Common PHI Threats and Vulnerabilities

THREATS

- Malware
- Social engineering and phishing
- Hackers
- Disgruntled or malicious employees (often referenced as the "insider threat")
- Untrained users (also an insider threat)
- Malicious contractors (think Edward Snowden and all of his National Security Agency revelations; another type of insider threat)
- Fires, earthquakes, tornadoes, floods, and so on

VULNERABILITIES

- OSs, databases, and applications with default passwords
- No data backup system
- Using and/or posting to social media sites
- Mobile devices and wireless access
- No procedures or technologies to update systems security exposures
- No full disk encryption on laptops
- SQL injection on web applications

Next, we will define *risk* as follows:

The likelihood that the confidentiality, integrity, or availability of PHI will be adversely affected if a threat exploits a vulnerability.

There are various levels of risk that need to be taken into consideration when analyzing risks to your PHI:

*   *Inherent Risk*: Built-in risks that do not consider any security measures taken to protect PHI
*   *Present Risk*: Risk that includes security measures taken to protect PHI
*   *Residual Risk*: Risk that is left over after all existing and recommended security measures have been taken to protect PHI; this will always be greater than zero

13.4 Stepping through the Process

The process of performing a risk analysis can be quite complex, but it does not have to be. There are various popular risk analysis methodologies and software applications that can be used during this process. See Appendix D for a listing of some of our favorites. We highly recommend using these as resources whenever possible. We could dedicate an entire book to performing a risk analysis, but we will spare you all those details for now! Instead, we have outlined in Exhibit 13.2 the high-level steps involved with

Exhibit 13.2   High-Level Steps in Performing a Risk Analysis

---

1. Identify your PHI and other supporting information systems and business assets.
    *   What PHI and associated systems is your organization dependent on?
        –Interview key personnel.
        –Take an inventory of all your hardware, software, and information.
        –Document your information flows.
    *   Review existing policies and procedures.
    *   Review your existing technology infrastructure supporting the privacy and security of PHI.
    *   Prioritize your findings based on criticality to the business.
2. Determine both tangible and intangible costs associated with your PHI and its supporting systems.
    *   Costs to acquire or create.
    *   Costs to replace.
    *   Costs to maintain and repair.

(*Continued*)

Exhibit 13.2   High-Level Steps in Performing a Risk Analysis (*Continued*)

- Costs to completely rebuild from scratch.
- Costs associated with any liabilities (such as the HIPAA penalties).

3. Identify the threats and vulnerabilities.
   - Use automated tools and manual assessments (looking at both technical and operational areas) to determine the specific threats and vulnerabilities associated with PHI—see Appendix D for a listing of some of these tools.

4. Calculate the specific risks.
   - Determine the actual risk factor involved (see Section 13.5 on calculating risk).

5. Analyze your actual results.
   - Identify and prioritize the specific risks that were discovered and determine the impact, including the following:
     - How certain are you of your calculations?
     - What could happen if the risk became a reality?
     - How often could it occur?
     - What security measures are currently in place to mitigate those risks?

6. Complete a cost–benefit analysis.
   - Determine how willing your organization is to accept those risks.
   - Decide whether or not the PHI you are trying to protect is as valuable as the costs, time, and effort it would require to protect it. Be sure to factor in the sanctions offered up by HHS for noncompliance!

7. Make management aware of the risks you have uncovered, putting it in terms they can understand.

8. Determine your risk mitigation plan—you have a few options.
   - Accept the risks—be sure to get it in writing from management if any risks are being accepted. Just make sure they have all the facts!
   - Reduce your risks through specific policies, procedures, and technologies.
   - Transfer your risks to another entity or via a contract or an insurance policy.
     - Be careful with this one! Transferring risks this way still will not keep you from getting in trouble with the law or having your reputation tarnished.

performing a risk analysis so you will know where to get started and what to expect.

When moving forward with your risk analysis, several factors will affect your approach and how detailed you will need to get. This includes the following:

- The various business processes that exist in your organization
- Your information systems complexity
- The number of business partners your organization deals with
- Your level of perceived risks
- How large of a mobile workforce you have and how they access and process PHI

- How you store PHI on medical devices such as ultrasound, cardiogram, and other equipment
- Whether or not you use wireless or dial-up connections (or both)
- The number of employees in your organization

13.5 Calculating Risk

There are several formulas for calculating risk. We will introduce you to a couple of the common ones here and show you an example of how to calculate risk. In general terms, risk is defined in the following formula:

$$\text{Risk} = \text{Threat} \times \text{Vulnerability} \times \text{Cost}$$

This essentially requires a numeric value to be assigned to both the threats and the vulnerabilities for a given situation and those values to be multiplied by the cost of the occurrence. Obviously, this is not a highly scientific formula. It is more of a guideline to show that the calculation of risk is dependent on how high or low the threat, vulnerability, and cost are for a particular scenario. For instance, in a given situation, imagine that the latest and greatest OS is installed on one of your computers but no security patches are applied. This in itself could be considered a high vulnerability. However, if you choose to only use the computer as a word processing workstation with minimal Internet access and no PHI stored on it, the threats to that computer are going to be pretty low. In addition, the costs associated with any sort of compromise of that computer are going to be low as well. Worst-case scenario, you will lose your word processing documents or perhaps have to replace the computer and its software. Overall, using the above formula, the risk will be low, and therefore you will not have to implement many security measures, if any, to ensure its viability. This, of course, assumes you have all the facts using the proper technologies and security testing procedures.

On the other hand, if you have that same OS installed on a practice management computer that stores and transmits PHI via the Internet, and the same security patches are not applied, you have a pretty serious situation on your hands. This is a high-threat, high-vulnerability, and potentially high-cost situation if that computer is compromised. Therefore, the risk is going to be much higher, and this system will in turn need to be much more secure to prevent unauthorized uses and disclosures of PHI.

Keep in mind that there are thousands of possible scenarios and calculations you can make using this formula, depending on your particular situation. If you choose to use this qualitative method to calculate your risks, just be sure to come up with a standard scale for rating your threats (e.g., 1 = lowest risk and 10 = highest risk or high, medium, and low), document how you came to your conclusions, and prioritize your risks that need to be addressed based on your findings.

Another, more academic and less practical, formula for calculating risk is the annual loss expectancy (ALE) formula. The formula for this quantitative method is as follows:

$$ALE = SLE \times ARO$$

where:

SLE (single loss expectancy) = value of the asset ($) × impact of the threat (%)

ARO (annual rate of occurrence) = frequency that a threat is expected to occur in a year

We will not go into specific details on this calculation, but you can see how the SLE and ARO can drive up the risk in certain situations. For example, if you have PHI, or even just a critical information system that is worth a lot of money to your organization combined with a specific virus or worm outbreak that you know will wreak havoc so many times a year on your systems that are not protected, you can calculate the ALE or specific risk involved. Regardless of how you calculate your risks, whether they are scientifically calculated using these formulas or unscientifically calculated using your experience or good old common sense, just pick a method and stick with it if it works for you and your organization. If you document how you have calculated your risks and provided reasonable supporting evidence that you can explain, you will be off to a great start with your Security Rule compliance efforts.

13.6 Managing Risks Going Forward

A risk analysis can be a complicated process from both a business and a technical perspective, so make sure you have the right person(s) for the job. Refer to Chapter 24 for more tips on outsourcing information technology services related to HIPAA. Keep in mind that you have got to balance the value of the PHI and systems you are protecting with how much it costs to protect them. Also remember that not implementing security simply because it costs money that you do not want to spend is *not* considered a reasonable or acceptable justification for not having the security. The best you can do is to reduce the window of exposure and minimize the impact of a breach once it does occur. Some solid efforts combined with some common sense will enable you to determine what is best for your organization.

Keep in mind that the final Security Rule requires everyone to reassess and update their security measures as needed on a regular basis. It specifically states as follows:

> Security measures implemented must be reviewed and modified as needed to continue provision of reasonable and appropriate protection of electronic protected health information.

We go into more detail on this subject in Chapter 26.

The outcome of your risk analysis depends on the results you want in return. Moving forward, you must manage your risks, not avoid the threats and vulnerabilities—they will always exist and most likely keep getting worse. As long as you try, in good faith, to reasonably balance cost-effectiveness with HIPAA compliance and maintain reasonable security measures on an ongoing basis, there is no reason you should not be successful in your HIPAA efforts. Just vow to not become one of those organizations that continually ignores security breaches and their consequences.

Practical Checklist

- You must determine what you are trying to protect before you can protect it.
- Threats are an indication of intent to inflict harm or damage.
- Vulnerabilities are weaknesses that can be exploited by a threat.
- Risk is the likelihood of threat exploiting a vulnerability.
- Perform a thorough analysis of your business processes, information systems, and PHI to determine where things stand.

- Make sure your costs do not outweigh the benefits of mitigating your risks.
- A risk analysis should not be a one-time deal—every day new information systems threats and vulnerabilities crop up that must be addressed on a regular basis, so do this *at least* on an annual basis.

14

WRITING EFFECTIVE
INFORMATION SECURITY
POLICIES

14.1 Introduction to Security Policies

There are many policies specific to the Security Rule and the breach notification requirements of the Health Information Technology for Economic and Clinical Health Act and 2013 Omnibus Rule updates that must be written so your organization can be in compliance with the Health Insurance Portability and Accountability Act (HIPAA). These security policies are such a critical staple item for your overall information security infrastructure that we decided to dedicate an entire chapter to the topic. So, what are security policies? Security policies basically define the framework around which your information security program is managed. They are the core of any successful information security initiative.

Security policies are documents that define the final "what" that must be accomplished with regard to your organization's information protection strategy. You will also need to create supporting documents that provide the "who, how, why, when, and where" information necessary to meet your policy requirements. These supporting documents will outline the following:

- Information systems roles and responsibilities
- Who has access to what information
- Acceptable usage for your employees
- Standards to which all employees must adhere
- Procedures to actually carry out the specific policies, standards, and guidelines

Some people might say, "We know what our security needs and technologies are so we don't need formal policies." This could not be further from the truth. Security policies should come first. Technically they usually come second in mid- to large-sized organizations, after your formal risk analysis, but they should be a top priority nonetheless. Security technologies are merely a way to enforce your policies and should not be seen as the only requirement for adequate security.

What people typically refer to as "security policies" are actually more than just policies. They usually also define security standards, guidelines, and procedures. In this chapter, although we will mostly refer to these documents as security policies, keep in mind that we are referring to the complete set of policies, standards, guidelines, and procedures. Before we go any further, we will take a look at the definitions of each of these terms as used in the context of security policy development.

- *Policy*: The overall definition of your organization's position on specific security topics. Policies state "this is how we do things here."
- *Standard*: Specific information on technology, business, and systems criteria that provide supporting details for meeting policy requirements. A standard might use words such as "will" or "shall" or "must."
- *Guideline*: Provides supporting details for a policy, but is less specific than a standard. A guideline might use words such as "should" or "consider."
- *Procedure*: Outlines the specific details of how a security policy will be implemented. These are often technical and very specific to a particular system, department, or organization.

We will not go into specific details on security procedures as they depend on specific technologies and will differ greatly among organizations. However, we have included a few tips for you to consider when developing your security procedures:

- Make sure they are thoroughly documented and stored in a safe and secure place.
- Make them detailed and succinct.
- Document every step in the process.
- A nontechnical person should be able to implement well-written procedures.
- Ensure any necessary procedures are tested on a regular basis.
- Update them as needed along with your security policies.

- Assign broad responsibilities for your procedures to the smallest number of people possible to ensure that the overall business objective of each policy is met without having too many people involved.
- Given their technical details, the procedures should not require the formal approval of management.

Well-written security policies are fairly high level and thus easy to manage over time. In addition, security policies should generally not be one large document. Instead, they should be short, individual documents that cover a specific security topic. Most policy documents should not be more than one to two pages in length. This might hold true for most of your policies even if you choose to document your standards, guidelines, and procedures along with them. The security or compliance officer should "own" and maintain the full set of information security policies in one location.

To simplify your policies, it is common (and preferable) to summarize each of them in a few sentences and have a reference back to the more detailed documentation. This is helpful for use in employee handbooks and other resources where you do not want to inundate your employees with a lot of details that they may not understand and probably will not read. We go into detail on how to handle this issue in Chapter 25 when we discuss HIPAA training, education, and awareness.

There are three main categories of policies:

1. *Organizational policies*: These cover specific organizations, departments, or offices within a company.
2. *Issue-specific policies*: These cover specific issues such as passwords and employee termination.
3. *System-specific policies*: These cover specific information systems, computers, or applications.

To be compliant with the HIPAA Security Rule, your organization will need several policies in each category. One of the most important factors you will want to consider is relating your security policies to specific business functions whenever possible. This will help with the integration of your security policies into everyday business processes as well as ensure that everyone has a fair chance of understanding how the policies apply to everyday business needs.

14.2 Critical Elements of Security Policies

On average, security policies either do not exist or are not enforced in today's health care environment. The first major hurdle that must be addressed to ensure security policies are implemented and managed properly is that of management support. Even though HIPAA compliance is federal law, health care organizations still need buy-in from management if security policies are to be successfully implemented and enforced. If you have reached the point of communicating the value and requirements of HIPAA to management and are already working toward compliance, this should not be a major issue for you as it is in other unregulated environments.

Beyond management buy-in, there are several other critical factors that will determine whether or not security policies are effective. In no particular order, these factors are as follows:

- *People must be aware of security policies.* Perhaps the greatest mistake in handling security policies is to create them and then put them on a shelf without making anyone aware of them. The organization would be just as well off without security policies in this case. Refer to Chapter 25 for details on the best ways to get the word on your security policies out to everyone involved.

- *Create a committee to develop and ensure the enforcement of your security policies.* You do not want to develop security policies all by yourself. This could be misconstrued as one-sided or biased (i.e., from the "IT department"), and this is certainly not the position any one individual wants to be in. Additionally, you must consider the expertise of your business leaders to ensure the security policies you create are feasible. Get other people involved. It is preferable to get human resources (HR), legal, and applicable business unit representatives to help with this.

- *Security policies must be specific to your organization.* You cannot simply buy a security policies book or download sample policies off the Internet and apply them verbatim to your immediate needs. Do not get us wrong; these policies are a great place to start—they can definitely save you a lot of time, money, and effort. Just remember to tailor these policies to your organization's specific needs and requirements. In fact, try to relate your security policies to your various privacy policies whenever possible. Tailoring these policies should not take a lot of work, and it is absolutely necessary to make sure your information systems and protected health information are properly protected in your particular environment.

- *Security policies must be readable and understandable.* Make sure you know your intended audience before you start writing your policies. Regardless of who will be reading them, use legal and technical jargon sparingly. All of your employees, regardless of their knowledge and intellect, need to be able to read any and all of your organization's security policies and completely understand them. This is not just an education or awareness issue. It also depends on how well written the policies are in the first place.

- *Security policies must be fair, reasonable, and legal.* Put yourself in your users' positions. Do the policies seem fair and reasonable so as not to interfere with your organization's way of doing business? If security policies are not fair and reasonable, people will break them, and that is the last thing anyone needs to have happen with their HIPAA policies. It really is possible to balance security, HIPAA compliance, and convenience. Make sure your organization is doing that. Also, do not forget to run your security policies by your HR manager and legal counsel before you publish them to make sure they are legal from an HR and employees' rights perspective.

- *Security policies must be enforced.* It is not enough for security policies to be fair, reasonable, and legal. They must also be enforced within the organization for all users, including management. Sure, HIPAA mandates security policies, but similar to the awareness issue discussed previously, if security policies are not enforced by the security policy committee, HIPAA officer(s), or management, then it is probably not worth the time, money, and effort to develop them in the first place. Not only this, but HIPAA also mandates sanction policies and requires documentation that you are actually enforcing the policies.

14.3 Sample Security Policy Framework

The following framework should be considered when developing security policies to ensure all the essential areas are covered. Even the most basic set of policies and supporting documents needs to have a structure such as this to ensure consistency, proper coverage, and ease of readability. Remember to create a separate policy for each issue you need to cover.

- *Introduction*: One or two sentences describing the specific policy such as passwords and event logging and monitoring. This may also include any background information.
- *Purpose*: The high-level goals and objectives of the policy.
- *Responsibilities*: What is expected by people or systems covered by the policies.
- *Scope*: What and who is actually covered by this policy.
- *Statement of policy*: The actual policy statement itself.
- *Procedures*: How the specific policy will be implemented. Consider documenting these separately to keep your policy simple.
- *Compliance*: How policy compliance will be measured and what the repercussions (sanctions) will be if the policy is not adhered to.
- *References*: Specific laws and regulations that apply to this policy.
- *Related documents*: Any other documentation that might play a role in this policy, including any standards the policy relies on or documentation that the policy replaces or outdates.
- *Revisions*: Any changes to the policy along with the date of the change and who made the change.

14.4 Security Policies You May Need for HIPAA Security Rule Compliance

Depending on the results of your risk assessment, your organization will need various security policies in place to become compliant with the Security Rule. Exhibit 14.1 contains a list of the basic security policies most organizations need, organized by the three major Security Rule safeguards sections. Emphasis here is on the word "may" because every organization's needs are different, but there are still specific policy topics that are necessary to be in compliance with HIPAA. This is not intended to be a comprehensive list, but should be a good starting point in your security policy development process. Keep in mind that security incident procedures, contingency plans, and evaluation methods are not listed here, as they are covered in depth in Chapters 15 and 26.

Exhibit 14.1 Possible HIPAA-Related Information Security Policies

ADMINISTRATIVE SAFEGUARD POLICIES	PHYSICAL SAFEGUARD POLICIES	TECHNICAL SAFEGUARD POLICIES
Security Management Process Risk assessment requirements Sanction/discipline for violations System logging requirements System monitoring requirements System auditing requirements System maintenance requirements Policy review and maintenance Incident response **Assigned Security Responsibility** Security officer roles and responsibilities Workforce security User authorization controls Administrative supervision methods Employee termination methods Background check requirements Outside consultant/vendor access controls	**Facility Access Controls** Building access and validation controls Emergency operation instructions Locks and other controls Facility maintenance record controls **Workstation Use** Permitted workstation uses **Workstation Security** Computer location and physical controls Device and media controls Information disposal instructions Media reuse controls Physical hardware accountability controls Data backup and storage controls	**Access Control** Unique user IDs Emergency operation instructions Automatic log-off time limits Systems or controls to ensure data confidentiality Server security settings Workstation security settings **Audit Controls** Technical methods used to enable system auditing **Integrity** Systems or controls to ensure data is not tampered with **Person or Entity Authentication** Requirement to ensure a user or entity is known and trusted **Transmission Security** Systems or controls to ensure data in transit is not tampered with Systems or controls to ensure data in transit is kept confidential

(Continued)

Exhibit 14.1   Possible HIPAA-Related Information Security Policies (*Continued*)

ADMINISTRATIVE SAFEGUARD POLICIES	PHYSICAL SAFEGUARD POLICIES	TECHNICAL SAFEGUARD POLICIES
Information Access Management System usage controls Instructions for privileged use of systems Isolation of clearinghouse functions User authorization controls User access establishment/ review controls Acceptable use of information assets (including social media use, bring your own device, and other employee-specific topics) **Security Awareness and Training** Security reminders Antivirus protection		

14.5 Managing Your Security Policies

As part of your ongoing HIPAA compliance initiatives, you will need to ensure that your security policies are kept up to date. Most mid- to large-sized organizations should perform an annual review of policies to ensure they are still appropriate for the information systems and business needs, as well as update them to reflect major organizational or technology changes as necessary. Small one- to five-person businesses will often not need to do the same types of formal reviews, but typically change their policies as needed whenever they have business changes, and when laws and regulations change or new ones emerge.

You may need to create new policies or revise or remove outdated ones. Staying abreast of your information security and policy needs will not be a simple task if you do not maintain them on an ongoing basis. We will talk more about this in Chapter 26 when we discuss performing HIPAA compliance reviews and audits.

With today's more advanced security infrastructure applications, many policies can be directly enforced by defining specific systems settings. For example, you can "program" some of your specific policies directly into firewalls, intrusion prevention systems, identity and access management systems, and centrally managed antimalware products for automated enforcement. In addition, with our modern software, everything from enterprise directory services to workstation operating systems have the ability to configure and enforce specific policies for items such as passwords, authentication, and logging. We will cover HIPAA technology infrastructures in more detail in Chapter 22, but we wanted to note this point here to remind you that many technologies you may already have in place can assist you with your security policy efforts. Keep in mind these programmable policies still must be documented and maintained as described in Sections 14.1 through 14.4.

For larger organizations where information systems and security policies are extremely complex, there are various third-party products that can assist in the ongoing management of them. These applications can help do the following:

- Store policies and track changes.
- Centrally host policies for easy access by everyone.
- Get the word out on policies through online tutorials and training sessions.
- Assess everyone's understanding of the policies via periodic quizzes.

Small organizations can often use a standardized set of information security policies that address the typical risks that exist in such businesses. For an example of such small business policies, and supporting procedures, see http://www.privacyprofessor.org.

Practical Checklist

- What most of us refer to as security "policies" can be more than just policies. Depending on how you structure your documentation, security policies will also likely include standards, guidelines, and procedures.
- Have you formed your security committee to help develop and enforce the necessary policies?

- Consider reviewing potential third-party products and Internet resources that can assist in your security policy development.
- Ensure that your policies are enforceable by making them fair and reasonable, and then ensure they are actually enforced. Management buy-in and ongoing support is critical.
- Remember that your current technologies may be able to assist in security policy enforcement.

15

CRAFTING A SECURITY IMPLEMENTATION PLAN

15.1 Background

Preparing for Security Rule compliance is very similar to preparing for Privacy Rule compliance in that it can be very complex and must be thoroughly planned out, utilizing virtually every department in your organization. A large portion of the Privacy Rule standards requires a solid information security infrastructure to be in place. Chapter 5 discussed the issue of how the rules are related. Many covered entities (CEs) and business associates (BAs) may already be well ahead of the Security Rule curve because of their Privacy Rule initiatives or simply because they have been following information security best practices or other compliance requirements as part of their daily business operations.

From a high-level perspective, Security Rule compliance requires determining where your organization stands compared to the Health Insurance Portability and Accountability Act (HIPAA) requirements, what protected health information (PHI) risks are present, what information security controls can be put in place to reduce those risks, and how you will go about implementing those controls. To reduce the overall burden of Security Rule compliance, the Department of Health and Human Services made the Security Rule and the subsequent Health Information Technology for Economic and Clinical Health (HITECH) Act and Omnibus Rule requirements as scalable and flexible as possible. This means that you can tailor your implementation plan based on your specific circumstances. According to the Security Rule documentation, it is "focused more on what needs to be done and less on how it should be accomplished." This will allow small CEs to reasonably comply without breaking the bank, and larger CEs to integrate the specific requirements into their current systems.

Exhibit 15.1 contains a plan to help you get started with your information security initiatives. You will, of course, have to modify

249

it depending on your organization's needs, size, and information systems' complexity. Keep in mind that this can be a complex subject, so we are keeping it at a fairly high level. For more detailed information and guidelines, you may consider referring to the ISO/IEC 27002 "Information technology—Security techniques—Code of practice for information security management" standard, found at http://www.iso.org, or other similar framework.

Exhibit 15.1 Security Rule Implementation Plan

1. Determine your CE status.
    a. Is your organization a HIPAA CE? If so, what type?
        i. Health care provider
        ii. Health plan
        iii. Health care clearinghouse
        iv. Hybrid entity (HIPAA-covered functions are not the primary functions of the organization)
    b. Is your organization a BA of an HIPAA CE? See Chapter 21 for more information on BA issues.
    c. We outline the steps to determine your HIPAA status in Part IV. Be sure to confirm your status with your legal counsel or other HIPAA expert.
2. Initiate your security project and start planning for your compliance activities.
    a. Determine who will sponsor your HIPAA security initiatives (business owner, executive management, board of directors, etc.), and document and communicate their commitment to your HIPAA compliance initiatives.
    b. Establish a steering committee that will plan, oversee, and guide your HIPAA security efforts. You do not want to go at this alone. Even if you are a small CE, get at least one other person involved. This can be the same committee used for your HIPAA privacy initiatives.
    c. Develop a high-level HIPAA strategic plan that involves all of your information security initiatives or determine how you can integrate compliance with an existing compliance program that you may already have such as the Payment Card Industry Data Security Standard. Make this available to everyone in your organization so they understand the mission, goals, and objectives of your HIPAA security efforts.
    d. Establish a HIPAA security compliance team that is responsible for project implementation. For small CEs and BAs, this could be the same people who are on the steering committee. This could be performed by internal personnel, external personnel, or a combination of both. See Chapter 24 for more information on outsourcing your information security initiatives.
    e. Develop detailed roles and responsibilities for your HIPAA security compliance efforts. To help prevent a "not invented here" culture as well as to maximize quality and efficiency, keep the roles broad and responsibilities specific as there will be overlap in certain areas.
    f. Organize people, processes, and methodologies to track and manage your HIPAA security initiatives. For small CEs and BAs, this could be the same people who are on the steering committee. Consider using a whiteboard, spreadsheet, or project management software to ensure everything is kept in line and addressed.

Exhibit 15.1   Security Rule Implementation Plan (*Continued*)

g. Develop a master HIPAA security plan and timeline for your overall goals and specific plans for each project phase (see Chapter 12 for specific information on what is required by the Security Rule, HITECH Act, and Omnibus Rule).

h. Determine how you are going to measure and keep track of your project results.

i. Establish a HIPAA security compliance budget or integrate your HIPAA initiatives into your existing budget.

3. Understand the activities covered by the Security Rule.

a. Communicate the noncompliance penalties mentioned in Chapter 1 to everyone in the organization, especially upper management.

b. Read and understand the HIPAA Security Rule (see Chapter 12).

c. Associate the specific administrative, physical, and technical safeguards outlined in the Security Rule to what your organization is doing.

4. Identify and prepare a security officer for the upcoming tasks.

a. Identify and appoint a qualified security officer to address HIPAA security-related issues. See Appendix B for a sample security officer job description.

b Identify the privacy officer and other HIPAA compliance team members with whom the security officer will have to work closely.

c. If necessary, ensure that the security officer has received the proper training. Outside of this book, HIPAA workshops and health care conferences are a great place to start. There are also various information security classes and conferences held around the United States where you can learn the essentials of information security. Kevin and Rebecca also each provide training, along with awareness tools, through each of their businesses.

5. Perform a Security Rule gap analysis and baseline the organization.

a. Develop an assessment methodology. There will be both IT and business issues to assess, so make sure you have the proper methodologies and resources. See Chapter 13 for detailed information on this. There are various tools available to assist as well, including the State of California Office of Health Information Integrity's HIPAA Security Toolkit (http://www.ohii.ca.gov/calohi/content.aspx?id=140) and those Rebecca offers at http://www.privacyprofessor.org.

b. Collect and review existing information security policies, procedures, and standards.

c. Collect and review existing network diagrams, information flow diagrams, and network hardware and software inventory lists.

d. Conduct interviews to collect and document security-related practices and procedures.

e. Identify all employees who have remote access capabilities to your information systems (virtual private network [VPN], remote desktop, GoToMyPC, etc.).

f. Collect the inventory of the PHI that you compiled for your Privacy Rule initiatives. Verify that this inventory is still accurate and comprehensive.

i. Be sure to include your operating systems, web applications, databases, and network infrastructure devices that either store or transmit PHI.

ii. Be sure to include mobile devices and network-connected medical equipment.

g. Create an inventory and sort all of the information you have collected based on its association with the HIPAA Security Rule standards and implementation specifications as well as the HITECH Act and Omnibus Rule updates.

h. Determine which areas of your organization are affected by the Security Rule requirements.

i. Where is PHI stored and transmitted within the organization?

ii. Which departments or people are responsible for this PHI?

(*Continued*)

Exhibit 15.1   Security Rule Implementation Plan (*Continued*)

---

     iii. Which departments utilize or otherwise rely on your organization's information systems?

     iv. Which facilities will need to be protected by the physical safeguards?

  i. Create an inventory of all your BAs (such as health care and IT vendors, lawyers, and contractors), and if you are a BA, of all your subcontractors and electronic trading partners with whom your organization shares PHI.

  j. Identify and diagram all BAs and subcontractors who have remote access to your information systems (VPN, remote desktop, GoToMyPC, etc.) for support purposes.

  k. Diagram all other electronic information flows with all of your BAs and subcontractors.

  l. Perform a risk analysis that includes vulnerability assessments and penetration tests for larger organizations, to determine specific risks to your information systems.

  m. Test all information systems to determine which authentication and access controls are currently being used.

  n. Compare existing organizational information security policies, procedures, and administrative functions with the Security Rule standards and document the differences.

  o. Compare existing organizational culture (the human element) with the Security Rule standards and document any areas of concern.

  p. Compare existing physical and technical security measures with the Security Rule standards and document the differences.

  q. Create a remediation/compliance plan for closing the gaps that were found and implement new systems to meet the Security Rule requirements.

  r. Document known and potential impacts the gaps present to your organization.

6. Plan remediation strategies.

  a. Document your administrative (policy and procedure) compliance strategy, implementation plan, and timeline.

  b. Document your technical compliance strategy, implementation plan, and timeline.

  c. Refine your Security Rule compliance budget as needed and seek additional funding commitment if necessary.

  d. Organize the teams necessary to close the gaps found. This can be performed by internal personnel, external personnel, or a combination of both. See Chapter 24 for more information on outsourcing your information security initiatives.

7. Remediate the organization.

  a. Update existing security policies, procedures, and standards and develop new ones where necessary.

  b. Update organizational policies and procedures to match your HIPAA security policy and procedure requirements.

  c Develop or outsource information security training for all personnel, including upper management. Be sure to document this training, including who was in attendance.

  d. Update existing BA contracts or develop new ones as necessary to include verbiage ensuring the protection of PHI and compliance with the HITECH Act and Omnibus Rule requirements. Chapter 12 provides the details on the latest changes impacting security.

  e. Work with legal counsel to ensure these BA agreements are properly executed.

  f. Modify business processes, technical systems, and physical facilities or create new ones as necessary to comply with the Security Rule standards.

  g. Transition the responsibility and maintenance of new processes and systems to the appropriate parties.

Exhibit 15.1   Security Rule Implementation Plan (*Continued*)

---

   h. Establish and document ongoing compliance procedures and implement the appropriate systems. See Chapter 26 for information on ongoing HIPAA compliance reviews and audits.

8. Monitor progress and changes in the HIPAA and related rules and update your organizational policies, procedures, and technologies appropriately.

   a. Keep current with changes to the HIPAA regulations.

   b. Keep current with new and updated state, federal, and international regulations related to information security.

   c. Keep current with various information security standards and best practices.

   d. Update policies and procedures as necessary to meet new regulatory requirements and to reflect organizational and business process changes.

   e. Monitor organizational procedures and follow up on areas of information security falling out of compliance.

   f. Regularly review information systems activity logs. With a few exceptions, this is the only way you will find out if any inappropriate computer activity is occurring. Better yet, outsource this service to a managed security (cloud) provider that specializes in this type of work.

   g. Manage BAs and other relationships related to the electronic storage or transmission of PHI.

   h. Perform periodic and consistent risk analyses and/or gap analyses (including technical vulnerability assessments that are often overlooked) at least annually, to ensure PHI is protected against newly discovered information threats and vulnerabilities. Perform these immediately after any major information systems or businesses process changes to ensure that no new threats or vulnerabilities were introduced with the changes.

   i. Perform regular internal audits for each aspect of Security Rule compliance. See Chapter 12 for the specific requirements on this.

   j. Perform ongoing information security training and awareness activities for all personnel, including management. If your BAs do not have such a program and you are in a position to offer this to them, that would be a great way to ensure they are doing the right things for compliance in this area.

   k. Maintain documentation on your HIPAA compliance activities and store it securely for future reference in the event of an audit or breach.

15.2 Some Points to Keep in Mind

The following are compliance facts to keep in mind when creating and applying your Security Rule implementation plan:

- The Security Rule, HITECH Act, and Omnibus Rule requirements are flexible and scalable depending on the size of a CE or BA, its internal culture, the complexity of its information systems, and the number of BAs it deals with.

- Information security is more than just technical safeguards. It is about business processes, organizational culture, and ensuring that everyone involved with PHI knows what to look for, what to do, and what not to do.

- The Security Rule does not require the use of specific technologies such as firewalls and operating systems that support access controls and logging; however, their use is implied.
- There is no such thing as 100% security. CEs, BAs, and their subcontractors are just expected to follow the Security Rule standards (along with any new updates such as the Omnibus Rule); implement the proper policies, procedures, and technologies; and reasonably show that the organization is making an effort to protect against common security threats and vulnerabilities.

15.3 Conclusion

As with Privacy Rule requirements and implementation efforts, Security Rule compliance initiatives will be an ongoing task that must be managed appropriately. You cannot simply create new policies, procedures, and technologies and expect that to be sufficient and not need any ongoing oversight. Remember, you must actually do what those policies and procedures say! In addition, there are newly discovered information threats and vulnerabilities every day. If you create your information security team, assess your gaps and risks, implement reasonable safeguards, document all of your compliance efforts, and manage your ongoing risks, you can in good conscience say that you have done everything you reasonably can to ensure that your PHI is properly secured.

Practical Checklist

- Determine your CE or BA status.
- Obtain Security Rule compliance sponsorship from management.
- Establish a Security Rule compliance project plan.
- Assign the appropriate responsibilities to your team and ensure any BAs are on board as well.
- Perform a gap analysis and risk analysis to determine where your organization stands.

- Create a remediation plan consisting of the appropriate policies, procedures, and technical systems that meet the compliance requirements.
- Implement your security plan.
- Monitor ongoing Security Rule compliance.
- Remember that there is no such thing as 100% security; however, there is a general expectation that reasonable security
  controls are in place.

16

SECURITY RULE
COMPLIANCE CHECKLIST

16.1 Introduction

As with the Privacy Rule compliance checklist in Chapter 11, we have created a Security Rule Checklist (Exhibit 16.1) for you as well. This is only high-level coverage, so be sure to refer to the other chapters on Security Rule compliance when moving forward—Chapters 12 and 15. The corresponding location in the regulatory text is listed for your reference. Some important notes to keep in mind as you use this checklist are as follows:

- The 2013 Omnibus Rule expanded these requirements to all business associates (BAs), and to the subcontractors of BAs.
- The term "addressable" does not mean optional! Addressable means that the control must be implemented based on the associated risks.

Exhibit 16.1 Security Rule Compliance Checklist

Administrative Safeguard Requirements

A. Security management process

_____ 1. Risk analysis (required)

§ **164.308(1)(a):** "Conduct an accurate and thorough assessment of the potential risks and vulnerabilities to the confidentiality, integrity, and availability of electronic protected health information held by the covered entity."

_____ 2. Risk management (required)

§ **164.308(1)(b):** "Implement security measures sufficient to reduce risks and vulnerabilities to a reasonable and appropriate level to comply with § 164.306(a)."

_____ 3. Sanction policy (required)

§ **164.308(1)(c):** "Apply appropriate sanctions against workforce members who fail to comply with the security policies and procedures of the covered entity."

(Continued)

Exhibit 16.1   Security Rule Compliance Checklist (*Continued*)

_____   4. Information system activity review (required)

§ **164.308(1)(d):** "Implement procedures to regularly review records of information system activity, such as audit logs, access reports, and security incident tracking reports."

B. Assigned security responsibility

_____   5. Assign a security official

§ **164.308(2):** "Identify the security official who is responsible for the development and implementation of the policies and procedures required by this sub-part for the entity."

C. Workforce security

_____   6. Authorization and/or supervision (addressable)

§ **164.308(3)(a):** "Implement procedures for the authorization and/or supervision of workforce members who work with electronic protected health information or in locations where it might be accessed."

_____   7. Workforce clearance procedure (addressable)

§ **164.308(3)(b):** "Implement procedures to determine that the access of a workforce member to electronic protected health information is appropriate."

_____   8. Termination procedures (addressable)

§ **164.308(3)(c):** "Implement procedures for terminating access to electronic protected health information when the employment of, or other agreement with, a workforce member ends or as required by determinations made as specified in paragraph (a)(3)(ii)(B) of this section."

D. Information access management

_____   9. Isolating health care clearinghouse functions (required)

§ **164.308(4)(a):** "If a healthcare clearinghouse is part of a larger organization, the clearinghouse must implement policies and procedures that protect the electronic protected health information of the clearinghouse from unauthorized access by the larger organization."

_____   10. Access authorization (addressable)

§ **164.308(4)(b):** "Implement policies and procedures for granting access to electronic protected health information, for example, through access to a workstation, transaction, program, process, or other mechanism."

_____   11. Access establishment and modification (addressable)

§ **164.308(4)(c):** "Implement policies and procedures that, based upon the entity's access authorization policies, establish, document, review, and modify a user's right of access to a workstation, transaction, program, or process."

E. Security awareness and training

_____   12. Security reminders (addressable)

§ **164.308(5)(a):** "Periodic security updates."

_____   13. Protection from malicious software

§ **164.308(5)(b):** "Procedures for guarding against, detecting, and reporting malicious software."

Exhibit 16.1 Security Rule Compliance Checklist (*Continued*)

_____ 14. Log-in monitoring (addressable)

§ 164.308(5)(c): "Procedures for monitoring log-in attempts and reporting discrepancies."

_____ 15. Password management (addressable)

§ 164.308(5)(d): "Procedures for creating, changing, and safeguarding passwords."

F. Security incident procedures

_____ 16. Response and reporting (required)—this is especially important for compliance with the Health Information Technology for Economic and Clinical Health (HITECH) Act's requirements for breach notification and the Omnibus Rule's additional requirements for analysis of breaches once they occur.

§ 164.308(6)(ii): "Identify and respond to suspected or known security incidents; mitigate, to the extent practicable, harmful effects of security incidents that are known to the covered entity; and document security incidents and their outcomes."

G. Contingency plan

_____ 17. Data backup plan (required)

§ 164.308(7)(a): "Establish and implement procedures to create and maintain retrievable exact copies of electronic protected health information."

_____ 18. Disaster recovery plan (required)

§ 164.308(7)(b): "Establish (and implement as needed) procedures to restore any loss of data."

_____ 19. Emergency mode operation plan (required)

§ 164.308(7)(c): "Establish (and implement as needed) procedures to restore any loss of data."

_____ 20. Testing and revision procedure (addressable)

§ 164.308(7)(d): "Establish (and implement as needed) procedures to enable continuation of critical business processes for protection of the security of electronic protected health information while operating in emergency mode."

_____ 21. Applications and data criticality analysis (addressable)

§ 164.308(7)(e): "Assess the relative criticality of specific applications and data in support of other contingency plan components."

H. Evaluation

_____ 22. Security evaluation

§ 164.308(8): "Perform a periodic technical and nontechnical evaluation, based initially upon the standards implemented under this rule and subsequently, in response to environmental or operational changes affecting the security of electronic protected health information, that establishes the extent to which an entity's security policies and procedures meet the requirements of this sub-part."

I. BA contracts and other arrangements

_____ 23. Written contract or other arrangement (required)—it is worth another reminder: keep in mind that all Health Insurance Portability and Accountability Act (HIPAA)/ HITECH compliance requirements extend to BAs and their subcontractors as a result of the 2013 Omnibus Rule changes.

(*Continued*)

Exhibit 16.1 Security Rule Compliance Checklist (*Continued*)

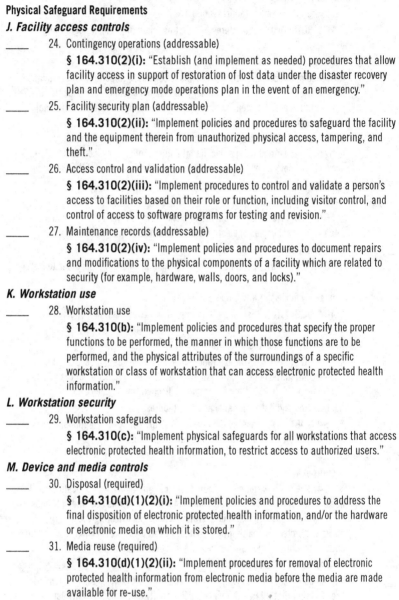

§ **164.308(b)(1)(4):** "Document the satisfactory assurances required by paragraph (b)(1) of this section through a written contract or other arrangement with the business associate that meets the applicable requirements of § 164.314(a)."

Physical Safeguard Requirements

J. Facility access controls

_____ 24. Contingency operations (addressable)

§ **164.310(2)(i):** "Establish (and implement as needed) procedures that allow facility access in support of restoration of lost data under the disaster recovery plan and emergency mode operations plan in the event of an emergency."

_____ 25. Facility security plan (addressable)

§ **164.310(2)(ii):** "Implement policies and procedures to safeguard the facility and the equipment therein from unauthorized physical access, tampering, and theft."

_____ 26. Access control and validation (addressable)

§ **164.310(2)(iii):** "Implement procedures to control and validate a person's access to facilities based on their role or function, including visitor control, and control of access to software programs for testing and revision."

_____ 27. Maintenance records (addressable)

§ **164.310(2)(iv):** "Implement policies and procedures to document repairs and modifications to the physical components of a facility which are related to security (for example, hardware, walls, doors, and locks)."

K. Workstation use

_____ 28. Workstation use

§ **164.310(b):** "Implement policies and procedures that specify the proper functions to be performed, the manner in which those functions are to be performed, and the physical attributes of the surroundings of a specific workstation or class of workstation that can access electronic protected health information."

L. Workstation security

_____ 29. Workstation safeguards

§ **164.310(c):** "Implement physical safeguards for all workstations that access electronic protected health information, to restrict access to authorized users."

M. Device and media controls

_____ 30. Disposal (required)

§ **164.310(d)(1)(2)(i):** "Implement policies and procedures to address the final disposition of electronic protected health information, and/or the hardware or electronic media on which it is stored."

_____ 31. Media reuse (required)

§ **164.310(d)(1)(2)(ii):** "Implement procedures for removal of electronic protected health information from electronic media before the media are made available for re-use."

_____ 32. Accountability (addressable)

§ **164.310(d)(1)(2)(iii):** "Maintain a record of the movements of hardware and electronic media and any person responsible therefore."

Exhibit 16.1 Security Rule Compliance Checklist (*Continued*)

_____ 33. Data backup and storage (addressable)

> **§ 164.310(d)(1)(2)(iv):** "Create a retrievable, exact copy of electronic protected health information, when needed, before movement of equipment."

Technical Safeguard Requirements

N. Access control

_____ 34. Unique user identification (required)

> **§ 164.312(2)(i):** "Assign a unique name and/or number for identifying and tracking user identity."

_____ 35. Emergency access procedure (required)

> **§ 164.312(2)(ii):** "Establish (and implement as needed) procedures for obtaining necessary electronic protected health information during an emergency."

_____ 36. Automatic log-off (addressable)

> **§ 164.312(2)(iii):** "Implement electronic procedures that terminate an electronic session after a predetermined time of inactivity."

_____ 37. Encryption and decryption (addressable)

> **§ 164.312(2)(iv):** "Implement a mechanism to encrypt and decrypt electronic protected health information."

O. Audit controls

_____ 38. Audit mechanisms

> **§ 164.312(b):** "Implement hardware, software, and/or procedural mechanisms that record and examine activity in information systems that contain or use electronic protected health information."

P. Integrity

_____ 39. Mechanism to authenticate electronic protected health information (addressable)

> **§ 164.312(c)(1)(2):** "Implement electronic mechanisms to corroborate that electronic protected health information has not been altered or destroyed in an unauthorized manner."

_____ 40. Person or entity authentication

> **§ 164.312(d):** "Implement procedures to verify that a person or entity seeking access to electronic protected health information is the one claimed."

Q. Transmission security

_____ 41. Integrity controls (addressable)

> **§ 164.312(e)(1)(2)(i):** "Implement security measures to ensure that electronically transmitted electronic protected health information is not improperly modified without detection until disposed of."

_____ 42. Encryption (addressable)—keep in mind the new Safe Harbor encryption requirements of the HITECH Act and Omnibus Rule.

> **§ 164.312(e)(1)(2)(ii):** "Implement a mechanism to encrypt electronic protected health information whenever deemed appropriate."

PART IV
COVERED ENTITY ISSUES

17
HEALTH CARE PROVIDER ISSUES

17.1 Background

If you are a person, business, or agency that furnishes, bills, or receives payment for health care in the normal course of business, then it is likely you are a health care provider. A health care provider provides health care services or supplies related to the health of an individual. It includes, but is not limited to, the following:

(1) Preventive, diagnostic, rehabilitative, maintenance, or palliative care, and counseling, service, assessment, or procedure with respect to the physical or mental condition, or functional status, of an individual or that affects the structure or function of the body; and (2) sale or dispensing of a drug, device, equipment, or other item in accordance with a prescription

See 45 CFR § 160.103 of the Privacy Rule for a complete definition.

17.2 Privacy Notices

Covered direct health care treatment providers must provide a Notice of Privacy Practices (NPP) to an individual on the date of first service delivery and, except in emergencies, attempt to obtain the individual's written acknowledgment of receipt of the notice. When an acknowledgment cannot be obtained, the provider must document the efforts to obtain the acknowledgment and provide an explanation why it was not obtained. If first service delivery to an individual is provided over the Internet through e-mail or using some other electronic method, the provider must send an electronic notice automatically at the same time of the individual's first request for service. The provider must try to obtain a return receipt or some other recognition from the individual in response to receiving the notice.

There are many situations in which providers must provide an NPP and some in which providing notice is not necessary. Here are some NPP pointers for providers:

- In emergencies, a provider must provide the notice to the individual as soon as possible after the emergency is over.
- Make the most recent notice available to individuals at their offices and facilities to allow individuals to obtain them there. In addition, providers must post the notice in a prominent location within the building.
- You may e-mail the notice if the individual agrees to receive it in this way.
- You can develop more than one notice, such as when you perform different types of covered functions. You should provide the most appropriate version of the notice to the individual as applicable.
- If you participate in an organized health care arrangement (OHCA), you can create a single, joint notice following some specific conditions. For example, the joint notice must describe the covered entities (CEs) and the service delivery sites to which it applies.
- If you choose to use consents for the use or disclosure of protected health information (PHI), you must try to obtain an acknowledgment of the NPP.
- You do not need to obtain a new acknowledgment of receipt of notice from patients when your privacy policy changes.
- You can obtain an electronic acknowledgment of the privacy notice from an individual if it was delivered electronically. An acknowledgment for a notice given face-to-face can also be an electronic version of the individual's handwritten signature.
- If your first treatment of a patient is not face-to-face (e.g., over the phone), you can mail the notice to the individual as soon as possible (the same day, if possible) and include some way for the individual to sign an acknowledgment and mail it back to you. Be sure to file a copy of the form sent to the patient to document the form and the accompanying acknowledgment.

- If the initial contact is simply to schedule an appointment, the notice may be given at the time the individual arrives for the appointment.
- For service provided electronically, the notice must be sent automatically and contemporaneously in response to the individual's first request for service. In this situation, an electronic return receipt or other return transmission from the individual is considered a valid written acknowledgment of the notice.
- Health care providers and other CEs that participate in an OHCA can use a single, joint notice that covers all of the participating CEs, or each can use their own separate notice. Each direct treatment provider within the OHCA must make an effort to obtain the individual's acknowledgment of the notice provided.
- When an individual, such as a child, has a personal representative, you may satisfy the notice distribution requirements by giving the notice to the personal representative (e.g., the child's parent), and make an effort to get the personal representative's acknowledgment of the notice.
- You must post your entire notice at your health care facility in a clear and prominent location. You cannot post just a brief description of the notice.
- You are not required to mail revised notices to patients when the notice changes. However, when the patient next receives care, the new notice must be given to the individual.
- If you make the notice available on a customer service website, it must be kept current.
- If you have direct treatment relationships with individuals, you must give the NPP to every individual on the first date of service delivery and try as best as possible to obtain a written acknowledgment of the receipt of notice. This is in addition to posting the entire notice in a prominent location. The only exception to this is during an emergency situation.
- If the initial contact with a patient is to collect preoperative information over the phone or collect some other information in anticipation of an appointment or procedure, you may satisfy the notice requirement by giving the notice at the time the individual arrives for the appointment.

- Pharmacists can have customers provide their acknowledgment of receipt of notice in a log book if the individual is clearly told what they are acknowledging, and if their acknowledgment is not also used for some other permission that appears in the log book.
- Notices can be distributed as part of other mailings or distributions. However, the notice cannot be combined into a single form that is mailed at the same time, such as an authorization.
- E-mails containing the notice may also contain other information as well. However, you must keep the notice separate from the other e-mail attachments and still make an effort to obtain the individual's written acknowledgment of receipt of the notice.

17.3 Fees for Record Review

Individuals must be given a copy of their corresponding PHI within a reasonable period of time after they request it. If the individual agrees to a summary or explanation of the information, you can request a reasonable fee based on the cost of providing that information. The fee must only consist of the costs involved in the following:

- Copying the PHI, including the cost of the supplies for the copy and the labor used for the copy
- Postage, if the individual has asked for the copy of PHI or the summary or explanation to be mailed
- Preparing the explanation or summary of the PHI, if the individual is told of this cost and agrees to it prior to its preparation

It is very important to understand that the Health Insurance Portability and Accountability Act (HIPAA) makes no provision for providers or any other CE to charge the individual for the cost involved for personnel who supervise the patient while they are reviewing their PHI within the facilities. In most if not all cases, state laws allowing such charges do not preempt the HIPAA prohibition on such supervisory costs. HIPAA also does not allow CEs to charge for the computing time, space, and storage that may be associated with providing a copy of the PHI. Carefully study your applicable state laws and discuss with your legal counsel to determine if this is a practice you can implement within your facility.

17.4 Mitigation Measures

The Privacy Rule requires CEs to follow mitigation procedures to address unauthorized use or disclosure of PHI, which includes a breach of PHI. A breach is defined in § 164.402 as follows:

> Breach means the acquisition, access, use, or disclosure of protected health information in a manner not permitted under subpart E of this part which compromises the security or privacy of the protected health information.

A CE must mitigate (to the extent practicable) any harmful effect that is known to the CE of a use or disclosure of PHI that is in violation of its policies or procedures (or the Privacy Rule) by the CE or its BA. Chapter 2 discusses breach response and mitigation in detail.

17.5 Fax Use

Providers often fax PHI to another physician's office for treatment purposes. In 2012, Professor Herold surveyed 20 of her health care provider clients to determine their most common source of privacy breaches. Far and away the most common sources stemmed from fax use: misdirected faxes, fax number changes that resulted in breaches, and documents left within faxes.

Reasonable and appropriate administrative, technical, and physical safeguards must be in place for these faxes to help ensure the privacy of the PHI. Besides putting a notice on the cover sheet of all faxes asking recipients to destroy misguided faxed information, you should also implement procedures to confirm the fax number is correct, to confirm successful transmission to the intended recipient, to ensure that the fax machine's physical location is secure, and other similar safeguards. You should also implement strong technical security controls, as described in Part III of this book.

17.6 Sign-In Sheets

Physicians' offices can use patient sign-in sheets or call out the names of patients in their waiting rooms. Be careful that the information disclosed is limited. The Privacy Rule permits certain incidental disclosures, such as in waiting rooms when patient names are called. However, they are allowed only as long as your office has implemented reasonable safeguards to ensure the minimum necessary standard. For example, consider calling out only the first name of the patient instead of the full name, or call Mr. or Ms. along with the last name. And, do not place medical information on the sign-in sheet that is not necessary for sign-in purposes.

17.7 Patient Charts

The HIPAA Privacy Rule allows providers to place patient charts in the plastic box outside an exam room, as is customarily done, as long as the clinic takes reasonable and appropriate safeguards to protect the patient's privacy. The physician and other health care professionals typically use the patient charts for treatment purposes. Incidental disclosures to others that might occur as a result of the charts being left in the box are permitted as long as reasonable safeguards are in place. The minimum necessary requirement needs to be met. For example, it could be reasonable and appropriate to safeguard the patient chart by limiting access to the area from the public, by supervising the area, by escorting all nonemployees who are in the area, or by putting the patient information within a folder so that the information cannot be viewed by anyone who happens to be passing by. Each provider needs to determine what safeguards, procedures, and measures are appropriate for his own unique situation and circumstances.

The situation is similar in hospital settings where patient names are often displayed by the doors. In this case, disclosure of patient names is permitted if the use or disclosure is for treatment, which it would be if the practice is to ensure that care is given to the correct individual, or for health care operations purposes such as providing a service to patients and their families. The disclosure of the patient name in this situation to other persons in the area would typically be considered an incidental disclosure. These incidental disclosures are allowed to the extent that the hospital has applied appropriate safeguards. By providing just the patient name by the door, it would likely seem the disclosure is the minimum necessary for the purposes described. Again, it is important for each CE to evaluate what measures are reasonable and appropriate in its particular circumstances.

17.8 Business Associates

Providers generally are not business associates (BAs) of payers. When a provider is a member of a health plan network and the only relationship between the health plan and the provider is that the provider submits claims for payment to the plan, then the provider is not a BA of the health plan. However, a BA relationship could arise if the provider performs a function on behalf of or provides services to the health plan, such as case management services.

Hospitals do not need to continuously monitor their BAs' activities with regard to PHI. However, they must have a written contract or some other formal arrangement with BAs in addition to obtaining reasonable assurances that appropriate safeguards are maintained, to ensure they appropriately protect the privacy of the health information. If a CE finds out there is a pattern of activity or practice of the BA that constitutes a material breach or violation of the BA's obligation under the contract or other arrangement, unless the CE took reasonable steps to cure the breach or end the violation, as applicable, and, if such steps were unsuccessful, then the CE should terminate the contract or arrangement, if feasible.

BAs are contractors or other personnel who are not part of the hospital workforce, hired to do work that involves the use or disclosure of PHI. Plumbers, electricians, photocopy repair technicians, and similar workers typically do not require access to PHI to perform work for a provider, so they do not meet the definition of a BA, and do not need a BA agreement. Janitorial services are typically not BAs either, because the work they perform usually does not involve the use or disclosure of PHI. Any disclosure of PHI that occurs in performing janitorial duties, such as when emptying trash cans, is likely limited in nature and is incidental to their janitorial functions.

When a service is hired to do work for a CE and the PHI disclosure is not limited, such as routine shredding of PHI documents, then the service would likely be considered a BA. If the work is performed under the direct control of the CE, for instance within the CE's facilities, then the CE treats the service as part of its workforce, and will typically not need a BA contract.

BAs typically do not need to create an NPP. However, a CE must contractually ensure the BA's use and disclosure of PHI is in compliance with the CE's NPP. This is a promise made within the CE's NPP. CEs may also use a BA to distribute the notices to individuals.

17.9 Authorizations

A CE cannot bypass getting an individual's authorization for a use or disclosure that is not permitted by the HIPAA Privacy Rule merely by notifying individuals of the use or disclosure in the NPP. A notice is not a substitute for an individual's authorization. An individual's written authorization must be obtained for any use or disclosure of PHI that is not permitted or required by the Privacy Rule. The NPP must describe the permitted uses and disclosures a CE may make without the individual's authorization, as well as state that any other uses or disclosures will be made only with the individual's written authorization.

17.9.1 Marketing

Health care providers are increasingly performing more marketing activities to create revenue. It is important for providers to thoroughly review and follow the HIPAA requirements for marketing. CEs generally cannot market health-related products and services without authorization from the patient. They also need to let patients know if they are receiving remuneration from a company for marketing the products they provide or recommend to patients. Providers need to review and assess their marketing plans to determine if current marketing activities or plans are in compliance with the HIPAA Privacy Rule. Chapter 6 discusses marketing issues in more detail.

17.9.1.1 Health Care Provider Marketing Checklist* Generally, except as discussed later, any communication that meets the definition of marketing is not permitted unless the CE obtains an authorization. If you receive direct or indirect payment for the marketing from a third party, you must state that such remuneration is involved. See 45 CFR § 164.508(a)(3).

- A communication is not "marketing" if it is made to describe your health-related product or service (or payment for such product or service) that is provided in communications about participants in a health care provider network or health plan network. This permits communications by a provider about its own products or services.
- It is not marketing when a hospital uses its patients list to announce the arrival of a new specialty group (e.g., orthopedic) or the acquisition of new equipment (e.g., X-ray or magnetic resonance imaging machine) through a general mailing or publication.
- A communication is not marketing if it is made for treatment of the individual. For example, it is not marketing when
  - A pharmacy or other health care provider mails prescription refill reminders to patients, or contracts with a mail house to do so.
  - A primary care physician refers an individual to a specialist for a follow-up test or provides free samples of a prescription drug to a patient.
- A communication is not marketing if it is made for case management or care coordination for the individual, or to direct or recommend alternative treatments, therapies, health care providers, or settings of care to the individual. For example, under this exception, it is not marketing when an endocrinologist shares a patient's medical record with several behavior management programs to determine which program best suits the ongoing needs of the individual patient.
- A hospital social worker shares medical record information with various nursing homes in the course of recommending

---

* Modified and paraphrased from the list provided by HHS.

that the patient be transferred from a hospital bed to a nursing home.

- Marketing in the form of a face-to-face communication does not need authorization.

- Providing a promotional gift of nominal value for marketing purposes does not require authorization. For example, no prior authorization is necessary when a hospital provides a free package of formula and other baby products to new mothers as they leave the maternity ward.

- You must obtain patients' authorization for the following types of uses or disclosures of PHI for marketing:
  - Selling PHI to third parties for their use and reuse. Thus, under the rule, a hospital or other provider may not sell names of pregnant women to baby formula manufacturers or magazines without an authorization.
  - Disclosing PHI to outsiders for their independent marketing use. Under the rule, doctors may not provide patient lists to pharmaceutical companies for those companies' drug promotions without an authorization.

- You may not give PHI to a telemarketer, door-to-door salesperson, or other third party you hired to make permitted communications (e.g., about your own goods and services) unless that third party has agreed by contract to use the information only for communicating on your behalf.

- You may not sell PHI to third parties for the third party's own marketing activities without authorization. For example, a pharmacist cannot sell, without patient authorization, a list of patients to a pharmaceutical company so it can market its own products to the individuals on the list.

- You can share PHI with a telemarketer only if you have either obtained the individual's prior written authorization to do so or have entered into a BA relationship with the telemarketer for the purpose of making a communication that is not marketing, such as to inform individuals about the CE's own goods or services.

- Disease management, health promotion, preventive care, and wellness programs generally do not fall under the HIPAA Privacy Rule's definition of marketing. To the extent the disease management or wellness program is operated by you or by a BA, communications about these programs are not marketing because they are about the CE's own health-related services. For example, a hospital's wellness department could start a weight-loss program and send a flyer to all patients seen in the hospital over the past year who meet the definition of obese, even if those individuals were not specifically seen for obesity when they were in the hospital.

- A communication that promotes health in a general manner and does not promote a specific product or service from a particular provider does not meet the definition of marketing. Such communications may include population-based activities in the areas of health education or disease prevention. Examples of general health promotional material include mailings reminding women to get an annual mammogram, or mailings providing information about how to lower cholesterol, new developments in health care (e.g., new diagnostic tools), support groups, organ donation, cancer prevention, and health fairs.

- Communications made to describe your health-related products or services (or payment for such product or service) are not marketing. It is not marketing for a physician who has developed a new "anti-snore" device to send a flyer describing it to all of her patients (whether or not each patient has actually sought treatment for snoring). It is not marketing for an ophthalmologist to send existing patients discounts for eye exams or eyeglasses available only to the patients.

- Communications describing the entities participating in your health care provider network is not marketing. For example, it is not marketing for an independent physicians' association to send its patients a preferred provider list.

- It is not marketing for you to make a prescription refill reminder even if a third party pays for the communication. The prescription refill reminder is considered treatment. The communication is therefore excluded from the definition of marketing and does not require a prior authorization. Similarly, it is not marketing when a doctor or pharmacist is paid by a pharmaceutical company to recommend an alternative medication to patients. Communications about alternative treatments are excluded from the definition of marketing and do not require a prior authorization. The simple receipt of remuneration does not transform a treatment communication into a commercial promotion of a product or service.

- You may use a legitimate BA to assist in making permissible communications. For instance, if a pharmacist that has been paid by a third party contracts with a mail house to send out prescription refill reminders to the pharmacist's patients, neither the mail house nor the pharmacist needs a prior authorization. However, a CE would require an authorization if it sold PHI to a third party for the third party's marketing purposes.

- Appointment reminders are considered part of treatment of an individual and can be made without an authorization.

- Alternative treatments are treatments that are within the range of treatment options available to an individual and do not need authorization. For example, it would be an alternative treatment communication if a doctor, in response to an inquiry from a patient with a skin rash about the range of treatment options, mails the patient a letter recommending that the patient purchase various ointments and medications described in brochures enclosed with the letter. Alternative treatment could also include alternative medicine. Alternative treatments include communications by a nurse-midwife who recommends or sells vitamins and herbal preparations, dietary and exercise programs, massage services, music, or other alternative types of therapy to her pregnant patients.

- Prior authorizations are not required when a doctor distributes promotional gifts of nominal value. You may distribute items commonly known as promotional gifts of nominal value without prior authorization, even if such items are distributed with the intent of encouraging the receiver to buy the products or services. This authorization exception generally applies to items and services of a third party, whether or not they are health-related, or items and services of the CE that are not health-related. A covered doctor, for instance, may send patients items such as pens, notepads, and cups embossed with a health plan's logo without prior authorization. Similarly, dentists may give patients free toothbrushes, floss, and toothpaste.

- You may give or discuss products or services, even when not health related, with patients without a prior authorization in face-to-face encounters. This prevents unnecessary intrusion into the doctor–patient relationship. Physicians may give out free pharmaceutical samples, regardless of their value. Similarly, hospitals may give infant supplies to new mothers. Moreover, the face-to-face exception allows providers to leave general circulation materials in their offices for patients to pick up during office visits.
- You may use information regarding specific clinical conditions of individuals to communicate about products or services for these conditions without a prior authorization. If the communication is for the individual's treatment or for case management, care coordination, or the recommendation of alternative therapies, the Privacy Rule permits the use of clinical information to the extent it is reasonably necessary for these communications. Similarly, population-based activities in the areas of health education or disease prevention are not considered marketing when they promote health in a general manner. Again, clinical information may be used for such communications, such as in a public education campaign.

The Health Information Technology for Economic and Clinical Health (HITECH) rule eliminated the ability of a CE to receive remuneration for the following treatment or health care operation communications:

- Communications to describe a health-related product or service that is provided by the CE
- Communications for the treatment of an individual
- Communications for case management or care coordination for the individual

As a result of the HITECH Act, a CE can still make these communications, but it cannot receive remuneration for doing so without an authorization from the individual. The rule has an exception for communications that describe a drug or biologic currently pre-scribed, such as a refill reminder, as long as any payment received by the CE for making the communication is reasonably related to the cost of making the communication; the CE cannot make a profit from such communications. However, some state laws, such as in California, also prohibit remunerated marketing and do not have this exception.

17.9.1.2 Fund-Raising It is a common practice within many health care providers to hold fund-raisers to help purchase new equipment, facilities, and so forth. Fund-raising for a provider's own benefit is defined to be part of health care operations. HIPAA provides restric-tions on how PHI may be used for such fund-raising purposes.

A CE may use, or disclose to a business associate or to an institutionally related foundation, the following PHI for the purpose of raising funds for its own benefit, without an authorization (45 CFR § 164.508[f][1]):

- Demographic information relating to an individual, including name, address, other contact information, age, gender, and date of birth
- Dates of health care provided to an individual
- Department of service information
- Treating physician
- Outcome information
- Health insurance status

Chapter 6 discusses fund-raising in more detail.

17.9.1.3 Real-World Challenges The following types of health care providers face some unique compliance challenges that must be addressed through careful consideration of risk assessment results, and thoughtful analysis of potential mitigation actions:

- *Hospitals.* The large number of patients and visitors requires hospitals to ensure patient charts are consistently handled and placed in ways that do not reveal patient information more than incidentally. There is also a challenge to ensure staff members do not keep their computers logged on, leaving them unsecured while they leave the workstation; this allows for unauthorized access to all the PHI they have access to through that workstation. As mentioned in Section 17.5, breaches involving faxes are also a large problem within hospital systems.

- *Health care clinics.* These are often short of resources and lacking the support necessary to know, understand, and appropriately safeguard all forms of PHI. Minimum necessary requirements are typically a significant challenge within clinics.
- *Homecare providers.* These have unique challenges in that the care environment is not under the control of the care provider. This makes it more important to implement physical and technical controls of the mobile computing devices, digital storage devices, and hard copy materials containing PHI that the providers take with them during their home visits. Theft and loss of these items is also a growing problem, further necessitating strong controls such as full disk encryption, tracking devices, frequent backups, and remote wipe capabilities.
- *Mental health and substance abuse.* One of the biggest challenges for these care providers is figuring out what can often be the confusing requirements for how, when, and with whom mental health and substance abuse records can be shared. On February 20, 2014, the Department of Health and Human Services (HHS) released new guidance on how the Privacy Rule protects patients' rights to mental health information and in what circumstances the Privacy Rule allows providers to communicate with others, including friends and family members. This guidance document, "HIPAA Privacy Rule and Sharing Information Related to Mental Health," was located at http://www.hhs.gov/ocr/privacy/hipaa/understanding/special/mhguidancepdf.pdf at the time this book was published. If it is no longer there, you should be able to find it by doing a search of the title along with ".gov" and "HHS."

For all of the above, training and ongoing awareness communications are typically completely lacking or severely insufficient and ineffective.

Practical Checklist

- Post your complete NPP in a conspicuous location within your facilities.
- Establish procedures for making best effort attempts to obtain individuals' receipts of the notices.
- Establish safeguards to limit incidental disclosure of PHI within your facilities.
- Include appropriate safeguard requirements within BA contracts.
- Review your marketing and fund-raising plans and determine what is allowed with and without authorization.
- Determine your fax risks, and implement appropriate controls to mitigate those risks.
- Implement safeguards for mobile computing and storage devices.

18

HEALTH CARE
CLEARINGHOUSE ISSUES

18.1 Background

The issue of whether or not an entity is a health care clearinghouse has been the center of much debate over the years. The Health Insurance Portability and Accountability Act (HIPAA) defines a health care clearinghouse as follows:

> A public or private entity … that does either of the following functions:
>
> 1. Processes or facilitates the processing of health informa-tion … in a nonstandard format or containing nonstan-dard data content into standard data elements or a standard transaction
> 2. Receives a standard transaction … and processes or facili-tates the processing of health information [in the standard transaction] into nonstandard format or nonstandard data content for the receiving entity

See 45 CFR § 160.103 for the complete definition.

If your organization processes or facilitates the processing of health information from nonstandard format or content into standard format or content, or from standard format or content into nonstandard for-mat or content, then you are likely a health care clearinghouse, and also a covered entity (CE) subject to HIPAA requirements. Unlike health care providers and plans, though, health care clearinghouses do not have to develop a Notice of Privacy Practices if the only pro-tected health information (PHI) they create or receive is as a business associate (BA) of another CE.

18.2 Requirements

First review the regulatory text that applies to health care clearing-houses to get a good feel for what you need to do. See § 164.500(b)(1) within the HIPAA regulatory text. To summarize, health care clear-inghouses must comply with the following HIPAA requirements:

- *Section 164.500 relating to applicability*: When health care clearinghouses are BAs to another CE, they may use and disclose PHI only as allowed by their BA agreement. When a health care clearinghouse functions as a CE, then it must abide by all of the applicable HIPAA requirements for CEs.

- *Section 164.501 relating to definitions*: The definitions made within the HIPAA regulations apply to all health care clearinghouses.

- *Section 164.502 relating to uses and disclosures of PHI*: Except that a clearinghouse is prohibited from using or disclosing PHI other than as permitted in the BA contract under which it created or received the PHI. Chapter 3 details the uses and disclosures requirements in detail.

- *Section 164.504 relating to the organizational requirements for CEs*: Including the designation of health care components of a CE, which apply to health care clearinghouses. See Chapter 5 for details.

- *Section 164.512 relating to uses and disclosures for which individual authorization or an opportunity to agree or object is not required*: Except that a clearinghouse is prohibited from using or disclosing PHI other than as permitted in the BA contract under which it created or received the PHI. This issue is discussed within Chapter 5.

- *Section 164.532 relating to transition requirements*: This will be of most significance with regard to BA agreements. A sample BA agreement can be found in Appendix B.

- *Section 164.534 relating to compliance dates for initial implementation of the privacy standards*: Health care clearinghouses were supposed to be compliant by April 14, 2003, with regard to being a CE. If a health care clearinghouse is considered a BA, it must be compliant with agreement revisions as indicated in the previous item.

Please be sure to discuss all these issues with your legal counsel. As we emphasize throughout this book, each organization has its own unique characteristics and business environment. You must determine what is applicable for your specific situation.

18.3 Transactions

HIPAA establishes requirements for processing financial electronic data interchange (EDI) transactions using uniform electronic standards. Although this is not the focus of this book, it is an important issue and helps demonstrate why health care clearinghouses are CEs and subject to Privacy Rule and Security Rule requirements. Because health care clearinghouses must edit electronic transactions according to HIPAA requirements, they must edit down to the data element level, which will involve accessing PHI, and also ensure all the medical codes are current and correct.

Clearinghouses and EDI translators may sometimes encounter transactions with missing information. Most of this missing information will need to be supplied by the underlying business applications that are generating the transaction information. This type of access and manipulation of information is another driver for making clearinghouses HIPAA CEs. These issues must be addressed within the BA agreements.

Network security requirements will vary between a clearinghouse's information-trading partners, and also between the various communications systems used. The Security Rule does not specify technology platforms, but focuses on the security issues and requirements for the exchange of PHI. The resulting disadvantage to clearinghouses is that each information-trading partner may be using a different system or technology. Health care clearinghouses may need to ensure Security Rule compliance (and, of course, Privacy Rule, HITECH Act, and Omnibus Rule compliance) for multiple systems and security solutions and technologies. This will likely require clearinghouses to invest money, knowledge, and people to achieve and maintain compliance.

If possible, you can minimize your health care clearinghouse's associated compliance resources and costs by using only one network security solution for your EDI network regardless of your BA relationship technologies. The key will be to ensure your systems are as compatible as possible with your EDI-trading partners, and also have your trading partners make changes in their systems as well. Because they are also impacted by the HIPAA requirements, chances are they are going to be making changes within their systems anyway.

18.4 Financial Institutions

A critical consideration for banks is determining what payment-processing activities qualify as CE and BA activities under HIPAA. If you look at the literal interpretation of the HIPAA definition of a health care clearinghouse, then it would seem it does cover financial institutions. In the normal course of business, many financial institutions may receive the following:

- Payment instruction from a HIPAA CE, such as a health care provider or insurance company, and will need to send automated clearinghouse (ACH) transactions with addenda in a HIPAA-compliant format
- ACH transactions with addenda in a HIPAA-compliant format, and will pass this information on to a CE after editing to a human-readable or other usable form

Banks and other financial institutions processing payments need to examine their payment processing activities closely to determine if they are, in fact, CEs. Many financial institutions may originate or receive HIPAA standard transactions (such as the Healthcare Claim Payment [835] and Premium Payment [820]), but they often will pass on the data without doing any conversions or reformatting. Even though these messages may be HIPAA transactions, the financial institution would not necessarily be considered a BA. There are some financial institutions, however, that provide value-added services for their health care customers that would then qualify them as a health care clearinghouse. For example, some health plans and providers may use financial institutions for support services to translate or edit files to meet the HIPAA criteria for electronic transactions. Some financial institutions may also translate specific transactions or addenda from nonstandard to HIPAA-compliant formats when requested by customers. In these situations, they will likely need to comply with the HIPAA Privacy Rule and Security Rule in addition to the other HIPAA rules.

If they are not CEs, financial institutions may very well be BAs to CEs if they process PHI for their customers. In this scenario, they will be subject to the security and privacy provisions of HIPAA as they relate to BA agreements. To complicate matters, these HIPAA requirements may conflict with federal banking laws. Accreditation by the Electronic Healthcare Network Accreditation Commission (EHNAC) is recommended. You can get more information at the EHNAC website at https://www.ehnac.org.

18.5 Conclusion

Health care clearinghouses will be CEs, BAs, or both. As such, all health care clearinghouses must understand and take action to comply with HIPAA and its subsequent updates in the HITECH Act and Omnibus Rule. Financial institutions that qualify as health care clearinghouses will generally be well positioned to meet the confidentiality requirements of HIPAA as a result of already taking actions to comply with the privacy and information security requirements imposed by the Gramm–Leach–Bliley Act (GLBA). Privacy practices notices for organizations that are covered by both HIPAA and GLBA will likely need to be revised to incorporate the following:

- Standard language for confidentiality assurances that is acceptable to financial institutions as well as the HIPAA requirements
- Definitions of the financial institution's HIPAA responsibilities to maintain records of and log access to the PHI using procedures that will likely be new within their organizations
- Breach response and notification policies and procedures (see Appendix C for an example)
- A mechanism to account for uses and disclosures
- Assurance that all BAs have signed BA agreements, and also can provide appropriate validation that they have proper safeguards in place

Practical Checklist

- Determine if you are considered a health care clearinghouse.
- Determine if you are considered a BA.
- Designate security and privacy officers and document your security and privacy responsibilities.
- Perform a security risk assessment to determine your baseline security posture, as well as a Privacy Rule gap analysis to identify your privacy vulnerabilities.
- Ensure that Internet and other external network connections are adequately protected from attack and are tested for vulnerabilities periodically.
- Review, revise as necessary, and periodically update security and privacy policies to meet HIPAA and related requirements.
- Review and update as necessary existing BA agreements to include the latest HITECH Act and Omnibus Rule changes.
- Inventory your PHI uses and disclosures.
- Provide privacy and security training for your personnel.
- Ensure that you only disclose PHI as required in BA agreements as they apply to the health care clearinghouse components of your organization.

19

HEALTH PLAN ISSUES

19.1 What Is a Health Plan?

The term "health plan" refers to an individual or group plan that provides or pays the cost of medical care. These include amounts paid for the following:

1. Diagnosis, cure, mitigation, treatment, or prevention of disease, or amounts paid for the purpose of affecting any structure or function of the body
2. Amounts paid for transportation primarily for and essential to medical care referred to in list item 1
3. Amounts paid for insurance covering medical care referred to in list items 1 and 2

See Title 42 U.S.C. 300gg-91(a)(2) for full details of health plan medical care costs.

A health plan, as defined in the Public Health Service (PHS) Act, includes any combination of the following:

- A group health plan (as defined in Section 2791[a] of the PHS Act), if the plan
  - Has 50 or more participants (as defined in Section 3[7] of the Employee Retirement Income Security Act [ERISA] of 1974)
  - Is administered by an entity other than the employer who established and maintains the plan
- A health insurance issuer (as defined in Section 2791[b] of the PHS Act)
- A health maintenance organization (as defined in Section 2791[b] of the PHS Act)

- Part A or B of the Medicare program under Title XVIII
- The Medicaid program under Title XIX
- A Medicare supplemental policy (as defined in Section 1882[g][1])
- A long-term care policy, including a nursing home fixed indemnity policy (unless the secretary of the Department of Health and Human Services [HHS] determines that such a policy does not provide sufficiently comprehensive coverage of a benefit so that the policy should be treated as a health plan)
- An employee welfare benefit plan or any other arrangement that is established or maintained for the purpose of offering or providing health benefits to the employees of two or more employers
- The health care program for active military personnel under Title 10 U.S.C.
- The veterans' health care program under Title 38 U.S.C. Chapter 17
- The Civilian Health and Medical Program of the Uniformed Services (CHAMPUS), as defined in Title 10 U.S.C. § 1072(4)
- The Indian Health Service Program under the Indian Healthcare Improvement Act (25 U.S.C. 1601 et seq.)
- The Federal Employees Health Benefit Plan under Title 5 U.S.C. Chapter 89

45 CFR § 144.103 defines a group health plan as the following:

Group health plan means an employee welfare benefit plan (as defined in Section 3[1] of ERISA) to the extent that the plan provides medical care (as defined in Section 2791[a][2] of the PHS Act and including items and services paid for as medical care) to employees or their dependents (as defined under the terms of the plan) directly or through insurance, reimbursement, or otherwise. For more information on what constitutes a group health plan, see our November 2000 Bulletin No. 00-06, Circumstances Under Which Health Insurance Regulated as 'Individual' Coverage Under State Law is Subject to the Group Market Requirements of the Health Insurance Portability and Accountability Act of 1996.

Government-funded health plans include the following:

- Medicare program under Title XVIII of the Social Security Act (Parts A, B, and C of 42 U.S.C. 1395, et seq.)
- Medicaid program under Title XIX of the Social Security Act (42 U.S.C. 1396, et seq.)
- Health care program for active military personnel (10 U.S.C. 1074, et seq.)
- Veterans' health care program (38 U.S.C. Chapter 17)
- CHAMPUS (10 U.S.C. 1061, et seq.)
- Indian Health Service program under the Indian Healthcare Improvement Act (25 U.S.C. 1601)
- Federal Employees Health Benefit Program (5 U.S.C. Chapter 89)
- Approved state child health programs under Title XXI of the Social Security Act (42 U. S. C. 1397, et seq.) (State Children's Health Insurance Program)

A third-party administrator (TPA) to a group health plan is not a covered entity (CE) based on TPA activities. A TPA of a group health plan is a business associate (BA) of the group health plan. It is possible that a TPA may meet the definition of a CE based on its other activities, for example, if it also provides group health insurance.

19.2 What Is a Small Health Plan?

The Health Insurance Portability and Accountability Act (HIPAA) defines a small health plan as one that has annual receipts of $5 million or less. Health plans should use the guidance provided by the Small Business Administration at 13 CFR 121.104 to calculate their annual receipts. Health plans that do not report receipts to the Internal Revenue Service (e.g., ERISA group health plans that are exempt from filing income tax returns) should use proxy measures to determine their annual receipts.

19.3 Health Plan Requirements

The Privacy Rule regulatory text has some very specific requirements for health plans as indicated in the following excerpts.

§ 164.504(f)(1)

1. Standard: requirements for group health plans.

    i. Except as provided under paragraph (f)(1)(ii) or (iii) of this section or as otherwise authorized under Sec. 164.508, a group health plan, in order to disclose PHI to the plan sponsor or to provide for or permit the disclosure of PHI to the plan sponsor by a health insurance issuer or HMO with respect to the group health plan, must ensure that the plan documents restrict uses and disclosures of such information by the plan sponsor consistent with the requirements of this subpart.

    ii. The group health plan, or a health insurance issuer or HMO with respect to the group health plan, may disclose summary health information to the plan sponsor, if the plan sponsor requests the summary health information for the purposes of:

        A. Obtaining premium bids from health plans for providing health insurance coverage under the group health plan; or

        B. Modifying, amending, or terminating the group health plan.

    iii. The group health plan, or a health insurance issuer or HMO with respect to the group health plan, may disclose to the plan sponsor information on whether the individual is participating in the group health plan, or is enrolled in or has disenrolled from a health insurance issuer or HMO offered by the plan.

§ 164.504(f)(2)

2. Implementation specifications: requirements for plan documents. The plan documents of the group health plan must be amended to incorporate provisions to:

    i. Establish the permitted and required uses and disclosures of such information by the plan sponsor, provided that such permitted and required uses and disclosures may not be inconsistent with this subpart.

ii. Provide that the group health plan will disclose PHI to the plan sponsor only upon receipt of a certification by the plan sponsor that the plan documents have been amended to incorporate the following provisions and that the plan sponsor agrees to:

A. Not use or further disclose the information other than as permitted or required by the plan documents or as required by law;

B. Ensure that any agents, including a subcontractor, to whom it provides PHI received from the group health plan agree to the same restrictions and conditions that apply to the plan sponsor with respect to such information;

C. Not use or disclose the information for employment-related actions and decisions or in connection with any other benefit or employee benefit plan of the plan sponsor;

D. Report to the group health plan any use or disclosure of the information that is inconsistent with the uses or disclosures provided for of which it becomes aware;

E. Make available PHI in accordance with § 164.524;

F. Make available PHI for amendment and incorporate any amendments to PHI in accordance with § 164.526;

G. Make available the information required to provide an accounting of disclosures in accordance with § 164.528;

H. Make its internal practices, books, and records relating to the use and disclosure of PHI received from the group health plan available to the Secretary for purposes of determining compliance by the group health plan with this subpart;

I. If feasible, return or destroy all PHI received from the group health plan that the sponsor still maintains in any form and retain no copies of such information when no longer needed for the purpose for which disclosure was made, except that, if such return or destruction is not feasible, limit further uses and disclosures to those purposes that make the return or destruction of the information infeasible; and

J. Ensure that the adequate separation required in paragraph (f)(2)(iii) of this section (§ 164.504(f) (2)) is established.

§ 164.504(f)(3)(iii)

3. Implementation specifications: uses and disclosures. A group health plan may

   i. Disclose protected health information to a plan sponsor to carry out plan administration functions that the plan sponsor performs only consistent with the provisions of paragraph (f)(2) of this section;

  ii. Not permit a health insurance issuer or HMO with respect to the group health plan to disclose protected health information to the plan sponsor except as permitted by this paragraph;

 iii. Not disclose and may not permit a health insurance issuer or HMO to disclose protected health information to a plan sponsor as otherwise permitted by this paragraph unless a statement required by § 164.520(b) (1)(iii)(C) is included in the appropriate notice; and

  iv. Not disclose protected health information to the plan sponsor for the purpose of employment-related actions or decisions or in connection with any other benefit or employee benefit plan of the plan sponsor.

19.4 Marketing Issues

Health plans depend heavily on their marketing activities to create revenue. For most if not all health plans, the HIPAA Privacy Rule marketing requirements will have a huge impact on their organizations. It is important for health plans to thoroughly review and follow the HIPAA requirements for marketing. CEs generally cannot market health-related products and services without authorization from the patient. Health plans need to review and assess their marketing plans to determine if current marketing activities or plans are in compliance with the HIPAA Privacy Rule. Chapter 6 discusses marketing issues in more detail.

19.4.1 Health Plan Marketing Checklist

- A CE can share PHI with a telemarketer only if the CE has either obtained the individual's prior written authorization to do so, or has entered into a BA relationship with the telemarketer for the purpose of making a communication that is not marketing, such as to inform individuals about the CE's own goods or services.
- The HIPAA Privacy Rule expressly requires an authorization for uses or disclosures of PHI for *all* marketing communications, except in two circumstances: (1) when the communication occurs in a face-to-face encounter between the CE and the individual and (2) when the communication involves a promotional gift of nominal value.
- Generally, disease management, health promotion, preventive care, and wellness programs do not fall under the HIPAA Privacy Rule definition of marketing.
- It is not marketing for a CE to describe products or services that are provided by the CE to its patients, or to describe products or services that are included in the health plan's plan of benefits to members of the health plan.
- It is not marketing for a CE to describe the entities participating in a health care provider network or a health plan network.
- It is not marketing for an insurance plan or health plan to send enrollees notices about changes, replacements, or improvements to existing plans.
- Health plans can communicate about health-related products or services to enrollees that add value to, but are not part of, a plan of benefits.
- Prior authorizations are not required when a doctor or health plan distributes promotional gifts of nominal value.
- Insurance agents who are BAs of a health plan do not need to seek a prior authorization before talking to a customer in

a face-to-face encounter about the insurance company's other lines of business.

- Nothing in the marketing provisions of the Privacy Rule can be considered as amending, modifying, or changing any rule or requirement related to any other federal or state statutes or regulations, including specifically antikickback, fraud, and abuse, or self-referral statutes or regulations, or to authorize or permit any activity or transaction currently proscribed by such statutes and regulations.

19.5 Notice of Privacy Practices

Health plans need to provide a Notice of Privacy Practices (NPP) to individuals covered by the plan and must provide an NPP to new enrollees at the time of enrollment. Health plans must also provide a revised notice to individuals then covered by the plan within 60 days of a material revision, and they must notify individuals then covered by the plan of the availability of the privacy practices notice, and how to obtain the notice at least once every three years.

The Privacy Rule does not require a group health plan to provide an NPP if it provides benefits only through one or more contracts of insurance with health insurance issuers or health maintenance organizations (HMOs), and if it does not create or receive PHI other than summary health information or enrollment or disenrollment information.

19.5.1 Health Plan NPP Checklist

- A health plan may e-mail the notice to an individual if the individual agrees to receive an electronic notice (see 45 CFR § 164.520(c) for the specific requirements for providing the notice).
- A health plan may develop more than one notice, such as when an entity performs different types of covered functions (i.e., the functions that make it a health plan, a health care provider, or a health care clearinghouse) and there are variations in its privacy practices among these covered functions.

- A health plan must have provided the NPP to individuals covered by the plan.
- A health plan must provide a revised notice to individuals then covered by the plan within 60 days of a material revision.
- A health plan must notify individuals covered by the plan of the availability of the NPP and information about how to obtain the notice at least once every three years.
- Health plans are not required to make a good-faith effort to obtain a written acknowledgment of the receipt of the notice from their enrollees.
- A health plan does not have to provide a copy of its notice to each dependent receiving coverage under a policy.
- A health plan must send its notice to each individual covered by the plan. A health plan can send the notice to the administrator of the group product or the plan sponsor for them to distribute to employees enrolled in the plan. However, if the other person or entity fails to distribute the notice to the plan's enrollees, the health plan may be in violation of the Privacy Rule.

19.6 Types of Insurance Plans Excluded from HIPAA

The following types of insurance generally are not considered health plans covered under HIPAA regulations:

- Long-term disability
- Short-term disability
- Workers' compensation
- Automobile liability that includes coverage for medical payments

HIPAA specifically excludes from the definition of a "health plan" any policy, plan, or program to the extent that it provides or pays for the cost of excepted benefits, which are listed in Section 2791(c)(1) of the PHS Act, 42 U.S.C. 300gg-91(c)(1). See 45 CFR § 160.103 for more details and direction about the type of insurance covered by HIPAA.

19.7 Communications

A health care provider may disclose PHI to a health plan for the plan's Health Plan Employer Data and Information Set. The Privacy Rule allows a provider to disclose PHI to a health plan for the quality-related health care operations of the health plan, provided the health plan has or had a relationship with the individual who is the subject of the information, and the PHI requested pertains to the relationship.

19.8 Government and Law Enforcement

19.8.1 Government Departments

State, county, and local health departments are required to comply with the Privacy Rule if the applicable department performs functions that make it a CE. For example, under the Privacy Rule a state Medicaid program is a CE (a health plan). Health departments that operate health care clinics are health care providers. If these health care providers transmit health information electronically in connection with a transaction covered in the HIPAA Transactions Rule, they are CEs. For more information, see the definitions of CE, health care provider, health plan, and health care clearinghouse in 45 CFR 160.103. There are also helpful "CE Decision Tools" at http://www.hhs.gov/ocr/privacy/hipaa/understanding/coveredentities to help determine whether a person, business, or agency is a covered health care provider, health care clearinghouse, or health plan. If the health department performs some covered functions and other noncovered functions, it should designate those components that perform covered functions as the health care component(s) of the organization. They will then be considered a hybrid entity.

19.8.2 Government Enforcement

HHS is responsible for investigating complaints that any provisions of the Privacy Rule, Security Rule, and Health Information Technology for Economic and Clinical Health (HITECH) Act have been violated, and to look into other information related to noncompliance. This will sometimes require reviewing PHI, such as situations in which individuals report that they believe a CE has handled their medical records improperly. The information to which they will need access will depend on the circumstances and associated allegations. The Privacy Rule limits the Office for Civil Rights' (OCR) access to only the information necessary to determine compliance. There may be situations where no PHI is needed. Examples of investigations where the OCR may need access to PHI include the following:

- Accusations that a CE did not appropriately respond to a request to correct a patient's medical record
- Accusations that a CE inappropriately used health information for marketing without first obtaining authorization as required by the Privacy Rule
- Accusations that a patient record was inappropriately modified

The HITECH Act granted state attorneys general the authority to enforce HIPAA Rules by bringing civil actions on behalf of state residents in federal district court. The HITECH Act Section 13410(e)(1) provisions describe the role of state attorneys general for enforcement of HIPAA Rules.[1]

19.8.3 Debt Collection Agencies

The Privacy Rule allows CEs to use the services of debt collection agencies. Debt collection is recognized as a payment activity within the HIPAA definition of "payment" in 45 CFR § 164.501. A CE may use a debt collection agency through a BA arrangement. Disclosures to collection agencies must occur as directed by the other Privacy Rule requirements, including the BA and minimum necessary requirements.

19.8.4 Law Enforcement

The Privacy Rule does not expand current law enforcement access to PHI. HHS had stated that in its opinion the Privacy Rule limits access to law enforcement to a greater degree than currently exists with the establishment of new procedures and safeguards that limit the situation under which a CE may give such information to law enforcement officers. The Privacy Rule limits the type of information that CEs may disclose to law enforcement without a warrant or similar document.

For example, it specifically prohibits disclosure of DNA information without a warrant or similar approval. The Privacy Rule requires CEs to obtain permission from persons who have been the victim of domestic violence or abuse in most circumstances before disclosing the information to law enforcement. Most state laws do not currently require this type of permission. When state laws impose additional restrictions on the disclosure of health information to law enforcement, those state laws continue to apply. Even when the Privacy Rule *allows* disclosure to law enforcement, the rule does not *require* CEs to disclose any information. Other federal or state laws may require such a disclosure, and in those cases the Privacy Rule does not take precedence over other laws. CEs should use their best professional and ethical judgment to determine whether to disclose information. Their decisions should mirror their organization's policies and ethical principles.

19.8.5 *Multistate Issues*

The Meaningful Use portion of the Patient Protection and Affordable Care Act resulted in implementations of electronic health information exchanges (HIEs) throughout the United States. The purpose of an HIE is to allow health care professionals and patients to appropriately access and securely share a patient's vital medical information electronically. There are many health care delivery scenarios driving the technology behind the different forms of health information exchange available today. This creates more complexity and information security and privacy risks to address. In addition to the associated meaningful use requirements for HIEs, which are generally extensions and more specific elaborations of the HIPAA requirements, there are now also additional state- and local-level laws to follow. See more about meaningful use in Chapter 2.

A large number of health insurance and managed care organizations have members in more than one state. Chapter 9 explores state preemption issues in detail. There are also implementation considerations for such organizations. If you are such an organization, following your state preemption analysis, you need to create or update your policies and procedures to comply with HIPAA and state laws based on the analysis results. This sounds easy, right? Well, it can really be quite a complicated activity, especially for health plans that sell multiple products in multiple markets across multiple states. Some actions you should take include the following:

- Identify the situations within the course of your business in which you are considered a CE. You may actually be a BA in some situations; identify these situations as well.
- Identify the federal and state agencies regulating your services and products in all your jurisdictions. A preemptive analysis will be necessary for some regulatory agencies, but may not be necessary for others.
- Determine how to combine all applicable state and federal requirements into your policies, procedures, and other relevant documents.

The most common definition applicable for health insurers and managed care companies within the regulatory text is "covered entity, health plan." There are situations when a health insurer or managed care organization is not a covered entity, health plan. If your organization is acting with a self-insured group health plan, you are not considered a CE; you are a BA of the group health plan.

However, if you sell an insured product to the employer, you may then become a "covered entity, health plan." In this case you would be both a CE and a non-CE to the same customer, depending on whether you assume insurance on some product lines. You must identify your customers and your products for which you must meet all HIPAA requirements as a CE health plan in addition to identifying when you have BA relationships to know how to comply with the laws.

Probably the most difficult activity for a multistate CE health plan is incorporating state requirements into your policies and procedures. It is not always feasible to create policies and procedures that will be applicable across all states. In these situations you will likely need to create not only multiple policies and procedures but also multiple forms and letters to cover the same issues.

For instance, right of access to PHI can vary greatly between states and agencies, starting with the definition of health information. The HIPAA definition of PHI usually allows individuals access to more types of information than state definitions of health information. However, some states use the definitions found in the National

Association of Insurance Commissioners' Insurance Information and Privacy Protection Model Act (http://www.naic.org/committees _index_model_description_i_q.htm). This model act also requires an accounting of disclosures along with information in response to infor-mation access requests.

Attention to privacy issues is increasing. It is likely health plans will receive more questions from consumers related to privacy, and could very well experience increased regulatory reviews, fines, and lit-igation. Because of the huge penalties and consequences, health plans must perform rigorous analysis, provide sufficient training, and create comprehensive policies and procedures.

Practical Checklist

- Determine if you are considered a health plan.
- See the HHS website (http://www.hhs.gov/ocr/privacy/hipaa /understanding/coveredentities/marketing.html) for detailed information about marketing and HIPAA.
- Generally, disease management, health promotion, preventive care, and wellness programs are not considered marketing.
- Determine if you should create more than one NPP.
- Health plans do not need to obtain a written acknowledg-ment of NPP receipt.
- Identify all state and federal PHI-related requirements and incorporate them into your policies and procedures.

20

EMPLOYER ISSUES

20.1 Background

Health Insurance Portability and Accountability Act (HIPAA) requirements are applicable to group health plans and issuers. In most cases, if you offer a group health plan to your employees, the health plan must comply with all HIPAA requirements. Eligibility for health plan enrollment is determined according to the terms of the health plan and the rules of the issuer, but not according to an individual's health status or that of an individual's dependent. These rules and terms must comply with all applicable state laws. This chapter examines some of the common issues related to employers and HIPAA, focusing on security and privacy issues. Because each organization is unique, you should consult with your organization's legal counsel to determine exactly how the regulations will apply to you. However, the information here can provide a good background for your meeting with legal counsel, in addition to helping you identify topics to discuss and address prior to the meeting.

A large percentage of employers believe that HIPAA does not apply to them if they do not sell health insurance or do not provide medical care and treatment. Many employers would be surprised or alarmed to learn how HIPAA can and likely will impact their operations. Employers must determine the nature of their relationship with their employee benefit plans, their use of protected health information (PHI), and how their activities must be modified to comply with HIPAA.

The Privacy Rule will apply to you indirectly as an employer or welfare benefit sponsor. The Privacy Rule will apply directly to you as a group health plan (as defined in the Employee Retirement Income Security Act [ERISA]) or a health plan (as defined in HIPAA). The only ERISA plans that are exempt are those self-administered with fewer than 50 participants. Most ERISA plans and multiemployer plans are covered entities (CEs) under the rule. The regulation also makes it applicable to "any other individual or group plan or combination of individual or group plans that provides or pays for the cost of medical care."

Most employers researching their health information uses and disclosures will discover that they receive health information in ways other than through the health plan. For instance, health information is received through the following:

- Workers' compensation
- Short-term disability/long-term disability
- Americans with Disabilities Act (ADA)
- Family Medical Leave Act (FMLA)
- Life insurance
- Long-term care
- Retiree coverage (e.g., Medigap and M+C)
- Drug and other employment screening tests
- Group health plan or preemployment physicals
- On-site health management programs
- On-site child care

Because health information in these situations was not created or received by the group health plan, its use is not a HIPAA issue for the employer. However, there may be other applicable federal or state laws covering the information, in addition to established company policies. With specific regard to HIPAA, this health information is not considered PHI for the employer. However, the provider may still need an authorization to release it. These other laws typically restrict distribution of employee health information as well as limit how employers can use such information to make employment decisions. HIPAA imposes additional requirements on all employers who sponsor employee health plans. Employers who are also CEs will usually be impacted in three major areas:

1. Organizational
2. Notice requirements
3. Use and disclosure requirements

Laws that also impact the use of health information include, but are not necessarily limited to, the following:

- ERISA
- Genetic Information Nondiscrimination Act
- ADA
- Federal substance abuse confidentiality requirements
- Gramm–Leach–Bliley Act
- Freedom of Information Act
- Family Educational Rights and Privacy Act
- FMLA
- European Union Data Protection Directive
- Canada's Personal Information Protection and Electronic Documents Act

20.2 "Small" and "Large" Employers

HIPAA defines a small employer as a company (or a nonfederal government employer) that has at least two but no more than 50 employees. Be aware that some states consider a business with only one employee a small employer. A large employer is defined as an organization (or a nonfederal governmental employer) that has at least 51 employees. Some HIPAA requirements apply only to large employers.

20.2.1 Small Employer Issues

HIPAA marketing rules apply to every employer group health plan that has at least two participants. HIPAA also guarantees access to health coverage for small employers. For the most part, no insurer can exclude a worker or family member from employer-sponsored coverage based on health status. Effective July 1, 1997, insurers were required to renew coverage to all groups, regardless of the health status of any member.

Your insurer should handle the HIPAA information collection activities for you when you purchase group health insurance coverage. Be sure to discuss this with your insurer to work out HIPAA process-related issues together. If you are self-insured, you are already performing a significant amount of insurance management and should have systems in place for executing your self-insurance. Incorporating the HIPAA requirements will be an addition to the processes you are already doing.

20.3 Health Benefits

Most employers now offer their employees wellness programs, on-site clinics, day care, employee assistance programs, and similar health-related benefits. Employers are generally not considered CEs under HIPAA definitions. However, employers qualify as CEs when they sponsor health care components such as self-insured health plans, wellness programs, on-site clinics, or employee assistance programs. The Privacy Rule impacts the use and disclosure of PHI by the health care component of the employer and the applicable personnel, and requires the establishment of "firewalls," or procedural and operational separations, to keep health-related functions separate from general, employment-related functions and personnel.

20.4 Enforcement and Penalties

States have the primary enforcement responsibility for the group and individual requirements imposed on health insurance issuers using sanctions available under the applicable state laws. If states do not take appropriate actions for their areas of responsibility, the secretary of the Department of Health and Human Services (HHS) may determine that they have failed to enforce the law, and then apply federal enforcement authority. This can result in sanctions on insurers as specified in HIPAA, as well as civil monetary penalties.

The secretary of HHS is responsible for enforcing nonfederal governmental plans, self-funded, and insured plans. HHS can impose sanctions on plans or plan sponsors as outlined within HIPAA, including civil monetary penalties. In addition, the secretary of labor enforces requirements on employment-based group health plans, including self-insured arrangements under ERISA. Individual employees can file suit to enforce ERISA.

Besides the indicated penalties and sanctions possible from HHS, the secretary of labor, and the states, the secretary of the treasury can impose tax penalties on employers or plans that are not compliant with HIPAA. The tax code obligates the employer or plan to pay the excise tax whether or not the secretary of the treasury has taken any enforcement action.

20.5 Organizational Requirements

20.5.1 Employer Obligations as CEs

As plan sponsors or plan fiduciaries, most employers need to implement the HIPAA requirements on behalf of their covered benefit plans, or to ensure that the insurance provider implements the HIPAA requirements or the Privacy Rule; plans must develop policies, procedures, and systems to address appropriate uses and disclosures of PHI. Plans must develop procedures to ensure that only those personnel with a need to know, use, or access PHI can comply with the minimum necessary requirements. The Privacy Rule does not apply to uses and disclosures of PHI made in accordance with individual authorizations.

Hybrid entities have components that fall under HIPAA. In general, a hybrid entity (such as a corporation) is one that qualifies as a CE, but whose covered functions are not the primary functions of the organization. For example, an employer in a non-health-related industry that self-administers a sponsored health plan is a hybrid entity, as is an employer that has an on-site medical clinic. (See Chapter 1 for more information about hybrid entities.) The Privacy Rule impacts hybrid entities as it applies only to the covered activities. Within hybrid entities there must be operational and procedural firewall separations between health care components and the other components. The transfer of PHI from the health care component to another area of the organization is considered a disclosure under the Privacy Rule.

At a high level, HIPAA requires employers acting as CEs to do the following:

- Amend health plan documents, such as ERISA-mandated summary plan descriptions, to include many specific privacy provisions when the employer, as a health plan sponsor, receives health information beyond that needed to enroll and disenroll participants.

- Negotiate or revise written contracts with third-party administrators, insurers, health maintenance organizations (HMOs), case managers, disease managers, utilization review and other managed care vendors, and other business associates (BAs). These contracts must include many specific privacy provisions.
- Appoint a privacy officer responsible for enterprise privacy issues, employee HIPAA and PHI training and awareness, and ensuring the implementation of privacy policies, practices, and procedures.
- Establish procedures for participants to inspect and copy their PHI, amend their records, and receive an accounting of all covered disclosures of their PHI.
- Implement procedures to resolve PHI-related complaints and grievances.
- Obtain authorization from each participant whose PHI will be used for any purpose other than treatment, payment, and operations.
- Separate health plan administration where PHI is used or disclosed from another organizational function, including the administration of other ERISA benefit plans.

20.5.2 Employer Obligations as Plan Sponsors

Plan sponsors must comply with several HIPAA requirements related to how PHI is handled and how health plan documents must be amended. Employers who are plan sponsors must assess how their organization handles employee health care information, determine who needs access to this information, and determine if the information gathered by the employer qualifies as PHI according to HIPAA. Plan sponsors typically do not need to sign BA agreements.

Most employers need access to the PHI in their plans, particularly for settlement purposes. HHS has indicated that it believes most employers are probably holding or gathering PHI, which in turn likely makes them subject to the HIPAA plan sponsor requirements. As a result, most employers that act as plan sponsors need to comply with the HIPAA plan sponsor requirements. Employers that are plan sponsors, with plans that qualify as group health plans, and employers that acquire PHI from the covered plans, need to address HIPAA requirements. These employers need to amend group health plan documents, agree to comply with these documents, and implement necessary safeguards. A group health plan must include provisions within the plan documents to establish the allowed and required PHI uses and disclosures before PHI can be disclosed to the sponsor.

20.5.3 Employer Organizational Requirements

Employers falling under one or both of the aforementioned descriptions will need to do the following to address these HIPAA requirements:

- Amend employee sanctions and disciplinary policies
- Communicate the employee HIPAA obligations
- Apply disciplinary actions for improper use and disclosure of PHI
- Confirm employee awareness and understanding of HIPAA policy
- Appoint a privacy official
- Develop complaint processes and sanctions
- Implement personnel training and awareness programs
- Establish a plan to comply with the minimum necessary requirements
- Implement physical, administrative, and technical safeguards for PHI
- Establish a minimum six-year records retention policy
- Implement procedures to ensure beneficiary rights
- Ensure the covered plan participants receive the Notice of Privacy Practices
- Obtain authorizations as applicable to HIPAA requirements

Exemption from HIPAA requirements may be available to group health plans that provide benefits only through insurance or HMO coverage, or who do not create or receive PHI except in summary form, and for premium and plan settlement purposes. Be sure to discuss this issue thoroughly with your organization's legal counsel; each situation is unique to the organization.

20.6 Health Information

Under HIPAA, employer health plan sponsors are typically allowed to have access to summary health information. Summary health information does the following:

- Summarizes the claims history, claims expenses, or type of claims experienced by individuals for whom a plan sponsor has provided health benefits under a group health plan
- De-identifies information by removing the following elements:
  - Names
  - All geographic subdivisions smaller than a state, including street address, city, county, precinct, zip code, and their equivalent geocodes (an exception is geographic information that can be aggregated to the level of a five-digit zip code)
  - All elements of dates (except year) directly related to an individual, including birth date, admission date, discharge date, and date of death, and all ages over 89 and all elements of dates (including year) indicative of such age, except that such ages and elements may be aggregated into a single category of age 90 or older
  - Telephone numbers
  - Fax numbers
  - E-mail addresses
  - Social Security numbers
  - Medical records numbers
  - Health plan beneficiary numbers
  - Account numbers
  - Certificate/license numbers
  - Vehicle identifiers and serial numbers, including license plate numbers
  - Device identifiers and serial numbers
  - Web URLs
  - IP address numbers
  - Biometric identifiers, including finger and voice prints
  - Full-face photographic images and any comparable images

- Genetic data that is individually identifying
- Any other unique identifying number, characteristic, or code

20.7 Medical Surveillance

A covered health care provider who provides health care to an individual at the request of the individual's employer, or provides the service in the capacity of a member of the employer's workforce, may disclose the individual's PHI to the employer:

- For the purposes of workplace medical surveillance
- For the evaluation of work-related illness and injuries when needed by the employer to comply with the Occupational Safety and Health Administration, the Mine Safety and Health Administration, or the requirements of state laws having a similar purpose

The PHI given to the employer must be limited to the provider's findings regarding the medical surveillance or work-related illness or injury. The provider must give the individual written notice that the information will be disclosed to his or her employer, or the notice may be posted at the worksite if that is where the service is provided. See 45 CFR § 164.512(b)(1)(v) for the regulatory text.

20.8 Workers' Compensation

The HIPAA Privacy Rule does not apply to entities that are workers' compensation insurers, workers' compensation administrative agencies, or employers, except if they are otherwise CEs. Nonetheless, these entities need access to the health information of individuals who are injured on the job or who have a work-related illness to process or settle claims, and to coordinate care under the workers' compensation systems. This PHI is typically obtained from health care providers who treat these individuals and whom the Privacy Rule may cover. Because of the significant number of state and other applicable laws relating to this topic, the Privacy Rule permits PHI disclosures for workers' compensation purposes in a number of different ways. Disclosures that do not require individual authorization by HIPAA generally include the following:

- As necessary to comply with laws relating to workers' compensation or similar programs established by law that provide benefits for work-related injuries or illness without regard to fault
- To the extent state and other applicable laws require the disclosure
- To obtain payment for any health care provided to the injured or ill worker

CEs must limit the amount of PHI they disclose to the minimum that is necessary to accomplish the workers' compensation purpose. PHI may be shared for such purposes to the full extent authorized by applicable state or other law. In addition, CEs must limit the amount of PHI disclosed for payment purposes to the minimum necessary. CEs are permitted to disclose PHI necessary to obtain payment for health care provided to an injured or ill worker. When a CE routinely makes disclosures for workers' compensation purposes or for payment purposes, the CE should develop procedures as part of its minimum necessary policies that detail the type and amount of PHI to be disclosed for these purposes. When PHI is requested by a state workers' compensation representative or other public official, CEs may rely on the official's representations that the information requested is the minimum necessary for the intended purpose. CEs are not required to make a minimum necessary determination when disclosing PHI required by state or other applicable law, or when having the individual's authorization.

20.8.1 HIPAA and Workers' Compensation Checklist

- For disclosures of PHI made for workers' compensation purposes, the minimum necessary standard permits CEs to disclose information to the full extent authorized by state or other law.
- For disclosures of PHI for payment purposes, CEs may disclose the type and amount of information necessary to receive payment for any health care provided to an injured or ill worker.

- Individuals do not have a right under the Privacy Rule to request that a CE restrict a disclosure of PHI about them for workers' compensation purposes when the disclosure is required by law or authorized by and necessary to comply with a workers' compensation or similar law.
- The Privacy Rule permits a health care provider to disclose an injured or ill worker's PHI without his or her authorization when requested for purposes of adjudicating the individual worker's compensation claim.
- The Privacy Rule permits a CE to disclose PHI as necessary to comply with state law. No minimum necessary determination is required in this situation.
- A CE may disclose PHI regarding an injured worker's previous condition, not directly related to the compensation claim, to an employer or insurer when the individual's written authorization has been obtained.

20.9 Training

Employers must provide training to their personnel regarding the safeguards necessary for PHI when the employer is self-insured or self-funded. Training appropriate to the job responsibilities related to PHI is required on an ongoing regular basis. Employers must also train their privacy officers and add privacy to their corporate compliance and orientation training programs. Employers should consider extending their training to BAs as well. See Chapter 25 for more information on training, education, and awareness.

20.10 Resources

There are as many unique HIPAA situations as there are employers. Some employers face especially interesting HIPAA issues because of their industries or size. Here is a short list of resources employers may find useful for their unique situations:

- *General HIPAA resources.* See the generic CMS HIPAA site at http://www.cms.gov/Regulations-and-Guidance/HIPAA -Administrative-Simplification/HIPAAGenInfo/index.html

- *Employer HIPAA responsibilities for church plans.* Contact the Internal Revenue Service at (202) 622-6080 or online at http://www.irs.gov/.
- *Individual or small group physicians.* See the Office of the Inspector General Compliance Program for individual and small-group physician practices at http://oig.hhs.gov /authorities/docs/physician.pdf.

20.11 Conclusion

The Privacy Rule helps address multiple fears that have been expressed by employees throughout the past several decades. Multiple news reports and research reveal common employee fears with regard to their employers and health information. Employees fear that

- Employers will use health information to make employment decisions.
- Prospective employers will have access to job applicants' health information and make hiring decisions based on the information.
- An inappropriate person, such as an ex-spouse, will get access to health information to use against the employee, such as in a custody battle.
- They will be found ineligible for loans or life and disability insurance.
- Privacy policies for their organizations will not provide them adequate protection.
- Requesting leave or accommodations will result in providing their employers access to their health information.

The requirements listed should demonstrate that employers must actively pursue compliance efforts, and that they will likely be focused on revising the policies and procedures, implementing training and education, and updating the plan documents, contracts, and other administrative forms. HIPAA likely will have a major impact on employers who provide or arrange for health care benefits for their workforce.

Practical Checklist

- Determine to what extent HIPAA impacts your organization.
- Conduct a CE analysis to determine if you are a CE under HIPAA.
- If you are considered a CE, conduct a CE analysis of benefit plans to determine the applicable HIPAA obligations.
- Determine if your employee benefit plan is a CE.
- If you offer covered benefit plans, identify the specific HIPAA requirements, and then develop and implement a compliance plan.
- Take into account your own specific identified exceptions, and take steps to comply with the Privacy Rule with respect to use and disclosure of PHI between the group health plan and the plan sponsor.

21

BUSINESS ASSOCIATE ISSUES

21.1 Is Your Organization a Business Associate?

As discussed in Chapter 1, a business associate (BA) is basically any individual or organization that performs an activity involving the use, storage, or disclosure of protected health information (PHI) on behalf of a covered entity (CE), or as a subcontractor of a BA. If you are a BA, this means that you or your organization must receive PHI from a CE or on behalf of a CE, and perform a function or activity for the CE using the PHI. In addition, this means that you are not part of the CE's workforce or in their control. Not sure if you are a BA? Odds are, you are considered a BA if you meet the previously mentioned criteria and are one of the following:

- Medical transcription companies
- Answering services
- Document storage or disposal (shredding) companies
- Patient safety or accreditation organizations
- Companies involved in claims processing, repricing, or collections (e.g., medical billing companies)
- Health information exchanges, e-prescribing gateways, and other health information organizations
- Third-party administrators and pharmacy benefit managers
- Medical billing companies
- Data conversion, deidentification, and data analysis service providers
- Utilization review and management companies
- HIPAA, information security, and/or privacy consultants
- IT consultants
- CEs working on behalf of another CE
- Subcontractors of BAs

- Accreditation bodies such as the Joint Commission on Accreditation of Healthcare Organizations
- Billing and printing service companies
- Outsourced radiology and other medical services providers
- Durable medical supplies providers
- Ambulance service companies
- Data aggregators
- Managed service providers
- Data backup storage services

The following are sometimes BAs:

- Accounting firms
- Auditors
- Law firms
- Collection agencies
- Banks
- Consulting firms
- Software vendors and consultants
- Management consultants
- Financial institutions (if engaging in accounts receivable or other functions extending beyond payment processing)
- Internet service providers, Active Server Pages, and cloud vendors
- Companies providing personal health records (if providing personal health records on behalf of a CE)
- Researchers (if performing HIPAA functions for a CE)

Keep in mind that HIPAA states that any activities performed as a CE employee or contractor (if a substantial amount of work is performed at the CE's facilities) do not fall into BA classification.

21.2 Business Associate Requirements

HIPAA is designed to protect the communication and handling of PHI between CEs and their BAs. As stated in the Security Rule, the overall responsibility of a BA originally was

> to implement administrative, physical, and technical safeguards that reasonably and appropriately protect the confidentiality, integrity, and

availability of the electronic protected health information that it creates, receives, maintains, or transmits on behalf of the covered entity as required by this sub-part

The Department of Health and Human Services (HHS) succinctly summarized the expanded responsibilities of BAs within the 2013 Omnibus Rules[1] by emphasizing that

- BAs must comply with the technical, administrative, and physical safeguard requirements under the Security Rule and are directly liable for violations.
- BAs must comply with the use or disclosure limitations expressed in the BA contract and those in the Privacy Rule, and are directly liable for violations.
- Subcontractors of BAs are now defined as BAs and BA liability flows to all subcontractors.
- Researchers are still not considered BAs by virtue of research activities.
- Institutional review boards are not BAs by virtue of their research review, approval, and oversight functions.

BA relationships with CEs are usually long term, and thus need to be established and managed carefully. Unfortunately, the days of a friendly handshake agreement are gone. Contracts must be in place before any business is transacted to protect both parties from certain liabilities and to ensure the confidentiality and privacy of PHI. These contracts should be reasonable and beneficial to both parties—not one-sided. They need to be kept as simple as possible so that there is no frustration or confusion over what is involved. There are, however, certain minimum requirements of a BA contract. The following is a list of obligations and requirements adapted from the HHS's "Obligations and Activities of Business Associate." For the optional statements, use only those that apply to the CE/BA contractual relationship:

- BA agrees to not use or disclose PHI other than as permitted or required by the BA contract or as required by law.
- BA agrees to use appropriate safeguards to prevent use or disclosure of the PHI other than as provided for by the BA contract.

- BA agrees to report to CE any use or disclosure of PHI not provided for by the agreement of which it becomes aware, including breaches of unsecured PHI, and any security incident of which it becomes aware.
  - Note: Consider including specificity regarding the breach notification obligations of the BA, such as a stricter time frame for the BA to report a potential breach to the CE and/or whether the BA will handle breach notifications to individuals, the HHS Office for Civil Rights, and potentially the media, on behalf of the CE.
- BA agrees to ensure that any agent, including a subcontractor to whom it provides PHI, agrees to the same restrictions and conditions that apply through the BA contract.
- BA agrees to provide access to PHI in a designated record set to an individual if directed to do so by the CE, or to the CE itself. (Not required if BA does not have PHI in a designated record set.)
- BA agrees to provide access to PHI in a designated record set to an individual if directed to do so by the CE, or to the CE itself, for amendment as needed; not required if BA does not have PHI in a designated record set.
- (Optional): BA may use PHI for the proper management and administration of the BA or to carry out the legal responsibilities of the BA.
- (Optional): BA may disclose PHI for the proper management and administration of BA or to carry out the legal responsibilities of the BA, provided the disclosures are required by law, or BA obtains reasonable assurances from the person to whom the information is disclosed that the information will remain confidential and used or further disclosed only as required by law or for the purposes for which it was disclosed to the person, and the person notifies BA of any instances of which it is aware in which the confidentiality of the information has been breached.
- (Optional): BA may provide data aggregation services relating to the health care operations of the CE.
- (Optional): CE shall notify BA of any limitation(s) in the notice of privacy practices of the CE to the extent that such limitation may affect BA's use or disclosure of PHI.

- (Optional): CE shall notify BA of any changes in, or revocation of, the permission by an individual to use or disclose his or her PHI, to the extent that such changes may affect BA's use or disclosure of PHI.
- (Optional): CE shall notify BA of any restriction on the use or disclosure of PHI that CE has agreed to or is required to abide by under law, to the extent that such restriction may affect BA's use or disclosure of PHI.
- (Optional): CE shall not request BA to use or disclose PHI in any manner that would not be permissible under HIPAA if done by CE. (Include an exception if the BA will use or disclose PHI for, and the agreement includes provisions for, data aggregation or management and administration and legal responsibilities of the BA.)
- BA agrees to make internal practices, books, and records, including policies and procedures and PHI relating to the use and disclosure of PHI, available to HHS for purposes of the secretary determining CE's compliance with the Privacy Rule, as well as to the CE when requested.
- BA agrees to document such disclosures of PHI and information related to such disclosures as would be required for CE to respond to a request by an individual for an accounting of disclosures of PHI.
- BA agrees to provide to CE or an individual, information collected to permit CE to respond to a request by an individual for an accounting of disclosures of PHI.

For a sample BA contract, refer to Appendix B.

21.3 What You Can Expect to See or Hear from Covered Entities

There are various questions and concerns that you as a BA can expect to hear from CEs, including the following:

Questions

- Do you know your HIPAA and Health Information Technology for Economic and Clinical Health (HITECH) obligations?
- Are you in full compliance with HIPAA and HITECH?

- Do you have someone with assigned responsibility for HIPAA compliance within your organization?
- Do you have fully documented information security and privacy policies and procedures?
- Can you demonstrate that you are following your policies and procedures?
- Are you providing extra preventative measures to ensure PHI is protected as mandated by HIPAA? If so, what are they?
  - Privacy safeguards
  - Security safeguards
- Does your company conduct background checks on employees that have access to PHI?
- Do you have an education program in place to train your employees in the HIPAA requirements? If so, how often is it being given? May we see the training materials?

Concerns

- Special letters of notification from their legal department regarding the HIPAA requirements and their expectations of your organization regarding HIPAA.
- Request for evidence that you have a documented security incident and breach response plan.
- Request that certain provisions be added to the BA contract, including the following:
  - Special insurance requirements
  - Indemnification against reasonable losses, damages, costs, or other expenses
  - Ability to review your policies, procedures, and records associated with the protection of PHI
  - Greater control over BA contract termination

21.4 Common Business Associate Weaknesses

Since 2001, Rebecca has performed over 250 BA HIPAA compliance audits. During that time, she compiled a tally list of the areas with the most findings. Here are the areas that were consistently either completely missing or grievously inadequate.

1. Incident response and breach notice. Very few of the BAs audited had documented security incident and breach response policies and procedures. Only one had actually tested them. The numbers of BAs that had such documented plans did not rise when the final Omnibus Rule was released in January 2013, even though that rule made it very clear that BAs needed to comply with the security incident and privacy breach response requirements.

To do:

- Create documented security incident and breach response policies and procedures.
- Assign team members for responding to breaches and incidents.
- Test the procedures at least once a year to ensure they will actually work when put into use.

2. Training and awareness. Most organizations, throughout all industries, simply do not provide good, effective training, and rarely provide ongoing awareness communications. This has been improving somewhat in financial organizations, where there are many different regulators to constantly audit and report on the need for them to do better in educating their staff. Rebecca found the following within her BA HIPAA audits:

- Only 21% of the BAs audited had training policies, with actual training materials and regular training, in place.
- Of those, only 12% had what would be considered to be effective, worthwhile training.
- Only 12% sent out ongoing awareness reminders.

Some of the most ineffective examples of training that were found, which actually were not training, included the following:

- One BA with over 1000 employees had copied all the HIPAA regulatory text into sections, filling close to 400 PowerPoint slides with the verbatim text, and nothing else. They then put this huge slide set onto their company intranet site, sent out an email with the link to the slide set, and told all the employees to go read it. That is what they considered to be their training. None of the employees I spoke with got past the first two or three slides before not continuing with the slide viewing.

To do:

- Assign responsibility for providing regular training and ongoing awareness communications.
- Ensure all employees participate in training.
- If you are not sure what to send out for ongoing awareness communications, sign up for the free Privacy Professor Monthly Tips message (sign up for it by filling out the box in the upper right corner of www.privacyguidance.com) and forward it to all employees each month when the new message arrives.
- For help with a full education program, see Rebecca's book, *Managing an Information Security and Privacy Awareness and Training Program*, published by Auerbach/CRC Press.

3. Disposal. In May 2012, documents containing patient data were placed in a publicly accessible dumpster at a Veterans' Affairs hospital in Maine. This was a HIPAA violation. Disposal problems do not just involve print materials. Digital equipment (computers, storage devices, printers, etc.) also needs to be properly disposed of.

- Ninety percent of the BAs audited had no documented policies or procedures requiring paper documents that contained PHI to be shredded upon disposal.
- Ninety-five percent of the BAs had no documented policies or procedures requiring the data to be completely removed from computing and digital storage devices upon disposal.
- Ninety-nine percent of the BAs had no documented policies or procedures requiring data to be removed from printers and copy machines before they were retired from use. Most of the BAs sold them to recoup their investment.

Possibly the worst policy found was a BA that had a "security policy" that basically read: "All computing equipment must be sold on eBay to recoup the ROI." No mention of removing the data.

To do:

- Assign a position with accountability for ensuring secure disposal of PHI in all forms.
- Document and implement policies and procedures to effectively and irreversibly dispose of all forms of PHI and the hardware or media where it exists.
- Ensure the procedures provide clear direction for irreversible data removal.
- Establish shredding solutions for print and other hard-copy media.
- Provide training to all personnel for the policies and procedures.
- If media and hardware will be reused elsewhere, establish procedures for completely and irreversibly removing the data before reuse.

4. Risk assessment. As pointed out more than once throughout this book, performing a risk assessment is one of the key activities necessary for HIPAA compliance. However, the BAs audited were largely lacking in actually performing risk assessments. These results were from prior to September 2013, when all BAs (and their subcontractors) were required to be in compliance with HIPAA.

- Ninety-six percent of BAs had not performed a risk assessment.
- Ninety percent of BAs did not plan to do a risk assessment.

To do:

- Assign a position with the responsibility of ensuring a risk analysis that meets HIPAA requirements will be performed at least once a year.
- Perform a risk assessment at least once a year and when major organizational or systems changes occur.

5. Cloud computing. More than 20 of the BA audits were for cloud service providers. Most of them initially believed they were not obligated to comply with HIPAA and HITECH. However, the 2013 Omnibus Rule made clear that cloud services providers used by CEs are indeed BAs.

A cloud service can store and process PHI for many clients in its data centers, making them responsible for their virtual tenants' HIPAA compliance. Any company maintaining PHI on behalf of a CE is considered a BA. Because cloud providers maintain or store PHI on a persistent basis (called "persistent possession" by the HHS in their public presentations on the subject), they are therefore BAs and must comply with all applicable HIPAA and HITECH requirements, including the Breach Notification Rule.

The HHS has publicly advised CEs that use cloud-based services to obtain a BA contract from those cloud providers, and if they refuse to sign one, the CE should look for another cloud service provider.[2]

To do:

- BAs that are cloud providers should anticipate, and plan how to answer, compliance questions from CEs that are, or who they would like to be, their clients.
- Establish responsibility for compliance within your organization.
- Document and implement HIPAA security and privacy policies and procedures to support full HIPAA compliance.
- If you still need help with compliance, contact Rebecca at www.hipaacompliance.org or www.privacyprofessor.org. For technical information security help, such as penetration testing, vulnerability assessments, and risk assessments, contact Kevin at www.principlelogic.com.

6. Subcontractors. The 2013 Omnibus Rule expanded the definition of BAs to include the subcontractors of BAs. As BAs, subcontractors must now comply with all applicable HIPAA and HITECH requirements. Most midsize to large subcontractors will already have staff with assigned responsibilities for information security, and some may have assigned responsibility for privacy. However, a large portion of these subcontractors are one- to five-person small shops with no prior experience with information security or privacy compliance. They can find it particularly challenging to meet all the HIPAA and HITECH requirements.

To do:

- Establish information security, privacy, and breach response policies and procedures appropriate for the subcontracting services.
- Perform a risk assessment appropriate for the subcontracting services.
- Obtain training and plan for receiving ongoing awareness communications appropriate for the subcontracting services.
- If you need help, Rebecca's Privacy Professor business (www.privacyprofessor.org) has services, tools, and products created for the smallest to largest of BAs.

7. Information technology. BAs need to ensure they have appropriately implemented and addressed all the necessary IT requirements under HIPAA, as described in detail in Part III of this book.

To do:

- Keep all software patches up to date.
- Use strong passwords.
- Implement anti-malware software.
- Use firewalls.
- Implement and follow an effective backup and recovery policy, procedure, and plan.
- Encrypt PHI in storage and in transit.
- Establish secure disposal of all computing and electronic storage devices.

21.5 Issues to Consider

You should consider the following items when dealing with CEs and working on BA contract issues:

- As a result of the 2013 Omnibus Rule, CEs will be held liable for the breaches, incidents, and noncompliance actions of their BAs, to a level based on the amount of due diligence that has been performed. Generally, the less oversight and assurances required by CEs of their BAs, the greater their liability.

- If you have not already done so, identify legal counsel that can assist with BA issues.
- Determine whether or not everyone that has access to PHI in your organization actually needs that access. Minimum necessary and need to know are important, and required, rules to live by.
- CEs are not required to train or educate BAs on the HIPAA requirements, but CEs must obtain assurances that such training occurs.
- If they have the ability to train and offer it, then go for it!
- Look for the following information in any training that is offered:
    - An overview of the HIPAA Administrative Simplification—the who and why.
    - Explanation of terminology used in HIPAA.
    - Outline of the three major rules: Privacy Rule, Security Rule, and Transaction and Code Sets Rule.
    - Compliance requirements.
    - You may also ask to hear about their HIPAA experiences and ask to see their plans.
- CEs may want only to share information that has been deidentified. Both parties will have to determine whether or not that is feasible based on the services provided by the BA, and if so, whether or not a BA contract is even necessary at that point.
- Find out who the HIPAA compliance officer(s) are within the CEs you work with and be sure you establish a good working relationship.
- Does the CE want you to create the HIPAA-compliant BA agreement, or does the CE want you to provide the agreement? You may want to consider creating such an agreement for those CEs who ask, and advise them to modify it and have it approved by their own legal counsel based on their own organization's needs.

21.6 Moving Forward

From trying to determine whether or not your organization is a BA to negotiating reasonable BA contracts, determining the most appropriate ways to get adequate assurances of compliance, and maintaining ongoing oversight, there are a lot of critical business decisions to be made. Now, you must also obtain assurances and BA contracts with your subcontractors, who are also BAs. Be sure to obtain legal advice if there is any gray area regarding your BA status. Also, obtain legal advice before establishing new business relationships with HIPAA CEs or before revising any existing contracts. Given that there is so much at stake with regard to business liability, it is absolutely critical to get an expert involved. You can perform all the research up front and even draft your own BA contract, but always be sure to run it by your attorney before conducting business with a CE.

Practical Checklist

- Any person or organization performing work on behalf of a CE that involves PHI is considered a BA.
- Any subcontracted person or organization performing work on behalf of a BA that involves PHI is also considered a BA and must comply with HIPAA and HITECH.
- CEs must obtain appropriate assurances that BAs are in compliance with HIPAA.
- CEs share in liability, to varying degrees based on their due diligence activities, for their BAs' noncompliance and breaches.
- CEs are not responsible for educating their BAs on HIPAA, but need to ensure such education occurs within the BA.
- Take advantage of any education that is offered from CEs.
- Be prepared to tell CEs how you protect PHI, in all forms.
- Make sure BA contracts meet HIPAA contract requirements and are reasonable and mutually beneficial.
- Obtain legal counsel or other HIPAA consultation if you are having trouble determining whether or not you or your organization is a BA.

PART V
HIPAA
TECHNOLOGY
CONSIDERATIONS

22

BUILDING A HIPAA-COMPLIANT TECHNOLOGY INFRASTRUCTURE

22.1 Overview

Both the Privacy and Security Rules specifically state that covered entities (CEs) must have certain administrative, physical, and technical safeguards in place to safeguard protected health information (PHI). Furthermore, the 2013 Omnibus Rule clarifies that business associates (BAs) and their subcontractors must also comply with the same requirements. In various places throughout this book, we have stressed that HIPAA compliance is less about technology and more about business processes and culture. Having said that, you can have all the policies, procedures, and culture changes in the world, but if certain technical controls are not in place, there is no way to ensure HIPAA compliance. You cannot have one without the other. The bottom line is that a lot of policies and procedures cannot be implemented properly or enforced at all without relying on certain technologies.

Both rules touch on this, but the Security Rule in particular presents a good combination of the information technology and security standards tailored for the health care industry. These best practices to protect PHI are all well known and proven. Some of them have been around since the days of the first mainframe computer! The drawback to the HIPAA rules is that they tell you what must be done but do not tell you how to do it. This chapter picks up where the HIPAA rules leave off. In this chapter, we focus on the technical safeguard requirements of HIPAA. We will not go into detail on how specific technologies work; instead we will give you ideas on certain technical controls that you can use to become HIPAA compliant and, more importantly, effectively manage your information risks. We also list some real-world experiences that we (and others) have had with these technologies, along with some practical tips that can save you some time, money, and effort. If you want to learn more about the specific technologies—how they work, how to best implement them, how to configure them, and so forth—there are many great books and resources to which you can refer.

There is not a one-size-fits-all solution when it comes to information technology. For example, a firewall or virtual private network (VPN) requirement for a large CE, such as a hospital, is not going to be the same as that for a small BA, such as a billing company. A lot of CEs and BAs may already have the necessary technologies in place and just need them to be configured properly. Others may have to make considerable hardware and software investments to be compliant.

22.2 Caution

Do not let anyone ever tell you that a firewall, antivirus software, or encryption alone is enough to protect your information systems and PHI. Firewalls are certainly part of the equation. So are intrusion prevention systems (IPSs), whole-disk encryption software, and mobile device management systems; however, you must layer your security to ensure that if one device fails or does not stop an attack, several more layers of protection will prevent penetration of your systems. This layered approach is referred to as "defense in depth."

You should not take the technology tips we outline in this chapter as specific requirements for your organization. Please keep in mind that the HIPAA requirements are scalable and flexible, depending on your business processes, size, and associated information risks. Given the technology guidance in this chapter combined with a comprehensive and accurate risk analysis and a little time, money, and effort, there is no reason that you cannot be well on your way to reasonably protecting PHI within your network environment. The point we are trying to make here is that it all just depends on your organization's specific situation.

22.3 Areas of Technology to Focus On

HIPAA, and specifically the Security Rule, is a set of requirements that essentially provides a framework for creating and managing an effective information security infrastructure. Without the proper technical controls in place, PHI can be put at risk. There are certain technical components that HIPAA mandates, such as

- Logical access controls
- Physical access controls
- Authentication controls
- Authorization controls
- Audit controls
- Data encryption and integrity mechanisms

Although HIPAA does not specify what technology solutions are needed to meet these requirements, some of the following are usually necessary:

- Authentication controls such as unique user names, passwords, or possibly biometric devices
- Operating system (OS), application, directory service (i.e., Active Directory or Lightweight Directory Access Protocol), and even identity access and management (IAM) systems that provide access controls to permit or deny access based on user, role, or context
- Network security devices such as a firewall, web application firewall (WAF), or an IPS
- Web and e-mail content filtering devices (or cloud services) and data leakage prevention (DLP) technologies to detect inappropriate computer usage or vulnerable PHI leaving the network and antivirus programs to detect malware
- Encryption software to protect PHI at rest or in transit
- VPNs to ensure secure network-to-network or remote access communications
- Logging systems, including the built-in logging functions of OSs and applications for real-time monitoring and audit trail purposes
- Policy management software for publishing and managing HIPAA policies and to assist in user awareness
- Patch management software to facilitate the ongoing management and deployment of critical software updates

22.4 Looking Deeper into Specific Technologies

The following are specific best practices and tips on certain technologies that may be a part of your overall HIPAA technology infrastructure. These are not comprehensive solutions and every business's needs are different. That said, these basic IT and security components are often implemented poorly or not at all, leading to most PHI-related technology breaches. You may very well come up with some additional ideas on your own. Regardless, this information can help you get started on building your HIPAA-compliant technology infrastructure.

22.4.1 Access Controls

- Ensure that every user has a unique user ID and password. IDs that are shared by two or more people are a definite security risk and provide no accountability for the activities performed using the ID.
- Disable unused user IDs or IDs for users that are on an extended leave of absence.
- Focus on granting people access based on the minimum necessary and "need to know" requirements to get the job done. Ensure that separation of duties via specific access control mechanisms is in place where possible.
- Access controls consist of identification, authentication, and authorization—these are all integral functions of OSs, applications, and databases.
  - Identification is the process of determining who a user is.
  - Authentication is the process of proving who a user is.
  - Authorization defines what a user is allowed to do.
- Consider implementing role-based access controls for your OSs, applications, and databases that define the access capabilities for a particular job role or computer system. Today's advanced IAM and single sign-on (SSO) technologies are great for this.
- User-based access is good but can be difficult to manage.
- Group-based access is easy to manage but it can be difficult to ensure that only specific users have access to certain resources.

- Whatever your access control methods are—just have *something*. Although we see it more often than not, in the interest of preventing malware infections, inadvertent mishaps, and unauthorized access, never give users full administrative rights to their computers (i.e., local administrator rights in Windows), applications, and related systems that process or store PHI; this is a security incident waiting to happen.
- Do not log on to OSs, applications, or databases with administrator or root privileges to perform daily job tasks that do not require those rights. This applies to users and to IT personnel.
- Create standard user IDs with limited rights for everyone and encourage their use except when administrative or root privileges are needed.
- There are three ways to authenticate a person or entity: something they know (password), something they have (secure token), and something they are (biometric).
- Implement at least one of these—there is simply no excuse not to. Ideally, you need two.
- A combination of any two—referred to as two-factor authentication or strong authentication—offers much greater information security.
- Biometrics can be a very effective way to authenticate users—just keep cost and system administration issues in mind before rolling out this technology system-wide.
- Make sure you have policies and procedures for the creation, maintenance, and revocation of access.
- SSO solutions (one password for everything) can help ease access-control administration burdens, but can be expensive and difficult to implement and administer if not done properly. SSO technology has, to an extent, evolved into IAM technology that, although still expensive, can offer a lot of flexibility and security for account management.
- Ensure that policies, procedures, and systems are in place to revoke accounts and passwords after termination. This is one of the most exploited vulnerabilities in a computer network.
- Have a plan for protecting PHI in case the administrator or root account is compromised. This may include encrypted offline databases, laptops, removable storage, failover systems, and so forth.

22.4.2 Malware Protection

- Antivirus software is rarely enough—look into the newer advanced malware and advanced persistent threat (APT) products for both computers and network traffic.
- Antivirus software needs to be loaded on every computer possible, including servers and computers that do not process or store PHI. Otherwise, the risk of infection is too great.
- This software needs to be configured to regularly and automatically download updates for the latest threats.
- This software must stay installed and enabled on your computers at all times to ensure proper protection. Disable the ability for your end users to uninstall or disable this software.
- This software should be centrally managed through the software's enterprise console. Having antivirus software installed on stand-alone machines is often too difficult to manage.
- Complete scans of your computer system are important after you first install the software and periodically throughout the week. Real-time protection against malware threats is a must and should never be disabled. Malware protection on e-mail servers, at the network perimeter (i.e., as part of your firewall), and even in the cloud (i.e., before e-mails ever reach your network) is highly recommended.

22.4.3 Applications, Databases, and Unstructured Information

- Certain clinical, practice management, and other health care applications have built-in user accounts.
- Use them only if necessary—use user ID and password integration with local OS or directory services if it is available.
- Create an account/password combination for each user.
- Ensure your mobile apps have the same level of protection.
- Ensure your PHI-centric web applications are tested periodically and consistently for web-specific security flaws using well-known, commercial web vulnerability scanners.
- Apply the latest vendor software updates—including updates for third-party software components—on a regular basis.
- Ensure that strong passwords are used/required—tips on passwords are discussed in Section 22.4.11.

- Ask your software vendor(s) how accounts and passwords are stored (cleartext, proprietary encryption format in a database, etc.) and take security precautions as necessary.
- Do not display the last user ID that logged in on the log-in screen.
- If it is displayed, a malicious user can use this against you and try to log in with that user ID.
- Use automatic screen/keyboard locking. There is no set time specified by HIPAA—just use common sense based on what you find in your risk analysis and what works best in your environment. Five to 10 minutes of inactivity (or less if in an open area) often works best in health care environments. There are multiple technologies available to allow for simple reauthentication (vicinity bracelets, fingerprint swipes, etc.), so there is no good excuse not to establish screen auto-locks.
- Some applications have built-in features that allow or even force users to log off manually or after a few seconds or minutes of inactivity.
- Treat databases as one of your most critical assets—this is where the "good stuff" is. This is where your PHI spends a lot of its waking hours.
- Databases are often the most highly targeted yet the most vulnerable part of your information systems.
- Specific attention must be given to your databases during and after your risk analysis.
- Leave database maintenance and administration up to the database experts or users that have received formal training.
- A great way to expose or otherwise damage a database and thus affect the confidentiality, integrity, and availability of PHI is for an untrained user to perform administrative functions in a haphazard fashion.
- PHI often resides in "unstructured" files (i.e., spreadsheets, documents, PDF files, and even log files) on various computer systems across the network. During your vulnerability assessments, you can use tools (often called personally identifiable information, or PII, search tools) to find these files stored in unprotected locations on the network. You will likely be amazed at how much PHI is being exposed to anyone who has a basic user account on the network!

22.4.4 Data Backups and Storage

- Consider backing up your data at least daily.
- Consider real-time backups for larger systems with heavy transaction volumes.
- Back up your OS and application files as well. This will help decrease system restoration times dramatically.
- Make complete backups of your system periodically—once a month or every few months—and keep them indefinitely.
- Backups can be made to tape, disk, or cloud-based service. (Note: If you use a cloud-based service, it will become one of your BAs.)
- Magnetic media, including tapes and disks, fail eventually, so consider replacing your media every few years or move away from it altogether.
- Backups must be tested to ensure they contain valid data that you may need in an emergency.
- Backups should be stored offsite—at least some of them, such as your weekly backups—in case a disaster destroys or damages them. Otherwise, you need to ensure that on-site storage is safe from unauthorized access and fires, floods, and so forth.
- Off-site backup media must be handled only by authorized and trusted personnel.
- Do not store backup tapes near a computer monitor or uninterruptible power supply—the electromagnetic interference coming from these devices can corrupt data on them or completely erase them.
- Ensure that backup media are adequately protected from extreme hot or cold temperatures and are readily accessible.
- Encrypt or at least password protect your backups.

22.4.5 Encryption

- Encryption was an "addressable" Security Rule implementation specification, but now that the Safe Harbor requirements state that data must be encrypted, if you are going to have Safe Harbor protections in the event of a PHI breach, encryption is the only viable solution to reduce the risk.

- It can be difficult and expensive to deploy and manage—but it might be a necessary evil.
- A common practice is to deploy encryption for data in transit and not for data at rest. This is not good!
- At a minimum, focus on data at rest, especially on mobile devices (i.e., phones, tablets, portable storage devices, and laptops) because this is where the true vulnerability lies.
- Ensure that strong passphrases are used for encryption keys—otherwise encryption's value is diminished.
- Any well-known 128-bit or greater encryption method such as AES, IDEA, or Triple-DES will suffice.
- Whole (or full) disk encryption is an excellent way to encrypt laptop, desktop, and even server hard drives.
- Zip utilities, such as 7-Zip, can encrypt files and are a cost-effective way to encrypt and share confidential information, including PHI.
- Never, ever rely on basic password protection in your word processor, spreadsheet, or file compression utility to ensure the security of the file's contents.
- There are dozens of utilities that can be downloaded for free that can crack most of these passwords in typically less than one minute.
- Encryption can be an inconvenience to users.
- You must balance security with convenience based on what was discovered in your risk analysis.
- Your goal with encryption should be to keep users out of the loop.
- Have ways to automatically encrypt PHI so that your users will not have to remember to do it.
- Implement data in transit encryption methods within your applications at the perimeter of your network instead of at the desktop level via PKI, SSL/TLS for e-mail and web applications, or e-mail firewalls for secure messaging.
- Always use the latest version of Secure Shell or a similar technology instead of telnet for encrypted remote computer access.

Refer to the HHS-recommended document developed by the National Institute of Standards and Technology (NIST).[1]

22.4.6 Faxes

- Traditional faxing is somewhat of a dying technology, but it is still used a good bit in health care. Faxes sent via computers (e-faxing) through fax modems are covered under the Security Rule. Regular fax machines are not considered "computers" in the context of the Security Rule.
- Faxes sent via a regular fax machine are covered by the Privacy Rule, however, if you fax PHI, make sure someone is at the other end to receive the fax by calling them while sending it or immediately thereafter.
- Do not let faxes sit around on fax machines.
- Make sure that fax machines are in a physically secure location away from public access.
- Immediately file or securely dispose of faxes (shred, etc.) before unauthorized people can see the fax.

22.4.7 Firewalls

- Use the best firewall you can afford—for a small network, you can get a really good firewall with most of the fancy bells and whistles for well under $1000.
- Use the built-in features of your existing network firewall, router, or other Internet connection device, including the following:
  - Block all traffic by default.
  - Open only the ports required for the traffic you need leaving or entering your network. If you allow all traffic by default, it will be much more difficult to secure and manage.
  - Block all outbound packets (this is called egress filtering) going to the Internet that do not originate from your network.
  - Block all inbound packets (this is called ingress filtering) coming from the Internet that are addressed from the broadcast address (0.0.0.0 or 255.255.255.255) or other reserved addresses such as 10.x.x.x, 172.16.x.x–172.31.x.x, or 192.168.x.x). This can help prevent IP spoofing and denial-of-service attacks involving your network.

- Use packet filtering to allow only specific types of traffic through.
- Make sure stateful packet inspection is enabled to increase security.
- Do not rely on IP addresses or Domain Name System (DNS) information to authenticate users or hosts via your packet filters as they can be forged to look like they are coming from anyone.
- Use network address translation. This is a good start for network security, but should not be the only security mechanism used.
  - It helps conceal your internal network configuration.
  - It helps restrict incoming and outgoing traffic.
- Use port forwarding if your firewall supports it. This forwards specific inbound traffic on to the proper host inside your network.
- Use application proxies, if possible, to help "hide" your systems behind the firewall and let the proxy software do all the work on behalf of your computers.
- Keep in mind that many firewalls cannot block application-specific or malicious software attacks.
- You can achieve much greater web application protection by using an application-friendly firewall, dedicated WAFs, or the newer "next-generation" IPSs.
- Enable malware protection on your firewall if possible.
- Log all firewall activity.
- Log locally or (ideally) to a remote syslog server—see Sub-subsection 22.4.10 for more information on logging.
- Consider outsourcing your firewall monitoring to make sure that security anomalies and attacks do not go unnoticed. This can take a huge burden off your IT and security staff and buy your network and PHI a lot of resiliency and security.
- Limit the number of applications running on your firewall device such as content filtering, antivirus, and so forth—you do not want to have your "layered" approach to security on a single point of failure device.
- Disable all unused user accounts on the firewall.

- Consider load balancing by adding a second firewall to increase firewall throughput and ensure the availability of your Internet connection in case your firewall fails.
- Change the default firewall password and assign a very strong passphrase—see Sub-subsection 22.4.11 for more information on passwords.
- Run the firewall service as an ID other than administrator or root if possible.
- Patch the firmware, OS, and application software for your firewall on a regular basis.
- Perform a firewall rule base analysis during your periodic security vulnerability assessments—especially if you have more than a dozen or so rules. This will help find security flaws that are otherwise very easy to overlook during normal security assessments and audits.
- Remember that a firewall might not be able to prevent security attacks originating from inside your network.
- Keep your firewall rule set as simple as possible and make sure that it stays in line with your security policies.

There is a good NIST document, titled Guidelines on Firewalls and Firewall Policy (SP 800-41), that provides more detailed information on firewall security.[2]

22.4.8 Intrusion Prevention Systems

- IPSs can be very effective to detect malicious use on your network, but they can also consume a lot of staff resources when monitored properly.
- Consider outsourcing the monitoring of your IPS.
- A common mistake is to install an IPS and forget about it.
- You (or a third party) must monitor your IPS constantly to be able to effectively respond to attacks.
- There are two types of IPS—network and host. Consider getting both.
  - Network-based IPSs can detect attacks across your entire network.
  - Host-based IPS can detect attacks on specific computer systems or applications.

- Typical network IPSs may be defeated fairly easily if the attack:
  - Is new or one the IPS does not recognize in its signature database or via its complex "heuristics" analysis.
  - Is encrypted.
  - Takes place on internal network segments that are not protected.
- Typical host IPSs can monitor system usage and detect local misuse of the system.
- Consider installing host-based intrusion detection system software that can check the integrity of files to determine whether or not they have been modified or tampered with by an unauthorized user.
- In a similar, yet more in-depth, manner to host-based IPS, DLP technologies can be used to monitor for malicious or unauthorized use on workstations and servers, and then block and alert on the findings. DLP is one of the best technologies you can use to help prevent HIPAA-related security breaches.
- Look for IPSs that have some or all of the following beneficial features:
  - Do not solely rely on attack signatures but can also detect network protocol anomalies and behavior-based attacks.
  - Can cut off an attack immediately.
  - Can monitor network bandwidth usage.
  - Can monitor web application traffic.
  - Can detect:
    - Trends
    - Malicious software including the latest APTs
    - Unauthorized hardware or software
    - Specific network events
    - Network analyzers
  - Can be distributed with multiple sensors across the various segments of your network.
  - Can track the attack back to its source.
  - Can reconstruct and playback network attacks.
  - Have good reporting capabilities—preferably through one centralized management console.

- Patch the firmware, OS, and application software for your IPS on a regular basis.
- Do not rely on IP addresses or DNS information to authenticate users or hosts as they can be forged to look like they are coming from anyone.
- We highly recommend outsourcing your IPS monitoring to make sure that security anomalies and attacks do not go unnoticed.

22.4.9 Operating Systems

- Centrally manage your client OSs via Group Policies in Windows.
- This will allow you to have granular control over client security features.
- Another benefit of Group Policies is that you can prevent users from modifying the OS settings that could inadvertently put PHI at risk.
- If group policies are not available, configure local client OS policies at a minimum to ensure PHI protection.
- Harden your OSs by implementing well-known best practices that are referenced in Appendix C.
- Disable all unnecessary services.
- Disable all unnecessary protocols.
- Make specific registry or configuration changes to plug known security holes.
- These will help reduce potential vulnerabilities as well as help the computer run at its optimum performance.
- Use personal firewall software on every computer possible inside your network to help prevent unauthorized drive access and malware infections.
- Apply the latest vendor software updates on a regular basis.
- Some OSs have an update feature built into them—use this at a minimum.
- Be careful not to install software updates on production computers that your business relies on without fully testing them first or having a quick and easy back-out plan in case they cause problems or fail.

- Patch third-party software such as Adobe and Java as these are the flaws exploited the most by malware. Use a third-party patch management product that you can use to centrally test, deploy, and manage these patches with. See Appendix C for a listing of some of these products.
- To prevent these automatic updates from occurring without your testing and approval, you can consider turning off the auto-update functionality within the OS.
- Ensure that strong passwords are used—see Sub-subsection 22.4.11 for tips on passwords.
- Turn on logging—all modern OSs support it.
- Enable system, application, security, and any other applicable logging features.
- This will help you create audit trails for PHI access.
- Do not display the last user ID that logged in on the log-in screen. If it is displayed, a malicious user can use this against you and try to log in with that user ID.
- Remove, or at least disable, any guest accounts on your systems.
- For automatic log-off, there is no set time specified by HIPAA—just use common sense based on what you find in your risk analysis and what works best in your environment.
- Some OSs have built-in features such as screen savers that will allow or even force users to log off manually or after a few minutes of inactivity.
- Consider using radio frequency–based proximity sensors to automate this when users come and go around workstations—especially nursing stations.

22.4.10 Logging

- Logging is required and is an essential element to create PHI audit trails.
- Turn on logging on every possible system. Logging-event successes and failures may prove to be too much information to sift through and store—consider logging-event failures and access to critical PHI files only.
- There are specific logging applications that can sift through all of your logging data to search for important security events.

Log to a remote syslog server that is running on dedicated hardware. This helps to ensure security of the logs and helps prevent tampering of the logs by a malicious user trying to cover his tracks.

- There are various free, open-source, commercial syslog products that can serve the purpose as well. Place strict access controls on any remote logging servers or log files.
- Make sure your log files are backed up periodically.
- Ideally, to maximize the utilization of your IT and security staff, you should outsource this service.

22.4.11 Passwords

- Do not make users choose complicated passwords or change them so often that they are difficult to remember and end up getting written down in obvious places such as on sticky notes placed on the monitor or keyboard.
- Never write down passwords.
- Enforce passwords within the OS, application, or database.
- Enforce password reuse and complexity such as minimum length, upper and lower case, and special characters at the OS, application, or database level—never rely on your users to create strong passwords.
- Eight characters is a good minimum length for passwords— just do not limit the number of characters. If a user wants to create a 25-character passphrase, let them do it.
- Encourage users to create passwords that are easy to remember yet difficult to guess.
- It is sufficient that passwords be changed every six–12 months as long as they are strong passwords that are difficult to guess—if users are required to change them more frequently, odds are they will be written down. A long *passphrase* (combination of real words such as *Itz_been_cold_outside* that is easy to remember yet very difficult to crack) that is changed maybe once every six or 12 months is better than short, more convoluted passwords that must be changed every 30–60 days.
- Make password cracking part of your ongoing security vulnerability tests.

22.4.12 Messaging

- HIPAA does not ban the use of e-mail or text messages to send PHI if no threats or vulnerabilities are found during the risk analysis. However, they are often there.
- Any e-mail or text message that is sent in cleartext is at risk— during transmission inside your network, across the Internet, and once it arrives at its destination, during transmission on the recipient's network, and while it is stored on the recipient's e-mail server or local computer.
- Without specific technologies in place, there is no way to prevent digital messages from being captured, printed, or forwarded on to another user.
- Users should not be given the option to encrypt e-mails or texts because if you give them that responsibility, it might not get done. Do it for them. Many e-mail firewalls have this capability.
- Have a policy against sending PHI via e-mail.
- If that is not possible, then you must have policies, procedures, and encryption technologies in place.
- Do not rely on an e-mail's subject line or the sender's e-mail address to verify the authenticity of the sender.
- E-mails can be forged or spoofed to look like they are coming from anyone and can be used to trick people or contain malicious code that can compromise PHI.
- Do not put PHI in the e-mail subject line.
- Use a perimeter or cloud-based e-mail firewall/encryption solution.
- These products encrypt/decrypt e-mails at the network perimeter (or in the cloud), thus taking e-mail security responsibilities away from users.
- Some cloud e-mail services have the ability to notify users that they have messages waiting for them; after clicking a link, the user is directed to a secure website to read the e-mail.
- If no risks are found to exist for internal e-mail, then encryption may be optional.
- Just make sure your e-mail server and message stores are secured from malicious attacks originating from inside or outside your network.

- Do not forget about instant messaging (IM) both on your traditional workstations and your phones and tablets. IM provides a great way to communicate—but it has many of the same threats and vulnerabilities an e-mail has (e.g., malware, cleartext network transmissions, storage of sensitive information in log files on unsecured systems).

There is a good NIST document titled Guidelines on Electronic Mail Security (SP 800-45) that provides more detailed information and guidance on e-mail security.[3]

22.4.13 *Remote Access/Virtual Private Networks*

- Only provide remote access to the systems necessary for your users to get their jobs done.
- Treat remote computers (workstations and mobile devices) as company computers when it comes to security policies and minimum system requirements.
- The trend today is for users to bring your own device (BYOD). Consider supplying company-owned equipment for remote access to eliminate any policy enforcement issues.
- Consider the following minimum system requirements for remote access:
  - Antivirus software installed
  - Personal firewall enabled
  - The latest OS and third-party software patches
  - Strong passwords
  - Secure authentication
  - Automatic log-off
  - Secure physical location
  - Contingency plan if the computer will be storing PHI
  - A VPN system that uses 128-bit encryption or greater
  - Strong encryption passphrases
  - Strong user authentication passwords
- Have a policy forbidding users to allow their VPN software to store, or "remember," their VPN password; for instance, if a

laptop is stolen, the thief could have a direct VPN connection into your network.

- Do not forget the physical security of remote clients—an unencrypted laptop with a VPN client that has a password saved in it can be very dangerous!
- Just because VPN information is encrypted does not mean that someone with access to the data stream cannot figure out what is going on, such as the time of day transmissions occurred, the length of the transmissions, and so forth, to help launch an attack on your VPN.
- You can even use VPN software built into your existing OSs, such as Point-to-Point Tunneling Protocol and Internet Protocol Security.

22.4.14 Physical Security

- Ensure that physical access to your critical infrastructure devices such as your firewall, IPS, router, and servers is tightly controlled, as unsecured areas can be one of the best ways for PHI to be compromised.
- Having a locked door on the computer room where only a limited number of people have access is ideal. Ask your cloud service providers to see a copy of their latest SSAE 16 SOC 2 audit report to validate there are no gaps of concern in their facilities. Bottom line: If you have an option or a way to lock it up, then do it—this can eliminate a lot of vulnerabilities.
- Biometrics and magnetic-strip ID badges work well.
- Limit physical access to network infrastructure equipment, including cables and patch panels.
- Limit the use of glass around computer rooms and equipment to prevent the possibility of someone gaining access.
- Place your computer systems in a safe place in the event of an earthquake or other threat that may cause structural damage to the building.
- Use physical tie-downs for computers and equipment that are susceptible to physical security risks.
- Ensure that media (CDs, tapes, external drives, etc.) are stored in locked containers or safes away from daily office traffic.

- Install heat and smoke detectors in your computer room, both above and below raised floors and ceilings.
- Ensure that fire suppression systems are installed, but do not unnecessarily put personnel or equipment at risk.
- Install humidity and temperature controls in your computer room to ensure that equipment is not damaged by too much or too little moisture or too high temperatures.
- Have a policy against eating, drinking, or smoking near any computer equipment.
- Install antiglare filters on computer monitors where there might be a chance of someone seeing what is on the screen—these not only help reduce glare, but also can prevent anyone from seeing what is on the screen unless directly in front of the computer.
- Use media shredders and bulk erasers to destroy media or data before disposing them.
- Use paper shredders or locked bins for paper that contains PHI.

22.5 Mobile Computing

22.5.1 Wireless Networks

Wireless local area networks (WLANs), also referred to as Wi-Fi, are everywhere. Medical professionals do not want to be tied to a desktop computer or take down notes on paper and have to reenter them later. They can just walk around with a laptop computer that is connected to a WLAN and enter or retrieve data immediately. Of course, along with such a useful and beneficial technology, there are various associated technical concerns and security risks, which are explained in Sub-subsections 22.5.1.1 through 22.5.1.3.

22.5.1.1 Technical Concerns

- Reliability concerns: Coverage and signal strength are not always optimal; this also depends on distance, antenna, and other factors such as the quality of the access point (APs) you are using.
- WLAN networks only support a limited number of hosts.

- In-depth technical skills are needed for large WLAN design and deployment.
- Network troubleshooting can be difficult.

22.5.1.2 Security Concerns

- Practically anyone can purchase a W-Fi router from an electronics department store, bring it into the office, and immediately connect it to your network, effectively bypassing all of your perimeter security controls.
- It can be difficult to know when these rogue APs are being used.
- Sensitive information (e.g., PHI) may go across WLANs—both inbound and outbound—unencrypted.
- PHI is also at risk while at rest if a malicious user gains access to the network via an insecure AP.
- The Wired Equivalent Privacy (WEP) encryption scheme can be cracked. This has been known for over 13 years, yet some people still use it in health care settings.
- Telecommuters use Wi-Fi (often any) and thus are subjecting their computers and communications sessions to unnecessary risks.
- Policy enforcement and system requirements must extend out to users' homes, when they are traveling, and so forth.
- A proper technical security vulnerability assessment will help determine where your wireless systems are weak.

22.5.1.3 What Can Be Done to Secure Wireless Networks?   It is not that difficult. At a minimum, you should do/have the following:

- Change default AP and wireless router passwords and use strong passphrases instead.
- Use Wi-Fi Protected Access version 2 for encryption. Preshared keys are fine as long as you use 20+ random characters.
- Turn on media access control (MAC) address access controls so you can specify which WLAN network cards can connect to your APs, if possible.

- Remember that MAC addresses can be forged or spoofed to allow unauthorized users on your network.
- Enable user authentication, if possible.
- Disable or at least change the default community string for Simple Network Management Protocol.
- Change the default network numbers known as service set identifiers.
- Physical security of your APs is a must—similar to other network infrastructure devices, if they are compromised, your entire system can be compromised.
- Consider adjusting AP signal strength to prevent stray signals that others could tap into.
- Install firmware and WLAN network driver updates on a regular basis.
- Consider adding a Wi-Fi device—see Appendix C for references to some of these products.
- Test to see what happens when your APs lose power. Can they be easily tapped into if physical access is available?
- Do not forget to turn on logging and monitor your wireless APs.
- Back up your log files or log to a remote syslog server.
- Save your AP configurations after any changes are made and store them somewhere safe and secure.
- Perform ongoing vulnerability assessments of your WLAN.
- Assess your WLAN from inside and outside.
- Ensure that client systems connecting to your WLAN meet these minimum requirements:
  - Antivirus software installed
  - Personal firewall enabled
  - The latest OS and third-party patches
  - Strong passwords
  - Secure authentication
  - Automatic log-off
  - Secure physical location
  - Contingency plan if the computer will be storing PHI

Do not let the security issues associated with WLANs keep you from using them. If properly secured, WLAN benefits can definitely outweigh the risks. As Chuck Yeager has said, "You do not concentrate on risks. You concentrate on results. No risk is too great to prevent the necessary job from getting done." Some WLAN security best practices and a little common sense will enable you to securely use WLANs in your health care setting. WLAN convenience and ease of use, when managed properly, can help to increase the overall efficiency and quality of patient care.

22.5.2 Mobile Devices

Mobile devices such as smartphones and tablets and their related apps are all the rage in health care today. If you are using these systems to store or process PHI, or in some other way to provide patient care, then you must follow the HIPAA Privacy Rule and Security Rule requirements. Mobile devices can easily become the source of inadvertent disclosure of PHI.

22.5.2.1 How Are Your Mobile Devices Used?   Whether you support BYOD or you provide mobile devices to your users, you must consider specifically how they will be used. The HIPAA Privacy Rule and Security Rule regulate securing PHI on mobile devices. Such devices must have safeguards implemented to guard against unauthorized use. In general, PHI may only be accessed and used within CEs for appropriate treatment, payment, or health care operation purposes. For example, physician-to-physician consultation for treating patients and sharing PHI stored on their mobile devices is an acceptable use of PHI. However, the size, portability, and storage capabilities of mobile devices make them extremely easy to lose or misplace, or to be stolen. In addition, the information stored on mobile devices must be secured so that others physically obtaining the device cannot get access to the PHI

Another consideration is the transmission of data from a mobile device to the computer network. Information may be intercepted while the mobile devices are transferring information to the network. The risks increase dramatically when the transmissions are wireless. Sending PHI from a mobile device to another individual outside the organization is most certainly covered by the Security Rule requirements. Encryption and other access control requirements may be established, and the transmissions must be planned and appropriately coordinated with the BAs. You also need to consider mobile devices (and any encryption they might be using) in your incident response procedures if you are going to have the benefit of the Safe Harbor protection outlined by the Omnibus Rule.

22.5.2.2 Mobile Device Risks If used correctly, mobile devices can increase efficiency and potentially decrease the rate of medical and insurance errors. However, they are inherently less secure than traditional workstations and servers. Their size and portability creates many risks, including but not limited to the following:

- Theft or loss
- Lack of passwords or bad password management
- Lack of file access controls
- Viruses
- Unauthorized network access using stolen mobile devices
- Wireless transmission concerns
- Difficulty retrieving devices from terminated employees

Mobile users must be responsible for knowing the information stored and processed on their mobile devices. Although it may be impractical for each person to know exactly the files that are on their mobile devices, they must know the apps and types of information, especially as it relates to PHI, that they have on their mobile devices. This is necessary to determine the information that has potentially been compromised in case of loss, theft, or inappropriate use, and to activate the appropriate mitigation procedures.

22.5.2.3 Securing Health Information on Mobile Devices If you are using mobile devices within your organization (and who is not?), you need to establish policies, procedures, and training covering their use to ensure the security of the information processed and stored in them. Consider establishing the following directives within your mobile policies and procedures to ensure the security and privacy of PHI on mobile devices. Determine the feasibility of each of these suggestions based on your business and environment.

- Management must approve the installation and use of synchronization software from corporate systems to and from mobile devices before use.
- Mobile users must participate in security training before using their mobile devices.
- Each mobile user must sign an acceptable usage agreement.
- Mobile devices containing PHI must be physically secured when left unattended.
- Corporate-approved access controls and encryption must be used on mobile devices containing PHI.
- A central inventory of all information stored, or allowed to be stored, on mobile devices must be maintained.
- Employees must back up data, using an approved corporate method, on a regular basis to avoid loss of valuable PHI.
- Mobile devices used for job responsibilities are subject to audits similar to any other electronic device, even if an employee owns it.
- Passwords must be used on all mobile devices.
- Mobile passwords must comply with corporate password policies.
- Mobile devices that are lost or stolen, or belong to terminated personnel, must be immediately locked out from network access.
- Only certain classification(s) of data are allowed to be accessible by mobile devices (this requires that you have a data classification process in place).
- Dynamic (single-use) passwords must be used on all mobile devices (e.g., via tokens).
- Antivirus software must be used on all mobile devices.
- Wireless transmission from mobile devices must be encrypted.
- Only mobile devices provided and configured by the organization can be used to process and access corporate information and PHI.
- Software must be implemented on mobile devices to create an audit trail of system activity, including log-in attempts, security incidents, and attempts to access files containing PHI.

- Mobile devices that will no longer be used must be wiped using the factory reset function to clear out or overwrite the PHI. If this is not possible, the PDA must be physically destroyed, or the storage removed and destroyed.

22.6 Additional Technology Considerations

The following are additional technologies that can help with HIPAA compliance that you will want to have on your radar:

- Software source code analysis for testing the security of your web applications and mobile apps
- Cloud services discovery/compliance technologies to ensure you understand which cloud services are being used on your network
- Forensics analysis tools for responding to and investigating security incidents

In the end, only you will know what is truly needed to build out a secure and compliant technology infrastructure. If your risk analyses are done properly, what is required should be obvious.

22.7 Conclusion

The tips we have provided in this chapter are not comprehensive, but we believe we have touched on many of the more important elements. What we have provided here is a lot of information to take in at once. Do not let this intimidate you. If you build your HIPAA-compliant technology infrastructure a little at a time and show reasonable effort, you will do fine.

Ultimately, there is no such thing as a 100% secure technology infrastructure, so do not strive for absolute perfection; strive for the most reasonable within your organization. Also, keep in mind that you cannot buy a complete, prepackaged HIPAA compliance solution, no matter what vendors tell you. HIPAA compliance does not come in a box. All of these technology considerations must be integrated with solid policies, procedures, and daily business practices to ensure HIPAA compliance.

Keep in mind that it is more difficult to add on to a system after it has been installed/deployed. We are not saying it is impossible—it is just not as easy, and it can be more costly. Instead, strive to design security in your technology systems and infrastructure from the beginning wherever possible. It will be cheaper and much easier to manage in the long run. Also, we cannot stress enough how important it is to keep in mind the scalable and flexible characteristics of HIPAA. As long as reasonable efforts are being made to protect PHI, you should have no problem attaining and maintaining HIPAA compliance.

Practical Checklist

- Perform a risk analysis to determine what PHI threats and vulnerabilities exist, which policies and procedures will have to be developed, and which technologies will have to be used to enforce your policies and facilitate your procedures.
- Remember that firewalls, antivirus, and basic passwords are not enough—you must have a layered security architecture to ensure "defense in depth" in the event one or more security controls fails.
- Encrypt e-mails if there is a chance they will contain PHI—e-mails sent and stored in cleartext may present too many vulnerabilities.
- Search unauthorized PHI access and transmission using DLP technologies.
- Harden your OSs to ensure they are not vulnerable to attack.
- Lock down your WLANs.
- The Security Rule requirements cover computer-based faxes and the Privacy Rule requirements cover hard-copy faxes.
- Do a walk-through of your facility and assess your physical security.
- All other security mechanisms can be defeated by lax physical security—make sure all electronic devices are under secure control.
- Determine how mobile devices are being used within your organization and make sure they are reasonably secure.
- Establish mobile usage policies and procedures, including acceptable mobile device hardware and software to use for processing and storing PHI.

23

CRAFTING SECURITY INCIDENT PROCEDURES AND CONTINGENCY PLANS

23.1 Background

The Security Rule sets forth very high-level standards and implementation specifications for dealing with information security incidents and unexpected information systems emergencies. The Breach Notification Rule in the Health Information Technology for Economic and Clinical Health (HITECH) Act of 2009 and the Health Insurance Portability and Accountability Act (HIPAA) Omnibus Rule published additional details that impact security incident response and contingency planning. Security incident procedures and contingency plans, as the Security Rule refers to these, are two different yet closely related areas of information security that are absolutely critical to the confidentiality, integrity, and availability of protected health information (PHI). They both define who, what, when, where, why, and how in planning for and responding to critical incidents involving your health care information systems. You certainly cannot expect to defend against all security incidents and disasters, but you do need to plan for the ones that could likely occur. Your overall goal should be to minimize the impact of a breach when it does occur.

In this chapter, we will explain the differences between security incident procedures and contingency plans, expand on what is required for these two standards by the Security Rule and more recent updates in the HITECH Act and Omnibus Rule, and provide some practical advice and checklists so you can ensure that your health care information systems are well protected from events such as hacker attacks, malware outbreaks, and natural disasters.

23.2 Handling Security Incidents

Computer security incidents are rarely thought of until they occur. In most situations, information security threats are not taken seriously until an organization suffers damage or loss. Security incidents can be caused by anything from malicious users inside or outside your network to a virus or worm outbreak that disables a system or deletes critical health care information. Massive amounts of computer security incidents occur on a daily basis. Although reporting is required and databases such as the Department of Health and Human Services breach website (http://www.hhs.gov/ocr/privacy /hipaa/administrative/breachnotificationrule/breachtool.html) and Chronology of Data Breaches (http://www.privacyrights.org /data-breach) are continually updated, many security incidents go unnoticed, unreported, or simply do not gain a spot in the media headlines.

Security incidents are becoming more frequent due to the ease of performing computer attacks and not getting caught, the increasing number of vulnerabilities found in the software we use, and the growing mobile workforce. A majority of organizations do not take information security seriously, and criminal hackers and malicious employees know that. Do not fret; there is no way to completely secure PHI. You can, however, put a set of procedures in place, which, combined with your other information security initiatives, will allow you to be assured that your systems are reasonably secured and you are well prepared to respond to an incident when that time does come.

An incident response program requires forming a team, developing incident handling and reporting procedures, testing those procedures, and being able to formally respond to security incidents when they occur. You may recall from Chapter 12 that a security incident is defined in the Security Rule as "the attempted or successful unauthorized access, use, disclosure, modification, destruction, or interference with system operations in an information system." The HITECH Act enacted requirements for breach notification once a breach was discovered, and the Omnibus Rule made some additional updates on what constitutes a breach and risk assessment steps that must be followed after a breach occurs. As it stands now, any disclosure or use of PHI not allowed by the Privacy Rule may very well be considered to be a breach. Refer to the Privacy Rule requirements in Chapter 6 for more information. Do not forget that these incident and contingency planning rules now apply equally to covered entities (CEs), business associates (BAs), and their subcontractors.

Given this, we provide guidance on developing procedures that will allow you to effectively respond if a security incident occurs. These security incident program building blocks are not application or operating system dependent. We have kept them at a high enough level that they can be applied within any organization, yet they are detailed enough to match up with the Security Rule requirements. For other security incident resources, please refer to Appendix C.

23.3 Security Incident Procedure Essentials

When the time comes to respond to a security incident, an expert team and a solid set of procedures must be in place to successfully maintain the confidentiality, integrity, and availability of your PHI and business operations. The following sections outline the Security Rule implementation specifications for security incidents along with some things you can do to meet these requirements.

23.3.1 Response and Reporting (Required)

The Security Rule lists security incident response and reporting as a required implementation specification. Response and reporting is defined in the Security Rule as follows:

- Identify and respond to suspected or known security incidents.
- To the extent practicable, mitigate harmful effects of security incidents that are known to the CE.
- Document security incidents and their outcomes.

Now consider the individual implementation specifications in Exhibit 23.1 for this standard and define what can be done to meet them.

Exhibit 23.1   Individual Implementation Specifications

1. Identify and respond to suspected or known security incidents.
   a. Security incident team
      i. First and foremost, you must have a team in place that can help plan for and formally respond to security incidents. This team, sometimes referred to as a Computer Emergency Response Team or Computer Security Incident Response Team (CSIRT), should consist of key internal employees who will formally respond to security incidents. Keep in mind that responding to security incidents is not just an IT issue. Anyone that plays a role in information systems management and compliance as well as health care operations should be included. The following is a list of people you need to consider having on your team:
         A. HIPAA Security Officer
         B. HIPAA Privacy Officer
         C. Network or security administrator(s)
         D. Security manager or executive (i.e., chief information security officer [CISO])
         E. Risk management executive
         F. Chief information officer
         G. Legal counsel
         H. Public relations representative
         I. Local, state, or federal law enforcement cybercrime investigator
      ii. Document in detail what each team member's roles and responsibilities are. If you choose to outsource your incident response to a consultant or other firm, be sure that someone in your organization still has ownership and responsibility for coordinating security incident response (most likely the HIPAA Security Officer).
      iii. Document each team member's full contact information, including the following:
         A. Home phone number
         B. Friend, relative, or spouse home or work number, if possible
         C. Mobile phone number
         D. Personal e-mail address, if possible
      iv. Determine which methods the team members will use to communicate in the event of a security incident.
   b. Security incident detection system. This could include one or more of the following items, some of which were discussed in detail in Chapter 22:
      i. Intrusion Prevention System (IPS)
      ii. Network analyzer
      iii. Antivirus software
      iv. Log monitoring and alerting system (or service)
   c. Formal response procedures. These procedures clearly define what steps your CSIRT will take when a security incident is detected. They should include the following at a minimum:
      i. What criteria will be used to determine if a security incident has occurred
         A. IPS alerts, system unavailability, loss of a mobile device, confirmed breach, and so on
      ii. The order in which CSIRT members will be contacted
         A. This should also include every member's detailed contact information
      iii. How the security incident will be analyzed
         A. What methods (IPS, log analysis, network analyzer, vulnerability scanner, etc.)
         B. Which tools will be used in the analysis

Exhibit 23.1   Individual Implementation Specifications (*Continued*)

   iv. Documentation on how you are currently collecting and storing your log files before the security incident occurred

     A. The word *before* is critical here. If you intend to pursue a formal investigation and prosecution of the perpetrator(s), you must ensure that logging is enabled before an incident occurs. If you start logging after you suspect a security incident has occurred, your logs may not be considered business records maintained in the course of normal business activities and thus may not be admissible in court.

   v. How you will communicate with the media, your customers, and the general public

     A. You should prepare a communications plan in advance of a security incident so that everyone is not scrambling to figure what to do and what to say.

     B. Be sure to include who will communicate the message of a security incident (internal or external public relations, HIPAA Security Officer, etc.), when it will be communicated, what will be said, and what is being done to resolve the issue and prevent further damage.

   vi. How your team will handle potential evidence

     A. How will log files (for systems and applications both on-site and off-site) be saved and stored?

     B. How will you interact with cloud service providers and other vendors?

     C. Who has primary responsibility for preserving evidence and leading the forensics collection?

     D. Will a forensics investigator be involved?

     E. What will be the chain of custody if a formal investigation is deemed necessary due to major losses or criminal activity?

   vii. What steps will be taken to restore or rebuild systems

     A. How will backups (including cloud-based and other off-site backups) be used?

     B. What other systems may be put in place of the victim systems (i.e., separate server instances or cloud service providers)?

     C. How will operating systems, applications, and configurations be reinstalled and reset?

     D. What is your estimated timeline to operate at a minimal level?

     E. What is your estimated timeline to be back to business as usual?

     F. Who will help with your recovery efforts?

   viii. What steps will be taken to meet the breach notification requirements

     A. Who will perform the risk assessment to determine how PHI was specifically impacted, who gained access, and whether PHI was accessed?

     B. What parameters are needed to determine the extent to which the risk has been mitigated?

     C. What if the information that was suspected to have been breached was encrypted and thus protected by Safe Harbor, discussed in Chapter 12?

     D. Who will handle the actual breach notification process if it is needed?

2. Mitigate, to the extent practicable, harmful effects of security incidents that are known to the CE.

   a. How you will protect your health care information systems from further intrusion or damage:

     i. Disconnect affected systems

     ii. Reboot affected systems

     iii. Place affected systems on different network segments

     iv. Patch or somehow fix the vulnerability

(*Continued*)

Exhibit 23.1   Individual Implementation Specifications (*Continued*)

---

3. Document security incidents and their outcomes.
   a. Document in as much detail as possible:
      i. What happened
      ii. When it happened
      iii. The symptoms of the incident
      iv. Systems or information that were damaged, lost, or stolen
      v. Outcomes of the investigation
4. Follow up actions with all members of the CSIRT and any others involved to discuss lessons learned and how to prevent this incident in the future.
5. Enact your breach notification procedure. Refer to Part II and also Appendix C for more information.

Once you document your security incident procedures, you should securely store them in a safe place that will be accessible to every member of your CSIRT when a security incident occurs. Because your business operations may change from time to time, remember to test these procedures and manage them on an ongoing basis as you would any other information security documentation.

23.4 Basics of Contingency Planning

Contingency planning involves preparing for the worst—anything from a system outage to outright loss of an entire database or data center. Although it is extremely difficult to protect against something that has not happened, certain fundamental steps can be taken to mitigate risks to information systems and critical business functions. Being unprepared for an information systems disaster can mean severe business interruption or even failure.

Although the terms "disaster recovery" and "business continuity" are often used interchangeably, technically there is a difference. Disaster recovery concerns the retrieval or recreation of information systems and business functionality to the state they were in before a disaster occurred. Business continuity refers to maintaining a minimum level of business operations to fulfill critical operating requirements in the midst of a disaster or other type of operational or systems disruption. Despite the differences in terminology, the concepts for implementing and managing successful disaster recovery and business continuity plans are basically the same.

As covered in Chapter 12, the Security Rule contains a contingency plan standard that requires establishing "policies and procedures for responding to an emergency or other occurrence (for example, fire, vandalism, system failure, and natural disaster) that damages systems that contain electronic protected health information." The specific implementation specifications for this standard include the following:

- Data backup plan
- Disaster recovery plan
- Emergency mode operation plan
- Testing and revision procedures
- Applications and data criticality analysis

Now consider the individual implementation specifications for this standard along with what can be done to meet them.

23.4.1 Data Backup Plan (Required)

The Security Rule defines the data backup plan requirement as "establish and implement procedures to create and maintain retrievable exact copies of electronic protected health information." Keep in mind that this rule (like all of the security rules) is flexible and scalable, depending on your organization's size. The following suggestions, although certainly not comprehensive for all situations, should be a good starting point for your data backup plan procedures:

- Specific backup technologies used
  - Tape backups
  - Optical disks (CDs and DVDs)
  - Disk-to-disk backups
  - Mirrored hard disks in servers and workstations
  - Redundant network-attached storage devices
  - Redundant storage area network devices
  - Cloud backups
  - Software or other methods used to create the backups
- Specific backup methodologies used
  - When data is backed up
    - In real time (constantly)
    - Hourly

- Daily
- Weekly
- Monthly
- Backup media (tape, disk, cloud, etc.) rotation schedule
  - Use the same media every day
  - Use different media every day
  - Have media labeled for each day, such as Monday–Thursday
  - Have other media labeled for Fridays, such as Friday 1 through Friday 4
- Type(s) of backups performed
  - *Full*: All data is backed up
  - *Incremental*: Backs up only the files that have changed since the last full or incremental backup and marks the files as being backed up (clears the archive file attribute)
  - *Differential*: Backs up only the files that have changed since the last full or incremental backup and does not mark the files as being backed up (does not clear the archive file attribute)

We strongly recommend backing up your workstations and mobile devices (both of which are rarely backed up yet often contain the only copy of sensitive information including PHI). Do not forget about your applications, databases, directory services, and network infrastructure systems (firewall, router, etc.) configurations associated with PHI to help minimize downtime.

- Backup management and media storage
  - Assigned backup responsibility
  - Who will manage your backups on an ongoing basis?
  - Backup testing methodology: this is very critical to ensure that your backup media actually contain valid data and will be reliable when you need them
  - Where the backup media will be stored, which is very critical to ensure that backups are not destroyed in the event of a disaster
    - In-house vault
    - In-house server(s)

- Off-site backup storage facility
- Cloud service provider
- Someone's home (not preferred but better than nothing)

23.4.2 Disaster Recovery Plan (Required)

Disaster recovery concerns the restoration or recreation of information systems and business functionality to the state they were in before a disaster occurred. Disaster recovery plans should address who is responsible for the information systems and various business operations; what information systems, PHI, and business functions are involved; and when the plan should be invoked. Keep in mind that there are parallels between disaster recovery and security incident response. If a security incident is bad enough, it could be considered a disaster. For example, if a malicious user deleted an entire patient database, this could lead to some, if not most, services coming to an abrupt halt. This might be considered a state of disaster for your organization.

All of the implementation specifications required for your contingency plan can help with your overall disaster recovery plan. The following is a set of minimum requirements needed to establish a disaster recovery plan to define the who, what, and when of disaster management:

- Disaster recovery team: Similar to your security incident team, you must have people in place that can help plan for and respond to information systems disasters. In the same fashion, anyone that plays a key role in your information systems and health care operations should be included. The following is a list of people you need to consider having on your team:

  - HIPAA Security Officer
  - HIPAA Privacy Officer
  - Network or security administrator (or both)
  - Security manager or executive (i.e., CISO)
  - Risk management executive
  - Operations manager

- Legal counsel
- Public relations representative
- Document in detail each team member's roles and responsibilities. If you choose to outsource your disaster recovery to a specialty firm, be sure that someone in your organization still has ownership and responsibility for coordinating disaster recovery (most likely your HIPAA Security Officer).
- Document each team member's full contact information, including
  - Home phone number
  - Friend, relative, or spouse home or work number, if possible
  - Mobile phone number
  - Personal e-mail address, if possible
- Determine which methods the team members will use to communicate in the event of a disaster.
- Anticipate that a disaster will occur eventually and plan for it. The disaster recovery team should consider beforehand
  - What could go wrong
  - What it would do in the event of a disaster
  - What is the worst that can happen
  - What is likely to happen
- Ensure that critical applications, systems, and data are distributed among facilities that are reasonably easy to get to but not so close that they could be affected by the same disaster (i.e., tornado, flooding, and related environmental events).
- Determine which information systems and business functions are involved.
  - Most of the systems and business functions involved along with the specific PHI that must be considered will have been determined during your information risk assessment.
  - More specifically, you can perform a business impact analysis that is outlined in Sub-subsection 23.4.5; this will help you obtain a detailed inventory of specific information, business processes, and other assets that must be protected and thus made part of this plan.
- Ensure that your system and data inventories and network diagrams are kept current.

- When the disaster recovery plan should be invoked? Your organization might categorize different levels of disasters, such as
  - A hacker or disgruntled employee attack that causes system outages or severe data losses
  - A computer virus, worm, or other malicious code that infects critical information systems and renders them unusable
  - A hardware failure on a critical computer system
  - An environmental catastrophe such as a tornado or fire
  - A building that is physically damaged or destroyed
- It should be top priority to ensure that people are protected and it is safe to implement your plan.
- When a disaster occurs, do not react impulsively and immediately; stop and think before acting. Get the facts first and find out
  - What has occurred
  - When it occurred
  - How it occurred
  - Who and what was involved
  - How you will communicate with the media, your customers, and the general public
- You should prepare a communications plan in advance of a disaster so that public relations decisions do not have to be made during a crisis and your organization will know what to say. Be sure to include
  - Who will communicate the message of the disaster (internal or external public relations)
  - When it will be communicated
  - What will be said
  - What is being done to resolve the crisis and get the business back on track
- Confirm that emergency shelter and other staple items for your workers are considered in your overall plan. Consider the following items at a minimum:
  - Shelter
  - Food
  - Water

- Clothing
- Backup communications devices such as mobile phones
- Determine who will facilitate all of this.
- What is the process of restoring data?
- Who will do it?
- What systems will the data be restored to?
- What data is most critical and will be needed first?
- How will data be tested for proper restoration and integrity?

A major objective of your disaster recovery planning should be to develop a plan that can be implemented by practically anyone in case the disaster recovery team becomes incapacitated and the organization's leadership becomes unreachable. Distribute copies of the written plans to everyone involved and also store extra copies in an off-site, fireproof vault to which each team member has access. Electronic copies should be stored off-site as well.

23.4.3 Emergency Mode Operation Plan (Required)

Emergency mode operation is essentially business continuity. As stated in the Security Rule, the goal here is to "establish procedures to enable continuation of critical business processes for protection of the security of electronic health information while operating in emergency mode."

There is a great amount of overlap between disaster recovery and business continuity, including forming a team and determining which systems and business processes are involved and when the plan should be invoked. These may be identical for both of these implementation specifications or perhaps combined into one document. The following items are specific to business continuity planning and should be considered in developing your overall emergency mode operation plan:

- On the basis of the results of your risk analysis, document the systems that are absolutely mission critical to keep your business running.
- Establish written policies, contracts, and service-level agreements with third-party hosting, collocation, telecommunications, and Internet service providers that facilitate business continuity.

- You will want to ensure that your service providers (if any) have the ability to provide redundant systems, Internet or wide area network connections, phone systems, and even technical expertise to assist in a crisis; this may involve
  - *Hot sites*: Facilities that have fully redundant systems that can take over within minutes.
  - *Warm sites*: Facilities that have partially ready computer systems such as hardware and network connections but no data or applications installed.
  - *Cold sites*: Facilities that have no equipment, applications, or data but are ready to be moved into.
- Confirm that not only is an emergency shelter available, but also that an off-site work facility is free to move into. Consider the following items:
  - Off-site office space
  - Backup communications devices such as mobile phones
  - Computers
  - Business supplies

23.4.4 Testing and Revision Procedure (Addressable)

The Security Rule states that testing and revision procedures must be in place for periodic testing and revision of contingency plans. This is an addressable implementation specification. Considering the criticality of contingency plans, we cannot imagine a scenario where they should not be tested and updated on an ongoing basis. Your information systems and business operations will change over time, thus requiring future testing and updating as necessary. Otherwise, you might not know that your plans are not going to work until the worst possible time. Here are a few tips on developing your contingency plan testing and revision procedures:

- Develop testing standards.
  - Determine what will be tested.
  - Team communication plans.
  - Data center failover plans.
  - Data backup plans.
  - Data restoration plans.

- If your information systems and business processes change regularly, consider performing a business impact analysis on a regular basis.
- Determine how often testing will occur.
  - Test plans at least annually and when major systems changes occur.
- Document and review your test results.
- Update the plans as needed.
- Analyze plans on an ongoing basis to ensure alignment with current business objectives and requirements.

23.4.5 Applications and Data Criticality Analysis (Addressable)

CEs and BAs must "assess the relative criticality of specific applications and data in support of other contingency plan components." This analysis is also known as a business impact analysis. This will help you to document and understand the interdependencies among business processes and determine how the business would be affected by an information systems outage. The Security Rule states that this is only a required implementation specification, but just like with the testing and revision procedure, we highly recommend integrating this step into your overall plan and your initial and ongoing risk analyses. In fact, we cannot imagine being able to effectively develop contingency plans without the information discovered in this analysis. Here are a few key steps to keep in mind when performing an applications and data criticality analysis:

- Take an inventory of information systems assets such as computer hardware, software, applications, medical devices, and sensitive information (including PHI).
- Identify single points of failure within the information systems infrastructure. For example, this could include the following:
  - A single computer or server that all employees rely on that only has a single hard drive as opposed to mirrored drives or a redundant array of inexpensive disks, or a single power supply as opposed to dual power supplies
  - A single Internet connection

- An on-site electronic medical record system or related internal application that is critical for the business
- A single administrator-equivalent user ID
- Only one network administrator or manager that knows all of the system passwords
- Identify critical applications, systems, and data.
  - What systems are must-haves?
  - What systems are needed but not critical?
  - What systems are not absolutely necessary until your team can restore business as usual?
- Prioritize key business functions. Business functions to consider are the following:
  - Emergency health care operations
  - Health care claims submissions
  - Supply chains
  - Lines of communication between patients and their caregivers

23.5 Moving Forward

Security incident and contingency plans are not only HIPAA requirements, but they are also an essential component of an overall information risk management program that makes good business sense. When developed and implemented properly, they are key to information systems and business survival. Moving forward, CEs and BAs can leverage the technological benefits inherent in the Internet/cloud to reduce the impact of a disaster.

Long term, it is much less expensive to implement proper security incident and contingency plans than it is to restore business operations and customer confidence. Computer intrusions and disasters cannot be stopped completely; however, if something does happen and the proper plans are in place, CEs and BAs will be able to minimize the impact with a fallback plan and be able to return to business as usual as quickly and efficiently as possible.

Practical Checklist

- Have you formed your security incident team?
- Have you formed your contingency plan teams?
- Have you documented everyone's full contact information?
- Do you have systems in place to detect security incidents?
- Are you prepared to notify all parties affected by a breach of unencrypted PHI?
- Do you feel that your BAs are capable of responding to an incident or outage effectively?
- Have you thought about all the different disaster scenarios that could occur?
- Have you performed a business impact analysis to determine what information and business processes are must-haves and which are optional during a crisis?
- Are off-site office facilities and emergency shelters available to move into in the event of a crisis?
- Do you have plans in place to test and update your security incident and contingency plans on an ongoing basis?

24

OUTSOURCING INFORMATION
TECHNOLOGY SERVICES

24.1 Background

Outsourcing is certainly nothing new to the health care industry. Health care executives and Health Insurance Portability and
Accountability Act (HIPAA) officers are constantly facing new
projects and technological changes, including compliance initiatives that force them to rethink their information technology (IT)
strategies. Health care in particular is faced not only with having
to embrace the information technologies of the twenty-first cen-
tury but also to perform overall health care operations more efficiently. These areas are the backbone of HIPAA Administrative
Simplification. With the growing HIPAA compliance pressures,
there simply is not enough manpower and expertise in-house to get
everything done, especially when it comes to information security.
Even if your organization has never outsourced IT or information
security services, you might be able to replicate the proven outsourcing methodologies used in other functions in your organization to make outsourcing work for you here as well.

24.2 Reasons to Consider Outsourcing

The "make or buy" decision on IT services is one that every covered
entity (CE) and business associate (BA) must consider. For many
businesses, there are simply too many complex HIPAA and information security issues to handle them all alone. IT and information
security are critical functions of all CEs and many of their BAs and
subcontractors, regardless of size.

If your organization is like most, your protected health information (PHI) is continuously at risk. You can put the policies, procedures, and technologies in place that we discuss in this book; however, they will still need constant nurturing and management. Sooner or later, one or more people will have to get involved in managing your security infrastructure. You will have to ask yourself if it makes good business sense to tie up your internal resources on managing these ongoing initiatives. Also, you will need to think long and hard about whether or not you and your team should be or want to be on call 24/7 to respond to those inevitable late-night security incidents.

Outsourcing can help your organization focus on what it does best: providing health care services. You must have a clear understanding of your organization's abilities in the IT and information security departments before moving forward. Here are some reasons to consider outsourcing your IT and information security work:

- IT, and specifically information security, is not a core competency of your business.
- Your current staff does not have the proper skill sets.
- Attracting and retaining employees with the proper skills is difficult.
- Outsourcing can make it easier to manage ongoing costs by allowing you to convert otherwise variable costs into fixed costs.
- It can be cheaper than hiring full-time staff to do it.
- If done properly, it can help reduce the overall cost of the IT and compliance functions.
- Effective, ongoing staff training is not cheap.
- Outside expertise is available and willing to help.
- Outside experts have less exposure to internal politics and can provide fresh and unbiased insight into what really needs to be done to secure your information and help you reach compliance.
- You will have access to the latest information technologies and aggregated expertise.
- It can allow you to obtain security trending intelligence that otherwise would be impossible to acquire.

24.3 What Functions to Outsource

Before outsourcing, you must first determine your specific needs and what makes the most business sense. You can outsource some or all of your IT and information security work. Just keep in mind that HIPAA requires information security responsibility to be assigned to one individual within the organization. This person can manage and oversee HIPAA security initiatives but certainly has the flexibility to outsource the needed services.

Do not outsource just for the sake of outsourcing. You must look at this decision from both a strategic and a tactical perspective. Do you really need to outsource? If so, then why? Is it because of lack of internal expertise? Time? Money? You must then determine (1) what areas you need to outsource and in what capacity, (2) how long the outsourcing will need to last, and (3) guidelines to which your out-sourcing vendors must adhere. All of this should be documented in service-level agreements (SLAs), which must be mutually beneficial, clearly articulate the opportunity and issues, and show the benefits to both parties. They should be flexible but at the same time outline specific deliverables, target dates, and expectations on responsiveness. They must be reasonable for both parties, with penalties clearly out-lined for breach of contract or sub-par service. Also, be sure to outline specific incentives to encourage the highest levels of performance.

The following is a list of areas that can be outsourced to help you with your HIPAA compliance:

- HIPAA Security Rule and Privacy Rule gap analysis
- Risk analyses
- Penetration testing
- Vulnerability assessments
- Information risk assessments
- Security and privacy policy and procedure development
- Network infrastructure design, installation, and maintenance
- Server and workstation security
- Web and application security
- Software development, quality assurance, and maintenance
- Security and privacy awareness and training
- Security planning and strategy development
- Security incident response plan creation and documentation

- Contingency (disaster recovery/business continuity) plan creation and documentation
- Data center operations
- Network security monitoring
- Cloud services including hosting and redundant systems
- Physical security design, installation, and maintenance
- Security incident response and forensics
- Ongoing security audits
- Breach response activities
- Breach notification activities

24.4 What to Look For in Outsourcing Firms

Given that IT and information security is one of the most critical functions of your business, you will need to make sure you find quality vendors with which to partner. Expertise can vary widely, so you must ask questions and check references from several potential vendors. Look at their credentials and focus more on experience than certifications. Consider the following certifications as a baseline requirement:

- CISSP® (Certified Information Systems Security Professional, sponsored by [(ISC)²])
- CIPP/US® (Certified Information Privacy Practitioner/U.S. specialization; sponsored by IAPP)
- CIPP/IT® (Certified Information Privacy Practitioner/IT specialization; sponsored by IAPP)
- CIPM® (Certified Information Privacy Manager; sponsored by IAPP)
- CGEIT® (Certified in the Governance of Enterprise IT, sponsored by [ISACA])
- CRISC® (Certified in Risk and Information Systems Control; sponsored by ISACA)
- HCISPP℠ (HealthCare Information Security and Privacy Practitioner, sponsored by [(ISC)²])
- CPHIMS (Certified Professional in Healthcare Information and Management Systems, sponsored by HIMSS)
- CAHIMS (Certified Associate in Healthcare Information and Management Systems, sponsored by HIMSS)

- CISA® (Certified Information Systems Auditor, sponsored by ISACA)
- CISM® (Certified Information Security Manager, sponsored by ISACA)
- GIAC (Global Information Assurance Certification, sponsored by SANS)
- Security+™ (sponsored by the Computing Technology Industry Association)
- Various vendor-specific certifications

Whatever you do, do not let certifications lead you to believe you are getting top-notch experts every time. As with medical doctors, there are many other factors to consider, such as technical and business experience, communication skills, and documentation skills. No matter what is on paper, nothing is better than real-world experience.

The more important the outsourced function, the more control you will want to maintain. Given the criticality of IT and information security not only regarding HIPAA compliance but also the fact that PHI needs to remain confidential, intact, and available at all times, you will certainly want to maintain input and control over what is done by your outsourcing vendors. Look for the following characteristics in your potential outsourcing vendors:

- Trustworthy, reliable people you can work with every day.
- Long track record of integrity—check several references.
- Proven expertise—check several references.
- Proven accomplishments (projects, writings, presentations, etc.).
- Flexible people that can change project direction and scope (within reason) when necessary.
- Avoid know-it-alls—it is practically impossible to know everything about all aspects of IT and information security; they need to know their limits and must be willing to pull in other subject matter experts when necessary.
- Team of resources (either internal or subcontract) that they can pull in almost immediately and rely on when more resources are needed.
- Specialized expertise in information security and preferably business management and health care as well.

- Solid and proven methodologies for all the services they perform.
- Open to recommending and implementing open-source, commercial off-the-shelf (COTS), and proprietary or in-house solutions, not just one single solution.
- Vendor neutrality so that there is no conflict of interest in them selling you products that are a better fit for them than they are for you.
- Reasonable and competitive rates for the particular service and expertise being provided.

24.4.1 Questions to Ask Outsourcing Firms and Related Business Associates

- How will you bill for projects—hourly or per project? (Both may be fine—you just need to know up front.)
- What is your regular system maintenance schedule to apply patches on our systems? (This needs to be done frequently—very soon following patch release.)
- Can you demonstrate you are complying with all the necessary HIPAA and HITECH requirements applicable to your organization?
- Do you outsource any activities to subcontractors? If yes, how do you ensure they are meeting HIPAA/HITECH compliance?
- Do you have an incident response plan in place to handle intrusions or disasters related to your own information systems that could affect our organization? (Their systems could be housing critical data that your organization is dependent on—make sure they have a Plan B.)
- Will you sign a HIPAA BA contract? (If the answer is no, you will be forced to look elsewhere.)
- How will you determine and evaluate the technologies and products we need? Is it based on our specific requirements, or certain vendor relationships you have? (Look for any signs of vendor bias and sales opportunities that you do not consider in your organization's best interest that take from your bottom line and add to theirs.)

- Are your solutions typically open-source, COTS, or proprietary? (Again, they should be open to all three, depending on
what is the best fit for your organization.)
- How do you plan to keep us informed regarding project status, milestones, reviews, and overall documentation? (They
must have a formal, documented methodology that will keep
you in the loop.)
- How does your staff keep up with new security threats and
vulnerabilities? (Look for answers such as subscribing to
security bulletins, attending security conferences, reading
information security trade publications, collaborating with
colleagues and other companies, etc.)
- Does your organization have both general liability and professional liability insurance? What other services do you offer?
Do you try to offer everything to everyone, or are you focused
solely on compliance or information security? Are general IT
services your core competency? Are you health care-industry
specific? (Keep in mind that greater specialization can result
in a better fit for your organization's HIPAA needs but it is not
always needed, especially in terms of information security.)
- If you will be monitoring my network, how and what will you
monitor?
- Do you simply monitor devices, or can you monitor my entire
network? (Look for an organization that can monitor anything
you have or may add in the future, including applications, database systems, and mobile devices. You do not want to limit your
network growth to their technical constraints and abilities.)
- Do you only monitor one technology (firewall, intrusion prevention systems, etc.) or one vendor's products? (A direct tie-in
to your specific products can be a plus, but you do not want to
be limited to just one vendor. They must be flexible and willing
to work with virtually all products that your needs require.)
- Will you also monitor for network performance that can help
me assess our future growth and needs? (This can be a nice
value-added service.)
- How do you keep abreast of and monitor for newly discovered
threats and vulnerabilities? (Look for partnerships with other

public [e.g., Computer Emergency Response Team] and private [partner company] security alert systems.)

- Do you monitor for unknown threats and vulnerabilities? If so, what techniques are used? (Look for behavior-based analysis that can search out anomalies in specific protocols and applications that would not otherwise be detected, such as advanced malware and phishing attacks.)

- How do you assess logs for attacks? Is it all automated? Is any of it done manually? (There should be a combination of both automated and manual assessments, because neither method is perfect or foolproof.)

- If a security anomaly or breach is detected, how will you respond? (There should be a formal security incident plan that you can review. This plan needs to be integrated with your security incident plan.)

- Is this service scalable regardless of how large my network grows? (If their systems cannot scale, then yours may be limited as well.)

- How is data correlated and analyzed to pick up specific anomalies? Do you look for specific trends across various systems?

- How will the information be presented to me? (They need to have formal procedures for presenting you with their ongoing reports; hard copy and web-based are preferable.)

- What expertise will my team need to have to read and interpret your monitoring information? (The reports should be presented in a nontechnical fashion that anyone can read and understand. If this is not done, it somewhat defeats altogether the purpose of outsourcing your security monitoring.)

- What will you require of our network? (You need to know if your network will have to be reconfigured or adapted to fit their monitoring technologies.)

24.5 Common Outsourcing Mistakes

Be sure not to do any of the following common actions and activities:

- Outsourcing solely to save money—certain outsourcing costs can be greater, especially up front.

- Outsourcing to fix a political, management, or operations problem that should be addressed internally.
- Viewing outsourcing from a short-term perspective without thinking about long-term goals, benefits, and relationships.
- Believing that your internal team has the time, energy, and wherewithal to handle everything.
- Failing to look at the context in which outsourcing will be done—outsourcing must be fit into the bigger picture of your organization's overall mission.
- Not requiring your outsourcing firms to keep track of what they do and report to you periodically.
- Not ensuring that solid SLAs are put in place that can facilitate quick problem resolution.
- Not monitoring the performance and stability of outsourcing vendors to stay ahead of any organization problems they may have.
- Not having a fall-back plan in case the outsourcing vendors have trouble. (This is especially important with cloud service providers that may have access to the only copy of critical information.)
- Relying on one vendor, which may amplify any problems that occur.
- Failing to communicate the decision to outsource to current employees.
- Not keeping management up to date on outsourcing initiatives.
- Not thinking through possible negative scenarios that could occur when outsourcing; it could be that outsourcing is really not worth the risks or is not the best option for your organization after all.

Practical Checklist

- Determine whether or not IT and information security is your organization's core competency—if not, consider outsourcing.
- Do not outsource for the sake of outsourcing; make a good business case for it based on skill sets, time, and money.

- Determine what areas of IT or information security need to be outsourced.
- Consider hiring an outside firm at least to help you get started on your HIPAA compliance efforts, including your initial risk analysis if you have not yet performed one.
- Perform your due diligence when interviewing and selecting your outsourcing partners—you will want to make sure you do this right the first time.
- Ensure a mutually beneficial SLA is in place to ensure outsourcing success.

PART VI
Managing Ongoing HIPAA Compliance

25

HIPAA TRAINING, EDUCATION, AND AWARENESS

25.1 Creating an Effective Awareness Program

Ensuring organizational awareness of privacy and security policies and practices is a requirement of the Health Insurance Portability and Accountability Act (HIPAA) regulations. It is also a good idea, and has been for many years. Your staff members are the foundation of ensuring your policy compliance. If they do not know and understand what is expected of them with regard to meeting HIPAA and other privacy and security requirements, then they will probably unwittingly do things that could very well put your organization at risk.

All covered entities (CEs) and business associates (BAs) must develop and implement an awareness program that meets the following goals:

- Ensures compliance with HIPAA privacy and security regulations.
- Establishes an executive owner or sponsor to champion, maintain, and ensure senior level involvement; this will be necessary to get the message across and secure support for HIPAA-compliance activities throughout the organization.
- Instills the privacy and security requirements and concerns into the organizational culture.
- Clearly communicates the HIPAA privacy and security issues and challenges.
- Supports your strategic and tactical HIPAA implementation strategies.

Your awareness strategy should include the following:

- An awareness budget that accounts for the communication, planning, and implementation activities that will be proportionate to this piece of the total amount of the HIPAA compliance budget.
- A timeline indicating target dates for all phases of the awareness and training program.
- A procedure or tool (or both) for measuring the overall effectiveness of the awareness program.
- Identification of integration points and windows to effectively coordinate the privacy and security awareness and education practices within the overall HIPAA compliance plan.
- A strategy to integrate the awareness processes throughout all departments and teams of the organization to help ensure a successful awareness program.
- Execution of an awareness risk assessment to identify awareness compliance gaps and form the baseline to use for measuring future awareness compliance success.
- A description of the tactical objectives of the awareness and education program.
- The development, implementation, communication, and enforcement of policies and procedures to mitigate risk and ensure ongoing compliance with HIPAA privacy and security regulations.

The privacy and security awareness and education program you create must address your organization's interpretation of HIPAA and support the activities your organization will take to mitigate risk and ensure patient privacy based on the results of the baseline assessment. Creation and delivery of a common message, interpretation of the regulations, and a process for addressing and communicating issues will speed the implementation and reduce the overall cost in complying with HIPAA.

Follow a structured process for the development and maintenance of your awareness program:

- Clearly define your HIPAA privacy message (why, value, strategic approach, policies, procedures, contacts, etc.)
- Clearly document the desired tactical outcomes

- Clearly document the details of what will be done (awareness activities and tasks)
- Provide examples of case studies and suggestions

Continue to assess, refine, and update the awareness program throughout all the phases of developing and maintaining your organization's HIPAA compliance.

Does your organization have the resources necessary to develop and deliver a privacy and security awareness and education program? If not, you will need to allocate or contract resources necessary to develop an awareness program. In the event you must obtain external resources, or an outsourced arrangement is desired, be sure to establish guidelines for qualifying an experienced consultant to develop your privacy and security awareness program, in addition to any other help you outsource for HIPAA compliance activities.

25.2 Identify Awareness and Training Groups

The following groups should be targeted for specialized privacy and security training and awareness. These will vary, depending on the type of CE and other business organization factors.

A. HIPAA implementation sponsors
B. Executive team and legal counsel
C. Department managers and supervisors
D. Information technology staff
E. Office managers
F. Medical practitioners
G. All employees, including newly hired
H. BAs impacted by HIPAA requirements
I. Call center and customer service staff
J. Human resources staff

Generally, there are six times when training should be given to one or more of these identified groups:

1. New employee orientation soon after employment start
2. Initial general training to all employees
3. Initial in-depth training to target groups

4. BA training following contract updates or when initiating new contracts
5. Specialized training when HIPAA policies or procedures change
6. Ongoing training for all groups; recommend at least once a year

Exhibit 25.1 visually represents training times and the associated groups, based on the groupings and descriptions previously discussed.

Exhibit 25.1   Privacy and Security Training Groups and Timing

TIMES	A	B	C	D	E	F	G	H	I	J
1		X	X	X	X	X		X		X
2	X	X	X	X	X	X	X			X
3	X	X	X	X	X	X				X
4					X				X	
5	X	X	X	X	X	X	X		X	X
6	X	X	X	X	X	X	X			X

25.3 Training

Training is more formal and interactive than an awareness program. The goal of training should be to build specialized skills and knowledge in the topic and to facilitate job responsibility, performance, and capabilities. Training should also motivate the participants. The importance of training to help ensure information security has been recognized in recent years as being one of the most effective ways to help secure information and protect privacy. In fact, the realization of this led to the National Institute of Standards and Technology (NIST) release of document Special Publication 800-16 in 1998. *IT Security Training Requirements: A Role- and Performance-Based Model* provides guidelines for federal agencies to develop their own IT security training programs. It provides a nice structure for nongovernment organizations to use as well, and will be helpful in building your privacy and security training program to meet HIPAA compliance requirements. NIST has released the following additional informative documents that contain training and awareness advice since SP800-16:

- NIST Special Publication 800-50, *Building an Information Technology Security Awareness and Training Program*

- NIST Special Publication 800-66 Revision 1, *An Introductory Resource Guide for Implementing the Health Insurance Portability and Accountability Act (HIPAA) Security Rule*

If you use any of these as guides, remember that you will need to modify the curriculum to match your own organization's unique training needs.

Keep in mind that it is job function and associated responsibilities that should determine what information security and privacy courses each target group needs. An employee may have multiple job responsibilities, and thus may need to attend more than one training session. This approach to training, although effective, may be a challenge to implement within some organizations because of time constraints or unwillingness to acknowledge that training is of such importance.

25.3.1 Specialized HIPAA Topics

Training content should be specialized for target groups based on specific issues that they must understand and with which they must comply. Match the course content to job responsibilities and roles as much as possible to be most effective. For instance, assume you have the following defined roles:

R1: Health care delivery personnel (e.g., physicians, nurses)
R2: Clinic and provider facility managers
R3: Health plan claims examiners
R4: Information technology personnel
R5: Privacy and security officers
R6: Plan member service representatives
R7: Billing personnel
R8: Health plan enrollment personnel
R9: Legal counsel and human resources
R10: Marketing and sales
R11: Customer services and call centers

You want the people filling these roles to know and understand their job responsibilities related to HIPAA compliance. Based on this, and taking into account your own unique business environment, you may determine the course content that should be given to the associated indicated roles. Exhibit 25.2 shows an example of how to do this.

Exhibit 25.2 HIPAA Training Matrix

COURSE TOPIC	ROLES										
	R1	R2	R3	R4	R5	R6	R7	R8	R9	R10	R11
Complete HIPAA Privacy Rule		X	X		X				X		
Complete HIPAA Security Rule		X		X	X				X		
Notice of Privacy Practices		X			X	X		X	X	X	X
Authorizations		X	X		X	X	X	X		X	
Business associates		X	X	X	X	X	X		X	X	
Accounting of disclosures	X	X	X		X	X	X				
Marketing		X			X			X	X	X	
Identity verification		X	X	X	X	X		X	X		X
Technical security mechanisms		X		X	X						
Penalties and preemption		X			X			X	X		
Exceptions for authorizations		X			X	X			X		
Access to information	X	X	X	X	X	X	X		X		X
Uses and disclosures	X	X			X		X				X

25.3.2 Training Delivery Methods

The size of your training groups may vary greatly. Large organizations may have as many as 50 in a classroom-setting training session. However, for the most effective training, we recommend you keep the number to 25 or less in this type of face-to-face training, to promote the most interaction and also to help reduce side discussions and maintain attention. Another good option for training, especially for the initial all-employee sessions, is via a computer-based training (CBT) method, an online interactive method (such as a webinar), or via a conference-call training session. The most effective delivery method will largely depend on your target audience. Methods for you to consider include the following:

- General classroom lectures to small- to medium-size groups
- Classroom training with group activities and tests to small- to medium-size groups
- Auditorium presentations to large groups
- Web-based interactive training
- CBTs with progress and achievement measures
- Audio instruction
- Video instruction
- Satellite or fiber-optic live distance training
- Outsourced training with professional education services
- Education provided by professional societies
- Government-sponsored training provided by regulatory agencies

25.4 Training Design and Development

Design the training curriculum based on the learning objectives for the associated target groups. The training delivery method should be based on the best way to achieve your objectives. In choosing a delivery method, select the best method for the learning objectives, the number of students, and your organization's ability to efficiently deliver the material.

During the design and development phase, keep these things in mind:

- Outline your class content.
- Divide into instructional units or lessons.
- Determine time requirements for each unit and lesson.
- Create content based on the things personnel need to know to perform their job responsibilities.
- Include interactive activities that can be taken back to their job and used right away.
- Be clear about the behaviors, actions, and activities expected of the students when performing their jobs.
- Describe the actions personnel should exhibit to successfully demonstrate meeting objectives being taught.

- Build on existing capabilities and experiences within the group.
- Sequence topics to build new or complex skills onto existing ones, and to encourage and enhance the students' motivation for learning the material.
- Use multiple learning methods.

When determining the best instructional method for your target groups, keep the following in mind:

- *Consider the people within your target group audience.* Consider the audience size and location. Consider experience levels. Consider time constraints. If the audience is large and geographically dispersed, a technology-based solution such as web-based, CD, satellite learning, or something similar may work best.
- *Consider the business needs.* If you have a limited budget, then a technology-based delivery may be appropriate, or you may want to bring in an outside instructor with already-prepared materials.
- *Consider the course content.* Some topics are better suited for instructor-led, video, web-based, or CBT delivery. There are many opinions about what type of method is best. Much depends on your organization. It will be helpful if you can get the advice of training professionals who can assess the material and make recommendations.
- *Consider what kind of student/teacher interaction is necessary.* Is the course content best presented as self-paced individual instruction or as group instruction? Some topics are best covered with face-to-face and group interaction, others are best suited for individualized instruction. For example, if the goal is just to communicate policies and procedures, a technology-based solution may be most appropriate. However, if students need to perform problem-solving activities in a group to reinforce understanding or demonstrate appropriate actions, then a classroom setting would be better.
- *Consider the type of presentations and activities necessary.* If the course content requires students to fill out forms, use a

specialized software program, or do role-playing, a classroom setting is best.

- *Consider the stability of the class content.* The stability of content is a cost issue. If content will change frequently (for instance, if procedures are expected to change as a result of mergers, acquisitions, or divestitures), or if new software systems are planned, the expense of changing the material needs to be estimated by considering difficulty, time, and money. Some instructional methods can be changed more easily and cost efficiently than others.

- *Consider the technology available for training delivery.* This is a critical factor in deciding the instructional strategy. Will all students have access to the technologies you require? If doing web-based training, will all students have access to the intranet or Internet? Do students have the necessary bandwidth for certain types of multimedia?

There are many instructional elements that will be consistent from course to course regardless of the instructional methods used. Most courses will involve delivery with voice, text, and graphics. To make instruction more effective you should also incorporate the use of pictures or graphics, video, demonstrations, role-playing, simulations, case studies, and interactive exercises. Several of these presentation methods will be used in most courses. Remember that it is generally considered most effective for students' understanding to deliver the same message and information multiple times using multiple methods. Your students have their own unique learning styles, and what works well for one person will not necessarily be effective for the others. Develop your instructional methods based on instructional objectives, course content, delivery options, implementation options, technological capabilities, and available resources.

Web-based training is often a good alternative for large audiences, to provide an overview of the topic and communicate policies and facts. However, this type of instruction is often not appropriate for audiences that are learning procedures or need to know how to act in specific types of situations for which role-playing is necessary.

If you decide you need to get outside help for your training, research the organizations you are considering and determine the following:

- Do they use trained and experienced instructors?
- Do they have health care (with providers, health plans, or clearinghouses) experience?
- Do they have metrics to support their training?
- Do they offer multiple training methods?
- Are their training offerings comprehensive for the HIPAA requirements?
- Do they have local training facilities or staff? Travel expenses can impact costs.
- Do they belong to an association with existing or proposed HIPAA certification authorities? Beware of vendor-created HIPAA certifications! These were not endorsed, or even recognized, by the Department of Health and Human Services at the time we wrote this book.

Effective privacy and security training is necessary to help you achieve HIPAA compliance. There are many resources freely available on the Internet. Keep in mind that these can be helpful, but that any training needs to be tailored to the organization's own unique environment and needs. To be effective, organizations must take advantage of different types of training methods. Training must support making HIPAA privacy and security policies and procedures a learned and consistently practiced behavior.

25.5 Awareness Options

Awareness activities are different from training activities. The objectives for delivering HIPAA privacy and security awareness are similar to training options. However, there are some very important differences between training and awareness activities. The options and methods for awareness activities are typically much different than the more formal and structured training. Awareness activities should:

- Occur on an ongoing basis
- Use a wide range of delivery methods
- Catch the attention of the target audience
- Be less formal than training

- Take less time than training
- Be creative and fun
- Reinforce the lessons learned during formal training

Think of positive, fun, exciting, and motivating methods that will give employees the message and keep HIPAA privacy and security issues in their minds as they perform their daily job responsibilities. The success of an awareness program is its ability to reach all personnel using a variety of techniques. Examples of awareness materials and methods include the following:

- Guest speakers
- Newsletters
- Intranet websites
- Posters
- Computer screen savers
- Lunch and "coffee break" presentations
- Departmental presentations
- Posting motivational or catchy slogans on screen savers, browser marquees, and so on
- Videotapes
- Computer-based awareness quizzes, games, and so on
- Brochures and flyers
- Pens, pencils, key chains, note pads, Post-it notes, and other types of promotional items with short privacy and security messages
- Stickers for doors and bulletin boards
- Cartoons and articles published monthly or quarterly in an in-house newsletter or department-specific notices
- Daily privacy or security thought or advice of the day
- Special topical bulletins
- Monthly e-mail notices related to privacy and security issues
- Privacy and security banners or messages that appear on the monitor at log-on
- Distribution of food items as an incentive; for example, packages of gummy bugs with an attached label that reads something similar to "Real Computer Viruses Are Not This Sweet"
- Travel first-aid kit with privacy or security slogan printed on the package such as "Help Ensure Customer Privacy Health"

- Badge holders with a privacy or security slogan such as "Protect Privacy" or "Think Security"
- Flashlight with a label such as "Spotlight Privacy"

It is critical to remember that an awareness program never ends. An effective awareness program must repeat your message many times in many ways. The more important the message, the more often it should be repeated using multiple methods. Because it is an ongoing activity, it requires creativity and enthusiasm to maintain the interest of all audience members. The awareness messages must demonstrate that privacy and security are important not only to your organization, but also to each employee and each customer and patient.

An awareness program must remain current. As HIPAA regulations change, and subsequently privacy and security policies and procedures, personnel must be notified. We recommend establishing a method to deliver immediate information and updates when necessary. Perhaps new information is sent as the first alert item that personnel see when logging on to the network for the day. The awareness messages and methods must also be simple. The purpose is to get messages and ideas out to personnel quickly and easily. The messages cannot be confusing or convoluted as this will dissuade personnel from reading them, and eventually they will not pay attention at all to the messages. Make it easy for personnel to get privacy and security information, and make the information easy to understand.

Depending on your available personnel, resources, and budget, you may need to consider outsourcing the design and development of your awareness program. Be sure to verify that any vendor you consider is experienced and qualified for the topic of health care privacy and security. You can review literally thousands of such vendors on the Internet. When you have narrowed the field, ask for references from the vendors to discuss their experiences and satisfaction. Asking your peers within professional organizations or on health care privacy or security mailing lists can also be revealing and help you with your decision.

25.6 Document Training and Awareness Activities

HIPAA regulations require privacy and security training for all members of your organization workforce, and all contractors who handle protected health information (PHI). Training must include coverage of privacy and security policies and procedures. All existing personnel must have been trained by the Privacy Rule compliance date of April 14, 2003. All new employees must be trained within a reasonably short period after starting work for your organization. You must log the people who have been trained and you must provide follow-up training when your policies and procedures change. Although it is not specifically required, it is a good idea to measure the understanding of the people who have participated in training and have received the awareness messages.

There are some automated systems that log the people who have taken training and received awareness messages. If you do not have the budget or resources for such a system, you need to log the people who have taken training and maintain this information for future reference and to provide to HIPAA regulators when they request to see who has taken training. Use a log similar to Exhibit 25.3 to keep track of training and understanding. Add rows and columns as appropriate for your training program. Make an entry only after the training has been completed. If you utilize a testing process you can add a column to indicate that the test was administered and the results of the test.

Exhibit 25.3   HIPAA Training Log

NAME	DEPARTMENT	PHONE	DATE	HIPAA TRAINING TOPIC	TEST RESULTS (%)
Sue Smith	Plan administration	X89356	04-02-03	Notice and acknowledgment	94
Dr. Herold	Family practice	X00000	05-03-03	Confidential channel requests	92
Dr. Beaver	Obstetrics	X99999	03-12-03	Minimum necessary	92
Joe Black	IT manager	X77777	05-13-03	Technology safeguards	71

25.7 Get Support

To be successful, senior management must support your HIPAA privacy and security training and awareness efforts. Not only must they provide financial support to effectively develop the program, but they must also provide visible support to demonstrate to the workforce the importance and necessity of your efforts. Create a project plan that includes your objective for HIPAA privacy and security awareness and training, and include estimates for necessary personnel, materials, time schedules, and any other associated costs (such as videos and manuals). Ask management to provide funds to support the organization's HIPAA privacy and security training and awareness compliance requirements. If you do not have perceived support from senior management, it is likely you will encounter passive resistance from a significant percentage of the workforce; they may not attend training for which they were scheduled, may ignore your requests to read and acknowledge policies and procedures, or may blatantly violate your policies and procedures. It is important to prevent this by having senior management clearly communicate the importance of everyone's participation before your training and awareness rollout.

25.8 Measure Effectiveness

All management programs must be periodically reviewed and evaluated for effectiveness. This holds true for your HIPAA privacy and security training and awareness program. The methods you use for quantitative and qualitative measurement to determine the effectiveness of your program will depend in large part on the size and composition of your organization. In small clinics it may be sufficient to discuss the issues and determine understanding with your workforce members. In large health plans you may need a sophisticated automated system to help determine effectiveness. Consider one or more of the following for determining effectiveness within your organization:

- Give quizzes immediately following training.
- Distribute a privacy and security awareness survey to all personnel or to a representative sample.
- Send follow-up questionnaires to people who have attended formal training approximately 4–6 months following the training to determine how well they have retained the information presented.
- Monitor the number of compliance infractions for each issue for which you provide training.
- Measure privacy and security knowledge as part of the yearly performance evaluation.
- Place feedback and suggestion forms on the intranet website.
- Track the number and type of privacy and security incidents that occur before and after the training and awareness activities.

- Conduct spot checks of personnel behavior. For instance, walk through work areas and note workstations that are logged in while unattended or patient information printouts that are not adequately protected.
- Record user IDs and completion status for web- and network-based training. Send a targeted questionnaire to those who have completed the online training.
- Have training participants fill out evaluation forms at the end of the class.

Your evaluation of training and awareness effectiveness has four distinct purposes to measure:

1. The extent that conditions were right for learning and the learner's subjective satisfaction
2. What the student learned from a specific course or awareness activity
3. A pattern of student outcomes following a specified course or awareness activity
4. The value of the class or activity compared to other training and awareness options

Besides obtaining these measurements, the evaluation should also help you identify how to

- Assist employees in determining their own performance success.
- Assist managers in determining their own workforce performance.
- Compile trend data to assist instructors in improving both learning and teaching.
- Create return on investment statistics to support training and awareness funds.

25.9 Conclusion

Until comparatively recently in the history of health care, physicians personally hand-wrote their patients' medical records, and they were typically locked in a file cabinet with very little access by anyone other than the nursing and support staff within the immediate office. Today, health care delivery and payment systems are some of the biggest industries within the United States, with many intermediaries touching the systems and associated data. Integrated processing systems and networks have virtually replaced the pen, paper, and locked file cabinets. There are now so many players, public and private, involved with the processing and handling of health information, it is almost impossible for all but the very smallest health care office to do business without some type of data processing. HIPAA regulations are leading the industries in many ways with privacy and security mandates. Complying with the multitude of requirements within all the HIPAA regulations will be a great challenge to most, if not all, health care organizations. Every health care organization covered by HIPAA must know, understand, and address the requirements set forth by HIPAA if it wants to remain a viable health care entity and maintain its patients' and customers' trust. To accomplish this, effective training and awareness activities are necessary.

For in-depth advice on this topic, see Rebecca's book, *Managing an Information Security and Privacy Awareness and Training Program.*[1]

Practical Checklist

- Analyze your organization's training and awareness needs and define the goals and objectives for the program.
- Create a training and awareness program.
- Obtain visible senior management support of the program.
- Obtain sufficient funding.
- Provide general and specialized training to all personnel, targeting specific groups according to their organizational roles.
- Use simple and straightforward awareness methods.
- Repeat messages using multiple methods to keep HIPAA awareness at the front of everyone's mind.
- Tell personnel what the threats are and how they are expected to address those threats.
- Constantly evaluate the effectiveness of your program and make changes accordingly.

26

PERFORMING ONGOING
HIPAA COMPLIANCE
REVIEWS AND AUDITS

26.1 Background

HIPAA compliance is not a onetime event. Once you have achieved HIPAA compliance, you are not finished with your efforts. You must now work to ensure your organization stays compliant, and this can be the hard part. This may become especially challenging in environments where there are many facilities in different locations and businesses that have very complex information systems. Even smaller covered entities (CEs) and business associates (BAs) that have the talent resources to do things properly can struggle.

Between the increasing demands of the Department of Health and Human Services (HHS), CEs and BAs simply cannot afford to be in a state of noncompliance. Performing ongoing reviews and audits will not only ensure HIPAA compliance but can also help build customer and business partner confidence and ultimately lower operating costs due to streamlined operations.

The Privacy and Security Rules must be managed on an ongoing basis indefinitely. In fact, as we have covered in this book, HIPAA specifically mandates creating audit trails and ongoing compliance efforts. Your business will change, people will come and go, new processes will evolve, new technologies will be developed, new information threats and vulnerabilities will emerge, and new policies and procedures will be put in place. All of these issues will require you to continuously manage HIPAA compliance as you would any other business matter.

Keep in mind that audits compare what an entity says it is doing to what is actually taking place. Audits are not necessary evils or negative HIPAA side effects. If the business value is understood and accepted

by everyone involved, HIPAA audits should be viewed as construc-
tive criticism that can help provide guidance to move forward. Before
starting any HIPAA compliance audits, you will need to gather as
much information as possible, including the following:

- Privacy policies and procedures
- Security policies and procedures
- All forms of protected health information (PHI) stored or
  transmitted both in hard copy and electronic formats
- The methods and systems in place to protect PHI

In this chapter, we outline both privacy and security areas you should
focus on, questions you should ask yourself and your HIPAA compliance team, along with some steps you can take to make this all happen.

26.2 Ongoing Cost of Compliance*

The HHS estimates the total cost of compliance with the 2013 Omnibus
Rule changes to be between $114 million and $225.4 million in the
first year of implementation and approximately $14.5 million annually
thereafter. Costs associated with the rule include the following:

- Costs to HIPAA CEs of revising and distributing new notices
  of privacy practices to inform individuals of their rights and
  how their information is protected.
- Costs to CEs related to compliance with breach notification
  requirements.
- Costs to a portion of BAs to bring their subcontracts into
  compliance with BA agreement requirements.
- Costs to a portion of BAs to achieve full compliance with the
  Security Rule.

Table 26.1 summarizes these costs. In Rebecca's experience doing BA
audits for CEs, she has found large CEs had up to 2500 or more BAs,
mid-size CEs averaged 500 BAs, and small CEs averaged 80 BAs—
not to mention all the additional BAs from the subcontractors.

---

* With the exception of the opinion content, all the information in this section is
taken from the HHS at http://www.gpo.gov/fdsys/pkg/FR-2013-01-25/pdf/2013
-01073.pdf.

Table 26.1   HHS's Estimated Costs of the 2013 Omnibus Rule

COST ELEMENT	APPROXIMATE NUMBER OF AFFECTED ENTITIES	TOTAL ESTIMATED COST
Notices of Privacy Practices	700,000 CEs	$55.9 million
Breach Notification Requirements	19,000 CEs	$14.5 million
BA Agreements	250,000–500,000 BAs of CEs	$21 million–$42 million
Security Rule Compliance by BAs	250,000–400,000 BAs of CEs	$22.6 million–$113 million
Total		$114 million–$225.4 million

This makes the HHS estimates for the number of BAs significantly too low in Rebecca's opinion, and therefore the resulting HHS cost estimates involving BAs too low. The HHS indicated that these estimated costs associated with breach notification will be incurred on an annual basis. All other costs are expected in the first year of implementation.[1]

26.3 Privacy Issues

Privacy compliance activities will become most effective on an ongoing basis when they become integrated within the business processes and functions they are intended to control. Incorporating a privacy architecture within your applications and business process development projects is the best way to ensure that privacy processes are addressed from the very beginning of planning a new process.

Certainly, another recommended method of staying compliant is to perform a yearly Privacy Rule gap analysis using the method described in Chapter 6. After performing the gap analysis, always compare the results to the previous gap analysis results to see where you have improved or where you have slipped and need to address new problems and issues.

In between the full gap analyses, you need to stay aware of ongoing privacy issues and changes. Items to review to determine whether privacy compliance and issues are continuing to be adequately addressed include the following:

- Does a privacy officer position, or at least the assigned responsibility, exist? Is this a dedicated role, or a role someone has assumed while performing other job responsibilities?

- Is the privacy official at the proper level within the organization?
- Does the privacy official have the authority to impose policies and procedures?
- Do communications regarding privacy and references to the privacy official regularly occur?
- Have privacy breach notice policies and procedures been documented, tested, and consistently followed?
- Have privacy noncompliance incidents been appropriately handled, and have sanctions been enforced?
- Have a privacy compliance budget and associated resources been identified?
- Have the security implications of privacy requirements been identified and documented?
- Are privacy activities scheduled and tracked?
- Have your applicable state laws been compared with HIPAA requirements to determine preemption issues?
- Is someone responsible for keeping up with new and updated privacy regulations, including the new requirements for BAs?
- Has a complete set of privacy requirements to meet HIPAA compliance been identified for your organizational environment?
- Has a Privacy Rule gap analysis been performed within your organization?
- Do you continue to update your PHI uses and disclosures as necessary?
- Has the privacy impact on business processes been determined?
- Do you continue to map your privacy practices to the Privacy Rule requirements as the practices change?
- Do you track privacy changes and identify where modifications within procedures must be made?
- Do you create new privacy policies, procedures, and forms as necessary?
- Are updates to your privacy policies and procedures planned as rules and business processes change?
- Does the appropriate staff receive regular privacy training and ongoing awareness communications?
- Does the privacy training get updated or completely changed each time it is given?

- Do you perform periodic privacy reviews within business units where PHI is processed?
- Do you ensure that your BAs have up-to-date privacy plans?
- Do you require BAs to participate in regularly scheduled privacy impact assessments?
- Has your organization implemented the technologies required to store, send, or receive encrypted PHI?
- Are new BA agreements created with privacy clauses?
- Have routers, firewalls, and intrusion prevention systems (IPSs) been implemented to control access to PHI on networks from outside sources?
- What about any cloud-based services that your business uses? How are they working to ensure privacy?
- Are new applications created that support your privacy policies and Notice of Privacy Practices?
- Are audit logs regularly reviewed and followed up?
- Are security events impacting privacy (i.e., unauthorized use) monitored for and properly responded to?
- Are regular (e.g., quarterly or biannually) reports created and submitted to upper management detailing privacy risk and impact, along with improvements and degradations to privacy compared to previous reports?
- Are auditors experienced and trained to do privacy impact assessments?

26.4 Security Issues

Similar to an automobile or even the human body, once a security infrastructure has been built, proper maintenance is by far the most critical element to ensure it stays in proper working order. There is the old saying, "An apple a day keeps the doctor away." Similarly, in the context of information security, a patch a day keeps the vulnerabilities away. The saying, "An ounce of prevention is worth a pound of cure," applies equally as well. A little tune up—a little monitoring, a little training, and a little maintenance of log files and configurations—can keep your information systems' infrastructure sound and secure.

The first step of security audits and reviews is to understand the business objectives and HIPAA requirements of what is being audited. The actual Security Rule verbiage[2] for ongoing monitoring, referred to as evaluation, is as follows:

> Perform a periodic technical and nontechnical evaluation, based initially upon the standards implemented under this rule and subsequently, in response to environmental or operational changes affecting the security of electronic protected health information, that establishes the extent to which an entity's security policies and procedures meet the requirements of this sub-part.

One key area to focus on to maintain your information's security is to perform a risk analysis on a regular basis. This is essentially the same analysis outlined in Chapter 12 that you need to perform at the beginning of your Security Rule compliance efforts. The only major differences will be that many new threats and vulnerabilities will exist and there will be new tools available for you to assess them. Speaking of new vulnerabilities, over 15,000 new security vulnerabilities were listed in the National Vulnerability Database[3] in the past three years alone! Here is another set of items to review to ensure that HIPAA security compliance is properly addressed:

- Does the security officer position, or at least assigned responsibility to an existing position, exist?
- Are security roles and responsibilities being adhered to?
- Do you suspect that BAs are reasonably handling PHI in a secure manner?
- Does the plan include testing both information systems and physical security systems?
- Are audits and reviews performed on a regular basis? What about vulnerability scans or penetration tests?
- Do budgets exist for audits and reviews?
- What specific metrics are in place for monitoring Security Rule compliance?
- Are there new methods of collecting and handling PHI since your last audit or review?
- Are your inventory and classifications of PHI current?

- Are your information flows, network hardware and software inventory, and network diagrams current?
- Can you honestly say that you know how PHI is being handled in the cloud?
- Is PHI being backed up and stored adequately?
- Are personnel security issues such as authorizations, access controls, and terminations being considered?
- Do you update your security policies and procedures as needed?
- Do you have security controls in place governing the use of employee-owned computing and storage devices (bring your own device [BYOD])?
- Are new policies and procedures being created as needed?
- Is security awareness training taking place periodically and consistently?
- How is training comprehension measured?
- Are you or your security team members subscribing to and reading security bulletins from vendors and organizations such as Microsoft, Cisco, and SANS?
- Are network and application vulnerability assessments being performed on a regular basis (monthly, quarterly, biannually, etc., depending on needs) or after any major system changes?
- Is your software (applications, operating systems, etc.), especially the software on critical computers or servers, checked for patches periodically and consistently?
- Are new security standards and best practices from the National Institute of Standards and Technology, SANS, and so forth, being kept up with and integrated into your security infrastructure?
- Do the incident and contingency plans cover the most critical information systems and reflect key business processes?
- Are the plans tested periodically?
- Do the resources required to test these plans exist?
- Is there a contingency plan that addresses partial or complete loss of access to PHI?
- Do you document who is making changes to your systems (applying patches, configuration changes, etc.), and along with the changes being made, why they are being made, and the necessary back-out procedures?

- Are you logging all system activities that are related to access, storage, or transmission of PHI to create sufficient audit trails?
- Do you monitor your systems' (firewalls, IPSs, servers, workstation, cloud applications, etc.) log files to ensure that signs of impending system failure are addressed and malicious activity is not occurring?
- Do you back up your log files in case you need to go back and determine what PHI was accessed at a specific time by a specific entity?

26.5 Making Audits Work

The results of your audits will, and probably should, vary from year to year. If everything turns up clean, you did not look hard enough. If your results get progressively worse over time, perhaps there is an internal process or management issue. Either way, any gaps or discrepancies found in your HIPAA privacy and security audits need to be addressed as soon as possible.

If the audits are performed by outside entities, make sure that they have your organization's best interests in mind. See Chapter 24 for more information on outsourcing. You will want to keep an eye out for auditors recommending that you fix all problems regardless of their significance or impact to your organization or the privacy and security of PHI. You will have to consider the cost of remediation for each issue versus the benefits remediation will provide. You cannot be expected to fix every single issue that turns up. If you cannot justify resolving certain problems that are uncovered, just make sure that you document the business reasons behind your decisions.

Ongoing HIPAA compliance is similar to any other compliance program. There needs to be a designated person in charge, the proper policies and procedures need to be maintained, and risk management techniques need to be applied in a common sense and business-oriented (not technical) fashion. The bottom line is to make sure your auditing practices can provide a critical view of the protective measures in place for PHI to help your organization reasonably comply with the HIPAA regulations moving forward.

Practical Checklist

- Is someone in charge of HIPAA privacy and security compliance?
- Are privacy and security audits and system reviews being performed at least annually?
- Are privacy and security policies and procedures being updated and added as needed?
- Does regular (at least annually, but more often is better) information security and privacy training occur?
- Are you clearly documenting the results of your ongoing HIPAA audits?
- Are you treating privacy and security compliance just as you would any other compliance program and integrating them into your overall risk management program?

PART VII
APPENDICES

Appendix A: Enforcement and Sanctions

The Office for Civil Rights (OCR) enforces the Privacy and Security Rules in several ways:[1]

- by investigating complaints filed with it,
- conducting compliance reviews to determine if covered entities are in compliance, and
- performing education and outreach to foster compliance with the Rules' requirements.

STATE	NO VIOLATION	RESOLVED AFTER INTAKE AND REVIEW	CORRECTIVE ACTION
Alaska	11%	57%	32%
Alabama	16%	59%	25%
Arkansas	18%	58%	24%
Arizona	13%	59%	28%
California	13%	64%	23%
Colorado	12%	60%	28%
Connecticut	15%	56%	29%
District of Columbia	11%	60%	29%
Delaware	13%	61%	26%
Florida	15%	59%	25%
Georgia	15%	61%	24%

(Continued)

STATE	NO VIOLATION	RESOLVED AFTER INTAKE AND REVIEW	CORRECTIVE ACTION
Hawaii	9%	62%	29%
Iowa	8%	75%	18%
Idaho	10%	57%	33%
Illinois	14%	60%	27%
Indiana	14%	62%	24%
Kansas	9%	73%	18%
Kentucky	15%	61%	25%
Louisiana	12%	66%	21%
Massachusetts	17%	53%	30%
Maryland	12%	63%	26%
Maine	22%	51%	27%
Michigan	12%	64%	24%
Minnesota	12%	60%	28%
Missouri	9%	71%	20%
Mississippi	21%	51%	28%
Montana	17%	58%	25%
North Carolina	16%	56%	28%
North Dakota	20%	51%	29%
Nebraska	7%	74%	18%
New Hampshire	16%	53%	31%
New Jersey	13%	63%	25%
New Mexico	13%	61%	26%
Nevada	10%	64%	26%
New York	11%	65%	24%
Ohio	12%	64%	24%
Oklahoma	16%	62%	22%
Oregon	12%	58%	31%
Pennsylvania	14%	59%	26%
Rhode Island	19%	37%	44%
South Carolina	15%	56%	28%
South Dakota	17%	56%	27%
Tennessee	15%	57%	28%
Texas	14%	62%	24%
Utah	15%	58%	27%
Virginia	14%	60%	27%
Vermont	19%	56%	26%
Washington	10%	57%	33%
Wisconsin	14%	61%	25%
West Virginia	14%	64%	22%
Wyoming	12%	59%	30%

OCR also works in conjunction with the Department of Justice (DOJ) to refer possible criminal violations of HIPAA.

Enforcement Results by State[2]

This data, for each state, represents the enforcement results for the period from April 14, 2003 through December 31, 2013. This includes the number

YEAR	NO VIOLATION		RESOLVED AFTER INTAKE AND REVIEW		CORRECTIVE ACTION OBTAINED		TOTAL RESOLUTIONS
Partial Year 2003	79	5%	1177	78%	260	17%	1516
2004	360	7%	3406	71%	1033	22%	4799
2005	642	11%	3888	68%	1162	21%	5692
2006	897	14%	4128	62%	1574	24%	6599
2007	727	10%	5017	69%	1494	21%	7238
2008	1180	13%	5940	63%	2221	24%	9341
2009	1211	15%	4749	59%	2146	26%	8106
2010	1529	17%	4951	54%	2709	29%	9189
2011	1302	16%	4466	53%	2595	31%	8363
2012	979	10%	5068	54%	3361	36%	9408
2013	993	7%	9837	69%	3470	24%	14300

Source: (From U.S. Department of Health and Human Services, http://www.hhs.gov/ocr/privacy/hipaa/enforcement/data/historicalnumbers.html.)

of complaints that OCR has resolved for these calendar years.

Enforcement Results by Year[3]

This table shows the enforcement results by calendar year according to the type of closure, which includes the percentage of the total resolutions for each category. These are the numbers of complaints for each year that OCR had resolved. The outstanding complaints that have not been resolved are not included.

Resolution Agreements and Civil Money Penalties[4]

A resolution agreement is a contract signed by HHS and a covered entity in which the covered entity agrees to perform certain obligations (e.g., staff training) and make reports to HHS, generally for a period of three years. During the period, HHS monitors the covered entity's compliance with its obligations. A resolution agreement likely would include the payment of a resolution amount. These agreements are reserved to settle investigations

ENTITY	VIOLATION	SANCTION
Skagit County, Washington. Announced March 7, 2014	Money receipts with electronic protected health information (ePHI) of seven individuals were accessed by unknown parties after the ePHI had been inadvertently moved to a publicly accessible server maintained by the County. OCR's investigation revealed a broader exposure of PHI involved in the incident, which included the ePHI of 1,581 individuals. Many of the accessible files involved sensitive information, including PHI concerning the testing and treatment of infectious diseases.	$215,000 fine in addition to correcting deficiencies (including creating policies, providing training, etc.) in its HIPAA compliance program.
Adult & Pediatric Dermatology, P. C., of Concord, Massachusetts (APDerm) Announced December 26, 2013	An unencrypted thumb drive containing the ePHI of approximately 2,200 individuals was stolen from a vehicle of one its staff members. The thumb drive was never recovered. The investigation revealed that APDerm had not conducted an accurate and thorough analysis of the potential risks and vulnerabilities to the confidentiality of ePHI as part of its security management process. APDerm also did not fully comply with requirements of the Breach Notification Rule to have in place written policies and procedures and train workforce members.	$150,000 fine and must also implement a corrective action plan (including creating policies, providing training, etc.) to correct deficiencies in its HIPAA compliance program.
Affinity Health Plan, Inc. Announced August 14, 2013	CBS Evening News reported that they had purchased a photocopier previously leased by Affinity. CBS informed Affinity that the copier that Affinity had used contained confidential medical information on the hard drive. Affinity estimated that up to 344,579 individuals may have	$1,215,780 fine plus must implement a corrective action plan (including creating policies, providing training, etc.) requiring Affinity to use its best efforts to retrieve all hard drives that were contained on photocopiers previously leased

ENTITY	VIOLATION	SANCTION
	been affected by this breach. OCR's investigation indicated that Affinity impermissibly disclosed the PHI of these affected individuals when it returned multiple photocopiers to leasing agents without erasing the data contained on the copier hard drives. In addition, the investigation revealed that Affinity failed to incorporate the ePHI stored on photocopier hard drives in its analysis of risks and vulnerabilities as required by the Security Rule, and failed to implement policies and procedures when returning the photocopiers to its leasing agents.	by the plan that remain in the possession of the leasing agent, and to take certain measures to safeguard all PHI.
WellPoint Inc. managed care company Announced July 11, 2013	Security weaknesses in an online application, managed by an outsourced third party (business associate) database left the ePHI of 612,402 individuals accessible to unauthorized individuals over the Internet.	$1,700,000 fine and must strengthen the security and privacy program (including creating policies, providing training, better third-party oversight, etc.).
Shasta Regional Medical Center (SRMC) Announced June 13, 2013	Two SRMC senior leaders met with media and discussed medical services provided to a patient, intentionally disclosing PHI to multiple media outlets on at least three separate occasions, without a valid written authorization. OCR's review indicated that senior management at SRMC impermissibly shared details about the patient's medical condition, diagnosis and treatment in an email to the entire workforce. In addition, SRMC failed to sanction its workforce members for impermissibly disclosing the patient's records pursuant to its internal sanctions policy.	$275,000 fine and a corrective action plan (CAP) required SRMC to update its policies and procedures on safeguarding PHI from impermissible uses and disclosures and to train its workforce members. Also requires fifteen other hospitals or medical centers under the same ownership to attest to their understanding of permissible uses and disclosures of PHI, including disclosures to the media.
Idaho State University (ISU) Announced May 21, 2013	ePHI of approximately 17,500 patients was unsecured for at least 10 months, after disabling firewall protections at servers maintained by ISU. OCR's investigation indicated that ISU's risk analyses and	$400,000 fine plus a comprehensive corrective action plan to address the issues uncovered (including creating policies, providing training, etc.).

ENTITY	VIOLATION	SANCTION
	assessments of its clinics were incomplete and inadequately identified potential risks or vulnerabilities. ISU also failed to assess the likelihood of potential risks occurring.	
Hospice of Northern Idaho (HONI) Announced January 2, 2013	An unencrypted laptop computer containing the ePHI of 441 patients was stolen in June 2010. OCR discovered that HONI had not conducted a risk analysis to safeguard ePHI.	$50,000 fine plus must follow a corrective action plan (including creating policies, providing training, etc.) with oversight for two years.
Massachusetts Eye and Ear Infirmary and Massachusetts Eye and Ear Associates, Inc. (MEEI) Announced September 17, 2012	An unencrypted personal laptop containing ePHI of MEEI patients and research subjects was stolen. MEEI failed to take necessary steps to comply with certain requirements of the Security Rule, such as conducting a thorough analysis of the risk to the confidentiality of ePHI maintained on portable devices, implementing security measures sufficient to ensure the confidentiality of ePHI that MEEI created, maintained, and transmitted using portable devices, adopting and implementing policies and procedures to restrict access to ePHI to authorized users of portable devices, and adopting and implementing policies and procedures to address security incident identification, reporting, and response.	$1,500,000 fine and must take corrective action to improve policies and procedures to safeguard the privacy and security of their patients' PHI and retain an independent monitor to report on MEEI's compliance efforts.
Alaska Department of Health and Human Services (DHHS) Announced June 26, 2012	A USB hard drive possibly containing ePHI was stolen from the vehicle of a DHHS employee. DHHS did not have adequate policies and procedures in place to safeguard ePHI; had not completed a risk analysis, implemented sufficient risk management measures, completed security training for its workforce members, implemented device and media controls, or addressed device and media encryption as required by the HIPAA Security Rule.	$1,700,000 fine and take corrective action to improve policies and procedures to safeguard the privacy and security of its patients' PHI.

ENTITY	VIOLATION	SANCTION
Phoenix Cardiac Surgery, P. C., of Phoenix and Prescott, AZ Announced April 17, 2012	The physician practice was posting clinical and surgical appointments for their patients on an Internet-based calendar that was publicly accessible. They also had implemented few policies and procedures to comply with the HIPAA Privacy and Security Rules, and had limited safeguards in place to protect patients' ePHI.	$100,000 fine and a corrective action plan that includes a review of recently developed policies and other actions taken to come into full compliance with the Privacy and Security Rules.
Blue Cross Blue Shield of Tennessee (BCBST) Announced March 9, 2012	Fifty-seven unencrypted computer hard drives containing PHI of over 1 million individuals were stolen from a leased facility in Tennessee. (NOTE: The enforcement action is the first resulting from a breach report required by the HITECH Act Breach Notification Rule.)	$1,500,000 fine and a corrective action plan which includes: reviewing, revising, and maintaining its Privacy and Security policies and procedures; conducting regular and robust trainings for all BCBST employees covering employee responsibilities under HIPAA; and performing monitor reviews to ensure BCBST compliance with the plan.
University of California at Los Angeles Health System (UCLAHS) Announced July 5, 2011	From 2005–2008, unauthorized employees repeatedly looked at the PHI of numerous other UCLAHS patients.	$865,500 fine and a corrective action plan to implement privacy and security policies and procedures approved by OCR, to conduct regular and robust trainings for all UCLAHS employees who use PHI, to sanction offending employees, and to designate an independent monitor who will assess UCLAHS compliance with the plan over 3 years.
General Hospital Corporation and Massachusetts General Physicians Organization, Inc. (Mass General)	Documents consisting of a patient schedule containing names and medical record numbers for a group of 192 patients, and billing encounter forms containing the name, date of birth, medical record number, health insurer and policy number, diagnosis and name of providers for 66 of those	$1,000,000 fine and required to develop and implement a comprehensive set of policies, procedures, and training to safeguard the privacy of its patients.

ENTITY	VIOLATION	SANCTION
Announced February 14, 2011	patients, were lost on March 9, 2009, when a Mass General employee, while commuting to work, left the documents on the subway train. The documents were never recovered.	
Cignet Health of Prince George's County, MD (Cignet) Announced February 4, 2011	Cignet violated 41 patients' rights by denying them access to their medical records. These patients, each of whom made a request to obtain their record between September 2008 and October 2009, individually filed complaints with OCR, initiating investigations of each complaint. The HIPAA Privacy Rule requires that a covered entity provide a patient with a copy of their medical records within 30 (and no later than 60) days of the patient's request. The CMP for these violations is $1.3 million. During the investigations, Cignet refused to respond to OCR's repeated demands to produce the records. Additionally, Cignet failed to cooperate with OCR's investigations of the complaints, including failure to produce the records in response to OCR's subpoena. On April 7, 2010, Cignet produced the medical records to OCR, but otherwise made no efforts to resolve the complaints through informal means. (NOTE: This represents "Willful Neglect," which resulted in the highest level of penalties.)	$4,300,000 fine.
Management Services Organization Washington, Inc. (MSO) Announced December 13, 2010	Disclosure between January 2007 and November 2010 of ePHI to Washington Practice Management, LLC, owned by MSO, which used the information for marketing purposes. An HHS investigation showed that MSO intentionally did not have in place or implement appropriate and reasonable administrative, technical, and physical safeguards to protect the privacy of the PHI.	$35,000 fine and implement a detailed corrective action plan (CAP) to ensure that it will appropriately safeguard PHI against impermissible use or disclosure. The CAP includes requirements for MSO to develop, maintain, and revise its policies and procedures and to appropriately train its workforce on these policies and procedures. HHS will monitor

ENTITY	VIOLATION	SANCTION
		MSO's compliance with the terms of the CAP and the Privacy and Security Rules for two years.
Rite Aid Corporation, its 40 affiliated entities, and 4,800 retail pharmacies Announced July 27, 2010	Television media videotaped incidents in which pharmacies were shown to have disposed of prescriptions and labeled pill bottles containing individuals' identifiable information in industrial trash containers that were accessible to the public. These incidents were reported as occurring in a variety of cities across the United States. Rite Aid pharmacy stores in several of the cities were highlighted in media reports.	$1,000,000 fine and follow corrective action to improve policies and procedures, and provide staff training, to safeguard the privacy of its customers when disposing of identifying information on pill bottle labels and other health information.
CVS Pharmacy, Inc. and all CVS retail pharmacies, over 6,300 stores Announced on January 16, 2009	PHI maintained by several retail pharmacy chains was disposed of in dumpsters that were not secure and could be accessed by the public. Among other issues, the OCR review indicated that: CVS failed to implement adequate policies and procedures to reasonably and appropriately safeguard PHI during the disposal process; CVS failed to adequately train employees on how to dispose of such information properly; and CVS did not maintain and implement a sanctions policy for members of its workforce who failed to comply with its disposal policies and procedures.	$2,250,000 fine and implement a detailed corrective action plan to ensure that it will appropriately dispose of PHI such as labels from prescription bottles and old prescriptions, which requires: 1. revising and distributing its policies and procedures regarding disposal of PHI; 2. sanctioning workers who do not follow them; 3. training workforce members on these new requirements; 4. conducting internal monitoring; 5. engaging a qualified, independent third-party assessor to conduct assessments of CVS compliance with the requirements of the corrective action plan and render reports to HHS; 6. new internal reporting procedures requiring workers to report all violations of these new privacy policies and procedures; and 7. submitting compliance reports to HHS for a period of three years.

ENTITY	VIOLATION	SANCTION
Seattle-based Providence Health & Services (Providence) Announced July 16, 2008	On several occasions between September 2005 and March 2006, backup tapes, optical disks, and laptops, all containing unencrypted electronic PHI, were removed from the Providence premises and were left unattended. The media and laptops were subsequently lost or stolen, compromising the protected health information of over 386,000 patients. HHS received over 30 complaints about the stolen tapes and disks, submitted after Providence, pursuant to state notification laws, alerted patients to the theft.	$100,000 fine and implement a detailed corrective action plan to ensure that it will appropriately safeguard identifiable electronic patient information against theft or loss. Also perform certain obligations (e.g., documented policies/procedure, and staff training) and make reports to HHS for a period of years, typically three years. During the period, HHS monitors the compliance of the covered entity with the obligations it has agreed to perform.

Source: (From The Privacy Professor®, http://www.privacyguidance.com. With permission.)

with more serious outcomes. When HHS has not been able to reach a satisfactory resolution through the covered entity's demonstrated compliance or corrective action through other informal means, civil money penalties (CMPs) may be imposed for noncompliance against a covered entity. To date, HHS has entered into 17 resolution agreements and issued CMPs to one covered entity.

The following table summarizes the 18 HHS-applied penalties and associated corrective action agreements that have occurred through March 7, 2014:

Breaches Affecting 500 or More Individuals[5]

As required by section 13402(e)(4) of the HITECH Act, the Secretary must post a list of breaches of unsecured PHI affecting 500 or more individuals. These breaches are now posted in a new, more accessible format that allows users to search and sort the posted breaches. Additionally, this new format includes brief summaries of the breach cases that OCR has investigated and closed, as well as the names of private practice providers who have reported breaches of unsecured PHI to the secretary. The full list of breaches involving more than 500 individuals that have been reported to the secretary are located at http://www.hhs.gov/ocr/privacy/hipaa/administrative/breachnotificationrule/breachtool.html.

Appendix B: HIPAA Glossary

General and Miscellaneous Terms

ACL: access control list. Generally, a list of users with privileges to a system.

APT: advanced persistent threat. Advanced malware that remains on a network for an extended period of time. APTs are typically harder to detect and remove from infected computers.

Audit trail: record of events, usually tracked by subject or object. For example, users' failed log-on attempts.

Authentication: verification of the identity of a user or other entity as a prerequisite to allowing access to computer resources.

Authorization: granting a user the right of access to computing resources, programs, processes, and data.

BYOD: bring your own device. A common way for users to access the network, email, and related resources using their own devices such as smartphones, tablets, and laptops.

Certification: formal written assurance that a system meets specified security controls.

CIA: with regard to information security: Confidentiality, Integrity, and Availability.

CISSP: Certified Information Systems Security Professional.

Cloud computing: a type of application, service, or similar resource that is made available and used over the Internet. Compared to in-house hardware and software, cloud computing takes less time, effort, and money to get running and to maintain over the long term. Cloud services are also referred to as software-as-a-service (SaaS) and cloud service providers are also referred to as application service providers and managed service providers.

CPRI: Computer-Based Patient Record Institute—organization formed in 1992 to promote adoption of health care information systems. It has created a security toolkit with sample policies and procedures (www.cpri-host.org).

DSL: digital subscriber line. A technology that dramatically increases the digital capacity of ordinary telephone lines (the local loops) into the home or office. DSL speeds are tied to the distance between the customer and the telephone company's central office.

EDI: electronic data interchange (computer-to-computer transactions).

Encryption: the process of transforming information into unintelligible form in such a way that the original information cannot be obtained without using the inverse decryption processes.

HHS or DHHS: U.S. Department of Health and Human Services.

IAM: Identity and Access Management. Technologies that allow for a more feature-rich and extensible means for managing user accounts across the network.

Incident: an unusual occurrence or breach in the security of a computer system.

IOM: Institute of Medicine. Prestigious group of physicians that studies issues and advises Congress. The IOM developed a report on computer-based patient records that led to the creation of CPRI. Its most recent popular work is its report on medical errors, *To Err Is Human: Building a Safer Health System* (Washington, DC, National Academy Press, 1999).

ISO/IEC 27001: ISO 27001:2013 is an information security standard. The official title of the standard is "Information technology—Security techniques—Information security management systems—Requirements." These provide the framework components for information security management systems (ISMS).

ISO/IEC 27002: ISO/IEC 27002 provides best practice recommendations on information security management for use by those responsible for initiating, implementing or maintaining information security management systems (ISMS). These support ISO/IEC 27001 requirements.

NIST: National Institute of Standards and Technology.

Nonrepudiation: strong and substantial evidence of the identity of the signer of a message and the message integrity, sufficient to prevent a party from successfully denying the origin, submission, or delivery of the message and the integrity of its contents.

NPRM: Notice of Proposed Rulemaking. The publication, in the Federal Register, of proposed regulations for public comment.

NRC: National Research Council. Quasi-governmental body that conducted a study on the state of security in health care, *For the Record: Protecting Electronic Health Information* (Washington, DC, National Academy Press, 1997).

PGP: Pretty Good Privacy. Public key cryptography software based on the RSA cryptographic method.

PKI: Public Key Infrastructure.

Smartphone: a smartphone is a mobile phone with more advanced computing capability and connectivity than basic feature phones. A smartphone has computing and digital storage capabilities.

SNIP: Strategic National Implementation Process. Sponsored by WEDI.

SSO: Single Sign-On or Standards-Setting Organization.

UPIN: Universal Provider Identification Number. To be replaced by National Provider Identifier under HIPAA.

URAC: The American Accreditation Healthcare Commission (formerly Utilization Review Accreditation Commission).

VPN: virtual private network. A private network that is configured within a public network.

WEDI: Workgroup on Electronic Data Interchange.

From the Regulatory Text

§ 160.103

Administrative simplification provision: means any requirement or prohibition established by:

1. 42 U.S.C. 1320d–1320d–4, 1320d–7, 1320d–8, and 1320d–9;
2. Section 264 of Pub. L. 104–191;
3. Sections 13400–13424 of Public Law 111–5; or
4. This subchapter.

ALJ: means Administrative Law Judge.

ANSI: stands for the American National Standards Institute.

Business associate:

1. Except as provided in paragraph (4) of this definition, business associate means, with respect to a covered entity, a person who:

    i. On behalf of such covered entity or of an organized health care arrangement (as defined in this section) in which the covered entity participates, but other than in the capacity of a member of the workforce of such covered entity or arrangement, creates, receives, maintains, or transmits protected health information for a function or activity regulated by this subchapter, including claims processing or administration, data analysis, processing or administration, utilization review, quality assurance, patient safety activities listed at 42 CFR 3.20, billing, benefit management, practice management, and repricing; or

    ii. Provides, other than in the capacity of a member of the workforce of such covered entity, legal, actuarial, accounting, consulting, data aggregation (as defined in § 164.501 of this subchapter), management, administrative, accreditation, or financial services to or for such covered entity, or to or for an organized health care arrangement in which the covered entity participates, where the provision of the service involves the disclosure of protected health information from such covered entity or arrangement, or from another business associate of such covered entity or arrangement, to the person.

2. A covered entity may be a business associate of another covered entity.

3. Business associate includes:

    i. A Health Information Organization, E-prescribing Gateway, or other person that provides data transmission services with respect to protected health information to a covered entity and that requires access on a routine basis to such protected health information.

    ii. A person that offers a personal health record to one or more individuals on behalf of a covered entity.

    iii. A subcontractor that creates, receives, maintains, or transmits protected health information on behalf of the business associate.

4. Business associate does not include:

    i   A health care provider, with respect to disclosures by a covered entity to the health care provider concerning the treatment of the individual.

    ii. A plan sponsor, with respect to disclosures by a group health plan (or by a health insurance issuer or HMO with respect to a group health plan) to the plan sponsor, to the extent that the requirements of § 164.504(f) of this subchapter apply and are met.

    iii. A government agency, with respect to determining eligibility for, or enrollment in, a government health plan that provides public benefits and is administered by another government agency, or collecting protected health information for such purposes, to the extent such activities are authorized by law.

    iv. A covered entity participating in an organized health care arrangement that performs a function or activity as described by paragraph (1)(i) of this definition for or on behalf of such organized health care arrangement, or that provides a service as described in paragraph (1)(ii) of this definition to or for such organized health care arrangement by virtue of such activities or services.

Civil money penalty or penalty: means the amount determined under § 160.404 of this part and includes the plural of these terms.

CMS: stands for Centers for Medicare & Medicaid Services within the Department of Health and Human Services.

Compliance date: means the date by which a covered entity or business associate must comply with a standard, implementation specification, requirement, or modification adopted under this subchapter.

Covered entity:

1. A health plan.
2. A health care clearinghouse.
3. A health care provider who transmits any health information in electronic form in connection with a transaction covered by this subchapter.

Disclosure: means the release, transfer, provision of access to, or divulging in any manner of information outside the entity holding the information.

EIN: stands for the employer identification number assigned by the Internal Revenue Service, U.S. Department of the Treasury. The EIN is the taxpayer identifying number of an individual or other entity (whether or not an employer) assigned under one of the following:

1. 26 U.S.C. 6011(b), which is the portion of the Internal Revenue Code dealing with identifying the taxpayer in tax returns and statements, or corresponding provisions of prior law.
2. 26 U.S.C. 6109, which is the portion of the Internal Revenue Code dealing with identifying numbers in tax returns, statements, and other required documents.

Electronic media:

1. Electronic storage material on which data is or may be recorded electronically, including, for example, devices in computers (hard drives) and any removable/transportable digital memory medium, such as magnetic tape or disk, optical disk, or digital memory card;

2. Transmission media used to exchange information already in electronic storage media. Transmission media include, for example, the Internet, extranet or intranet, leased lines, dial-up lines, private networks, and the physical movement of removable/transportable electronic storage media.

   Certain transmissions, including of paper, via facsimile, and of voice, via telephone, are not considered to be transmissions via electronic media if the information being exchanged did not exist in electronic form immediately before the transmission.

Electronic protected health information: means information that comes within paragraphs (1)(i) or (1)(ii) of the definition of protected health information as specified in this section.

Employer: is defined as it is in 26 U.S.C. 3401(d).

Family member: means, with respect to an individual:

1. A dependent (as such term is defined in 45 CFR 144.103), of the individual; or
2. Any other person who is a first-degree, second-degree, third-degree, or fourth-degree relative of the individual or of a dependent of the individual. Relatives by affinity (such as by marriage or adoption) are treated the same as relatives by consanguinity (that is, relatives who share a common biological ancestor). In determining the degree of the relationship, relatives by less than full consanguinity (such as half-siblings, who share only one parent) are treated the same as relatives by full consanguinity (such as siblings who share both parents).
   i. First-degree relatives include parents, spouses, siblings, and children.
   ii. Second-degree relatives include grandparents, grandchildren, aunts, uncles, nephews, and nieces.
   iii. Third-degree relatives include great-grandparents, great-grandchildren, great aunts, great uncles, and first cousins.
   iv. Fourth-degree relatives include great-great grandparents, great-great grandchildren, and children of first cousins.

Genetic information:

1. Subject to paragraphs (2) and (3) of this definition, with respect to an individual, information about:
    i. The individual's genetic tests;
    ii. The genetic tests of family members of the individual;
    iii. The manifestation of a disease or disorder in family members of such individual; or
    iv. Any request for, or receipt of, genetic services, or participation in clinical research which includes genetic services, by the individual or any family member of the individual.
2. Any reference in this subchapter to genetic information concerning an individual or family member of an individual shall include the genetic information of:
    i. A fetus carried by the individual or family member who is a pregnant woman; and
    ii. Any embryo legally held by an individual or family member utilizing an assisted reproductive technology.
3. Genetic information excludes information about the sex or age of any individual.

Genetic services:

1. A genetic test;
2. Genetic counseling (including obtaining, interpreting, or assessing genetic information); or
3. Genetic education.

Genetic test: means an analysis of human DNA, RNA, chromosomes, proteins, or metabolites, if the analysis detects genotypes, mutations, or chromosomal changes. Genetic test does not include an analysis of proteins or metabolites that is directly related to a manifested disease, disorder, or pathological condition.

Group health plan: (also see definition of health plan in this section) means an employee welfare benefit plan (as defined in section 3(1) of the Employee Retirement Income and Security Act of 1974 (ERISA), 29 U.S.C. 1002(1)), including insured and self-insured plans, to the extent that the plan provides medical care (as defined in section 2791(a)(2) of the Public Health Service Act (PHS Act), 42 U.S.C. 300gg-91(a)(2)), including items and services paid for as medical care, to employees or their dependents directly or through insurance, reimbursement, or otherwise, that:

1. Has 50 or more participants (as defined in section 3(7) of ERISA, 29 U.S.C. 1002(7)); or
2. Is administered by an entity other than the employer that established and maintains the plan.

Health care: means care, services, or supplies related to the health of an individual. Health care includes, but is not limited to, the following:

1. Preventive, diagnostic, therapeutic, rehabilitative, maintenance, or palliative care, and counseling, service, assessment, or procedure with respect to the physical or mental condition, or functional status, of an individual or that affects the structure or function of the body; and
2. Sale or dispensing of a drug, device, equipment, or other item in accordance with a prescription.

Health care clearinghouse: means a public or private entity, including a billing service, repricing company, community health management information system or community health information system, and "value-added" networks and switches, that does either of the following functions:

1. Processes or facilitates the processing of health information received from another entity in a nonstandard format or containing nonstandard data content into standard data elements or a standard transaction.
2. Receives a standard transaction from another entity and processes or facilitates the processing of health information into nonstandard format or nonstandard data content for the receiving entity.

Health care provider: means a provider of services (as defined in section 1861(u) of the Act, 42 U.S.C. 1395x (u)), a provider of medical or health services (as defined in section 1861(s) of the Act, 42 U.S.C. 1395x (s)), and any other person or organization who furnishes, bills, or is paid for health care in the normal course of business.

Health information: means any information, including genetic information, whether oral or recorded in any form or medium, that:

1. Is created or received by a health care provider, health plan, public health authority, employer, life insurer, school or university, or health care clearinghouse; and
2. Relates to the past, present, or future physical or mental health or condition of an individual; the provision of health care to an individual; or the past, present, or future payment for the provision of health care to an individual.

Health insurance issuer: (as defined in section 2791(b)(2) of the PHS Act, 42 U.S.C. 300gg-91(b)(2) and used in the definition of health plan in this section) means an insurance company, insurance service, or insurance organization (including an HMO) that is licensed to engage in the business of insurance in a State and is subject to State law that regulates insurance. Such term does not include a group health plan.

Health maintenance organization (HMO): (as defined in section 2791(b)(3) of the PHS Act, 42 U.S.C. 300gg-91(b)(3) and used in the definition of health plan in this section) means a federally qualified HMO, an organization recognized as an HMO under State law, or a similar organization regulated for solvency under State law in the same manner and to the same extent as such an HMO.

Health plan: means an individual or group plan that provides, or pays the cost of, medical care (as defined in section 2791(a)(2) of the PHS Act, 42 U.S.C. 300gg-91(a)(2)).

1. Health plan includes the following, singly or in combination:
    i. A group health plan, as defined in this section.
    ii. A health insurance issuer, as defined in this section.
    iii. An HMO, as defined in this section.

iv Part A or Part B of the Medicare program under title XVIII of the Act.

v. The Medicaid program under title XIX of the Act, 42 U.S.C. 1396, et seq.

vi. The Voluntary Prescription Drug Benefit Program under Part D of title XVIII of the Act, 42 U.S.C. 1395w-101 through 1395w-152.

vii. An issuer of a Medicare supplemental policy (as defined in section 1882(g)(1) of the Act, 42 U.S.C. 1395ss (g)(1)).

viii. An issuer of a long-term care policy, excluding a nursing home fixed indemnity policy.

ix. An employee welfare benefit plan or any other arrangement that is established or maintained for the purpose of offering or providing health benefits to the employees of two or more employers.

x. The health care program for uniformed services under title 10 of the United States Code.

xi. The veterans health care program under 38 U.S.C. chapter 17.

xii. The Indian Health Service program under the Indian Healthcare Improvement Act, 25 U.S.C. 1601, et seq.

xiii. The Federal Employees Health Benefits Program under 5 U.S.C. 8902, et seq.

xiv. An approved State child health plan under title XXI of the Act, providing benefits for child health assistance that meet the requirements of section 2103 of the Act, 42 U.S.C. 1397, et seq.

xv. The Medicare Advantage program under Part C of title XVIII of the Act, 42 U.S.C. 1395w-21 through 1395w-28.

xvi. A high-risk pool that is a mechanism established under State law to provide health insurance coverage or comparable coverage to eligible individuals.

xvii. Any other individual or group plan, or combination of individual or group plans, that provides or pays for the cost of medical care (as defined in section 2791(a)(2) of the PHS Act, 42 U.S.C. 300gg-91(a)(2)).

2. Health plan excludes:

i. Any policy, plan, or program to the extent that it provides, or pays for the cost of, excepted benefits that are listed in section 2791(c)(1) of the PHS Act, 42 U.S.C. 300gg-91(c)(1); and

ii. A government-funded program (other than one listed in paragraph (1)(i)-(xvi) of this definition):

    a. Whose principal purpose is other than providing, or paying the cost of, health care; or

    b. Whose principal activity is:

        1. The direct provision of health care to persons; or

        2. The making of grants to fund the direct provision of health care to persons.

HHS: stands for the Department of Health and Human Services.

Implementation specification: means specific requirements or instructions for implementing a standard.

Individual: means the person who is the subject of protected health information.

Individually identifiable health information: is information that is a subset of health information, including demographic information collected from an individual, and

1. Is created or received by a health care provider, health plan, employer, or health care clearinghouse; and

2. Relates to the past, present, or future physical or mental health or condition of an individual; the provision of health care to an individual; or the past, present, or future payment for the provision of health care to an individual; and

    i. That identifies the individual; or

    ii. With respect to which there is a reasonable basis to believe the information can be used to identify the individual.

Manifestation or manifested: means, with respect to a disease, disorder, or pathological condition, that an individual has been or could reasonably be diagnosed with the disease, disorder, or pathological condition by a health care professional with appropriate training and expertise in the field of medicine involved. For purposes of this subchapter, a disease, disorder, or pathological condition is not manifested if the diagnosis is based principally on genetic information.

Modify or modification: refers to a change adopted by the Secretary, through regulation, to a standard or an implementation specification.

Organized health care arrangement:

1. A clinically integrated care setting in which individuals typically receive health care from more than one health care provider;
2. An organized system of health care in which more than one covered entity participates and in which the participating covered entities:
   i. Hold themselves out to the public as participating in a joint arrangement; and
   ii. Participate in joint activities that include at least one of the following:
      a. Utilization review, in which health care decisions by participating covered entities are reviewed by other participating covered entities or by a third party on their behalf;
      b. Quality assessment and improvement activities, in which treatment provided by participating covered entities is assessed by other participating covered entities or by a third party on their behalf; or
      c. Payment activities, if the financial risk for delivering health care is shared, in part or in whole, by participating covered entities through the joint arrangement and if protected health information created or received by a covered entity is reviewed by other participating covered entities or by a third party on their behalf for the purpose of administering the sharing of financial risk.
3. A group health plan and a health insurance issuer or HMO with respect to such group health plan, but only with respect to protected health information created or received by such health insurance issuer or HMO that relates to individuals who are or who have been participants or beneficiaries in such group health plan;
4. A group health plan and one or more other group health plans, each of which are maintained by the same plan sponsor; or

5. The group health plans described in paragraph (4) of this definition and health insurance issuers or HMOs with respect to such group health plans, but only with respect to protected health information created or received by such health insurance issuers or HMOs that relates to individuals who are or have been participants or beneficiaries in any of such group health plans.

Person: means a natural person, trust or estate, partnership, corporation, professional association or corporation, or other entity, public or private.

Protected health information: means individually identifiable health information:

1. Except as provided in paragraph (2) of this definition, that is:
   i. Transmitted by electronic media;
   ii. Maintained in electronic media; or
   iii. Transmitted or maintained in any other form or medium.
2. Protected health information excludes individually identifiable health information:
   i. In education records covered by the Family Educational Rights and Privacy Act, as amended, 20 U.S.C. 1232g;
   ii. In records described at 20 U.S.C. 1232g (a)(4)(B)(iv);
   iii. In employment records held by a covered entity in its role as employer; and
   iv. Regarding a person who has been deceased for more than 50 years.

Respondent: means a covered entity or business associate upon which the Secretary has imposed, or proposes to impose, a civil money penalty.

Secretary: means the Secretary of Health and Human Services or any other officer or employee of HHS to whom the authority involved has been delegated.

Small health plan: means a health plan with annual receipts of $5 million or less.

Standard: means a rule, condition, or requirement:

1. Describing the following information for products, systems, services, or practices:
   i. Classification of components;
   ii. Specification of materials, performance, or operations; or
   iii. Delineation of procedures; or
2. With respect to the privacy of protected health information. Standard-setting organization (SSO) means an organization accredited by the American National Standards Institute that develops and maintains standards for information transactions or data elements, or any other standard that is necessary for, or will facilitate the implementation of, this part.

State: refers to one of the following:

1. For a health plan established or regulated by Federal law, State has the meaning set forth in the applicable section of the United States Code for such health plan.
2. For all other purposes, State means any of the several States, the District of Columbia, the Commonwealth of Puerto Rico, the Virgin Islands, Guam, American Samoa, and the Commonwealth of the Northern Mariana Islands.

Subcontractor: means a person to whom a business associate delegates a function, activity, or service, other than in the capacity of a member of the workforce of such business associate.

Trading partner agreement: means an agreement related to the exchange of information in electronic transactions, whether the agreement is distinct or part of a larger agreement, between each party to the agreement. (For example, a trading partner agreement may specify, among other things, the duties and responsibilities of each party to the agreement in conducting a standard transaction.)

Transaction: means the transmission of information between two parties to carry out financial or administrative activities related to health care. It includes the following types of information transmissions:

1. Health care claims or equivalent encounter information.
2. Health care payment and remittance advice.

3. Coordination of benefits.
4. Health care claim status.
5. Enrollment and disenrollment in a health plan.
6. Eligibility for a health plan.
7. Health plan premium payments.
8. Referral certification and authorization.
9. First report of injury.
10. Health claims attachments.
11. Health care electronic funds transfers (EFT) and remittance advice.
12. Other transactions that the Secretary may prescribe by regulation.

Use: means, with respect to individually identifiable health information, the sharing, employment, application, utilization, examination, or analysis of such information within an entity that maintains such information.

Violation or violate: means, as the context may require, failure to comply with an administrative simplification provision.

Workforce: means employees, volunteers, trainees, and other persons whose conduct, in the performance of work for a covered entity or business associate, is under the direct control of such covered entity or business associate, whether or not they are paid by the covered entity or business associate.

§ 160.202

Contrary: when used to compare a provision of State law to a standard, requirement, or implementation specification adopted under this subchapter, means:

1. A covered entity or business associate would find it impossible to comply with both the State and Federal requirements; or
2. The provision of State law stands as an obstacle to the accomplishment and execution of the full purposes and objectives of part C of title XI of the Act, section 264 of Public Law 104-191, or sections 13400-13424 of Public Law 111-5, as applicable.

More stringent: means, in the context of a comparison of a provision of State law and a standard, requirement, or implementation specification adopted under subpart E of part 164 of this subchapter, a State law that meets one or more of the following criteria:

1. With respect to a use or disclosure, the law prohibits or restricts a use or disclosure in circumstances under which such use or disclosure otherwise would be permitted under this subchapter, except if the disclosure is:
   i. Required by the Secretary in connection with determining whether a covered entity or business associate is in compliance with this subchapter; or
   ii. To the individual who is the subject of the individually identifiable health information.
2. With respect to the rights of an individual, who is the subject of the individually identifiable health information, regarding access to or amendment of individually identifiable health information, permits greater rights of access or amendment, as applicable.
3. With respect to information to be provided to an individual who is the subject of the individually identifiable health information about a use, a disclosure, rights, and remedies, provides the greater amount of information.
4. With respect to the form, substance, or the need for express legal permission from an individual, who is the subject of the individually identifiable health information, for use or disclosure of individually identifiable health information, provides requirements that narrow the scope or duration, increase the privacy protections afforded (such as by expanding the criteria for), or reduce the coercive effect of the circumstances surrounding the express legal permission, as applicable.
5. With respect to recordkeeping or requirements relating to accounting of disclosures, provides for the retention or reporting of more detailed information or for a longer duration.
6. With respect to any other matter, provides greater privacy protection for the individual who is the subject of the individually identifiable health information. Relates to the privacy

of individually identifiable health information means, with respect to a State law, that the State law has the specific purpose of protecting the privacy of health information or affects the privacy of health information in a direct, clear, and substantial way.

State law: means a constitution, statute, regulation, rule, common law, or other State action having the force and effect of law.

§ 160.401

Reasonable cause: means an act or omission in which a covered entity or business associate knew, or by exercising reasonable diligence would have known, that the act or omission violated an administrative simplification provision, but in which the covered entity or business associate did not act with willful neglect.

Reasonable diligence: means the business care and prudence expected from a person seeking to satisfy a legal requirement under similar circumstances.

Willful neglect: means conscious, intentional failure or reckless indifference to the obligation to comply with the administrative simplification provision violated (74 FR 56130, Oct. 30, 2009, as amended at 78 FR 5691, Jan. 25, 2013).

§ 160.402 Basis for a Civil Money Penalty

a. General rule. Subject to § 160.410, the Secretary will impose a civil money penalty upon a covered entity or business associate if the Secretary determines that the covered entity or business associate has violated an administrative simplification provision.

b. Violation by more than one covered entity or business associate.

1. Except as provided in paragraph (b)(2) of this section, if the Secretary determines that more than one covered entity or business associate was responsible for a violation,

the Secretary will impose a civil money penalty against
each such covered entity or business associate.

2. A covered entity that is a member of an affiliated covered
entity, in accordance with § 164.105(b) of this subchapter,
is jointly and severally liable for a civil money penalty for a
violation of part 164 of this subchapter based on an act or
omission of the affiliated covered entity, unless it is established that another member of the affiliated covered entity
was responsible for the violation.

c. Violation attributed to a covered entity or business associate.

1. A covered entity is liable, in accordance with the Federal
common law of agency, for a civil money penalty for a
violation based on the act or omission of any agent of the
covered entity, including a workforce member or business
associate, acting within the scope of the agency.

2. A business associate is liable, in accordance with the
Federal common law of agency, for a civil money penalty for a violation based on the act or omission of any
agent of the business associate, including a workforce
member or subcontractor, acting within the scope of the
agency.

§ 160.502

Board: means the members of the HHS Departmental Appeals
Board, in the Office of the Secretary, who issue decisions in
panels of three.

§ 162.103

Code set: Any set of codes used to encode data elements, such as
tables of terms, medical concepts, medical diagnostic codes,
or medical procedure codes. A code set includes the codes and
the descriptors of the codes.

Code set maintaining organization: An organization that creates
and maintains the code sets adopted by the Secretary for use

in the transactions for which standards are adopted in this part.

Controlling health plan (CHP): means a health plan that:

1. Controls its own business activities, actions, or policies; or
2. i. Is controlled by an entity that is not a health plan; and
   ii. If it has a subhealth plan(s) (as defined in this section), exercises sufficient control over the subhealth plan(s) to direct its/their business activities, actions, or policies.

Covered health care provider: means a health care provider that meets the definition at paragraph (3) of the definition of "covered entity" at § 160.103.

Data condition: The rule that describes the circumstances under which a covered entity must use a particular data element or segment.

Data content: All the data elements and code sets inherent to a transaction, and not related to the format of the transaction. Data elements that are related to the format are not data content.

Data element: The smallest named unit of information in a transaction.

Data set: A semantically meaningful unit of information exchanged between two parties to a transaction.

Descriptor: The text defining a code.

Designated Standard Maintenance Organization (DSMO): An organization designated by the Secretary under § 162.910(a).

Direct data entry: The direct entry of data (for example, using dumb terminals or Web browsers) that is immediately transmitted into a health plan's computer.

Format: Refers to those data elements that provide or control the enveloping or hierarchical structure, or assist in identifying data content of, a transaction.

HCPCS: Stands for the Health (Care Financing Administration) Common Procedure Coding System.

Maintain or maintenance: Refers to activities necessary to support the use of a standard adopted by the Secretary, including technical corrections to an implementation specification, and enhancements or expansion of a code set. This term excludes the activities related to the adoption of a new standard or implementation specification, or modification to an adopted standard or implementation specification.

Maximum defined data set: All of the required data elements for a particular standard based on a specific implementation specification.

Operating rules: means the necessary business rules and guidelines for the electronic exchange of information that are not defined by a standard or its implementation specifications as adopted for purposes of this part.

Segment: A group of related data elements in a transaction.

Stage 1 payment initiation: means a health plan's order, instruction or authorization to its financial institution to make a health care claims payment using an electronic funds transfer (EFT) through the ACH Network.

Standard transaction: A transaction that complies with the applicable standard and associated operating rules adopted under this part.

Subhealth plan (SHP): means a health plan whose business activities, actions, or policies are directed by a controlling health plan

§ 160.103

Act: The Social Security Act.

ANSI: Stands for the American National Standards Institute.

Business associate:

1. Except as provided in paragraph (2) of this definition, business associate means, with respect to a covered entity, a person who:

   i. On behalf of such covered entity or of an organized health care arrangement (as defined in § 164.501 of this subchapter) in which the covered entity participates, but other than in the capacity of a member of the workforce of such covered entity or arrangement, performs, or assists in the performance of:

      a. A function or activity involving the use or disclosure of individually identifiable health information, including claims processing or administration, data analysis, processing or administration, utilization review,

quality assurance, billing, benefit management, practice management, and repricing; or

    b. Any other function or activity regulated by this sub-
chapter; or

  ii. Provides, other than in the capacity of a member of the
workforce of such covered entity, legal, actuarial, accounting, consulting, data aggregation (as defined in § 164.501
of this subchapter), management, administrative, accreditation, or financial services to or for such covered entity, or
to or for an organized health care arrangement in which
the covered entity participates, where the provision of the
service involves the disclosure of individually identifiable
health information from such covered entity or arrangement, or from another business associate of such covered
entity or arrangement, to the person.

2. A covered entity participating in an organized health care
arrangement that performs a function or activity as described
by paragraph (1)(i) of this definition for or on behalf of such
organized health care arrangement, or that provides a service
as described in paragraph (1)(ii) of this definition to or for such
organized health care arrangement, does not, simply through
the performance of such function or activity or the provision of
such service, become a business associate of other covered entities participating in such organized health care arrangement.

3. A covered entity may be a business associate of another covered entity.

Compliance date: The date by which a covered entity must comply
with a standard, implementation specification, requirement,
or modification adopted under this subchapter.

Covered entity:

1. A health plan.
2. A health care clearinghouse.
3. A health care provider who transmits any health information
in electronic form in connection with a transaction covered by
this subchapter.

Group health plan: (Also see definition of health plan in this section.) An employee welfare benefit plan (as defined in section 3(1) of the Employee Retirement Income and Security Act of 1974 (ERISA), 29 U.S.C. 1002(1)), including insured and self-insured plans, to the extent that the plan provides medical care (as defined in section 2791(a)(2) of the Public Health Service Act (PHS Act), 42 U.S.C. 300gg-91(a)(2)), including items and services paid for as medical care, to employees or their dependents directly or through insurance, reimbursement, or otherwise, that:

1. Has 50 or more participants (as defined in section 3(7) of ERISA, 29 U.S.C. 1002(7)); or
2. Is administered by an entity other than the employer that established and maintains the plan.

HCFA: Healthcare Financing Administration within the Department of Health and Human Services.

Health care: Care, services, or supplies related to the health of an individual. Health care includes, but is not limited to, the following:

1. Preventive, diagnostic, therapeutic, rehabilitative, maintenance, or palliative care, and counseling, service, assessment, or procedure with respect to the physical or mental condition, or functional status, of an individual or that affects the structure or function of the body; and
2. Sale or dispensing of a drug, device, equipment, or other item in accordance with a prescription.

Health care clearinghouse: A public or private entity, including a billing service, repricing company, community health management information system or community health information system, and "value-added" networks and switches, that does either of the following functions:

1. Processes or facilitates the processing of health information received from another entity in a nonstandard format or containing nonstandard data content into standard data elements or a standard transaction.

2. Receives a standard transaction from another entity and processes or facilitates the processing of health information into nonstandard format or nonstandard data content for the receiving entity.

Health care provider: A provider of services (as defined in section 1861(u) of the Act, 42 U.S.C. 1395x (u)), a provider of medical or health services (as defined in section 1861(s) of the Act, 42 U.S.C. 1395x (s)), and any other person or organization who furnishes, bills, or is paid for health care in the normal course of business.

Health information: Any information, whether oral or recorded in any form or medium, that:

1. Is created or received by a health care provider, health plan, public health authority, employer, life insurer, school or university, or health care clearinghouse; and
2. Relates to the past, present, or future physical or mental health or condition of an individual; the provision of health care to an individual; or the past, present, or future payment for the provision of health care to an individual.

Health insurance issuer: (As defined in section 2791(b)(2) of the PHS Act, 42 U.S.C. 300gg-91(b)(2) and used in the definition of health plan in this section.) An insurance company, insurance service, or insurance organization (including an HMO) that is licensed to engage in the business of insurance in a State and is subject to State law that regulates insurance. Such term does not include a group health plan.

Health maintenance organization (HMO): (As defined in section 2791(b)(3) of the PHS Act, 42 U.S.C. 300gg-91(b)(3) and used in the definition of health plan in this section.) A federally qualified HMO, an organization recognized as an HMO under State law, or a similar organization regulated for solvency under State law in the same manner and to the same extent as such an HMO.

Health plan: An individual or group plan that provides, or pays the cost of, medical care (as defined in section 2791(a)(2) of the PHS Act, 42 U.S.C. 300gg-91(a)(2)).

1. Health plan includes the following, singly or in combination:
    i. A group health plan, as defined in this section.
    ii. A health insurance issuer, as defined in this section.
    iii. An HMO, as defined in this section.
    iv. Part A or Part B of the Medicare program under title XVIII of the Act.
    v. The Medicaid program under title XIX of the Act, 42 U.S.C. 1396, et seq.
    vi. An issuer of a Medicare supplemental policy (as defined in section 1882(g)(1) of the Act, 42 U.S.C. 1395ss (g)(1)).
    vii. An issuer of a long-term care policy, excluding a nursing home fixed-indemnity policy.
    viii. An employee welfare benefit plan or any other arrangement that is established or maintained for the purpose of offering or providing health benefits to the employees of two or more employers.
    ix. The health care program for active military personnel under title 10 of the United States Code.
    x. The veterans' health care program under 38 U.S.C. chapter 17.
    xi. The Civilian Health and Medical Program of the Uniformed Services (CHAMPUS) (as defined in 10 U.S.C. 1072(4)).
    xii. The Indian Health Service program under the Indian Healthcare Improvement Act, 25 U.S.C. 1601, et seq.
    xiii. The Federal Employees Health Benefits Program under 5 U.S.C. 8902, et seq.
    xiv. An approved State child health plan under title XXI of the Act, providing benefits for child health assistance that meet the requirements of section 2103 of the Act, 42 U.S.C. 1397, et seq.
    xv. The Medicare + Choice program under Part C of Title XVIII of the Act, 42 U.S.C. 1395w-21 through 1395w-28.
    xvi. A high-risk pool that is a mechanism established under State law to provide health insurance coverage or comparable coverage to eligible individuals.
    xvii. Any other individual or group plan, or combination of individual or group plans, that provides or pays for the

cost of medical care (as defined in section 2791(a)(2) of the PHS Act, 42 U.S.C. 300gg-91(a)(2)).

2. Health plan excludes:

    i. Any policy, plan, or program to the extent that it provides, or pays for the cost of, excepted benefits that are listed in section 2791(c)(1) of the PHS Act, 42 U.S.C. 300gg-91(c)(1); and

    ii. A government-funded program (other than one listed in paragraph (1)(i)-(xvi) of this definition):

        A. Whose principal purpose is other than providing, or paying the cost of, health care; or

        B. Whose principal activity is:

            a. The direct provision of health care to persons; or

            b. The making of grants to fund the direct provision of health care to persons.

HHS: Department of Health and Human Services.

Implementation specification: Specific requirements or instructions for implementing a standard.

Individually identifiable health information: Information that is a subset of health information, including demographic information collected from an individual, and:

1. Is created or received by a health care provider, health plan, employer, or health care clearinghouse; and

2. Relates to the past, present, or future physical or mental health or condition of an individual; the provision of health care to an individual; or the past, present, or future payment for the provision of health care to an individual; and

    i. That identifies the individual; or

    ii. With respect to which there is a reasonable basis to believe the information can be used to identify the individual.

Modify or modification: Refers to a change adopted by the Secretary, through regulation, to a standard or an implementation specification.

Secretary: The Secretary of Health and Human Services or any other officer or employee of HHS to whom the authority involved has been delegated.

Small health plan: A health plan with annual receipts of $5 million or less.

Standard: A rule, condition, or requirement:

1. Describing the following information for products, systems, services or practices:
   i. Classification of components;
   ii. Specification of materials, performance, or operations; or
   iii. Delineation of procedures; or
2. With respect to the privacy of individually identifiable health information.

Standard-setting organization (SSO): An organization accredited by the American National Standards Institute that develops and maintains standards for information transactions or data elements, or any other standard that is necessary for, or will facilitate the implementation of, this part.

State: Refers to one of the following:

1. For a health plan established or regulated by Federal law, State has the meaning set forth in the applicable section of the United States Code for such health plan.
2. For all other purposes, State means any of the several States, the District of Columbia, the Commonwealth of Puerto Rico, the Virgin Islands, and Guam.

Trading partner agreement: An agreement related to the exchange of information in electronic transactions, whether the agreement is distinct or part of a larger agreement, between each party to the agreement. (For example, a trading partner agreement may specify, among other things, the duties and responsibilities of each party to the agreement in conducting a standard transaction.)

Transaction: The transmission of information between two parties to carry out financial or administrative activities related to health care. It includes the following types of information transmissions:

1. Health care claims or equivalent encounter information.
2. Health care payment and remittance advice.

3. Coordination of benefits.
4. Health care claim status.
5. Enrollment and disenrollment in a health plan.
6. Eligibility for a health plan.
7. Health plan premium payments.
8. Referral certification and authorization.
9. First report of injury.
10. Health claims attachments.
11. Other transactions that the Secretary may prescribe by regulation.

Workforce: Employees, volunteers, trainees, and other persons whose conduct, in the performance of work for a covered entity, is under the direct control of such entity, whether or not they are paid by the covered entity.

§ 142.103

Code set: Any set of codes used for encoding data elements, such as tables of terms, medical concepts, medical diagnostic codes, or medical procedure codes.

Health care clearinghouse: A public or private entity that processes or facilitates the processing of nonstandard data elements of health information into standard data elements. The entity receives health care transactions from health care providers or other entities, translates the data from a given format into one acceptable to the intended payer or payers, and forwards the processed transaction to appropriate payers and clearinghouses. Billing services, repricing companies, community health management information systems, community health information systems, and "value-added" networks and switches are considered to be health care clearinghouses for purposes of this part.

Health care provider: A provider of services as defined in section 1861(u) of the Social Security Act, 42 U.S.C. 1395x, a provider of medical or other health services as defined in section 1861(s) of the Social Security Act, and any other person who furnishes or bills and is paid for health care services or supplies in the normal course of business.

Health information: Any information, whether oral or recorded in any form or medium, that

1. Is created or received by a health care provider, health plan, public health authority, employer, life insurer, school or university, or health care clearinghouse; and
2. Relates to the past, present, or future physical or mental health or condition of an individual, the provision of health care to an individual, or the past, present, or future payment for the provision of health care to an individual.

Health plan: An individual or group plan that provides, or pays the cost of, medical care. Health plan includes the following, singly or in combination:

1. Group health plan. A group health plan is an employee welfare benefit plan (as currently defined in section 3(1) of the Employee Retirement Income and Security Act of 1974, 29 U.S.C. 1002(1)), including insured and self-insured plans, to the extent that the plan provides medical care, including items and services paid for as medical care, to employees or their dependents directly or through insurance, or otherwise, and:
   i. Has 50 or more participants; or
   ii. Is administered by an entity other than the employer that established and maintains the plan.
2. Health insurance issuer. A health insurance issuer is an insurance company, insurance service, or insurance organization that is licensed to engage in the business of insurance in a State and is subject to State law that regulates insurance.
3. Health maintenance organization. A health maintenance organization is a Federally qualified health maintenance organization, an organization recognized as a health maintenance organization under State law, or a similar organization regulated for solvency under State law in the same manner and to the same extent as such a health maintenance organization.
4. Part A or Part B of the Medicare program under title XVIII of the Social Security Act.

5. The Medicaid program under title XIX of the Social Security Act.

6. A Medicare supplemental policy (as defined in section 1882(g)(1) of the Social Security Act, 42 U.S.C. 1395ss).

7. A long-term care policy, including a nursing home fixed-indemnity policy.

8. An employee welfare benefit plan or any other arrangement that is established or maintained for the purpose of offering or providing health benefits to the employees of two or more employers.

9. The health care program for active military personnel under title 10 of the United States Code.

10. The veterans' health care program under 38 U.S.C. chapter 17.

11. The Civilian Health and Medical Program of the Uniformed Services (CHAMPUS), as defined in 10 U.S.C. 1072(4).

12. The Indian Health Service program under the Indian Healthcare Improvement Act (25 U.S.C. 1601 et seq.).

13. The Federal Employees Health Benefits Program under 5 U.S.C. chapter 89.

14. Any other individual or group health plan, or combination thereof, that provides or pays for the cost of medical care.

Medical care: The diagnosis, cure, mitigation, treatment, or prevention of disease, or amounts paid for the purpose of affecting any body structure or function of the body; amounts paid for transportation primarily for and essential to these items; and amounts paid for insurance covering the items and the transportation specified in this definition.

Participant: Any employee or former employee of an employer, or any member or former member of an employee organization, who is or may become eligible to receive a benefit of any type from an employee benefit plan that covers employees of that employer or members of such an organization, or whose beneficiaries may be eligible to receive any of these benefits. "Employee" includes an individual who is treated as an employee under section 401(c)(1) of the Internal Revenue Code of 1986 (26 U.S.C. 401(c)(1)).

Small health plan: A group health plan or individual health plan with fewer than 50 participants.

Standard: A set of rules for a set of codes, data elements, transactions, or identifiers promulgated either by an organization accredited by the American National Standards Institute or HHS for the electronic transmission of health information.

Transaction: The exchange of information between two parties to carry out financial and administrative activities related to health care. It includes the following:

1. Health claims or equivalent encounter information.
2. Health care payment and remittance advice.
3. Coordination of benefits.
4. Health claims status.
5. Enrollment and disenrollment in a health plan.
6. Eligibility for a health plan.
7. Health plan premium payments.
8. Referral certification and authorization.
9. First report of injury.
10. Health claims attachments.
11. Other transactions as the Secretary may prescribe by regulation.

§ 164.103

Common control: exists if an entity has the power, directly or indirectly, significantly to influence or direct the actions or policies of another entity.

Common ownership: exists if an entity or entities possess an ownership or equity interest of 5% or more in another entity.

Covered functions: means those functions of a covered entity the performance of which makes the entity a health plan, health care provider, or health care clearinghouse. Health care component means a component or combination of components of a hybrid entity designated by the hybrid entity in accordance with § 164.105(a)(2)(iii)(D).

Hybrid entity: means a single legal entity: (1) that is a covered entity; (2) whose business activities includes both covered and noncovered functions; and (3) that designates health care components in accordance with paragraph § 164.105(a)(2)(iii)(D).

Law enforcement official: means an officer or employee of any agency or authority of the United States, a State, a territory, a political subdivision of a State or territory, or an Indian tribe, who is empowered by law to:

1. Investigate or conduct an official inquiry into a potential violation of law; or
2. Prosecute or otherwise conduct a criminal, civil, or administrative proceeding arising from an alleged violation of law

Plan sponsor: is defined in section 3(16)(B) of ERISA, 29 U.S.C. 1002(16)(B)

Required by law: means a mandate contained in law that compels an entity to make a use or disclosure of protected health information and that is enforceable in a court of law. Required by law includes, but is not limited to, court orders and court-ordered warrants; subpoenas or summons issued by a court, grand jury, a governmental or tribal inspector general, or an administrative body authorized to require the production of information; a civil or an authorized investigative demand; Medicare conditions of participation with respect to health care providers participating in the program; and statutes or regulations that require the production of information, including statutes or regulations that require such information if payment is sought under a government program providing public benefits.

§ 164.304

Access: means the ability or the means necessary to read, write, modify, or communicate data/information or otherwise use any system resource. (This definition applies to "access" as used in this subpart, not as used in subparts D or E of this part.)

Administrative safeguards: are administrative actions, and policies and procedures, to manage the selection, development, implementation, and maintenance of security measures to protect electronic protected health information and to manage the conduct of the covered entity's or business associate's workforce in relation to the protection of that information.

Authentication: means the corroboration that a person is the one they claim to be.

Availability: means the property that data or information is accessible and useable upon demand by an authorized person.

Confidentiality: means the property that data or information is not made available or disclosed to unauthorized persons or processes

Encryption: means the use of an algorithmic process to transform data into a form in which there is a low probability of assigning meaning without use of a confidential process or key.

Facility: means the physical premises and the interior and exterior of a building(s).

Information system: means an interconnected set of information resources under the same direct management control that shares common functionality. A system normally includes hardware, software, information, data, applications, communications, and people.

Integrity: means the property that data or information have not been altered or destroyed in an unauthorized manner.

Malicious software: means software, for example, a virus, designed to damage or disrupt a system.

Password: means confidential authentication information composed of a string of characters.

Physical safeguards: are physical measures, policies, and procedures to protect a covered entity's or business associate's electronic information systems and related buildings and equipment, from natural and environmental hazards, and unauthorized intrusion.

Security or security measures: encompass all of the administrative, physical, and technical safeguards in an information system.

Security incident: means the attempted or successful unauthorized access, use, disclosure, modification, or destruction of information or interference with system operations in an information system.

Technical safeguards: means the technology and the policy and procedures for its use that protect electronic protected health information and control access to it.

User: means a person or entity with authorized access.

Workstation: means an electronic computing device, for example, a laptop or desktop computer, or any other device that performs similar functions, and electronic media stored in its immediate environment.

§ 164.402

Breach: means the acquisition, access use, or disclosure of protected health information in a manner not permitted under subpart E of this part which compromises the security or privacy of the protected health information

1. Breach excludes:
   i. Any unintentional acquisition, access, or use of protected health information by a workforce member or person acting under the authority of a covered entity or a business associate, if such acquisition, access, or use was made in good faith and within the scope of authority and does not result in further use or disclosure in a manner not permitted under subpart E of this part.
   ii. Any inadvertent disclosure by a person who is authorized to access protected health information at a covered entity or business associate to another person authorized to access protected health information at the same covered entity or business associate, or organized health care arrangement in which the covered entity participates, and the information received as a result of such disclosure is not further used or disclosed in a manner not permitted under subpart E of this part.
   iii. A disclosure of protected health information where a covered entity or business associate has a good faith belief that an unauthorized person to whom the disclosure was made would not reasonably have been able to retain such information.

2. Except as provided in paragraph (1) of this definition, an acquisition, access, use, or disclosure of protected health information in a manner not permitted under subpart E is presumed to be a breach unless the covered entity or business associate, as applicable, demonstrates that there is a low probability that the protected health information has been compromised based on a risk assessment of at least the following factors:

   i. The nature and extent of the protected health information involved, including the types of identifiers and the likelihood of re-identification;

   ii. The unauthorized person who used the protected health information or to whom the disclosure was made;

   iii. Whether the protected health information was actually acquired or viewed; and

   iv. The extent to which the risk to the protected health information has been mitigated

Unsecured protected health information: means protected health information that is not rendered unusable, unreadable, or indecipherable to unauthorized persons through the use of a technology or methodology specified by the Secretary in the guidance issued under section 13402(h)(2) of Public Law 111-5.

§ 164.501

Correctional institution: means any penal or correctional facility, jail, reformatory, detention center, work farm, halfway house, or residential community program center operated by, or under contract to, the United States, a State, a territory, a political subdivision of a State or territory, or an Indian tribe, for the confinement or rehabilitation of persons charged with or convicted of a criminal offense or other persons held in lawful custody. Other persons held in lawful custody include juvenile offenders, adjudicated delinquents, aliens detained awaiting deportation, persons committed to mental institutions through the criminal justice system, witnesses, or others awaiting charges or trial.

Data aggregation: means, with respect to protected health information created or received by a business associate in its capacity as the business associate of a covered entity, the combining of such protected health information by the business associate with the protected health information received by the business associate in its capacity as a business associate of another covered entity, to permit data analyses that relate to the health care operations of the respective covered entities.

Designated record set:

1. A group of records maintained by or for a covered entity that is:
   i. The medical records and billing records about individuals maintained by or for a covered health care provider;
   ii. The enrollment, payment, claims adjudication, and case or medical management record systems maintained by or for a health plan; or
   iii. Used, in whole or in part, by or for the covered entity to make decisions about individuals.
2. For purposes of this paragraph, the term record means any item, collection, or grouping of information that includes protected health information and is maintained, collected, used, or disseminated by or for a covered entity.

Direct treatment relationship: means a treatment relationship between an individual and a health care provider that is not an indirect treatment relationship.

Health care operations: means any of the following activities of the covered entity to the extent that the activities are related to covered functions:

1. Conducting quality assessment and improvement activities, including outcomes evaluation and development of clinical guidelines, provided that the obtaining of generalizable knowledge is not the primary purpose of any studies resulting from such activities; patient safety activities (as defined in 42 CFR 3.20); population-based activities relating to improving health or reducing health care costs, protocol development, case management and care coordination, contacting of health care

providers and patients with information about treatment alternatives; and related functions that do not include treatment;

2. Reviewing the competence or qualifications of health care professionals, evaluating practitioner and provider performance, health plan performance, conducting training programs in which students, trainees, or practitioners in areas of health care learn under supervision to practice or improve their skills as health care providers, training of non-health care professionals, accreditation, certification, licensing, or credentialing activities;

3. Except as prohibited under § 164.502(a)(5)(i), underwriting, enrollment, premium rating, and other activities related to the creation, renewal, or replacement of a contract of health insurance or health benefits, and ceding, securing, or placing a contract for reinsurance of risk relating to claims for health care (including stop-loss insurance and excess of loss insurance), provided that the requirements of § 164.514(g) are met, if applicable;

4. Conducting or arranging for medical review, legal services, and auditing functions, including fraud and abuse detection and compliance programs;

5. Business planning and development, such as conducting cost-management and planning-related analyses related to managing and operating the entity, including formulary development and administration, development or improvement of methods of payment or coverage policies; and

6. Business management and general administrative activities of the entity, including, but not limited to:

   i. Management activities relating to implementation of and compliance with the requirements of this subchapter;

   ii. Customer service, including the provision of data analyses for policy holders, plan sponsors, or other customers, provided that protected health information is not disclosed to such policy holder, plan sponsor, or customer.

   iii. Resolution of internal grievances;

   iv. The sale, transfer, merger, or consolidation of all or part of the covered entity with another covered entity, or an entity that following such activity will become a covered entity and due diligence related to such activity; and

v. Consistent with the applicable requirements of § 164.514, creating de-identified health information or a limited data set, and fundraising for the benefit of the covered entity.

Health oversight agency: means an agency or authority of the United States, a State, a territory, a political subdivision of a State or territory, or an Indian tribe, or a person or entity acting under a grant of authority from or contract with such public agency, including the employees or agents of such public agency or its contractors or persons or entities to whom it has granted authority, that is authorized by law to oversee the health care system (whether public or private) or government programs in which health information is necessary to determine eligibility or compliance, or to enforce civil rights laws for which health information is relevant.

Indirect treatment relationship: means a relationship between an individual and a health care provider in which:

1. The health care provider delivers health care to the individual based on the orders of another health care provider; and
2. The health care provider typically provides services or products, or reports the diagnosis or results associated with the health care, directly to another health care provider, who provides the services or products or reports to the individual.

Inmate: means a person incarcerated in or otherwise confined to a correctional institution.

Marketing:

1. Except as provided in paragraph (2) of this definition, marketing means to make a communication about a product or service that encourages recipients of the communication to purchase or use the product or service.
2. Marketing does not include a communication made:
   i. To provide refill reminders or otherwise communicate about a drug or biologic that is currently being prescribed for the individual, only if any financial remuneration received by the covered entity in exchange for making the

communication is reasonably related to the covered entity's cost of making the communication.

ii. For the following treatment and health care operations purposes, except where the covered entity receives financial remuneration in exchange for making the communication:

a. For treatment of an individual by a health care provider, including case management or care coordination for the individual, or to direct or recommend alternative treatments, therapies, health care providers, or settings of care to the individual;

b. To describe a health-related product or service (or payment for such product or service) that is provided by, or included in a plan of benefits of, the covered entity making the communication, including communications about: the entities participating in a health care provider network or health plan network; replacement of, or enhancements to, a health plan; and health-related products or services available only to a health plan enrollee that add value to, but are not part of, a plan of benefits; or

c. For case management or care coordination, contacting of individuals with information about treatment alternatives, and related functions to the extent these activities do not fall within the definition of treatment.

3. Financial remuneration means direct or indirect payment from or on behalf of a third party whose product or service is being described. Direct or indirect payment does not include any payment for treatment of an individual.

Payment:

1. The activities undertaken by:

i. Except as prohibited under § 164.502(a)(5)(i), a health plan to obtain premiums or to determine or fulfill its responsibility for coverage and provision of benefits under the health plan; or

ii. A health care provider or health plan to obtain or provide reimbursement for the provision of health care; and

2. The activities in paragraph (1) of this definition relate to the individual to whom health care is provided and include, but are not limited to:

   i. Determinations of eligibility or coverage (including coordination of benefits or the determination of cost sharing amounts), and adjudication or subrogation of health benefit claims;

   ii. Risk adjusting amounts due based on enrollee health status and demographic characteristics;

   iii. Billing, claims management, collection activities, obtaining payment under a contract for reinsurance (including stop-loss insurance and excess of loss insurance), and related health care data processing;

   iv. Review of health care services with respect to medical necessity, coverage under a health plan, appropriateness of care, or justification of charges;

   v. Utilization review activities, including precertification and preauthorization of services, concurrent and retrospective review of services; and

   vi. Disclosure to consumer reporting agencies of any of the following protected health information relating to collection of premiums or reimbursement:

      a. Name and address;
      b. Date of birth;
      c. Social Security number;
      d. Payment history;
      e. Account number; and
      f. Name and address of the health care provider and/or health plan.

Psychotherapy notes: means notes recorded (in any medium) by a health care provider who is a mental health professional documenting or analyzing the contents of conversation during a private counseling session or a group, joint, or family counseling session and that are separated from the rest of the individual's medical record. Psychotherapy notes exclude medication prescription and monitoring, counseling session start and stop times, the modalities and frequencies of treatment furnished, results of clinical tests, and any summary of the following items: diagnosis, functional status, treatment plan, symptoms, prognosis, and progress to date.

Public health authority: means an agency or authority of the United States, a State, a territory, a political subdivision of a State or territory, or an Indian tribe, or a person or entity acting under a grant of authority from or contract with such public agency, including the employees or agents of such public agency or its contractors or persons or entities to whom it has granted authority, that is responsible for public health matters as part of its official mandate.

Research: means a systematic investigation, including research development, testing, and evaluation, designed to develop or contribute to generalizable knowledge

Treatment: means the provision, coordination, or management of health care and related services by one or more health care providers, including the coordination or management of health care by a health care provider with a third party; consultation between health care providers relating to a patient; o the referral of a patient for health care from one health care provider to another.

§ 164.504

Plan administration functions: means administration functions performed by the plan sponsor of a group health plan on behalf of the group health plan and excludes functions performed by the plan sponsor in connection with any other benefit or benefit plan of the plan sponsor.

Summary health information: means information, that may be individually identifiable health information, and:

1. That summarizes the claims history, claims expenses, or type of claims experienced by individuals for whom a plan sponsor has provided health benefits under a group health plan; and

2. From which the information described at § 164.514(b)(2)(i) has been deleted, except that the geographic information described in § 164.514(b)(2)(i)(B) need only be aggregated to the level of a five-digit zip code.

Appendix C: MODEL INCIDENT AND PRIVACY RESPONSE PROCEDURES

The following was provided by The Privacy Professor® as a model Health Insurance Portability and Accountability Act (HIPAA) Security Incident and Privacy Breach Response Plan. Customizable copies of this plan can be purchased from The Privacy Professor site at http://www.privacyprofessor.org. There is also a free incident response overview at the site that corresponds to the procedures below.

Security Incident and Privacy Breach Response Procedure

This procedure covers the following topics:

- Initial Reporting Procedure
- Incident Response Procedure

1. Initial Reporting Procedure
   A. Report the incident to <<Put appropriate title or office here, such as Information Security and Privacy Office, or whatever is most appropriate for your organization>>. Be prepared to provide the following information:
      a. Name

   b. Phone number (primary and secondary)

   c. E-mail address of the point-of-contact at the reporting
       site

B. Document a description of the incident using the "Security
    Incident and Privacy Breach Response Report" form,
    including the following:

    a. The initial assessment of the incident category is as
        follows:

        1. Category 6: Event involves protected health infor-
            mation (PHI) or some other type of personal
            information

        2. Category 5: Port or vulnerability scan, social engi-
            neering, phishing, and so on

        3. Category 4: Inappropriate website, website deface-
            ment, blackmail, unapproved software, unap-
            proved hardware, and so on

        4. Category 3: Virus/worm, spyware, bot/botnet,
            Trojan/backdoor, malicious network activity,
            smartphone malware, and so on

        5. Category 2: Denial-of-service attack, other type
            of network-based attack, and so on

        6. Category 1: Website defacement, lost or stolen
            equipment, and so on

    b. The affected location and/or named system.

    c. The date and time (including time zone) that the inci-
        dent occurred.

    d. If the incident involves, or may involve, PHI or any
        other type of personal information, also provide the
        following:

        1. Estimated number of individuals, and/or records,
            affected

        2. The type of PHI/personal information involved,
            including (if possible) the specified data fields
            involved

    e. If any law enforcement organization has been
        mobilized.

   f. Note: Do NOT delay initial reporting to gather the information below. This information may be provided later, as determined by the <<Put the appropriate title here>>. It may be researched and reported as part of the response phase of the incident handling process.

C. If available and applicable, also report the following:
   a. Source IP, port, and protocol
   b. Destination IP, port, and protocol
   c. Operating system (including version, patches, etc.)
   d. System function (e.g., DNS/web server, workstation)
   e. Antivirus software installed, including version, and latest updates
   f. Method used to identify the incident (e.g., IPS, audit log analysis, system administrator)

2. Incident Response Procedure
A. If it is a Category 6 incident, immediately initiate the Section 3 "Privacy Breach Response Procedure" concurrently while completing this procedure section. Category 6 (Privacy) incidents must be reported to the <<Put appropriate title or office here, such as Information Security Office, or whatever is most appropriate for your organization>> within one hour of discovery.
B. Coordinate with the <<Put appropriate title or office here, such as Privacy Office, or whatever is most appropriate for your organization>> to perform the following applicable actions. (Note: Several of these procedures may be required—some may need to be performed in parallel.)
   a. For Category 6: <<Put appropriate title or office here, such as Information Security Office, or whatever is most appropriate for your organization>> must work with <<Put appropriate title or office here, such as Privacy Office, or whatever is most appropriate for your organization, such as Legal Counsel, Systems Administrator, Compliance Officer, and so on>> during the application of Privacy Breach Procedure.

    b. For Categories 5 through 1: <<Put appropriate title or office here, such as Information Security Office, or whatever is most appropriate for your organization>> must work with <<Put appropriate title or office here, such as IT Department, or whatever is most appropriate for your organization>>.

C. Reassess the incident category to verify and update the initial incident categorization. This process may need to be performed again several times, as facts and conditions are updated.

D. If not already created, document the occurrence of an incident in the "Security Incident and Privacy Breach Response Report" form.

E. If criminal activity is suspected:

    a. Report the incident to the <<Put appropriate title or office here, such as Safety Office, Lawyer, or whatever is most appropriate for your organization>>.

    b. If the <<Put appropriate title or office here, such as Safety Office, Lawyer, or whatever is most appropriate for your organization>> determines outside help is necessary, the "Outside Investigation" form will be completed.

    c. Continue with this procedure.

F. If a forensic response is required, coordinate the forensic response as follows:

    a. Identify possible sources of forensic data. Coordinate with <<Put appropriate title or office here, such as Safety Office, or whatever is most appropriate for your organization>> as required.

    b. Acquire the forensic data. Coordinate with <<Put appropriate title or office here, such as Information Security and Privacy Office, or whatever is most appropriate for your organization>> as required.

    c. Develop a plan to acquire forensic data.

    d. Coordinate with appropriate onsite personnel to acquire the forensic data.

        1. Secure/confiscate applicable equipment.

2. Secure/confiscate applicable software.
3. Secure/confiscate applicable system logs.
4. Coordinate with <<Put appropriate title or office here, such as Information Security Office, or whatever is most appropriate for your organization>> to verify the integrity of the forensic data.

G. After management approval has been acquired to recover from the incident, do the following:

a. Monitor the applicable resources to determine if the malware (if any was involved) has been removed effectively. If ANY indications of infection reemerge, stop the process and combat the attack before proceeding to the next step.

b. Reopen the network traffic that was used as a propagation method by the attack.

c. Reconnect the affected subareas together.

d. Reconnect the mobile devices to the affected area.

e. Reconnect the affected area to the local network.

f. Reconnect the affected area to the Internet.

H. Collaborate with appropriate legal teams if a legal action is in process.

I. In case of a new vulnerability discovery (e.g., a zero-day-exploit):

a. Report to the applicable vendor.

b. Follow-up with the vendor to receive applicable patches and fixes as soon as they become available.

J. Collect lessons learned. This should occur no less than seven days after recovery from the incident.

a. Consider what preparation steps could have been taken to respond to the incident faster or more effectively.

b. If necessary, adjust assumptions that affected the decisions made during incident preparation.

c. Assess the effectiveness of the organization's response process, involving people and communications.

d. Consider what relationships inside and outside of organization could help with future incidents.

K. Debrief and close out the incident as follows:

a. Measure response effectiveness. Determine if the organization responded too quickly, if the organization needs to improve response time and add new steps, and so on.

b. If required, update these procedures based upon the experiences.

c. Prepare a final report using the "Security Incident and Privacy Breach Response Report" form.

d. Include an evaluation of the team's response, damage estimates, and any major recommendations for procedural changes. Distribute the final written report to <<List the positions/individuals who should receive this report. The following is a list to work from and update as necessary. Delete these instructions before submitting for approval.

1. Company Manager
2. CISO
3. CPO
4. IT Director>>

3. Privacy Breach Response Procedure

This procedure covers the following topics:

- Defining a breach
- Breach discovery
- Breach risk assessment procedure
- Breach notification
- Harm variables guidance
- Documentation
- Providing notification

A. Defining a breach

a. "Unsecured protected health information" is PHI that is not secured through the use of a technology or methodology specified by the Department of Human and Health Service (HHS) guidance that specifies the technologies and methodologies that render PHI unusable, unreadable, or indecipherable to unauthorized individuals.

b. A "breach" is the unauthorized acquisition, access, use, or disclosure of unsecured PHI, in a manner not permitted by HIPAA, which compromises the security or privacy of such information.

c. Situations where an unauthorized person to whom such information is disclosed would not reasonably have been able to retain such information is NOT considered to be a breach.

d. Impermissible use or disclosure of PHI is presumed to be a breach unless the Company or business associate (BA) demonstrates a low probability that the PHI has been compromised or an exception applies.

e. Perform a breach risk assessment (see C. Breach risk assessment procedure) to determine if there is a significant risk of harm to the individual as a result of the impermissible use or disclosure. The risk assessment must include consideration of the following and document the answers:

1. Who impermissibly used the PHI or received it?
2. Has any mitigation of the risk of harm occurred?
3. Was the PHI accessed?
4. What type or amount of PHI was impermissibly used or disclosed?

B. Breach discovery

a. Personnel must report known or possible breaches without delay to the <<Put appropriate title or office here, such as Information Security and Privacy Office, or whatever is most appropriate for your organization>>.

b. A privacy breach must be treated as discovered on the first day the breach is known to the Company, or by exercising reasonable diligence would have been known to the Company <<Put appropriate title or office here, such as Information Security and Privacy Office, or whatever is most appropriate for your organization>>.

c. HIPAA requires that the time countdown for making any necessary notifications must start from the day when the breach is discovered or should have been discovered.

C. Breach risk assessment procedure

   a. Risk assessment under HIPAA requires consideration of

      1. The nature and extent of the PHI involved

      2. The types of identifiers and the likelihood of reidentification

      3. The unauthorized person who used the PHI, or to whom the disclosure was made, and whether the PHI was actually acquired or viewed

      4. The extent to which the risk to the PHI has been mitigated

   b. Use the "Security Incident and Privacy Breach Response Report" form to identify and record the following risk factor information.

      1. Factor 1: Evaluate the nature and the extent of the PHI involved, including types of identifiers and likelihood of reidentification of the PHI. For example:

         i. Social Security numbers, credit cards, financial data (risk of identity theft or financial fraud), and so on

         ii. Clinical details, diagnosis, treatment, medications, and so on

         iii. Mental health, substance abuse, sexually transmitted diseases, pregnancy, and so on

         iv. All other PHI items

      2. Factor 2: Consider the unauthorized person who impermissibly used the PHI, or to whom the impermissible disclosure was made. For example:

         i. Does the unauthorized person who received the information have obligations to protect its privacy and security?

         ii. Does the unauthorized person who received the PHI have the ability to reidentify it?

         iii. Does the unauthorized person who received the PHI refuse to communicate or cooperate with the incident investigation?

3. Factor 3: Consider whether the PHI was actually acquired or viewed or if only the opportunity existed for the information to be acquired or viewed. For example:

   i. Does IT analysis show that the PHI on a computer that was stolen, then later recovered, was never accessed, viewed, acquired, transferred, or otherwise compromised? If yes, the Company can determine the information was not actually acquired by an unauthorized individual, although opportunity existed.

   ii. Does IT analysis show that the PHI on a computer that was stolen, then later recovered, may have been accessed, viewed, acquired, transferred, or otherwise compromised? If yes, the Company can determine the information was acquired by an unauthorized individual.

   iii. A stolen computer containing clear-text PHI was never recovered. The Company can determine the information was probably acquired by an unauthorized individual.

4. Factor 4: Consider the extent to which the risk to the PHI has been mitigated. For example:

   i. Obtaining the recipient's satisfactory assurances that the information will not be further used or disclosed (through a confidentiality agreement, etc.) or will be destroyed (if credible, with reasonable assurance)

   ii. Obtaining verbal assurance from the recipient that the information will not be further used or disclosed, but nothing in writing is obtained

   iii. Not being able to communicate with the recipient; thus not obtaining any assurances that the information will not be further used or disclosed

   c. Evaluate breach risk.

      1. No breach notification is required for PHI encrypted as per the "Encryption and Decryption Policy."

      2. For PHI that is not encrypted, use the results from the breach risk assessment to determine overall probability that the PHI has been compromised by considering all four risk factors and using the "Security Incident and Privacy Breach Response Report" form.

      3. If evaluation of the factors fails to demonstrate low probability that the PHI has been compromised, breach notification is required.

   d. Refer to section 4 "Harm variables guidance." If the following harm variables are determined by the <<Put appropriate title or office here, such as Information Security and Privacy Office, or whatever is most appropriate for your organization>> to be a sufficiently significant factor for each specific breach incident, the Company will provide notification even if the breach risk was determined to be low:

      1. Number of individuals affected

      2. Time period during which the violation occurred

      3. Nature and extent of the harm resulting from the violation, consideration of which may include but is not limited to

         i. Whether the violation caused, or likely could cause, physical harm

        ii. Whether the violation resulted, or likely could result, in financial harm

      iii. Whether the violation resulted, or likely could result, in harm to an individual's reputation

      iv. Whether the violation hindered an individual's ability to obtain health care

4. Harm Variables Guidance

A. *Nature of the Data Elements Breached.* The nature of the data elements compromised is a key factor to consider in determining when and how notification should be provided to affected individuals. It is difficult to characterize data elements as creating a low, moderate, or high risk simply based on the type of data because the sensitivity of the data element is contextual. A "name" in one context may be less sensitive than in another context. In assessing the levels of risk and harm, consider the data element(s) in light of their context and the broad range of potential harms resulting from their disclosure to unauthorized individuals.

B. *Number of Individuals Affected.* The magnitude of the number of affected individuals will influence the method(s) chosen for providing notification, but should not be the determining factor for whether the Company should provide notification.

C. *Likelihood the Information is Accessible and Usable.* Upon learning of a breach, the Company <<Put appropriate title or office here, such as Information Security and Privacy Office, or whatever is most appropriate for your organization>> must assess the likelihood PHI, or other sensitive personally identifiable information, will be, or has been, used by unauthorized individuals. An increased risk that the information will be used by unauthorized individuals will increase the need for notification.

D. *Likelihood the Breach May Lead to Harm.*

   a. The Company must protect against any anticipated threats or hazards to the security or integrity of PHI that could result in substantial harm, embarrassment, inconvenience, or unfairness to any individual about whom information is maintained. The Company <<Put appropriate title or office here, such as Information Security and Privacy Office, or whatever

is most appropriate for your organization>> must consider the following to make this determination:

1. The potential for blackmail
2. The disclosure of private facts about the associated individuals
3. Mental pain and emotional distress
4. The disclosure of address information for victims of abuse
5. The potential for secondary uses of the information which could result in fear or uncertainty
6. Unwarranted exposure leading to humiliation or loss of self-esteem

b. The likelihood a breach may result in harm will depend on the manner of the actual or suspected breach and the type(s) of data involved in the incident. The following are some situations to consider:

1. Social Security numbers and account information are useful to committing identity theft, as are date of birth, passwords, and mother's maiden name.
2. Names and addresses, or other personally identifying information, may pose a significant risk of harm if, as one of many potential examples, it appears on a list of patients at a clinic for treatment of a contagious disease.

E. *Ability of the Company to Mitigate the Risk of Harm.* The "risk of harm" will depend on how the Company is able to mitigate further compromise of the system(s) affected by a breach. In addition to containing the breach, appropriate countermeasures, such as monitoring system(s) for misuse of the personal information and patterns of suspicious behavior, should be taken. Such mitigation may not prevent the use of the personal information for identity theft, but it can limit the associated harm. Some harm may be more difficult to mitigate than others, particularly where the potential injury is more individualized and may be difficult to determine.

5. Breach Notification

A. Under HIPAA, the Company has the discretion to provide the required notifications following an impermissible use or disclosure of PHI without performing a risk assessment.

B. BAs must notify the Company <<Put appropriate title or office here, such as Information Security and Privacy Office, or whatever is most appropriate for your organization>> in the event of a breach of unsecured PHI as soon as they discover the breach, or suspect a breach.

C. Breach notice to involved individuals.

   a. Notice to individuals must be made without unreasonable delay, within 10 days whenever possible, and not more than 60 days from when the breach was discovered.

   b. Discovery is when the Company, or a Company BA, knew or "should have known" of the breach.

   c. BA breach notice to the Company must identify the individuals whose PHI was involved in the breach.

   d. BA breach notice to the Company must also provide any other available information that the Company is required to provide in its notice to individuals.

D. Breach notice to the HHS secretary.

   a. The Company is required to submit breach reports to HHS.

   b. Notice of each breach affecting 500 or more individuals must be made to the HHS within 60 days of knowledge of the breach.

   c. Notice of all breaches affecting fewer than 500 must be made to the HHS within 60 days after end of the calendar year for when breaches occurred.

E. Communications with news media.

   a. A designated spokesperson, who understands the basics of HIPAA and Health Information Technology for Economic and Clinical Health (HITECH) Act, must be appointed to be part of the Company breach response team.

    b. The designated spokesperson must know the facts that are available, including the projected time of the internal investigation, and the information that can and cannot be made to the public.

    c. The designated spokesperson will be the only individual within the Company to speak with any outside news media and other entities about the breach.

6. Documentation

  A. The Company must document all reasoning for the decisions supporting the decision to provide, or not provide, breach notification.

  B. The Company must document all reasoning that an impermissible use or disclosure did not constitute a breach.

  C. The Company must retain and appropriately safeguard all breach documentation for at least six years.

  D. Breach notifications must be provided in writing and should be concise, conspicuous, and in plain language.

  E. The Company must include the following within breach notifications:

    a. A brief description of what happened, including the date(s) of the breach and of its discovery.

    b. To the extent possible, a description of the types of personal information involved in the breach (e.g., full name, Social Security number, date of birth, home address, account number, and disability code).

    c. A statement as to whether the information was encrypted or protected by other means, when determined that such information would be beneficial and would not compromise the security of the system.

    d. What steps, if any, individuals should take to protect themselves from potential harm.

    e. What the Company is doing, if anything, to investigate the breach, to mitigate losses, and to protect against any further breaches.

    f. Persons or positions the affected individuals should contact at the Company for more information, including a toll-free telephone number, e-mail address, and postal address.

7. Providing Notification

A. The <<Put appropriate title or office here, such as Information Security and Privacy Office, or whatever is most appropriate for your organization>> must determine the way to provide notification for each breach incident. The best means for providing notification will depend on the number of individuals affected and the contact information that is available about the affected individuals.

B. Notice provided to individuals affected by a breach should be commensurate with the number of people affected and the urgency with which they need to receive notice.

C. The following types of notice may be considered:

a. Telephone

1. Telephone notification may be appropriate in cases where urgency may dictate immediate and personalized notification and/or when a limited number of individuals are affected.

2. Telephone notification, however, should be at the same time as, or in parallel with, written notification by first-class mail.

b. First-class mail

1. First-class mail notification to the last known mailing address of the individual in the Company records should be the primary means for providing notification.

2. The notice should be sent separately from any other mailing so that it is conspicuous to the recipient.

3. If the Company contracts a third party to facilitate mailing, care should be taken to ensure that the Company is identified as the sender, and not the contracted third party.

4. The front of the envelope should be labeled to alert the recipient to the importance of its contents, for example, "Data Breach Information Enclosed"

and should be marked identifying the Company as the sender to reduce the likelihood the recipient thinks it is advertising mail.

c. E-mail
   1. E-mail notification should be avoided when possible, because individuals change their e-mail addresses and often do not notify third parties of the change. In addition, such notifications are susceptible to being viewed as spam.
   2. Notification by postal mail is preferable. However, where an individual has provided an e-mail address and has expressly given documented consent to use e-mail as the primary means of communication with the Company, and no known mailing address is available, notification by e-mail may be appropriate if approved by the Company <<Put appropriate title or office here, such as Information Security and Privacy Office, or whatever is most appropriate for your organization>>.
   3. E-mail notification may also be employed in conjunction with postal mail if the circumstances of the breach warrant this approach.

d. Newspapers or other public media outlets
   1. The Company may supplement individual notification with placing notifications in newspapers or other public media outlets.

e. Substitute notice
   1. Substitute notice may be made in those instances where the Company does not have sufficient contact information to provide notification.
   2. Substitute notice should consist of a conspicuous posting of the notice on the home page of the Company website and notification to major print and broadcast media, including major media in areas where the affected individuals reside.
   3. The notice to media should include a toll-free phone number where an individual can learn

whether or not his or her personal information is included in the breach.

D. The <<Put appropriate title or office here, such as Information Security and Privacy Office, or whatever is most appropriate for your organization>> must determine, based on the privacy breach situation, if the Company will set up toll-free call centers staffed by trained personnel to handle inquiries from the affected individuals and the public.

Related Policies, Procedures, and Forms

- Security Incident and Privacy Breach Response Policy
- Security Incident and Privacy Breach Response Report form
- Outside Investigation form

Supports the Following Regulations and Standards

- HIPAA § 164.308 Administrative safeguards. (a)(6)(i) Standard: Security incident procedures
- HITECH ARRA SEC. 13402. Notification in the case of breach.
- NIST SP 800-66 Guide for Implementing the Health Insurance Portability and Accountability Act (HIPAA) 4.6. Security Incident Procedures
- NIST SP 800-53 Security Controls Mapping: IR-4, IR-5, IR-6, IR-7
- ISO/IEC 27002: 2005 Section 13 Information security incident management
- ISO/IEC 27001: 2005 Section A.13 Information security incident management

Appendix D: HIPAA Resources

Links to HIPAA Regulatory Texts

HIPAA 2013 Omnibus Rule:
  http://www.hhs.gov/ocr/privacy/hipaa/administrative
  /omnibus/index.html
HIPAA Privacy Rule:
  http://www.cms.hhs.gov/hipaa/hipaa2/regulations/privacy
  /default.asp
  http://www.hhs.gov/ocr/privacy/hipaa/administrative
    /combined/hipaa-simplification-201303.pdf
HIPAA Security Rule:
  http://www.hhs.gov/ocr/privacy/hipaa/administrative
  /securityrule/
Transaction Standards and Code Sets:
  http://www.hhs.gov/ocr/privacy/hipaa/administrative/other
  /index.html
HIPAA Identifiers Standards:
  http://www.hhs.gov/ocr/privacy/hipaa/administrative/other
  /index.html
OCR Civil Money Penalties: Procedures for Investigations,
  Imposition of Penalties, and Hearings:

http://www.hhs.gov/ocr/privacy/hipaa/administrative
/privacyrule/extension.pdf

HIPAA Websites and Related Organizations

Centers for Medicare and Medicaid Services:
  https://www.cms.gov/Regulations-and-Guidance/HIPAA
    -Administrative-Simplification/HIPAAGenInfo/index
    .html
CMS ACA System Security Plan Attachment 1 SSP Workbook:
  http://www.cms.gov/CCIIO/Resources
  /Regulations-and-Guidance/Downloads/ACA-SSP
  -Workbook-v-1-0-08012012-a.pdf
Covered Entity Decision Support Tool Home Page:
  http://www.cms.gov/hipaa/hipaa2/support/tools
  /decisionsupport/default.asp
Final Privacy Rule Preamble—Discussion of Comments:
  http://aspe.hhs.gov/admnsimp/final/PvcPre03.htm
Final Privacy Rule Preamble—Final Regulatory Analyses:
  http://aspe.hhs.gov/admnsimp/final/PvcPre04.htm
Health Insurance Association of America:
  http://www.hiaa.org
HHS Data Council Privacy Committee:
  http://aspe.hhs.gov/datacncl/privcmte.htm
Workgroup for Electronic Data Interchange Strategic National
  Implementation Process:
  http://www.wedi.org/
HIPAA Privacy Rule and Its Impact on Research:
  http://privacyruleandresearch.nih.gov/resources.asp
HIPAA Source Links:
  http://www.himss.org/ResourceLibrary/
HHS Initial Regulatory Flexibility Analysis for the HIPAA
  Privacy Rule:
  http://aspe.hhs.gov/admnsimp/nprm/pvc53.htm
NIST Special Publication 800-111 Guide to Storage Encryption
  Technologies for End User Devices:
  http://www.hhs.gov/ocr/privacy/hipaa/administrative
  /securityrule/nist800111.pdf

NIST Special Publication 800-45 Guidelines on Electronic Mail Security:
http://csrc.nist.gov/publications/nistpubs/800-45-version2/SP800-45v2.pdf

NIST Special Publication 800-41 Guidelines on Firewalls and Firewall Policy:
http://csrc.nist.gov/publications/nistpubs/800-41-Rev1/sp800-41-rev1.pdf

Office for Civil Rights—Privacy of Health Records:
http://www.hhs.gov/ocr/privacy/

Practice Brief Defining the Designated Record Set:
http://library.ahima.org/xpedio/groups/public/documents/ahima/bok1_048604.hcsp?dDocName=bok1_048604

The Top Fifteen Privacy Concerns Quiz—DHHS:
http://www.regreform.hhs.gov/HIPAAQUIZ_0204171/sld001.htm

State of California Office of Health Information Integrity's HIPAA Security Toolkit:
http://www.ohii.ca.gov/calohi/content.aspx?id=140

NCVHS—National Committee on Vital and Health Statistics:
http://www.ncvhs.hhs.gov

U.S. Government Printing Office:
http://www.access.gpo.gov

Workers' Compensation Guidelines:
http://www.hhs.gov/ocr/hipaa/guidelines/workerscompensation.pdf

Related HIPAA Resource Books by the Authors

Rebecca Herold:

- *The Privacy Papers*, Auerbach Publishing/CRC Press
- *Managing an Information Security and Privacy Awareness and Training Program*, 2nd Edition, Auerbach Publishing/CRC Press
- Multiple compliance e-books
- http://www.realtimepublishers.com/author?id=19, Realtimepublishers.com

Kevin Beaver:

- *Healthcare Information Systems,* 2nd edition, Auerbach Publishing/CRC Press
- *The Definitive Guide to Email Management and Security,* Realtimepublishers.com
- *Implementation Strategies for Fulfilling and Maintaining IT Compliance,* Realtimepublishers.com
- *Hacking For Dummies,* Wiley

Software Tools Supporting HIPAA Compliance

Privacy Professor Information Security and Privacy Compliance Tools:
  http://www.privacyprofessor.org
Compliance Helper:
  http://www.compliancehelper.com

Security Policy Products and Resources

Privacy Professor Information Security and Privacy Compliance Tools:
  http://www.privacyprofessor.org
Compliance Helper:
  http://www.compliancehelper.com
SIMBUS:
  http://www.hipaacompliance.org

HIPAA and Information Security and Privacy Training, Education, and Awareness-Related Organizations and Vendors

Classes and Certifications

The Privacy Professor:
  http://www.privacyprofessor.org
Principle Logic, LLC:
  http://www.principlelogic.com

HIMSS:
   http://www.himss.org
AHIMA:
   http://www.ahima.org
(ISC)^2:
   http://www.isc2.org
ISACA:
   http://www.isaca.org
IAPP:
   http://www.privacyassociation.org
MIS Training Institute:
   http://www.misti.com
SANS:
   http://www.sans.org

Risk Assessment Resources

Principle Logic, LLC:
   http://www.principlelogic.com
ISO/IEC 27002 Information Technology—Security Techniques
—Code of Practice for Information Security Management:
   http://www.iso.org
NIST Special Publication 800-30 Guide for Conducting Risk
Assessments:
   http://csrc.nist.gov/publications/nistpubs/800-30-rev1
   /sp800_30_r1.pdf

References

Chapter 1

1. Seacoast Radiology Computer Server Breached—231,400 Patients Notified. *Office of Inadequate Security*, accessed November 6, 2013, http://www.databreaches.net/seacoast-radiology-computer-server-breached-231400-patients-notified/.
2. U.S. Department of Health and Human Services. Breaches Affecting 500 or More Individuals, accessed November 15, 2013, http://www.hhs.gov/ocr/privacy/hipaa/administrative/breachnotificationrule/breachtool.html.
3. South Carolina Department of Health and Human Services. Improper Release of Beneficiary Information, accessed November 3, 2013, https://www.scdhhs.gov/press-release/improper-release-beneficiary-information.
4. Brown, E. Court okays firing FDNY lieutenant who posted 911 caller info to Facebook, Internetcases, accessed November 1, 2013, http://blog.internetcases.com/2013/01/31/court-okays-firing-fdny-lieutenant-who-posted-911-caller-info-to-facebook/.
5. El Centro Regional Medical Center. Notice Regarding Missing X-Rays for El Centro Regional Medical Center Patients, accessed November 10, 2013, http://www.ecrmc.org/news-&-updates/&/view/event/id/118/.
6. Gorman, A. and A. Sewell. Six people fired from Cedars-Sinai over patient privacy breaches, Los Angeles Times, accessed November 16, 2013, http://articles.latimes.com/2013/jul/12/local/la-me-hospital-security-breach-20130713.
7. Healthcare Data Breaches Are on the Rise infographic, ID Experts, accessed October 15, 2013, http://www2.idexpertscorp.com/ponemon2012/Infographic/.

8. U.S. Department of Health and Human Services. HIPAA Enforcement Highlights, accessed November 3, 2013, http://www.hhs.gov/ocr/privacy/hipaa/enforcement/highlights/index.html.

9. U.S. Department of Health and Human Services. HITECH Act Enforcement Interim Final Rule, accessed October 1, 2013, http://www.hhs.gov/ocr/privacy/hipaa/administrative/enforcementrule/hitechenforcementifr.html.

10. U.S. Department of Health and Human Services. Equal Employment Opportunity Commission: Regulations Under the Genetic Non discrimination Act of 2008; Final Rule, Federal Register, November 9, 2010, http://www.hhs.gov/ocr/privacy/hipaa/understanding/special/genetic/ginafinalrule.pdf.

11. U.S. Department of Health and Human Services. New rule protects patient privacy, secures health information, accessed October 1, 2013, http://www.hhs.gov/news/press/2013pres/01/20130117b.html.

12. U.S. Department of Health and Human Services. Modifications to the HIPAA Privacy, Security, Enforcement, and Breach Notification Rules Under the Health Information Technology for Economic and Clinical Health Act and the Genetic Information Nondiscrimination Act; Other Modifications to the HIPAA Rules, Federal Register, accessed July 15, 2013, https://www.federalregister.gov/articles/2013/01/25/2013-01073/modifications-to-the-hipaa-privacy-security-enforcement-and-breach-notification-rules-under-the#h-8.

13. U.S. Department of Health and Human Services. Breach Notification Rule, http://www.hhs.gov/ocr/privacy/hipaa/administrative/breachnotificationrule/index.html.

14. U.S. Department of Health and Human Services. HIPAA Privacy Rule Accounting of Disclosures under the Health Information Technology for Economic and Clinical Health Act, Federal Register, May 31, 2011, http://www.gpo.gov/fdsys/pkg/FR-2011-05-31/pdf/2011-13297.pdf.

15. U.S. Department of Health and Human Services. CLIA Program and HIPAA Privacy Rule; Patients' Access to Test Reports, Federal Register, September 14, 2011, http://www.gpo.gov/fdsys/pkg/FR-2011-09-14/pdf/2011-23525.pdf.

16. U.S. Department of Health and Human Services. Health Insurance Portability and Accountability Act (HIPAA) Privacy Rule and the National Instant Criminal Background Check System (NICS), Federal Register, January 7, 2014, https://www.federalregister.gov/articles/2014/01/07/2014-00055/health-insurance-portability-and-accountability-act-hipaa-privacy-rule-and-the-national-instant.

17. U.S. Department of Health and Human Services. HIPAA Administrative Simplification, Regulation Text, February 16, 2006, http://www.hhs.gov/ocr/privacy/hipaa/administrative/privacyrule/adminsimpregtext.pdf.

18. FTC Bureau of Consumer Protection. Health Breach Notification Rule, accessed January 1, 2014, http://business.ftc.gov/privacy-and-security/health-privacy/health-breach-notification-rule.

19. Basics of Health IT, HealthIT.gov, accessed November 2, 2013, http://www.healthit.gov/patients-families/basics-health-it.
20. Health Information Exchange (HIE), HealthIT.gov, accessed October 2, 2013, http://www.healthit.gov/providers-professionals/health-information-exchange.
21. Garrett, P. and J. Seidman, PhD. EMR vs EHR—What is the Difference? Health IT Buzz, accessed November 2, 2013, http://www.healthit.gov/buzz-blog/electronic-health-and-medical-records/emr-vs-ehr-difference/.

Chapter 2

1. U.S. Department of Health and Human Services. Breach Notification for Unsecured Protected Health Information, Federal Register, August 24, 2009, http://www.gpo.gov/fdsys/pkg/FR-2009-08-24/pdf/E9-20169.pdf.
2. U.S. Department of Health and Human Services. Disposal of Protected Health Information, http://www.hhs.gov/ocr/privacy/hipaa/faq/disposal_of_protected_health_information/.
3. NIST Computer Security Publications, SP 800-88 Rev. 1, Draft Guidelines for Media Sanitization, September 6, 2012, http://csrc.nist.gov/publications/PubsDrafts.html#SP-800-88-Rev.%201.
4. FCRA, PART 682—Disposal of Consumer Report Information and Records, last modified May 8, 2014, http://www.ecfr.gov/cgi-bin/text-idx?c=ecfr&tpl=/ecfrbrowse/Title16/16cfr682_main_02.tpl.
5. U.S. Department of Health and Human Services. HIPAA Privacy Rule and Sharing Information Related to Mental Health, accessed July 8, 2014, http://www.hhs.gov/ocr/privacy/hipaa/understanding/special/mhguidance.html.

Chapter 3

1. Third Annual Patient Privacy & Data Security Study, Ponemon Institute, accessed December 1, 2013, http://www.ponemon.org/library/third-annual-patient-privacy-data-security-study.
2. Health Privacy Project, "Medical Privacy Stories," https://www.cdt.org/files/healthprivacy/20080311stories.pdf.

Chapter 4

1. U.S. Department of Health and Human Services. Final Omnibus Rule version of HIPAA and the Health Information Technology for Economic and Clinical Health (HITECH) Act, last modified January 17, 2013, https://s3.amazonaws.com/public-inspection.federalregister.gov/2013-01073.pdf. 5.

2. HIPAA Privacy Officer Job Salaries in United States, PayScale, accessed December 4, 2013, http://www.payscale.com/af/calc.aspx?job=HIPAA+ Privacy+Officer&state=&country.

3. Chief Privacy & Security Officer Job Salaries in United States, PayScale, accessed December 4, 2013, http://www.payscale.com/af/calc.aspx?job= Chief+Privacy+%26+Security+Officer&state=&country.

4. McMann, Erin. Healthcare CIOs earn big bucks, *Healthcare IT News*, accessed December 4, 2013, http://www.healthcareitnews.com/news /healthcare-cios-paid-big-bucks.

Chapter 12

1. U.S. Department of Health and Human Services. Breach Notification Rule, http://www.hhs.gov/ocr/privacy/hipaa/administrative/breach notificationrule/index.html.

2. U.S. Department of Health and Human Services. Omnibus HIPAA Rule-making, http://www.hhs.gov/ocr/privacy/hipaa/administrative/omnibus /index.html.

3. U.S. Department of Health and Human Services. The Security Rule, http://www.hhs.gov/ocr/privacy/hipaa/administrative/securityrule /index.html.

4. U.S. Department of Health and Human Services. Guidance to Render Unsecured Protected Health Information Unusable, Unreadable, or Indecipherable to Unauthorized Individuals, http://www.hhs.gov/ocr /privacy/hipaa/administrative/breachnotificationrule/brguidance.html.

5. Freeman, N. Horizon Blue Cross Blue Shield tells 840,000 of data breach, *Health IT Security*, December 10, 2013, http://healthitsecurity .com/2013/12/10/horizon-blue-cross-blue-shield-tells-840000-of-data -breach/.

Chapter 19

1. U.S. Department of Health and Human Services. Section 13410, Impr-oved Enforcement of the HITECH Act, subsection (e) for Enforcement through State Attorneys General.

Chapter 21

1. U.S. Department of Health and Human Services. *HIPAA/HITECH Omnibus Final Rule*, last accessed February 6, 2014, http://www.hhs.gov /ohrp/sachrp/mtgings/2013%20March%20Mtg/hipaa/hitechomnibus _finalrule.pdf.

2. Munro, D. HIPAA Support Widens In Cloud Vendor Community, *Forbes*, last accessed February 15, 2014, http://www.forbes.com/sites /danmunro/2013/05/01/hipaa-support-widens-in-cloud-vendor -community/.

Chapter 22

1. National Institute of Standards and Technology (NIST). *Guide to Storage Encryption Technologies for End User Devices (SP 800-111)*, http://www.hhs.gov/ocr/privacy/hipaa/administrative/securityrule/nist800111.pdf.
2. National Institute of Standards and Technology (NIST). *Guidelines on Firewalls and Firewall Policy (SP 800-41)*, http://csrc.nist.gov/publications/nistpubs/800-41-Rev1/sp800-41-rev1.pdf.
3. National Institute of Standards and Technology (NIST). *Guidelines on Electronic Mail Security (SP 800-45)*, http://csrc.nist.gov/publications/nistpubs/800-45-version2/SP800-45v2.pdf.

Chapter 25

1. Herold, R. 2010. *Managing an Information Security and Privacy Awareness and Training Program*, Ed. 2. CRC Press: Boca Raton, FL.

Chapter 26

1. U.S. Department of Health and Human Services. Modifications to the HIPAA Privacy, Security, Enforcement, and Breach Notification Rules Under the Health Information Technology for Economic and Clinical Health Act and the Genetic Information Nondiscrimination Act; Other Modifications to the HIPAA Rules. Federal Register, http://www.gpo.gov/fdsys/pkg/FR-2013-01-25/pdf/2013-01073.pdf
2. U.S. Department of Health and Human Services. *The Security Rule*, http://www.hhs.gov/ocr/privacy/hipaa/administrative/securityrule/.
3. National Institute of Standards and Technology. *National Vulnerability Database Automating Vulnerability Management, Security Management and Compliance Checking*, http://web.nvd.nist.gov/view/vuln/search.

Appendix A

1. U.S. Department of Health and Human Services. Enforcement Process, http://www.hhs.gov/ocr/privacy/hipaa/enforcement/process/index.html.
2. U.S. Department of Health and Human Services. Enforcement Results by State, http://www.hhs.gov/ocr/privacy/hipaa/enforcement/data/bystate.html.
3. U.S. Department of Health and Human Services. Enforcement Results by Year, http://www.hhs.gov/ocr/privacy/hipaa/enforcement/data/historicalnumbers.html.
4. U.S. Department of Health and Human Services. Case Examples and Resolution Agreements, http://www.hhs.gov/ocr/privacy/hipaa/enforcement/examples/index.html.

5. U.S. Department of Health and Human Services. Breaches Affecting 500 or More Individuals, http://www.hhs.gov/ocr/privacy/hipaa/administrative/breachnotificationrule/breachtool.html.

Further Reading

Chapter 1

U.S. Department of Health and Human Services. Administrative Simplifi-
cation: Adoption of a Standard for a Unique Health Plan Identifier,
Federal Register, September 5, 2012, http://www.gpo.gov/fdsys/pkg
/FR-2012-09-05/pdf/2012-21238.pdf.

U.S. Department of Health and Human Services. HIPAA Administrative
Simplification Rule links, last modified June 25, 2007, http://aspe.dhhs
.gov/admnsimp.

U.S. Department of Health and Human Services. HIPAA Electronics
Transactions and Code Sets, http://aspe.hhs.gov/admnsimp/bannertx
.htm.

Chapter 2

National Conference of State Legislatures. HIPAA Impacts and Actions
by States, last modified February 2013, http://www.ncsl.org/research
/health/hipaa-a-state-related-overview.aspx.

National Conference of State Legislatures. State Security Breach Notification
Laws, last modified April 11, 2014, http://www.ncsl.org/research
/telecommunications-and-information-technology/security-breach
-notification-laws.aspx.

Chapter 3

Health Privacy, Center for Democracy & Technology, https://cdt.org/issue
/health-privacy/.

Chapter 6

Designated Record Sets: Know What They Are!, *Privacy Professor*®, http://
    privacyguidance.com/blog/designated-record-sets-know-what
    -they-are-ad-nprm-discussion-1/.
If It Was Intentional It Is Not Incidental, *Privacy Professor*®, http://
    privacyguidance.com/blog/if-it-was-intentional-it-is-not-incidental/.
Implementing a Data De-Identification Framework, *Privacy Professor*®,
    http://privacyguidance.com/blog/implementing-a-data-de-identification
    -framework/.
UCLA Health System Pays $865K to Settle Celebrity Privacy HIPAA
    Violations, *Privacy Professor*®, http://privacyguidance.com/blog/ucla
    -health-system-pays-865k-to-settle-celebrity-privacy-hipaa-violations/.

Chapter 15

State of California Office of Health Information Integrity. HIPAA Security
    Toolkit, http://www.ohii.ca.gov/calohi/content.aspx?id=140.

Chapter 19

National Association of Insurance Commissioners. Model Descriptions, http://
    www.naic.org/committees_index_model_description_i_q.htm.

Chapter 20

Centers for Medicare & Medicaid Services. HIPAA—General Information,
    last modified April 2, 2013, http://www.cms.gov/Regulations-and
    -Guidance/HIPAA-Administrative-Simplification/HIPAAGenInfo
    /index.html.
U.S. Department of Health and Human Services. OIG Compliance Program
    for Individual and Small Group Physician Practices, Federal Register,
    October 5, 2000, http://oig.hhs.gov/authorities/docs/physician.pdf.

Index

access control and information
integrity, 64–65
administrative safeguard
requirements, 214–220
applications and data criticality
analysis, 372–373
business associate
agreements, 66
compliance, 67, 249, 257–261
contingency plans, 66
data backup plan, 365–367
designing, 206–207
emergency mode operation plan,
370–371
general rules for, 210–211
goals of, 206
implementation plan, 249–255
individual rights, 67
initiatives, 225–226
key terms in, 207
organizational requirements,
213, 225
overlaps with Security Rule,
62–63
PHI data flows mapping, 64
physical safeguard requirements,
220–222
policies and procedures, 65–66
vs. Privacy Rule, 59–61
Privacy Rule overlaps with,
62–63
protecting appropriate
information, 64
required *vs.* addressable, 211–213
requirements, 94, 208–210
response and reporting, 361
risk analysis, *see* Risk analysis of
Security Rule
safeguards, 63
sanctions, 67
security and privacy
accountability, 65

security implementation costs,
51–53
security officer costs, 55–57
security ongoing maintenance
costs, 53–55
security policies, 244–246
stepping process, 233–235
technical safeguard requirements,
222–225
testing and revision procedure,
371–372
training and awareness, 66
Service-level agreements (SLAs), 377
Sign-in sheets, health care provider,
270
SLAs, *see* Service-level agreements
Small Business Administration at 13
CFR 121.104, 289
Small employer issues, 303–304
Small health plan, 289
Software source code analysis for
testing, 356
South Carolina Department of
Health and Human
Services, 4
State breach notification laws, 36
State health information laws, 36
State law, 165
State preemption, 165–166
analysis, 169–171
contrary, 166–168
decision tree, 171
exceptions to, 168–169
information websites, 172–175
issues, 171
Stepping process, 233–235
Stimulus Act, *see* American Recovery
and Reinvestment Act
Storage, data, 338
Subcontractors, 13–15
Substitute notice, company, 482
System-specific policies, 241

Printed in the United States
by Baker & Taylor Publisher Services